Archaeological Artefacts as Material Culture

How can material culture studies enrich archaeology?

This colourful book combines practical and theoretical information to provide a fresh approach to analysing and interpreting artefacts. In its study of the used and modified objects unearthed during excavations and surveys, archaeological enquiry is already steeped in material culture: here, Linda Hurcombe shows how an awareness of the discipline can deepen our understanding of the social context of past cultures. She also explores the manner in which objects from the past become part of the present.

Issues of materiality and its perception lie at the heart of her discussion. Examining the characteristics of a full range of raw materials – organic, stone, clay and metal – and the objects made from them, Hurcombe explains how to approach these materials with a detailed analysis of methods and theories both scientific and sociological. Diverse approaches from a variety of disciplines are brought together, including the most recent research and developments, to provide an holistic overview of the field.

Including over seventy illustrations with almost fifty in full colour, this book not only provides the tools an archaeologist will need to interpret past societies from their artefacts, but will also enable the reader to develop a keen appreciation of the beauty and tactility involved in working with these fascinating objects. This is a book no archaeologist should be without, but it will also appeal to anybody interested in the interaction between people and objects.

Linda Hurcombe is Head of the Department of Archaeology, Exeter University. She has particular interests in a range of artefact studies including stone tools, functional analysis and organic material culture. She has undertaken fieldwork in Pakistan, Britain and Europe and published books on gender and material, cultural and functional analysis.

Archaeological Artefacts as Material Culture

Linda M. Hurcombe

Routledge
Taylor & Francis Group

LONDON AND NEW YORK

First published 2007
by Routledge
2 Park Square, Milton Park, Abingdon, Oxon OX14 4RN

Simultaneously published in the USA and Canada
by Routledge
270 Madison Ave, New York, NY 10016

Reprinted 2008, 2009

Routledge is an imprint of the Taylor & Francis Group, an informa business

Typeset in Joanna by
Keystroke, 28 High Street, Tettenhall, Wolverhampton
Printed and bound in Great Britain by
MPG Books Ltd, Bodmin, Cornwall

British Library Cataloguing in Publication Data
A catalogue record for this book is available from the British Library

Library of Congress Cataloging in Publication Data
A catalog record for this book has been requested

ISBN10: 0–415–32091–7 (hbk)
ISBN10: 0–415–32092–5 (pbk)
ISBN10: 0–203–06852–1 (ebk)

ISBN13: 978–0–415–32091–7 (hbk)
ISBN13: 978–0–415–32092–4 (pbk)
ISBN13: 978–0–203–06852–6 (ebk)

For Patrick and Matthew

for the pleasure of seeing them learn about 'things',
how they behave, what they can do,
and, in some cases, what they once were.

Contents

Tables and figures

Tables

Figures

Colour figures appear between pages 176 and 177

Preface

Artefacts allow a tactile and tangible connection between present and past which can be 'felt', as tangible implies. This is not a whimsical fancy but simply a statement that more of the senses are directly involved with the past – a practical as well as a mental engagement with another material world. Having taught students about artefacts and material culture for a number of years, I wrote this book in part to encapsulate something missing from the available literature – a sense of materiality and a place where close observation, scientific analysis, and theoretical concepts of material culture could all be brought together. At the time of writing Hodges's 1964 book *Artefacts* is still on library shelves and in university bookshops, because the factual manual he created as part of the functionalist paradigm of the 1950s still has validity, but it was time to set down a more postmodernist critique of artefact studies whilst not ignoring the practical issues of materials and matter realities. This book is written by somebody who loves objects and the information which can be read from them in the hope that others will feel likewise. I hope that this book speaks to its readers in straightforward ways and perhaps this will make the ideas and concepts within it seem obvious or even simple. If so I will have done my job as communicator and also made a good argument. The ideas brought together here have become more obvious to me over a number of years and were further crystallised by the process of writing them down. I see them as persuasive evaluations of archaeological processes and the value of studying artefacts.

In recent years, I have also realised that the way children learn about things, the material world, and their own material culture are powerful parts of their development and, with them, society's perpetuation and change. I have watched my son, Patrick, explore and learn about the world of things and my close friend's son, Matthew, learn about and pass away from the world of things. The objects we touch and transform have a life-cycle as much as we do. Though some objects are transient, others outlast us and stand witness to past human lives. That is what the study of archaeological artefacts is all about.

Linda Hurcombe
Exeter, 2006

Acknowledgements

This book has had a very long gestation and because of its diversity has benefited from many contacts. I should especially like to thank my parents Betty and Jack for fostering a love of objects from broken clay pipes to antiques, Pat Phillips and Robin Torrence for the chance and guidance to pursue that interest through research, Jane Prendergrast and Pam Jenkin for a wealth of practical and mental support over the years, and Robin Dennell for unfailing constructive criticism and encouragement.

My colleagues at Exeter University have all offered useful comments but Bruce Bradley, Bryony Coles, John Coles, Gill Juleff, Carl Knappett, Val Maxfield, Robert van de Noort, Alan Outram, and Steve Rippon deserve especial thanks for loans of objects, help with images and extensive discussions. Our technicians Seán Goddard and Mike Rouillard have overseen the creation of all of the images and made my concepts of these a reality. In this and other production issues I have been assisted by Adam Wainwright, Chris Smart, and Sue Rouillard. Bryn Morris and Ann Oldroyd also assisted with in-putting the references.

Other colleagues have provided useful information and comment including Marie-Claude Boileau, Richard Fullagar, Annelou van Gijn, Matthew Johnson, Dave Killick, Jennifer Moody, and John Waddell. Graham Langman, Exeter Archaeology Unit's finds officer for the Princesshay excavations generously discussed his role and the processing of finds on site with me, and Thomas Cadbury of the Royal Albert Memorial Museum and Art Gallery, Exeter, allowed me to borrow some objects for the photographs. Current students on our MA programme in Experimental Archaeology generously lent objects they had made and offered photographs, so particular thanks to Andrew Young, Erin Schroeder, Caroline Jeffra, and Julia Wiecken. Lee Bray also offered comments.

The images form an important contribution to the book, and creating these and obtaining copyright clearance for others has been a major endeavour. The sources of the images are sometimes complex and so these have been listed as part of the captions. However, I should like to thank here all who gave their permission and the helpfulness encountered from so many of you: Piran Bishop and the Devon Archaeological Society, figure 8.6; Bruce Bradley, figure 8.3 pestle and mortar, figure 8.4c and 8.4e, figure 8.8b, figure 9.2b, figure 9.3b and figure 9.3c, figure 9.5; Jacqui Carey, figure 7.17; Bryony Coles, figure 7.13; Adrien Hannus, figure 7.11; Staffan Hyll, Per Karsten and the Swedish National Heritage Board, figure 2.7; Caroline Jeffra, figure 7.14g, figure 9.6a; author and Gill Juleff, figure 10.5, figure 10.6e–f, figure 10.7; Gill Juleff, figure 10.8, figure 10.9; Bryony Kelly, figure 9.3e; Carl Knappett, figure 9.2c, figure 9.3d, figure 9.6b, figure 9.12; Valerie Maxfield, figure 7.20c, figure 8.5f; Peter Montanez, figure 7.18i for photograph, annotation by author; the Royal Albert Memorial Museum and Art Gallery, Exeter, figure 7.14f; author, Julia Wiecken and Andrew Young, figure 10.6a–d. All the other illustrations are by the author except for figure 5.2 which reproduces Pitt-Rivers 1875 reprinted 1906: plate II.

In addition, the late Malti Nagar kindly gave me the Indian courting comb during a visit to Deccan College, India, and colleagues from Tashkent University, Uzbekistan, hosted a visit during which I took some of the images used in this book. I should also like to acknowledge the insights and images gained from the professional craft specialists who regularly demonstrate on our Experimental Archaeology MA programme: Dave Budd (iron), Neil Burridge (copper and bronze), and Linda Lemieux (basketry). I am grateful to all these people for their kindness and the opportunities they created for me.

Finally, such a vast subject has inevitably been tackled in phases – projects funded by the British Academy and Leverhulme have contributed to this book – and work was progressing on small sections in and around other responsibilities. This changed when the AHRC provided funding for a period of research leave. This has enabled me to focus entirely on this project and has directly led to significantly more coherence and coverage as a result. Thanks go to AHRC for their timely and crucial support in bringing this project to fruition.

Cover illustration: a detail of Suzanne Bellamy's 'The Goddess of Glebe', part of her art performance and installation project entitled 'The Lost Culture of Women's Liberation, the Pre-Dynastic Phase, 1969–1974'. The figure is a satiric reference to the snake goddess and also refers to the 'ritual' drinking of endless cups of tea during the founding of Women's Liberation. Glebe is an inner city suburb of Sydney Australia. (55cm in height, clay and reassembled china pieces).

I would like to thank Suzanne Bellamy for permission to use this image from her installation project which I saw in Sydney in 1999. The reuse of artefacts and exemplification of complex object meanings and biographies made it a very apt choice for the cover of this book. The installation project continues to evolve and this book will now form a part of the story.

Part I

Deconstruction and analysis

1 Introduction

Artefacts as evidence

We live in a material world. Artefacts – modified objects, tools, used objects and structures – houses, buildings, fences, sheds – are all around us. Our material culture is made up of all of these things and reveals as much about our preferences as any other source of evidence is likely to do, including the written word. Our material culture reveals our spending power, it reinforces our sense of gender and age group, it emphasises the cultural affiliations we hold, and sets them out for other people to see our social status. We have objects that reveal our travels as souvenirs, and objects from the general past as antiques, or our personal past as heirlooms or mementos. Our contemporary world is dominated by material culture. The objects communicate things about us and the society in which we live. All human societies have material culture. The reason we study this material culture of past societies is to use the objects of the past as the means of seeing archaeological societies. They may have left a written record as well but their material culture is always informative. Furthermore the archaeological record of artefacts is immeasurably longer than the history of the written word. The oldest stone tools in the world date to around 2.7 million years ago, but this is just the record of the surviving inorganic artefacts, as many organic items leave few traces. Archaeology deals with the physical remains of the past, but it is about people.

Archaeology has many different kinds of physical evidence, so what do artefact studies contribute? From the earliest development of archaeology as a discipline, they have provided crucial information but the use made of that information and approaches to their study have varied over time along with paradigm shifts within the discipline. It could be said that artefact studies have at times gone out of fashion but they are the very expression of fashion. An artefact is defined as anything made or modified by people, so artefacts are not just 'things' but are intricately linked with people's needs, capabilities, and aspirations. All societies and the individuals within them use objects to define, punctuate, perpetuate, and manipulate their social personae. It would be hard to find out much about past societies and individuals without artefactual evidence. The social clues would be reduced to those based on the biological parameters of race, sex, age, and posture. Language could add to the personal impression, but hair arrangements and body scarification or other physical manipulation (bound feet or heads, elongated necks) are actually artefacts. Clothing and adornments are universal adjuncts to human personae even where the prevailing climate does not dictate their adoption. It follows then that the study of artefacts is fundamental to seeing people in their social contexts. If archaeology is the study of individuals or societies, artefacts are made, used, and discarded by individuals acting within their society. Even an individual seen as an 'outcast' is defined in relation to a society. Cross-cultural adaptations and movements are there to be seen. Thus studying the prevailing styles and traits of the artefactual remains of a society is not to reduce everything to 'norms', but to define normal parameters, so that the abnormal – the individuals who have chosen to stand out within that society – can be seen archaeologically.

Artefacts form a major category of archaeological evidence, so any archaeological project will look for objects from a past society. These will provide information on the past activities at a site or in a landscape. The objects may themselves give dating evidence or the project will use other forms of archaeological information, such as stratigraphy, to show the relationships in time at a site and thus date the objects. It will also look at groups of objects that occur together, perhaps to show a related set of activities or a set of objects contemporary in time, or synonymous with a particular culture or group within that culture. As much as societies today communicate via objects, so the objects of the past are the means by which we can try and extract information about past societies. All forms of archaeological fieldwork will collect artefacts, whether the projects are the traditional excavation of an activity area, monument or settlement site (one place in time) or a cemetery (with items of personal adornment or goods placed as grave furniture by the living), or broad-scale field surveys across ploughed fields (e.g. prehistoric or Roman sites in areas now intensively farmed), or eroding landscapes (for example ancient fossils and tools in Africa or Asia). The cultural remains will be dominated by artefact evidence. Artefacts thus reveal the particular sequence at a site, and the intensely personal as well as the very general cultural landscape of a people.

It follows then that artefacts and material culture are always going to be at the heart of an archaeological investigation. Anyone who works within archaeology on sites or surveys needs to be able to distinguish an artefact from an unmodified object and to see the sense behind what that artefact can reveal about the society which made and used it. No matter where in the world archaeological work takes place, or whatever the time period that archaeologists are interested in investigating, material culture forms a major category of evidence. This is why this book reveals how archaeologists approach studies of material culture, and the means by which archaeologists extract that encoded social information from the material remains that they excavate or find on field surveys.

Artefacts, tools, manuports, and material culture: defining terms

It is essential to recognise whether an object has been modified by humans, or is simply a fortuitously shaped piece of natural material, and to also appreciate when an object has been used or simply moved by human agency. There are a number of words that archaeologists use which have very specific meanings. Archaeologists discussing objects commonly use the terms 'artefacts' and 'tools' but these are not synonymous. Archaeological and dictionary definitions state that an *artefact* is something changed or modified by people. It may be an incidental waste product of making another item, but, if it is modified, it is an artefact and can reveal choices made in the manufacture of other objects which might themselves have been taken away and used. *Tools* are objects which have been used as implements or instruments. Not all tools need be artefacts (for example a natural pebble makes a good hammer), though in practice most are. One further term for an object of material culture is used by archaeologists but is not commonly found in dictionaries. A '*manuport*' (e.g. Oakley 1981) is a natural object moved to a new location by people, though it remains unaltered. A beach pebble picked up and used to hammer a wooden peg into the ground is a tool and could be modified by use with tiny fractures in the surface but it is not recognisable as an artefact. If someone picked it up from a beach and took it to use at a site inland it might be possible to recognise it as a manuport but it still might have no discernible traces of modification. If it is used more intensively and becomes worn as a result of usage then technically it becomes an artefact, something altered by people.

A tool is something that is used but it also has to be identified as such archaeologically so, strictly speaking, it needs to show traces of use. In practice archaeologists usually call artefacts 'tools' where their shape is distinctive and their purpose as an implement is surmised. A clear example would be a stone scraper or polished stone axe because these objects have recognisable shapes and their surmised use is as implements to do something else. Ceramic vessels are not necessarily thought of as instruments to use on something else so they are more often referred to as artefacts than tools. However some of the objects called tools need not have been used in the ways envisaged. Thus, to be really sure that an object is indeed a tool, one would need to recognise the traces of use from all of the other traces on the surface of an object.

With each of these words there is a consequence about the kinds of things that archaeologists need to be able to do. To identify a manuport, one requires knowledge of what is naturally present in the landscape contemporary to the site and to know whether any natural transport mechanisms, such as seasonal streams, may have affected the site. In other words the background information on the natural objects present in that area is a prerequisite for the successful identification of manuports. In a similar way, recognising an artefact requires an understanding of the natural material and the circumstances of its formation, transport, and incorporation into the archaeological record. Traces of deliberate modification need to be distinguished from natural wear, breaks, or growth patterns. For example, an antler will acquire wear during a deer's life because it is used in the rut and for browsing. A rounded or worn piece of antler would be an artefact only if it were subsequently altered by humans *and* recognised as such by archaeologists – for example perhaps the wear traces did not conform to those expected from natural causes. So here the skill that needs to be acquired is that of recognising natural modifications and the original shape of the natural piece of material, from the traces distinguishable as deliberate and due to the action of people.

By recognising artefacts, tools, and manuports, archaeologists can look at what people did in the landscape under study: the taskscapes where they performed certain actions, and left debris from manufacturing processes or from subsistence activities. In all of these ways, material remains enter the archaeological record. This record is also composed of some deliberate depositional acts and also chance loss. An arrowhead may simply enter the record by being lost during its use, whereas objects contained in burials have been deliberately placed into the ground. In their different ways, all of the objects that find their way into the ground constitute the archaeological record for an area. This archaeological record of material remains is the surviving material culture of the past but is not a complete record.

Using words such as artefacts, tools, and manuports immediately suggests that these objects will yield information on the technologies available in a society and the range of tools created and used. This is true; most objects serve a purpose but this is not to say that they are utilitarian. Function is not a simple concept. Objects can perform both utilitarian and social tasks. Clothes keep us warm but they do much more than this. Most people possess a comb, but it is not a true necessity and its functional form may vary according to hair style and texture while the choice of material, colour, and decoration depend upon prevailing fashion, status, and individual choice. Technologies and developments within them and the function of objects are key aspects of artefact studies, but they are not the only ones and there is a social dimension to all artefact studies. '*An artefact is always active – tying together heterogeneous things, material and human*' (Shanks 1998: 27). It is this that turns the building blocks of artefacts, tools and manuports into material culture.

A keen eye will have discerned a schism in the above discussion. If material culture includes everything made or moved, then the term 'artefact studies' seems to reduce this to small objects rather than structures such as houses and monuments or fields and landscapes. In fact material culture does incorporate these: Stonehenge (UK) is a good example of a very large collection of both moved and modified objects (Cleal et al. 1995: plate 7.1 shows the fine tooling on sarsen stone 16, an example of a large artefact). Barrows or huge earthmoving creations such as Serpent Effigy Mound, (Ohio, USA) and the laid-out fields of Bronze Age Dartmoor are also part of material culture. Altered landscapes are part of the diversity of material culture. As ever, there are practical constraints limiting what can be covered in one book and there are different branches of archaeology. Landscape studies tend to incorporate these large-scale aspects of material culture, and this discipline has developed significantly over the last twenty years. Artefact studies, whilst concentrating on the smaller items, does not exclude large items such as boats and logically also houses. It has developed along two paths: the study of material culture and meanings, and the development of scientific techniques of analysis. The application of these to actual objects has at times been piecemeal, and the whole field could do with a renaissance of reintegration. Issues of 'materiality' arise (Chapter 6). Pottery, mud brick, and fired brick all start as clay. The term *materiality* has tended to be appropriated by a highly social approach to material culture, but the raw materials are the basis for all forms of 'made or moved' aspects of material culture. Understanding the materials is fundamental to appreciating the choices made by people. Thus, this book has chosen to concentrate on artefact studies as material culture mediated by an emphasis on materials.

There is one final definition, that of material culture itself. Artefacts, tools, and manuports collectively make up *material culture*, so at one level it comprises anything made or moved by people. However, material culture is about more than the sum of its parts, in this case the individual objects. Societies do have sets and subsets of artefacts and tools which vary across time and space but even these grouped objects offer only a reductionist idea of material culture. One view sees culture – and thus, I would argue, also material culture – as 'man's extrasomatic means of adaptation' (Binford 1962: 218, White 1959: 8). This view has the advantage that it conveys a sense of the pragmatic benefits to be obtained from the use of material culture but also places these within a strong social category where benefits or disadvantages are more fluid concepts for individuals and societies. Over and beyond the utilitarian aspects, material culture is about the social significance of objects and the way they can interact to create bold or nuanced meanings. Material culture is thus a set of social relationships between people and things, and above all it is a way of communicating as well as enabling. Language can be seen as a way of describing the world but it is not a passive depiction: words and the meanings of them frame schools of thought and ways of seeing. In the same way the objects that make up material culture influence and shape ways of thinking. If words are about verbal communication, material culture is about non-verbal communication. It is that aspect which allows objects of material culture to communicate information about the past activities and lifestyles of individuals and communities even down to their ways of thought. Many subjects are now engaged in material culture studies, including disciplines which can use existing documentary evidence. In these fields, perhaps because of a need to stress the contribution of non-verbal sources to an understanding of past societies formerly based primarily on texts, the phrase 'visual culture' has been creeping into use almost as a synonym for material culture. Visual information is certainly a very powerful communication media which can be processed from a distance: before a stranger utters a word another person can read from their appearance their status, cultural affiliations, gender, and age. However, material culture engages all the senses: ethnic cooking styles can be discerned by smell and taste and styles of vessels, the temperature of a furnace can be heard as well as seen and felt, clothing can be felt, crystals in metal can be heard by bending a bar; it is possible to hear a well-struck flint flake or hear the flaw in a cracked cup or piece of rock; one can feel a dull edge, a handle polished by years of use, the drape of a textile, or when a hide has been well processed; chemical and textural compositions can be tasted and the way a hide or cord has been prepared may be smelt. Thus the term visual culture should be reserved for seen elements of culture but should not be used as an alternative to material culture since the latter acts on all five senses.

The conceptual framework

A major concern of any discipline is to provide a means of communicating ideas, and systems for ordering and making sense of particularistic data. Those studying artefacts need to describe and make sense of the plethora of objects. If all objects were treated as unique – which they are – all discussion would be drowned out by endless description, so each discipline creates categories and gives them names in order to describe and communicate issues with other people. A category might be 'pottery' or 'chipped stone' or even more specific terms such as 'scrapers' or 'hand axes', 'cups' or 'storage jars'. Categories divide up the mass of unique objects into those which share common traits but the selection of which traits to use is a subjective one. A classification system is devised and the objects are grouped into humanly created divisions. These units both describe and make common discussion possible, but they do neither neutrally. They add their own influences. To complicate matters further, the archaeologists creating the categories and trying to understand the past system have several world views to consider: the discipline of archaeology (since each discipline has its own schools of thought), the contemporary society of the archaeologist (everyone is influenced by their own society), the other society that they are trying to study (this would also occur for an anthropologist), and, finally, the distance in time which limits access to knowledge about the society studied. This complexity, described as the fourfold hermeneutic (Shanks and Tilley 1992: 107–8), is particular to subjects like history and archaeology and, I would argue, extinct languages such as Latin. To continue the linguistic analogy, it can be likened to one discipline replete with its own specialist terms, being studied by people speaking one contemporary language but whose goal is to investigate another society with both a different language and a more ancient language system. All this adds an extra dimension to the study of archaeological artefacts as material culture and, whilst it is not easy, it is a worthwhile endeavour. Without objects the chronological study range for humankind would be reduced to historic societies alone and of course the physical evidence can often be used to reinforce or contest the written sources.

There are a few other useful concepts when discussing material culture. First and foremost there need to be names to go with the very specific categories of different kinds of cultural object. Archaeologists call these *types*, usually distinguished by both a kind of material and a particular shape, for example, a polished stone axe (universally understood) or a Folsom point (a particular kind of North American stone arrowhead). Different types combine to form a classification system. There are various purposes behind the way in which archaeologists classify objects. First and foremost a classification system makes sense of the vast array of archaeological material culture. It gives us 'handles', names with which to describe the things we see and communicate with others; it makes sense of that wealth of particularist information. There are many different types of arrowheads, e.g. for North America see Kooyman (2000: 107–127), and similar complex typologies exist for Britain (Green 1980). Thus arrowheads can be infinitely divided into various forms, for example barbed and tanged, and 'Breton' arrowheads in Europe or Clovis, Folsom, and Holcombe points in North America. Such names originate from several common sources. Sometimes they are a straightforward description of the shape or the name of the areas where the type is common, for example a Breton arrowhead, or a reference to the sites where the 'type' was first described or found and whose name became synonymous with the object. The shape descriptions are fairly obvious, for example a 'horseshoe scraper' or a 'button scraper', but site-based names such as Clovis and Folsom points are relevant only because the basic descriptions in the site reports have left a definition of what constitutes this type so that if someone reads this term they can look up details about it. Common usage makes the name a generally accepted type. All classification systems may have slightly different usages of particular terms but, as long as they are fully described, another archaeologist or reader can understand what is being discussed.

The classification system is thus the order that we impose upon the data and, as such, there are a number of ways of doing it, serving a number of purposes. Objects can be classified by material. They can also be classified by size or shape, or by period, or according to their function. From this statement it follows that a set of objects can be classified in several different ways according to the information desired. Archaeological researchers set their own agenda and use existing classification systems and types, or devise their own. Some classification systems outline the technology employed in the manufacture of the object. For example, one way of classifying stone flakes is to call them primary, secondary, or tertiary, depending upon whether they have one side totally covered with the whitish skin of the original cortex, or a part of it, or none of it, respectively. In this way, the flake classification system gives some indication of which stages of the manufacturing process have lead to the current spread of cultural debris recovered from a site. Types can singularly or collectively serve as cultural markers. The objects signal their cultural affiliations.

Some types tend to define a whole material culture system standing for a particular period or a region. One example is polished stone. Here, a particular technology is characteristic of a period known in Europe as the Neolithic. Polished stonework does exist later on, but it tends to be used for different objects. Thus in this case, the technology identified by the term is serving to define a difference in the material culture of that period. Transverse, leaf, and barbed and tanged arrowheads are all forms known from the later prehistory of Europe, but each one is characteristic of the subdivision within this general time period. The function of them is, broadly speaking, the same, but the precise way in which the culture has chosen to shape its arrowheads, or projectile points, has varied slightly over time. A Clovis point or barbed and tanged arrowhead has a particular shape and form. It is both a functional type and distinctive of a particular period. A long cross silver penny is a very distinctive and specific archaeological type. It has a period of usage, being a medieval coin, but it is not marking out one period because it is a relatively rare find and other contemporary objects have greater potential as chronological markers. Object types used as chronological markers and culture names tend to come from prehistoric periods. This remark makes it clear that there are historiographical issues in artefact studies. Different problems in the study of archaeology have caused artefact studies to treat nomenclature and ways of studying objects in a variety of ways rather than as a uniform system.

One further example is used to introduce the concept of cultures. Kossinna (1911 in Trigger 1989: 163–6) sets out the idea of cultural groups who would express their ethnic identity using material culture. Sets of recurring groups of objects were thus to be read by archaeologists as 'cultures' or groups of people affiliated with one another. These could be recognised in the archaeological record which could then locate these cultures in time and space. The idea of an assemblage, a recurring set of associated objects, remains an important archaeological tenet though Kossinna himself used his ideas to further nationalistic ends in a way which today is unequivocally condemned. A slightly later but allied concept of 'traditions' is relevant here. Cultures can change but often the changes are not across all areas in one time (otherwise they would not be seen as the same culture). In fact there might be considerable periods of time when certain aspects of material culture hold constant or change gradually, building on what has gone before. This gives the notion of 'cultural traditions' which in an archaeological sense are about broad similarities through time or space. Sometimes a particular technology can be referred to as a tradition, for instance blade-making traditions. Occasionally one particular aspect of technology is so distinct that an object type is used to name a 'culture'. For example, LBK or Linear Band Keramic pottery is marked by a particular kind of ceramic decoration, but LBK is now the shorthand term used for a culture that spread over central Europe as part of the Neolithic. In a similar way one aspect of material culture, basketry, has been so distinctive of a southwestern American group that there is a 'basketmaker culture'.

It is no coincidence that many of the examples so far are of stone, pot, or metal types. These three materials dominate the finds on a site and it is these hardy materials which offer the first means of ordering the artefact collections made by antiquarians last century. Readily identifiable archaeological types, such as barbed and tanged arrowheads, have been picked up and noticed for centuries. In the past people believed that these arrowheads were made by fairies and called them elfshot. Thunderbolts were believed to have caused the polished stone axes. The reason behind these, to us farfetched, ideas about how such artefacts came into existence are tied up with the prevailing thought at the time. At one stage the Christian church dominated the thinking of large areas of the world and its teaching held that the world was created in 4004 BC. There were rigid dictates in that kind of society against the notion that people had evolved gradually or that there might be artefacts of different materials from a period much further back in time than the written word recorded. The nineteenth-century antiquarians thus had a difficult starting point. Many of them were collecting artefacts but could offer no satisfactory explanation for them given their own society's worldview. A turning point came in 1859 when Darwin published his book *The Origin of Species*, outlining his theory that different species had evolved gradually and over a long period of time. This requirement to think of very long time periods was supported by the work of geologists such as Sir George Lyell, who stressed that geological strata were produced by long-term processes. Archaeology too had played a role. Early work had discovered extinct types of animals associated with stone tools. All of these different disciplines working together eventually managed to give a much longer chronology to the past and, with this expansion of the time period before the present, so too there was a need to order it and to find some way of defining the sequence of events that led to the present.

Early antiquarians collected many artefacts. These were characteristically of those hardy substances of stone and metal. It was these that survived most easily and in forms that were readily identifiable as humanly worked. There were collections of arrowheads, spearheads, axes and the shapes of these could be placed in rows to suggest how they had changed gradually over time. Using these principles of progressive and gradual change to show how one type evolved into another, the early antiquarians were able to classify their objects, not by an individual type but by major divisions of that time period.

Thus the materials and the artefacts gave archaeology its first major periods. This was called the three age system. It was invented by Thomsen in the early nineteenth century (Trigger 1989: 73–9) and consisted of the Stone Age, the Bronze Age, and the Iron Age. This three-age system is still with us. It has been refined slightly so that now the Stone Age is divided up into the Palaeolithic and the Neolithic, the Neolithic having pottery and polished stonework. More recently the Mesolithic has been added as an additional period of the Stone Age. But by and large the principles that were laid down by the antiquarians have withstood the test of time. Modern dating methods provide much more fine detail and a welcome additional and independent source of evidence. But it is none the less true that certain kinds of artefacts can be picked up and immediately assigned to a period on the basis of this very ancient principle of the three-age system.

Interesting arte(facts)

It is scarcely surprising that the objects found by the antiquarians and by ourselves, seem to be a source of endless fascination. When you hold a stone tool or a polished stone axe in your hand, you are holding the work of someone who lived millennia ago. Their objects survive for us to find and in the objects we can find the people. So what is it that we want to know from the objects about those people and how can that information be read? These questions lie at the heart of archaeology.

There are many different ways of being interested in artefacts. The obvious one is archaeology. But collectors of all kinds and metal detectorists are, in their own way, curious about the past and about the objects from it. Each one of those different professions has, at their root, an interest in objects and material culture. The difference between an archaeologist and, in particular, a metal detectorist is that the former also wants to know about the context of artefacts, and it is this that is really crucial to getting the most out of artefact studies.

As soon as an artefact is picked up, it is removed from its context, where perhaps it was discarded or brought to rest in an ancient living system. If we were interested in these objects only for their artistic value then it would not really matter. We can pick up an object, place it somewhere where it can be seen and appreciated by ourselves or by a wider audience, perhaps in an art gallery, in which case we have served our purpose – we have collected an object from the past and valued it in our own contemporary world. However, we have taken it out of its context, and it has a lot more to reveal than simply our appreciation based on our aesthetic sense of what was once an object valued within its own community. An archaeologist is trying to read the value and the role of an object in the past system and this is why archaeologists are so concerned to get details of the location and artefact associations. It is a fundamental concern to understand the context of an artefact, as well as to study it for itself.

This idea is followed up in the next two chapters which explain why archaeologists spend so much time and money dealing with artefacts and studying them, both as they get them out of the ground, categorising them and cataloguing them, and also by subsequently sending them off to specialists and conducting specialist scientific techniques on them. All of these are a necessary part of getting the full value out of archaeological material culture and to fulfil the duty of putting in the public domain that which has been both discovered (objects, associations, strata, features, samples) and destroyed. An excavation can never be conducted twice because that area of a site, or objects from a field, has been taken away for ever.

The tripartite divide

The way in which this book is organised reflects the divisions and conflicting interests in the study of artefacts. There is a need to understand the materials of which artefacts are made because their properties as raw materials, and their availability in terms of their quantity, shapes, and seasonality, all influence fundamental aspects of their use by a society and equally their survival and the techniques available and most productive for their study by archaeologists. That is why the latter part of the book is divided into groups of raw materials. However, all specialist studies have to integrate with other evidence from both different materials and other kinds of archaeological evidence to present a context-based discussion of material culture issues. There is a tripartite divide in archaeological artefacts as material culture. Objects are recovered from excavations or field survey by field archaeologists who may have a generalised knowledge of artefacts but may be neither period nor material specialists. It would be impossible for any one person to have detailed specialist knowledge of all finds from all periods. Instead the objects are passed on to myriad specialists for post-excavation analysis but even these specialists may call on the services of others for very technical analyses. Furthermore research analyses of artefacts has fallen into two distinct fields: the highly technical scientific studies of artefacts (such as composition analysis, technologies, characterisation, genetic sequencing, and wear analysis), and a social-science approach to material culture based on psychology, cognition, semiotics, perception, and agency. Few bring these two different knowledge spheres together. Thus the people who bring the objects in from the field, the hard scientists, and the social scientists all contribute to an understanding of archaeological artefacts as material culture but rarely cross into the other fields. Students tend to grasp one of these and are doing well if they manage two, not least because each field has its own pressures of funding and knowledge systems and, in some cases, a seemingly impenetrable terminology. What this book hopes to achieve is the melding together of these different aspects of artefact studies so that it will cover how to recognise an object and the properties of raw materials – a concept explored more fully as materiality in Chapter 6 – as well as the technical analyses that are possible and the social interpretations of these, and all, it is hoped, in technically precise but jargon-free language. In doing so I hope to show the central place of artefact studies and encourage an approach which is rooted in an appreciation of raw material properties, and recognises the merits and pitfalls of the artefactual evidence and the manner of its recovery and study.

2   Artefacts from the ground

Pragmatic issues are never far away in studies of objects, and archaeology never deals with unbiased collections because there are cultural and natural patterns affecting what goes into or on the ground to form an archaeological record, what is preserved for archaeology to discover, and what archaeologists remove and retain from the ground to study. This chapter tries to make explicit some of these basic issues of bias and deconstructs some archaeological practices as they affect the study of artefacts as material culture.

In many fieldwork projects not all material is recovered for a variety of reasons. There may be bias amongst individual excavators or surveyors on recognising materials, or selective recovery and publication of objects based on the research design. Examples of the latter practices are leaving more recent (however this is defined) material in the field, collecting only samples of frequently found or heavy materials such as bricks and tiles, the use of sieving or screening programmes for the systematic recovery of smaller pieces, or the hierarchical treatment of objects for analysis and publication. Some artefacts are seen as more important and accorded different levels of study and description across and within different material categories. Other artefacts may not be covered in detail in the final report or be accorded less analysis because they are believed to have no causal relationship with the period or feature being studied. It is possible neither to collect every piece of cultural information from fieldwork nor to publish each item in detail. In practice there is always a mixture of conscious choices and inadvertent bias in getting objects out of the ground, retaining and publishing them, then archiving or displaying them, but any fieldwork-to-publication project should have a planned strategy for dealing with data collection and the handling of artefacts (Alexander 1970, Andrews 1991, Balme and Paterson 2005, Redman 1973, Shopland 2006). Strategies for artefact recovery and processing vary according to site type and academic traditions (Shott 2005) though methods are not necessarily detailed in the final publications (but Holtorf 2002 presents a detailed account of the discovery and study of one sherd, see also Shanks 1998). For those who have never experienced such strategies, figure 2.1 (pp. 16–17) presents an overview and a case study from a developer-funded excavation at Princesshay in 2005 in the historic centre of Exeter city, UK, where the important underlying themes are the phased flow of information resulting from fieldwork and the fact that such work generates physical objects and written or visual data pertaining to them.

Recovery strategies

Some experiments have been conducted looking at how material is collected from the surface of arable fields, often called the plough zone (Shennan 1985: 33–46, Yorston et al. 1990). In these, the dispersion of objects in a field has been shown to have a relationship to where those objects were originally. The material is scattered, but where the ground is flat it is scattered around the initiation point and so there is still a relationship between the points at which the objects were buried and their general distribution in the plough soil. However, the picking up of objects need not be a reflection of what is genuinely there. Shennan (1985) observed that different field walkers could pick out different categories of material better than another person, and that some people were particularly good at recognising shapes, such as flint arrowheads or flint flakes. It is quite likely that these sorts of collection biases are contributing to what is picked up off ploughed fields, especially where the collecting strategy uses widely dispersed walkers rather than the grid collection method.

With all collection, whether it is plough zone archaeology or excavation, the training and the initiation of the excavation or field walking teams is an important aspect of the overall research design. Some long-term excavations provide their own set of pages or manuals on how to fit the data that is being collected into the general systems prevalent in that organisation or at that particular site. For example, Augustana College, USA, has a manual as part of its archaeological laboratory, the Crow Canyon Archaeological Centre, USA, has a set of data sheets covering provenience (context) designation and finds records available on its website, and the Museum of London Archaeological Services produced a manual which has been adopted by others and has recently been translated into Chinese (MOLAS 1994, and Parker Pearson pers. comm.). Where there is one supervisor for a small team of people engaged in short-term fieldwork, points of information might be controlled by personal discussions, but often fieldwork seasons are short and teams are large, with supervisors acting as a middle layer between the fieldworkers and the overall site director or the finds officer. In these cases, everybody needs to be briefed and newcomers to the fieldwork process need to be placed with more experienced team members.

These are just small examples of how good practice creates a more definitive database for subsequent analysis. Archaeological endeavour takes material from the ground and so destroys its context with no repetition possible. This places the responsibility on archaeologists to maximise the information available. The project strategy should take account of the soil type, the period of the site, the likely range of artefacts, the materials and their probable condition, and the level of skill of the team that will be doing the physical work. Some sites use sieving programmes to ensure that small artefacts are systematically recovered, and the density and quantity of finds expected will affect recovery, processing, and storage strategies. At a Mesolithic settlement site in Sweden over 2100 kilos of flint were recovered and there were over 478,000 separate finds (Knarrström 2001: 310). A large proportion of the work at a site will be devoted to recovering finds and then processing them,

IMMEDIATE INFORMATION (HOURS)

Informs excavation and collection strategies

FIELDWORK (excavation or survey)

OBJECTS COLLECTED / EXCAVATED
hand-collected, sieved, bulk sampled

PLACED IN FINDS TRAYS OR BAGS

TEMPORARILY STORED

DIRECTOR(S)—SUPERVISOR(S)—DIGGER(S)

QUICK INFORMATION (DAYS)

Informs fieldwork and processing strategies

FINDS PROCESSING (often at or near fieldwork base)

OBJECTS CLEANED & LABELLED (see box 1)

BAGGED/BOXED
by context material and type
(see box 2)

DIRECTOR(S) —— CATALOGUES
FINDS OFFICER(S)   *CONTEXT LISTINGS*
short summary of types by context e.g. for approx. dates

POST-FIELDWORK ANALYSIS (assessment of finds study needs)

WRITTEN RECORDS   +   **FINDS**
incl. context info, listings + plans, initial phasing

TRAVEL BY SPECIALISTS / FINDS

INTERIM INFORMATION (MONTHS)

Informs data analysis and study

HOLISTIC REVISIONS
ideally discussion at themed meetings

SPECIALIST STUDY
for materials / periods / types
(see fig 2.2)

DIRECTOR
collates, integrates, revises, illustrates

SPECIALIST REPORTS
catalogues, archive reports, draft publication reports, images recommended / undertaken

POST-PUBLICATION

INFORMATION (IN PERPETUITY?)

PUBLISHED REPORTS   +   *ARCHIVE REPORTS*   +   **OBJECTS**
descriptions, images + interpretation   *usually organised by site, material, type*

PUBLICLY AVAILABLE IN LIBRARIES   **PUBLICLY AVAILABLE IN DISPLAYS OR IN MUSEUM STORES**
for comparisons + further study   *for comparisons, further study + analysis by arrangement*

INFORMS OTHER FIELDWORK, ANALYSIS AND RESEARCH

FINDS PROCESSING: EXAMPLES OF DETAILS

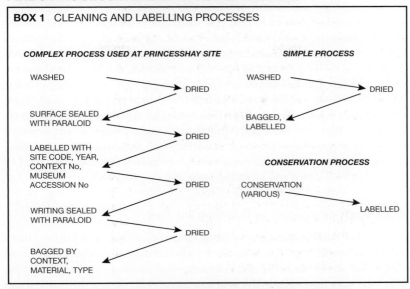

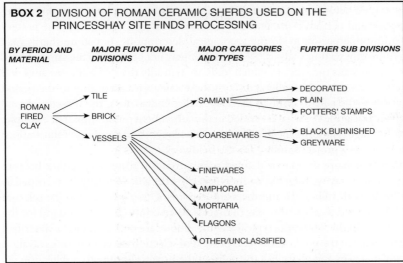

Figure 2.1 Stages in the treatment of archaeological finds and the information available at different phases

Source: author

and consequently a large section of the preparatory process will be planning for the finds that are recovered and formalising the archaeological project's research design for the finds. It is good practice to brief specialists and excavation assistants before the project commences, so that there is clear liaison and mutually agreed objectives and systems. If one type of material is going to be crucial, for example pot sherds for dating, then it needs to be agreed how this information will be collated quickly in the field and sent back to those responsible for organising the digging process. The cleaning, labelling, and marking, similarly, need clarifying at the outset. With most excavations it is possible to lay out a preliminary listing of the groups of objects that will be significant. For example, if graves are found, it might be important to list sets of grave objects found from one grave, or, if a floor or rubbish pit is found, all of the material from that feature may need to be placed together. This kind of information can be collated and recorded as excavation progresses.

The finds analysis process as information flow

The processing of finds in respect of washing, cleaning, sorting, and marking them so that their contextual information cannot be lost is crucial, and is usually done on site or nearby as part of the fieldwork. Following this, the material is sent off to the specialists who may have several layers of speciality. At this point the material can be fragmented between a range of different specialists depending upon the variety of materials and periods represented in the fieldwork (see figure 2.1). The pottery may require one person to do the typological descriptions, but some sherds may then require thin section analysis, which may or may not be done by the same person. Figure 2.2 presents the ways in which finds are typically divided but most sites will in practice have a much smaller subset of these categories according to the period and nature of the site. Within all these specialist endeavours, the director should have given a clear idea of what is needed in the subsequent publication. For example, English Heritage typically expects estimates of text length and numbers of illustrations before approving project funding for the fieldwork.

Objects which are unique or defined as important in some way, either because of their context, rarity, fragility, or individual worth, will generally be recorded as 'small finds' with individual numbers and records. Other objects may be selected because they are typical of large sets of objects so descriptions of them stand for the whole group. In this sense, the typical and the unique are picked out to be described in greater detail in the publication. This process of selection starts with the excavation or survey practices and continues throughout the process leading to publication. As finds leave a site, or the immediate processing of finds, there is already a hierarchy of objects. Some will be 'typed' and simply given as summary statistics in tally sheets; some will never leave the site or go beyond this primary analytical phase. Groups of objects may also have been presented as listings with preliminary quantities and tallies by contexts as part of the phasing interpretation during the ongoing excavation. Others will have been individually photographed and perhaps conserved in situ, or singled out in a listing of important finds because of their rarity, value, or delicacy. These kinds of hierarchies of finds treatments continue throughout the

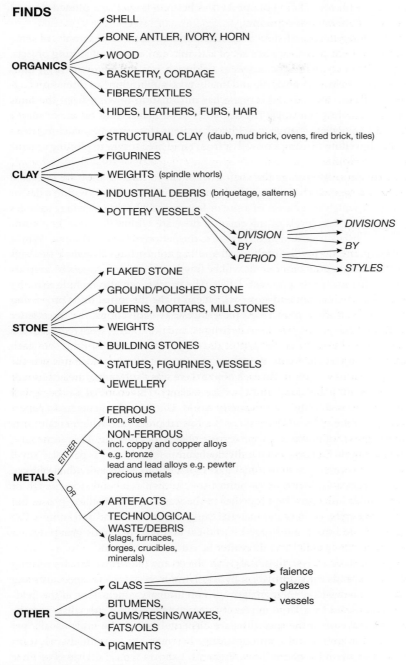

FINDS

ORGANICS
- SHELL
- BONE, ANTLER, IVORY, HORN
- WOOD
- BASKETRY, CORDAGE
- FIBRES/TEXTILES
- HIDES, LEATHERS, FURS, HAIR

CLAY
- STRUCTURAL CLAY (daub, mud brick, ovens, fired brick, tiles)
- FIGURINES
- WEIGHTS (spindle whorls)
- INDUSTRIAL DEBRIS (briquetage, salterns)
- POTTERY VESSELS
  - *DIVISION BY PERIOD*
    - *DIVISIONS BY STYLES*

STONE
- FLAKED STONE
- GROUND/POLISHED STONE
- QUERNS, MORTARS, MILLSTONES
- WEIGHTS
- BUILDING STONES
- STATUES, FIGURINES, VESSELS
- JEWELLERY

METALS
- *EITHER*
  - FERROUS
    iron, steel
  - NON-FERROUS
    incl. coppy and copper alloys
    e.g. bronze
    lead and lead alloys e.g. pewter
    precious metals
- *OR*
  - ARTEFACTS
  - TECHNOLOGICAL
    WASTE/DEBRIS
    (slags, furnaces,
    forges, crucibles,
    minerals)

OTHER
- GLASS
  - faience
  - glazes
  - vessels
- BITUMENS,
  GUMS/RESINS/WAXES,
  FATS/OILS
- PIGMENTS

Figure 2.2 Divisions of finds specialists

Source: author

post-excavation phases. The whole process is best envisaged as a phased flow of information to different user-groups.

Figure 2.1 shows the overall flow of information from finds and examples of some of the details of finds processing as a set of activities and as ways of sorting objects. The diagram presents the major phases as fieldwork (excavation or survey), finds processing, post-fieldwork analysis, and finally post-publication, an often unrecognised phase of finds analysis. Each phase has information flowing from the finds and being used in different ways. The discovery of particular finds on site or survey can lead to an immediate change in fieldwork strategy, for example switching from picking and shovelling to using a trowel or from rapid field survey to plotting specific find spot relationships.

In the finds processing stage the swift assessment of finds as they are collected and washed can provide chronological or functional interpretations within a day or so which affect which other areas of a site or features will be dug or where samples should be taken. These levels of information flow are within the close-knit community of a fieldwork team and mostly relate to the period of fieldwork alone. Whilst excavators at many sites will simply wash and bag robust finds, labelling the bags with context information, other items will be fragile and require conservation treatment with individual packaging with labels. The process can also include marking individual finds such as pot and stone which can make the initial finds processing complex (see box 1 in figure 2.1). At the Princesshay excavations, the three-letter excavation code, the year expressed as two digits, and the context were required data put on to each and every sherd as part of the on-site processing of finds, but each one was also being labelled with the museum accession number since this was the material's ultimate destination. On each object there was a substantial area of surface covered with writing and paraloid (a surface sealant). This material has been well and truly appropriated by the contemporary world. The finds also generated a paper-based adjunct to the objects. Often there is a formal procedure which creates lists of finds by context, and indicates approximate phases for contexts. Also, some rare, important, or fragile finds are given individual numbers and listed as part of a 'small finds' separate processing system which takes greater care with individual objects. Most objects from a distinct layer or unit of soil, known as a context in the UK or provenience in America, are kept together in the washing and labelling phases but are then bagged up by context and material categories such as 'pot' and 'stone'. The finds leave the site boxed and bagged into these accepted materials groupings, in which divisions the material will thereafter be studied and stored.

The post-fieldwork analysis thus deals with objects and the written archive relating to them, and expands the information by involving more people as specialists and also amassing the results of their analysis into preliminary conclusions. If the fieldwork was conducted by a large university department, all the specialists may be together, but more often the specialists are dispersed and so the finds usually get sent to them for study, and communication between the post-fieldwork team becomes part of the information flow. Figure 2.2 shows typical divisions of finds within archaeology, though few sites will feature all of them. The director and specialists may be presenting overviews in public talks or research seminars. At this stage a formal interim report may be written and published. All these activities widen the flow of information to a larger audience. The specialists and director may circulate draft reports or hold group workshops to improve the flow of information to one another, and further analyses may follow. The finds specialists' contributions to the final publication (text and figures) are honed, and specialists usually also finalise the archive reports which may include databases or raw analytical results, all of which have to be organised and presented with explanatory statements, and also bag and box the material systematically. The finds, archive reports, and final publication reports all go back to the control of the director who puts together the final edited report and assembles the material to go into an archive.

The final publication serves as a point of reference. It is on the one hand a primary data set for subsequent archaeological studies and an indication of the further information potential of the unpublished archive of full reports, plans and records, and the physical objects and samples. In some ways the illustrations and the material that is indicated in the published report act as an advertisement for what the site has revealed and for the objects that are then held in an archive. Good practice in an archaeological report would be to indicate where the site archive is held so that people reading the publication who want to study a particular object themselves will know where to go and perhaps even have a very clear indication of how to locate the object further (for example museum accession number, feature number, or illustration number). Certainly looking at other reports and trying to use them soon shows problems and examples of best practice.

It may be that the best and most typical examples of a range of objects are drawn and some are then selected further for photography to show particular surface features, perhaps microscopic details, or colours, or mottling of the surface and a particular surface effect. Photographs are good for surface texture and for beautiful objects, but archaeological illustration conventions allow a great deal of information to be succinctly conveyed. Archaeological illustration itself is a set of interpretations. It is not a subject for photographic renditions. Modern digital cameras make photographs very easy, but often those photographs show details which are extraneous to some aspects of the interpretation. For example, mottling of flint is quite common but it is the flake scar features that another person reading the report might want to see and these may not be obvious where there is a strong patterning on the surface of the flint. That is why archaeological illustration is a specialist branch of archaeology in its own right, with its own publications (e.g. Adkins and Adkins 1989, Griffiths and Jenner 1990), its own craft traditions, and its own organisations supporting those who are specialists in this activity. Space is a crucial issue in any report: the objects to be drawn need to be kept to a minimum and are usually reproduced at a smaller scale, all of which keeps the costs of the final publication down. Preferably, all such illustrations have a drawn scale so that, no matter what the scale of reproduction, the object's measurements are clear. Some objects might be too delicate or complex to draw (for example a fragment of embroidered cloth) and, in these cases, photographs with scales may serve as the basis of the illustrations. Because drawings take so much time, they will be one of the last things to be undertaken before publication. Typically archaeological reports will use tables, histograms, pie charts, or other ways of representing the data. All these will require clear legends and labelling, as well as captions numbered in sequence and referred to in the text. The whole archive will then need ordering and placing into a system suitable for the museum for which it is intended. Many museums also require the objects to be boxed into their standard box sizes and will want some discussion of how the material should be ordered for their storage systems. The museum then takes over issues of care and access and in many cases this is assumed to be in perpetuity though in practice many museums are facing storage problems.

If the end point is to see the finds safely delivered to a museum, the process of getting finds from the ground into a final publication is fraught with problems. It is a complicated business interweaving directors and specialists with storage and access to objects. Once the full publication is produced and the archive is in the museum, the information available from the finds enters a new phase. Archaeological site reports typically have a print run of five hundred to a thousand copies. Many of these will go not to individuals but to libraries, mostly to university libraries. Libraries have thousands of members and virtually all allow books to be consulted by non-members. Whilst some books may be taken out only a handful of times a year, others will be used more frequently. The publication allows the greatest number of people to 'see' the material from a site, without ever having visited the excavation or seen the material in the museum. Objects in the final report are not merely described but ideally placed in context. This can mean drawing attention to so-called 'parallels' – similar finds. These parallels are often found using the publications of other sites and surveys, and so individual fieldwork publications do not merely accumulate descriptions but accrue contextualised significance, and incrementally build interpretations and knowledge. The results outlined in the publication will be used to inform other research and fieldwork. Nor is the fieldwork report the last word. The objects and the paper archive together constitute another resource on which further analysis may be undertaken. In the post-publication phase, the initial fieldwork has created a stored resource of useful material to answer new research questions. This latter phase offers opportunities for studying existing information and gathering new data, if not in perpetuity, at least for the foreseeable future.

The finds analysis process as objects and people interactions

Though the procedures for finds can be presented as a system for dealing with objects, the process is not objective. All the stages involve the interaction of people with objects and the nature of this interaction can be seen as changing their meaning and significance and is subject to human strengths and foibles. A discussion of some of the practical details and the nature of human–object interactions highlights this subjectivity.

Objects can have a use life which outlasts their makers. An extreme example comprises the stones that make up Stonehenge. Those particular humanly modified objects are now thousands of years old and have been highly visible throughout their existence. They have been used in very different ways and have meant very different things to societies over this time. They have never left a living context. In contrast, smaller objects usually leave the living context which created them to become part of a deposit, and re-enter a living context when they are discovered by archaeologists or others. In a living context objects can be seen and handled by different groups of people which tend to change as the object enters different phases of manufacture and use. These object–people interactions through time can be envisaged as spirals. These spirals can go from small origins outwards, or they can close down. Figure 2.3 shows these interaction spirals and the variety of profiles they present. An every-day practical object is created. Perhaps there are one or two makers, with more people who will see the object being made, and perhaps one or more users, or a family of users. The object might be hung up when not in use on the inside wall of a house, so that a family and even a community can see and have contact with that object. Thus the object interacts initially with a small number of people, but the interaction spiral opens outwards to encompass a family or community. More public, perhaps ritual, objects might start life in much the same way with a small group of makers but have a wider spiral of interaction as part of community or inter-community events (for example wrapping and unwrapping wear on some large polished stone axes suggests their use in rituals; Wentink 2006: 62). Secret ritual objects could similarly begin interactions with a few makers but, in contrast, never go much beyond this and so their spiral will be a very narrow column of tight lines. Thus objects have different interaction spirals with people in their initial living context. My contention is that these different interaction spirals can once more be recognised when the object enters the modern world of the living. Recovery from the ground might involve the digger, the supervisor, possibly a few others such as the washer, marker, finds director, and then the subject specialist. In some ways this is at the level of a family looking at the object. Then it enters the museum storage and might only ever see the light of day intermittently for a long period of time to come. Occasionally objects are involved in activities which allow them to be touched: for example the Princesshay site held an open day which, unusually, included the chance to handle objects found on the site (figure 2.4), and museum education visits in Exeter can involve artefact handling (Osborne 2005). In both cases the objects had been specially selected and the activity was managed but it was evident that people were enjoying this direct contact even if these opportunities were only for a relatively local and self-selecting community. In contrast, if an object is selected for public display in a museum, then it can be seen (usually behind glass but see alternatives such as Lundström and Adolfsson 1993) by any visitor and in this sense it can have a very wide public usage. In these ways, access to archaeological objects can be closed down once they enter the museum storage, making them almost secret objects, accessed on limited occasions by specialists, or they can become public parts of cultural heritage and, as such, can become fetishised objects in our own society.

A good example of a venerated object is the Dead Sea Scrolls, where the whole museum room is designed to echo the object in the case (figure 2.5). In some ways it is a shrine for the object concerned. Another example of veneration is the 'stone of Scone', a stone associated with Scottish kingship which was taken to England and kept under the coronation chair in Westminster Abbey for seven hundred years. It was returned to Scotland in 1996 with due ceremony on a significant date,

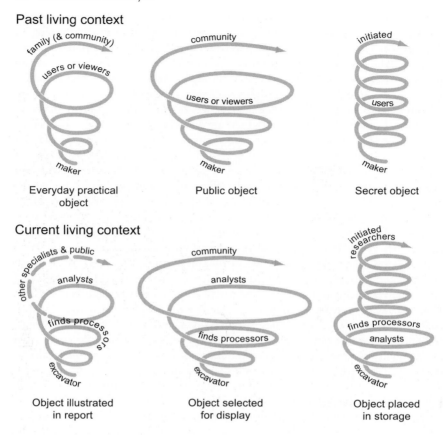

Past living context

Everyday practical object

Public object

Secret object

Current living context

Object illustrated in report

Object selected for display

Object placed in storage

Figure 2.3 Spirals of object/people interactions

Source: author

St Andrew's day, as St Andrew is the patron saint of Scotland (Welander et al. 2003). As an artefact it has held its symbolic appeal for all this time. Objects from the past matter to us in the present. The place and manner of their storage and display link to contemporary society, and the manner in which ancient objects are used can be termed 'symbolic capital' (Hamilakis and Yalouri 1996). That is why the spirals of object–people interactions shown in figure 2.3 have mirrored variations for both the past society and the contemporary one.

The very fact that we bother to store objects from the past suggests that we value them. However, this conceptual valuation is sometimes at odds with pragmatic issues and financial constraints. All museums try to make best use of their display and storage space as part of the effective deployment of resources. Many museums already have to think about how they will store collections because they are only ever being asked to take more without being allowed to let some finds go. Unless public funds are forthcoming to increase their storage space in line with their expected role as

Figure 2.4 All ages enjoy handling objects at the Princesshay open day

Source: author

endless repositories of objects from the past, eventually they will no longer be able to fulfil that function. This is already an issue in museum studies and, in some cases, developers are being asked not just to pay for fieldwork, analysis, and publication but also to contribute to storage costs. Most developers will not be in a position to

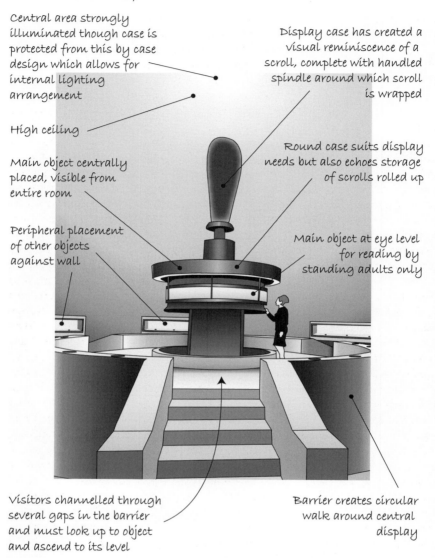

Central area strongly illuminated though case is protected from this by case design which allows for internal lighting arrangement

High ceiling

Main object centrally placed, visible from entire room

Peripheral placement of other objects against wall

Display case has created a visual reminiscence of a scroll, complete with handled spindle around which scroll is wrapped

Round case suits display needs but also echoes storage of scrolls rolled up

Main object at eye level for reading by standing adults only

Visitors channelled through several gaps in the barrier and must look up to object and ascend to its level

Barrier creates circular walk around central display

Figure 2.5   Deconstructing the use of space and allusions in the museum setting of the Dead Sea Scrolls in 'the Shrine of the Book', Israel

Source: author based on Broshi 1994: fig. 11.9

commit themselves to storage costs through infinity because the ideal is that the finds from fieldwork are placed in museums to preserve them for posterity. This supposition is really based on a concept of the 'forseeable future'.

It could well be that some objects get redeposited on site if they are not giving sufficient information. For example, some wet timbers are reburied in wet contexts.

If the objects cannot be taken out of the ground and conserved, or if only a limited selection of those taken out of the ground can be conserved, then one way of preserving objects is to redeposit some of them. There are difficult choices which will affect the material we have to study now and in the future.

Time is also an important factor in seeing the fieldwork finds through to publication. A classic example of some of the problems of post-excavation analysis is that of Stonehenge. An English Heritage volume (Cleal et al. 1995) brings together the previously unpublished material from all of the twentieth century unpublished excavations at the monument. This spans the period between 1901 and 1964, and five different directors of fieldwork. As could be expected, the standard of work and the surviving archives were of varying quality and geographically dispersed. Some excavators had originally intended the finds to be located via grid references, but unfortunately the grid pegs that served as the reference were not recorded on the monument as a whole and so there was no means of tying these into the present monument. Unusually perhaps, but illuminatingly, space within the 1995 volume is devoted to addressing precisely how to draw such disparate features and a variety of recording methods together. Walker and Gardiner (in Cleal 1995) discuss the nature of the archives and state where these currently reside. In particular, they present their post-excavation rationale (1995: 20–2). As an example the site records might state that finds were from the base of a fill of one of the holes. Their strategy was to assign the identified finds a modern context number so that they could be talked about together and assign another context number for the general fill of this hole. Standard pottery recording sheets were completed and individual record numbers were devised. In effect, the modern authors had to 'excavate' the associations of objects from the old archives and used standard archaeological tools such as context numbers and recording sheets to do this as a means of standardising disparate archives and presenting the information in a more accessible form for future research. Although the finds that exist now are described and quantified, it is noted that, in each excavation, some proportion might have been reburied or simply not kept and so overall quantities are now impossible to determine. These problems are exemplified by Stonehenge because it has attracted so much attention, but they are mirrored in smaller ways on so many other excavations which have spanned broad periods of time or where the excavators have died. Since the finds were often dispersed to specialists or to the director's institution in the post-excavation phase, if the final act of publication is incomplete, then the finds remain dispersed. In the Stonehenge example, although most finds went to the local museum in Salisbury, material was also placed at the National Museum of Wales and the Fitzwilliam Museum, Cambridge, as well as the British Museum.

In many ways, excavation reports have to be fairly standardised so that other people can find the information they need from them quickly. They are about conveying the essentials of the site and the interpretations of it. That is the key role of the monographs or small published articles detailing excavations or projects such as field walking exercises. Table 2.1 gives an overview of the role of finds in an ad hoc set of projects from a variety of environments and periods; some are 'type sites' for cultures. Together they show that finds take up half or more of most fieldwork publications. Where the percentage was lower this was because of extensive environmental or subsistence data (Agate Basin site) and/or spatial analysis (Çatalhöyük and the Stonehenge Environs publications). Some of the latter were still related to artefacts. They also show that, in general, the number of authors involved with finds rises according to the diversity of objects on a site, which in turn depends in part upon the period of the site and the preservation conditions and also the date of the fieldwork. There are, however, some surprises. Croes (1995) mentions other

Table 2.1 Finds in fieldwork publications

Project name (place), period(s) (other data); vol.(s) published, no. of pages devoted to finds and no. of authors for finds sections	Categories of finds: organics, stone, ceramics, metals
Selevac (Balkans 'Eastern Yugoslavia'), Neolithic/ Eneolithic research excavation Tringham and Krstić 1990, 310 of 616 pages (50%); 12 finds authors	*Organics:* bone tools *Stone:* use of stone resources (incl. use wear), macro-crystalline artefacts. *Ceramics:* ceramic technology, quantitative (incl. stats and typology), non-ceramic clay, figurines *Metals:* exploitation of copper minerals (incl. provenance)
Mons Claudianus (Egypt), Roman research excavation (*arid environment*) Peacock and Maxfield 1997, 151 of 338 pages; Maxfield and Peacock 2006, 110 of 456 pages; 2005, 450 of 450 pages Total, 711 of 1244 (57%); 17 finds authors	*Organics:* leather; bone, horn and shell; wooden objects *Stone:* quarries; routes and transportation; characterisation studies and use; portable stone artefacts *Ceramics:* Egyptian pottery fabrics; red slipped wares; thin walled; Egyptian faience; flagons beakers and mugs; jars and cooking pots; bowls, dishes, and casseroles; lids; misc.; amphorae, dipinti (written texts on pots); reworked vessels *Metals:* metalwork (comprising copper alloy, iron, lead organised by functional purpose); jewellery (incl. pearls and glass beads); fibulae, buckles, and fastenings; needles; pins; styli; seals and seal boxes; fish-hooks; vessels and utensils; lead fastenings; tools; fittings for furniture and furnishings; structural fittings and fastenings; assorted features and offcuts
Hoko River (Washington State, USA), Locarno Beach phase (3000–1700 BP) research excavation (*Wet and dry sites*) Croes 1995, 150 of 236 pages (64%); one author for entire volume but 19 'student researchers' and others as 'academic support' in acknowledgements	*Organics:* perishables (incl. fishhooks, basketry, cordage, wooden splitting wedges, woodworking debitage, pointed wooden objects, formed wooden artefacts, anchor stones with bindings, hafted stone tools) *Stone:* lithics (incl. vein quartz debitage), anvil stones, hammer stones, 'handwedges' sandstone, chipped schist, irregular sandstone abraders, formed sandstone whetstones, ground stone celts, ground slate, misc. ground slate, bifacially flaked points, stone beads, incised bone art, handstones and stone bowl, stone slab-lined pit, boiling stones and thermally altered rock *Ceramics:* − *Metals:* −

Agate Basin (Wyoming, USA), Palaeoindian research excavation (*type site*) Frison and Stanford 1982, 54 of 370 pages (15%); 6 finds authors

Organics: bone, antler, ivory artefacts and technology; cultural modification of bone
Stone: stone flaking material sources: flaked stone technology and typology; fluting of Folsom projectiles
Ceramics: —
Metals: —

La Gravette (France), Palaeolithic research excavation (*type site*) Lacorre 1960, c. 259 of 360 pages (72%); one author for entire volume

Organics: osseous industries
Stone: lithic industry; engraved stone blocks
Ceramics: —
Metals: —

Çatalhöyük (Turkey), Research site surface collection prior to excavation Hodder 1996, 151 of 366 pages (41%); 7 finds authors

Organics: worked bone
Stone: knapped stone
Ceramics: surface pottery; figurines, clay balls, small finds (incl. stone vessels, groundstone, stone and bone beads, coins, glass, plaster, shell objects, and various grave items); luminescence dating of mud brick
Metals: —

Stonehenge environs, (Wiltshire, UK), multi-period research survey with sample excavations Richards 1990, 54 of 289 pages (19%); 5 finds authors

Organics: —
Stone: lithics from the surface collections; lithics studies incl. analysis of specific assemblages and non-local stone
Ceramics: ceramics from the surface collection; prehistoric pottery (incl. divisions by periods)
Metals: —

Source: author

researchers and research students who contributed to the project, but the publication is sole authorship throughout. It is more common to see the director given as the author but with clear attribution to other specialist authors where appropriate. In effect, the director usually acts as both a major author and an editor of other authors' contributions but in bibliographical listings the work is treated as authored rather than edited. This is not the only idiosyncrasy of fieldwork publication.

In most subjects, books written more than a hundred or even twenty years earlier would be consulted mostly for their historical value because they would have been superseded by more recent work. Excavation reports present primary data from a unique source which can never be exactly repeated by more fieldwork. Reports, whenever they were written, are still consulted. Some of the standard ways of doing things have been described but there is some discussion on the role of finds reports (Stephenson 2005), and every so often someone tries to express things in a different way. Hodder (1989) randomly ordered one thematic book on object meanings so that a structural flow through it could not be read. He has also tried to use the different experiences of all the participants on the dig at Çatalhöyük, to show that there are multiple voices, not just one voice, producing the overall report. Renfrew et al. (2004) wanted to use film and texts as new ways of seeing objects. Barratt et al. (2000: 44–5) used different divisions to try to group discussions thematically along the lines of subsistence and food, and clothing and decoration, rather than the normal materials-based finds presentation. Likewise, for the five-volume series of *Mary Rose* publications, Gardiner (2005) tried to develop themes in each volume in the series and within these to group objects in ways that reflect their role in life: for example basketry, sacking, and chests are part of a chapter on storage on board the ship. The Tågerup volume (Karsten and Knarrström 2003) is similarly themed to make it a very readable report. Figure 2.6 reproduces its cogent illustration of the paradox of objects by grouping the same set of contemporary objects by 'in life' functional themes versus 'in archaeology' material themes. This report draws attention to publication issues.

These are brave and interesting attempts to get away from standard archaeological narratives, that is the formulaic storylines followed by the texts that explain sites and finds. Often the narrative framework is either a chronology or a set of material themes, but sometimes those narratives need to shift so that things can be seen in different ways. All such attempts have to live with the requirements of the profession to make a publication a useful resource for other specialists through time and a preservation by record, as well as a useful discussion and overview. The publication and its illustration act as written and pictorial advertisements for the information that is still in the archives and for the value of the site reports. In much the same way as the objects on display in a museum will be seen by anyone who goes into that museum, so too archaeological publications will allow others to access that material, even if they are then at a distance from it. In an era before modern mass publications, one of the reasons why finds were dispersed across vast areas was that people who were digging the sites gave sets of objects away, because this would then act as an advertisement for their work and would show other people, working in different areas of the world, what was being found. That is why in Exeter's Royal Albert Memorial Museum there are sets of objects from the late nineteenth century excavation of lake sites in the circum-Alpine regions. At first sight this might seem unusual and wrong because the material should not have been separated in this way, but, in an era without adequate ways of reaching a large audience, this was the excavators' way of publicising the work being undertaken in the archaeology of a particular region. People used ancient objects to communicate their results to their contemporaries.

Deconstructing the practice of finds analysis

There is a sense in which finds studies are seen as descriptions after the fact of excavation or fieldwork and, within the discipline, this area is regarded as in some ways straightforward; the objects are archaeological facts. Yet modern archaeology continues to encourage critical self-reflection and there is a trend towards seeing how the practice of doing something affects the manner and outcome of it. What follows is an attempt to put into words those issues of practice which have lurked on the edges of my consciousness over a number of years and imparted a growing sense of unease. Such reflection could be called a postmodernist deconstruction but it is not intended to be angst-ridden, simply an exposition of aspects of practice which usually go unrecorded.

Objects grouped by material

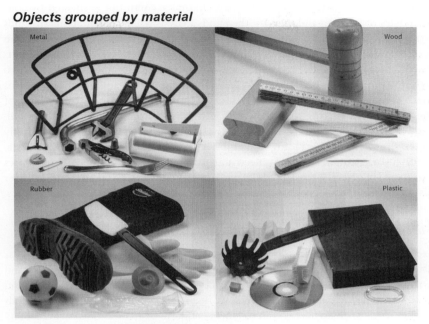

Objects grouped by function

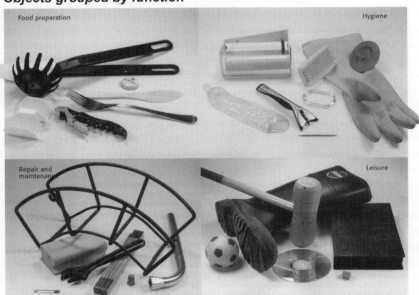

Figure 2.6 Modern objects grouped by material versus function

Source: photographs by Staffan Hyll in Karsten and Knarrström 2003, figs 1 & 2, National Heritage Board, Sweden

If archaeology does not take place in a cultural vacuum but is affected by contemporary regulations and agendas, then finds analysis will be no different. The finds analysis should really start with the research design. Inevitably, a theoretical plan is constrained by weather, safety, politics, or practical issues. Not many early reports discuss their goals and limitations in a self-reflective way. However, a more modern reflective overview is often useful in seeing how theoretical and practical concerns mesh together. For example a research design may be constrained by the laws of the country, such as the requirement to excavate any trench down to sterile soil, and restrictions imposed by the fieldwork permit, such as the need to keep mostly to the site itself, so precluding an emphasis on survey (e.g. Tringham and Krstić 1990: 8–9). A combination of reflective statements and personal experience shows that there are several issues about the practice of finds analysis which deserve wider discussion within the profession.

Fieldwork versus analysis: time and relative status

Excavation or survey field seasons are just the tip of the iceberg, and the analysis usually takes much more time. As an example, the Selevac project (Tringham and Krstić 1990: 3) had three excavation and preliminary processing field seasons and three of detailed material analysis. Such work is often organised into annual periods of three to six weeks to fit best with weather conditions or accommodation availability or to be outside university terms in so-called 'vacations'. The field seasons reflect concentrated effort from a team of people assembled in one place and dedicated to one task. If the finds analysis is not scheduled into this period, or into separate study field seasons, then the specialists disperse and so does the effort. For a research excavation, goals and information cannot be so easily communicated between researchers, and the finds analysis loses momentum because the specialists have other calls on their time such as other projects, university teaching and administration, or simply the need to return to their *paid* job. That is why some excavations have taken twenty years or more to produce the final publication. They are also complex pieces of choreographed movements and datasets which can span immense changes in technology: there are tales of records on punch cards giving way to 1960s coded data on central computers, then large personal desktop computers with limited memory, to laptops able to easily handle databases and graphics. Developers and research funding bodies have tightened procedures to ensure prompt publication. Time for the finds analysis should be built into all projects but often there is just preliminary processing on site. More rewardingly, excavations discover new data which can change systems of analysis or thought, and these take time to be incorporated into the previous dataset and worked up into a coherent whole. However, there is also a sense within archaeology that fieldwork has primacy over the finds analysis. The latter, famously has been likened to archaeological housework (Gero 1994). It is this primacy of fieldwork that has lead to some specialist contributors' names being only marginally visible in the finished publication. Excavation reports are rarely treated as edited volumes, though in practice that is what some are. The person who had the vision to conduct the project and organise both excavation and post-excavation work is seen as the driving force behind a resulting *authored* book in a way which the organiser of a conference resulting in an *edited* volume is not. There may be good reasons for the attribution of primary authorship to the person who devised and ran the major undertaking of a fieldwork project, but it tends to leave the finds specialists less significant by comparison, even though their work is an important contribution to the whole process.

Archaeological fieldwork is the high-profile visible tip of the iceberg but the post-fieldwork analysis leading to final publication is the less visible but much larger body of work, and the finds analysis forms a major part of this.

Boundaries and frontiers

Many archaeologists work on the archaeology of other countries. In some ways host countries welcome this as international recognition of the importance of their heritage, but it can create problems and it has formed part of colonial or patronising attitudes. Many countries now ban the export of cultural antiquities. In many cases permits state that objects must stay within a country boundary, or in a particular museum or secure store and researchers must travel to the objects. This is partly a security and conservation issue but it is also a reaction against the period when foreign nationals would dig and then take away objects. Many of these were lost to the home country for ever. Now it is possible to get permits to study some material outside a national boundary but this is tightly controlled and often allowed only where a particular study technique requires equipment not available in the host country.

During excavation finds are usually held at the field base and access to them for study purposes is usually freely available. However, once the field season is over the finds will go into secure museum or other stores. Getting access to them then requires permission and may be restricted, for example one box per day available at a particular time and often for only a short working day such as 10 am to 4.00 pm. It may be impossible to browse the collection and, depending upon permits and conditions in the working area, photography may be forbidden or very difficult. In one extreme case, local political conditions mean that it is possible to travel to the area where the finds are held in store only with a police convoy which leaves at a set time. The scheduled arrival time is after the deadline for requests for access to boxes from the store, so a set of two conditions makes it impossible for this material to be studied at this moment in time. Researchers have learned to live with access restrictions and they are the understandable legacy of a very different era. In practice, some problems can be sidestepped. For example the Fitch Laboratory based at the British School in Athens will produce thin sections which can be exported for analysis elsewhere from ceramic sherds which cannot leave the country. The artefacts are transformed into artefact and 'scientific sample', with the latter generally being more easily exported. This shows that it is not pieces of 'data' which are being denied an export permit but a 'culturally valued object' from the past – samples are not necessarily part of the emotional value system of cultural objects.

Division

In most cases it would be impossible for the directors of a project to take responsibility for all of the finds reports. These have become specialisms within archaeology and are the preserve of other academic contributors or self-employed or government-based specialists working within local or national bodies. Often the reports show that aspects of the artefact analyses were undertaken by PhD, master's and undergraduate students (Croes 1995: xi, Tringham and Krstić 1990). There is a trend away from specialist reports as appendices because the integration of all the contributing data is seen as important and a strong research goal will be explored using the different categories of evidence to address the problems from the special strengths of the particular category of evidence (e.g. Tringham 1990: 9–11). However, in many cases the specialists will be widely dispersed and working on their own material. Exchange of drafts or presentations to other researchers is desirable but not always possible in practice. It is not unusual to see more than ten contributors to a site report, and figure 2.2 shows why. Specialisms can be pursued in physical isolation and some specialists will even need to pass some items on to other specialists. Those studying the material may never have seen the region or site of the fieldwork and may lack a context for the other finds and know nothing of the work on them conducted by others. It is up to the director to ensure that specialists are briefed and receive the information needed, but many specialists do work in isolation.

Objects in their current living context

Once out of the ground, objects have only a brief period where a few people may have relatively free access to them, then they are removed and placed in secure stores where access is very restricted. They are guarded closely and only a few people may see the objects again. Access to them is highly controlled and is often possible only for initiates who have gained approval and who have performed prescribed rituals – signing in at the entrance, leaving bags and coats in an antechamber, wearing gloves lest their skin pollute the objects. This might seem a fanciful way of describing these acts but if an anthropologist were observing similar practices in another living society that is precisely the way these actions would be seen. If archaeologists recorded for an ancient society the physical remains of special store rooms full of objects within locked secure areas, with some items in public rooms but behind glass, we would interpret these as venerated objects, perhaps secretly sequestered and available for viewing or touch only for a few initiated people within that society. The fact that some objects are behind barriers may send a clear signal that they are on public display, but only to look at, and with no contaminating touches. Likewise, many objects will be visible only in low light in windowless rooms, where temperatures and light levels can be controlled. These dark secretive areas with lights placed to show some features at the expense of others, or some surfaces at the expense of others, could be seen as detailed restrictive practices. A small amount of deconstruction shows that objects from the past are seen as valuable, and practices can be read as 'closely guarded from the uninitiated and preserved for future generations'.

Thus even the scraps of cooking pot from the past can become venerated objects and part of in some sense a hoarded treasure of ancestral heritage. An anthropological deconstruction of the analysis of finds is quite revealing in this respect.

Public displays form an important aspect of the communication spirals. Objects must be specially selected for display for a particular reason supported by those who now control these objects. Even if, in most cases, this shadowy controller of the venerated objects of the past is, in reality, a friendly curator who is a public servant preserving objects for a community, and selecting display items as examples of common and special practices and achievements, the whole system can easily control access to the past and make that past give a message serving contemporary political agendas or personal gain. It would be possible to close off access to some objects or knowledge and emphasise others as described in figure 2.3. In some ways, those objects selected for full description and illustration in the publication are not subject to the same possibilities for restrictions. Books have the potential to reach a far larger audience and, once publication disperses copies, it is much harder to control access. Internet information is even harder to control. Thus publication of objects puts their information in the public domain of their current living context in a way that is difficult to retract or reduce, whereas this deconstruction shows that a physical object is much easier to control simply because it can be hidden and physical contact restricted. This difference in information flow possibilities has implications for how people used objects in the past.

Type sites and type descriptions

Some of the publications analysed in Table 2.1 were chosen because they are consciously defining a set of cultural material which has been encoded with a modern word. The Agate Basin Site is the type site of the Agate Basin Cultural complex. Likewise, the material from La Gravette and the site name have been used to define a major stage of the Palaeolithic – the Gravettian spanning some seven thousand years of the Upper Palaeolithic and stretching across Europe. These publications take especial care to illustrate as well as describe the finds. New material found elsewhere can then be compared to the original in order to assess whether it can it be given the same cultural label and thus be used to give general dates to material. These questions are still important because they set new discoveries in context. It is extraordinarily difficult for one expert to describe a type to someone else without an illustration. The human brain makes sense of a picture (even a schematic one) much more rapidly than if that same object is conveyed in descriptive prose. Illustration conveys information not only more quickly but more selectively. That is why it is a substantial feature of any artefact report, and why, despite the production of measured drawings being lengthy and thus costly, there is still no better alternative. Archaeological illustration is a technical drawing skill which has come to use a series of codes to present aspects of information in a very succinct way. It is not often that a researcher goes cold to a museum store to just look through objects. The published information is much more widely accessible and it is only after reading this that most will know that they do want to go back to the original material. Thus, if material is not published sufficiently, its value as a long-term set of research material is diminished. The terms used as types in reports need to be fully explained in words and images because they are a fundamental building block. These terms use words to create object semiotics, a language of signs from objects. Types make explicit archaeological concepts about objects and enable communication about them: they are created by close observation of the finds.

Becoming a specialist

It is possible to read and learn how to study objects, but in the end there is a practical skill base and, much as one would worry if a doctor had read books but had no practical experience, so a finds specialist who is learning their trade needs more than just books, films and DVDs. Therefore to become a finds specialist is to oneself become a specialist in the *craft* of finds analysis. This may include practical expertise in the craft skill under study but certainly involves the craft skill of physical analysis, textural recognition of key features and the knowledge base to reject certain possible causes and accept others. All this sounds dangerously like the sort of expert knowledge which can be restricted or made into a secret rite for the chosen few. In one sense it is just that: funding and access to a knowledgeable practitioner would both be ideal in learning the craft of finds analysis but neither is easy and both rely on circumstances beyond the control of an individual. There are concerns about the status of finds specialists and the passing on of specific finds analysis skills (Geary 2005, Hancocks and Powell 2005, Peachy 2005). In practice some people learn on the job as part of fieldwork employment. They start by completing minor reports and gradually build up their expertise. Others undertake PhDs and, whilst they are pursuing a unique aspect of study to fulfil the goal of a PhD, also pick up general skills in the analysis of particular kinds of material. There is no formal apprenticeship or mentoring system for learning the craft of finds analysis and there are current and likely future shortages of specialists in some fields (Peachy 2005). Archaeology values the crafts of the past more than it values the craft of finds analysis.

Overview

Artefacts which were once part of another cultural context come out of the ground and are reborn into our world. Contemporary artefact recovery and study strategies affect the flow of information arising from objects, and the whole process can be envisaged as a new set of object/people interactions as the ancient artefacts become part of a new cultural context, with relationships as complex as in their original cultural setting. A deconstruction of practices within artefact studies reveals some general concerns.

When freshly emerged from the archaeological deposits, artefacts are at their most free unless they are encased for conservation reasons. Shortly after this, they are likely to enter a period of seclusion and restriction from which most never emerge. A small minority will be selected for displays which serve benign or malign contemporary agendas. Researchers may have to travel to the finds and may even then have limited and restricted access to the objects. Finds specialists can be divorced from the archae-ological context and also isolated from one another or operate within a limited group. Objects which were once associated with each other are divided because of the knowledge base and scholarship traditions of archaeological practice. People learn to study finds in much the same way as an apprentice learns a craft. There are physical skills to learn as well as knowledge and a language of finds analysis. As with all crafts there are different levels of ability and degrees of expertise. Access to the knowledge base of a particular specialist craft can be restricted by geography, funding, aptitude, or circumstance. Archaeology values and studies the crafts of the past more than it values and reflects on the craft of finds analysis and publication practices.

3   Learning from contexts

Object histories and contexts

There are three different aspects to object histories and the way archaeologists can view them. The first is the living contexts of the past – what did people do with the object, and how can the life histories of objects reveal the activities and thoughts and strategies of that past society? In order to do this researchers from the 1960s onwards have become more aware of depositional contexts and the different ways in which the archaeological record is created. Schiffer (1972) wrote a classic paper trying to articulate some aspects of how objects were created and modified, and how material entered the archaeological record. He produced a division between, in his terms, the 'systemic' context, meaning the living archaeological societies' cultural context, and the archaeological context, which meant the post-depositional phase. In practice, there is another living context, our own, because, as soon as an object is dug out of the ground, it becomes part of our living cultural heritage system and we value or change it, or allow it to be changed by natural processes.

Schiffer (1983, 1987, 1995; Schiffer and Miller 1999) has further elaborated these formative concepts and specified a clear distinction between cultural and natural modifications which he termed 'cultural' and 'non-cultural' transformations. He divided up the life history of an object within its living cultural system as procurement (obtaining raw materials), manufacture, use and then its possible reuse, either with modification, in which case he termed it recycling, or without modification, in which case it was lateral recycling in the way that we would use a screwdriver as an impromptu chisel. He also invented three terms for different ways in which the debris of cultural activities entered the archaeological record. One he called 'de facto refuse' which was really the incidental leaving of objects in their situations. The key aspect here is that objects which were used in a place, or the trimmings of objects which were made in a place, would be left there and be associated with the remnants of that cultural task or activity. This is very useful archaeologically because sets of associated objects remain together at the location of manufacture or use. But there are two other ways in which objects can enter the archaeological record via a more conscious discard process. These he called 'primary refuse', where the objects that might have been associated together in a task or in life were deposited deliberately in one place as refuse, and 'secondary refuse', where objects were transported some distance to go into a special place. These concepts incorporated ideas about object associations, the spatial proximity of these to their places of manufacture or use, and also some distinction between unintentional and conscious discard practices. All of these different forms of refuse have different interpretive possibilities for an archaeologist. Furthermore, objects do not necessarily have one simple use. Schiffer's terms of lateral recycling or modification and maintenance recognised that objects changed use or were transformed during their life history.

These concepts offer a useful outline but need some updating. Firstly, there are other ways in which objects enter the archaeological record. They can simply be lost. This is rather different from inadvertently leaving material near a place where debris was created. The owner might well have placed value on the object that is lost, but simply cannot retrieve it. Also archaeology is not composed of 'refuse' in any simple sense and the idea of 'rubbish' is now challenged (Appadurai 1986, Bradley 2000, Brück 1995, 1999a, 1999b, Hill 1995, Kopytoff 1986, Needham 1989, Needham and Spence 1997, Schiffer 1987 and Woodward 2000). The formation of the archaeological record is a complex interaction of chance loss, deliberate leaving where an object was last used, deliberate leaving where it was last placed, the return and collection of something that was previously left and the deliberate accumulation and then deposition of objects as a conscious act of discard or as a way of placing objects outside their normal interactions with people. In particular, patterns of material emerge which have been termed 'structured deposition' (Richards and Thomas 1984, Hill 1995, Pollard 2001). Some such patterning may be socially determined: for example in Africa, Endo society links some kinds of refuse to a particular gender so that in this case depositions of ash and dung will be differently structured (Moore 1996: 110). This innately social practice, whether or not it is seen as 'ritual', will affect the archaeological record in a structured way. Nor is material that is deliberately put outside the immediate living context by deposition ignored, forgotten or unmeaningful. Thomas (1996: 59–60) criticises Schiffer for seeing the deposited material as outside of social awareness, whereas it may be consciously alluded to in the subsequent deposition of other material or placement of later structures. An Iron Age midden in the Scottish Brochs can be seen as a rich heap surrounding and enveloping the settlement not with rubbish but with ancestral debris. This could then serve as a metaphor and as a resource from which objects could be mined to be reused and reincorporated into the living contexts (Parker Pearson 2001).

Object histories becoming object biographies

Figure 3.1 incorporates modern variations on the means by which objects enter the archaeological record and covers the treatment of objects in more than one living context and as they are discovered and exist in our own society. It also includes the operational chain and object biographies. This is a holistic overview of archaeological artefacts as material culture using understandable terms.

In figure 3.1 the first cultural context incorporates Schiffer's notions of maintenance (also resharpening, mending, rehafting), lateral cycling, and recycling. Whilst these terms originally served as very pragmatic notions they lend themselves

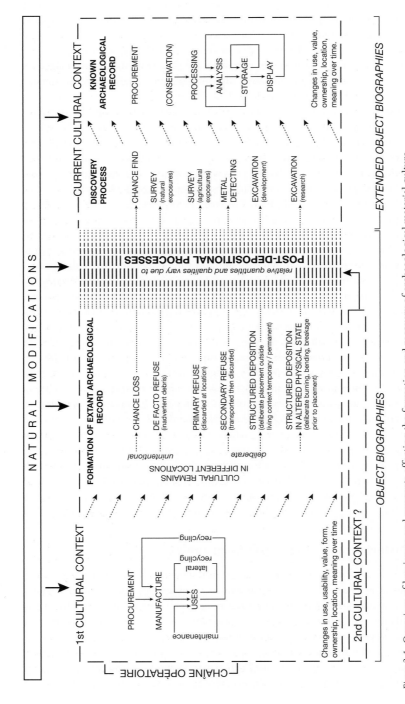

Figure 3.1 Overview of key issues and concepts affecting the formation and recovery of archaeological material culture

Source: author, incorporating data from Schiffer 1972: figs 1 and 3

to more esoteric reconceptualising of objects. Likewise with the addition of concerns of location, stages, set sequences, and cultural variations this section of the diagram encapsulates what is meant by the *chaîne opératoire*. The operational sequence or operational chain approach has been developed by French archaeologists starting with Leroi-Gourhan (1964) and incorporates the reduction sequence approach propounded for lithics (the archaeologist's general term for stone tools and flaking debris) (Bradley 1975). The term *chaîne opératoire* has now gained a wider and more general usage (Lemonnier 1986, 1993, Pelegrin 1993, Schlanger 2004, 2005) because the operational sequences of producing an artefact, the locations of the different steps and the debris left from each are all part of this approach and they can provide a framework for investigating any technological production systems. However, they can also go on into repair, curation, and, lastly, discard processes (e.g. Schiffer and Skibo 1997). The approach is as much about social practices as technologies and has gained prominence as a way of approaching material culture studies. When examined in detail, it shows that any one part of the chain can combine different aspects of the utilitarian, social and ideological because all of these, in practice, overlap and interact. The operational chain follows a time and space sequence to investigate different steps in the life cycles of objects.

The *chaîne opératoire* approach has some common aspects to seeing artefacts as 'categories' as proposed by Miller (1985). He recognises that the categories are part of the production process and are the way the people making things envisage each part of the process and situate it within their lives, though archaeologist's categories may not be those adopted by the past artisans. Hence the argument runs into emic (originating inside the culture) versus etic (imposed from outside) approaches to categorisation and classification. In some ways this is a non-argument because, essentially, what all of these authors are trying to say is that there is a sequence of operations and that those steps are culturally situated but, at the same time, contain pragmatic, necessary phases of manufacture, use, and eventually discard.

Life histories and the way in which structures and objects are used within a society are perhaps less utilitarian than the term suggests, which is why 'object biographies' is now a more common term. It can be used to describe any objects, some of which endure beyond one person's lifetime, whose values change over time and who perhaps have periods where they are dormant or go out of circulation and then are regenerated and reintroduced into society after a period of time. The meaning of an object changes over the period of use, and that change is part of the continuing negotiation of objects and people and the way in which the one interacts with the other (Gosden and Marshall 1999). However in the drive to place object biographies as a social agenda, there is some neglect of mundane issues which still leave their mark in the archaeological record. Factors such as human and animal trampling are known to affect both what enters a deposit by being 'trodden in' and also the condition in which it enters it (McBrearty et al. 1998, Nielsen 1991, Tringham et al. 1974). The objects that eventually enter museums are at the end point of their use as cultural objects – or are they? Visitors to museums place some kind of value on the objects, otherwise they would not be going to see them. The visitors will have different reasons for their visit and will see the objects from their own world-view, spending longer at some exhibits than others. Somebody who understands the significance of a deep colour in ivory, because this signifies that it has been in existence for a long time as hand oils gradually darken the colour of the tooth, will be able to read different information from it than somebody coming without that knowledge of material and a value system which appreciates this (Gosden and Marshall 1999: 171).

There are ethnographic examples (Strathern 1988) where objects are not something external to a person but embody the people who have touched or made them, and have intimate relations with the social connections that lie behind that object (see also Gell 1998). The notion of a cultural biography of objects incorporates these social dimensions as well as the more pragmatic considerations. Figure 3.1 shows the range of cultural contexts (possibly several) and cultural formation processes which are usually meant by 'object biographies' and demonstrates that it is only logical to extend this into the current living context. To make this clear, I have used the term 'extended object biographies'.

Although archaeologists have commonly dealt with fragments of objects, it is only recently that they have begun to question how those fragments have come into being – by chance or by deliberate acts of breakage (Grinsell 1960, Talalay 1987). Recent studies have, moreover, confirmed that some objects in the past are deliberately broken and the pieces dispersed as a way of enchaining social relationships by the fragment being viewed as a 'synecdoche', with the one part standing for the whole, or 'prescencing', conjuring a spirit of something by having one piece of it (Chapman 2000: 70–9, Talalay 1993, Skeates 1995). The body of evidence which suggests that fragments were kept after perhaps a deliberate act of breakage or the storage of the material in something like a midden or barrow is growing. Deposits can include sherds with very abraded edges from a more ancient period mixed in with much later sherds, and yet the contexts are secure. Objects are not simply entering the archaeological record, they are being reused by societies; fragments are being kept, perhaps after a period where they have been stored or buried, and then they are passed round, becoming relics and heirlooms before entering the archaeological record for a second time. It is suggested that sherds, perhaps stored in a midden at one point, are picked up and go back into circulation, functioning as relics or heirlooms. The same phenomenon can be seen in different classes of objects, for example beads, where the placement of holes or wear suggests that what was once a spacer plate in a composite necklace becomes a pendant. These complicated ideas have been advanced for the Neolithic, Copper, and Bronze Ages of southeastern Europe by Chapman (2000) and for Britain in the Bronze Age by Woodward (2002). This sophisticated recognition of fragmentation and deliberate acts of deposition and structures of deposition is part of this important means of distinguishing between cultural transformations and natural modifications and is all a part of recognising and analysing the objects that come out of the ground from archaeological sites. Furthermore, there is evidence for deliberate breakage, burning, or other acts of transformation as part of the cultural treatment of objects prior to structured deposition (Chapman 2000, Pryor 2001, Larsson 2000). The more archaeologists have investigated these processes, the more cultural practices have been discerned.

People have treated objects and their formation in simplistic ways in the past, but archaeologists can no longer do this. It may not be simple yet it does make for some really interesting interpretive possibilities, but only if we look at objects in different ways, for example by recording the abrasion on sherds.

Getting into the archaeological record

Concepts of object biographies and the way in which objects enter the record offer a way of thinking about the archaeological artefacts found in a particular place, or a particular society. Artefacts can enter the archaeological record in different conditions, after a time delay or a considerable period of use, or in very biased ways. What do we do with broken objects? In some cases they are taken away for mending or recycling. It is only when things are no longer *perceived* as useful that our society treats objects as rubbish. But usefulness is person and context dependent. Thus, the way in which different artefacts entered the archaeological record can reveal different value systems and perceptions in the past.

Curation and expediency

At perhaps a more basic level but none the less on this same theme, there is Binford's (1973) notion of curation versus expediency in the formation of the archaeological record. Curated objects are retained for future use, whereas expedient ones are made for immediate use and not retained. 'Expedient' means that it is for a short-term need, and if the object is still usable when it is discarded it does not matter. Curated tools can be very simple so the distinction is not one of technological complexity. However, because they are retained objects which are curated, they enter the archaeological record less frequently and perhaps in a slightly altered state compared with their expedient tool counterparts. A society moving around the landscape might use expedient tools in one place and curated tools in another, or particular kinds of tools might be curated with the remainder more expedient. The archaeological record is not simply an issue of curated versus expedient tools, it is about how people have used curated and expedient tools in a given situation and is essentially about cultural practices. One problem is that technological efficiency and tool curation are two parts of a complicated equation. Efficiency and the need to have effective use of raw materials usually requires there to be limited supplies of the raw material, either for reasons of distance or for social access. Curation can thus be a very complicated concept, with efficiency just one aspect of its measure (Bamforth 1986). Of course it is not just tools themselves that have to be efficient or curated. Time too, is optimised and can be curated and guarded closely (Torrence 1983). Though the concept originated with stone tools it is applicable to other artefacts.

DeBoer and Lathrap (1979: 127) describe a case study where ceramic objects are difficult to replace, and vessels are kept or 'curated' until they can no longer be repaired. Food bowls and beer mugs have a rapid turnover rate because they are frequently used and portable. Their fine construction renders them quite fragile. Despite this, most objects are made, used, broken, and discarded within a small defined household area. Even here, though, some objects will disappear because sherds are reused and ground up for use as temper in other batches of pottery. This is true too, where Harrison et al. (1994 in Chapman 2000: 54) suggests that the incorporation of old ancestral elements of sherds gives the past a physical presence in the present, and perhaps up to 25 per cent by bulk of the pots in the site in question consisted of grog temper. That would mean a loss to the archaeological record of a considerable number of sherds and thus of evidence of pottery use.

Size and usefulness

These two factors interweave as some of the following examples show. After making a small rabbit hutch in a garden, the 'waste' products are the wood offcuts; the large ones might be stored for reuse or perhaps used as kindling, but pieces too small to be of much use might be left on the ground. If the same task used small, readily available nails, some of which had dropped to the ground during the project, these might either be left as unimportant or be partially trodden in and not noticed. If, in the act of hammering in a nail on a post, the hammer head breaks, then the hammer itself is not effective and it might be impossible or uneconomic to mend, so it could be recycled or thrown away, in which case it might be left in some bushes out of the way and not deliberately discarded into a primary refuse context. If it was the handle that broke, the hammer head could be retained with the intention of mending it. Thus a complex web of usefulness, mending and technological possibilities, and economic value affect the object. If a house and contents are inherited the objects will be reviewed. Tools can be kept, for example something like a saw might be taken away for reuse, but an object that is a little bit more specialist, such as a gimlet, may not be recognised as a tool that is still useful to someone because it is not useful to everyone. It could be left in a shed or discarded as rubbish. Thus the size and perceived value of objects are important factors in how they enter the archaeological record (de facto, primary, and secondary refuse are just some of the possibilities) and in what condition (unused, used and usable, or broken).

Recyclable materials which can be remanufactured

There are materials and technologies which allow complete remanufacture. In our own society, metals and glass can be collected and can go back into the manufacturing process and be completely lost to the archaeological system. This is more than recycling-as-modification which might leave traces of former use, but might be better distinguished as remanufacturing. It is possible only in some materials and technologies, but although the possibility would be recognised in the archaeological record vast numbers of objects would never enter the record in the form they originally held.

Longevity, functional contexts, and quantities entering the archaeological record

Though some objects are used for a few moments and then discarded, there are others whose longevity means that they enter the archaeological record infrequently. Ethnographic evidence suggests that some stone objects such as querns could have been used for 70 to 80 years (Curwen citing examples from Scotland, 1937: 144). Some are dowry items and they are also inherited objects (Caulfield 1977). Thus some objects may occur less frequently in the archaeological record because, despite daily use, they lasted for 70 or 80 years rather than for one day. Objects such as sickles could have been used for one or more weeks each year, but would have had a season of use. The handles could have been far more long-lived items than the functioning elements that formed the flint blades set into the handle. Juel Jensen (1994: 85–160) showed, via use wear evidence, that in the early Neolithic of Denmark the implements used for harvesting seemed to have one season's wear on them and were not kept, whereas in the middle Neolithic the wear is much more developed and her explanation for this is that they were keeping sickles and using them from year to year. All of these things make up the archaeological record, but there is also another very pragmatic bias that enters into the formation of the objects we find on sites and in the plough zone. This is one where, inherently, some objects are more breakable than others and some, because of their context of use, are more often lost than others, and some get used up more quickly than others. All of these mean that simple counts of how many objects of different types are found on one site are absolutely meaningless unless these other factors are taken into account. Various authors discuss issues relating to discard practises and quantities in relation to different kinds of tools, their use lives and the formation of the archaeological record. (e.g. DeBoer 1974, Foster 1960, Hildebrand 1978, Nelson 1991, Shott 1989, 2001, Shott and Sillitoe 2001, Varien and Potter 1997, Wilson et al. 1991). Disposal patterns have been studied (Clark 1991, Deal 1985) but it is recognised that objects can be abandoned in different stages of their usable life, and Schlanger (1991) has tried to link the contexts of use into the contexts of discard and abandonment for specific types of tools. They can be broken in production, abandoned during different phases of this process, lost or broken in use, recycled, or deliberately abandoned in use. Abandonment itself is a very important archaeological concept involving deliberate 'finishing off', or discarding of objects and houses (e.g. Cameron and Tomka 1993, Tringham 1991, 1994, Chapman 2000 and Nowakowski 1991, 2001). Abandonment processes are known to have an effect on the range and quantities of objects entering an assemblage (Kent 1993, Tomka 1993). There are areas in the archaeological record where abandonment processes are now thought to have had significant effects on the archaeological remains, for example in Pueblos (Lightfoot 1993 and Montgomery 1993).

The implications of this work challenge some of the ideas about assigning particular tool types idealised functions, and then having simple measures of counts of different types within and between sites as an indication of the relative proportions of particular activities. This is too simplistic because there are obviously different rates of tool use for different tasks. For example, some skinning and hide preparation tasks performed by obsidian scrapers in Ethiopia require very sharp edges which need to be maintained by resharpening the tool every couple of minutes (Gallagher 1977, Clark and Kurashina 1981). So, earlier ideas based on simplistic assumptions on the making of the archaeological record have had to be revised and further developed to incorporate more complicated ideas of use lives and use histories (Ammerman and Feldman 1974, David 1972, Dibble 1987, Braun 1983, Hildebrand 1978, and Longacre 1985). Ideas can be tested using ethnographic data which, in some cases, have shown that the rules archaeologists have proposed are not followed. In part, this is because, where tools are highly curated and camps are occupied for short time spans, there is not a sufficient number of tools abandoned for them to be statistically representative of the activities that took place there (Shott 1989: 12). There is no straightforward relationship between the numbers and kinds of tools and the kinds of activities and the frequencies of those activities in a particular site. There is some merit in looking at use life values of tool classes so that these sorts of figures can be mediated. There are some sites with what has been called the 'Pompeii Premise' (Binford 1981), where objects have been abandoned in the midst of being used owing to a major disruption such as a volcanic eruption. But there are other pragmatic factors affecting the relative quantities of objects.

In pottery, the vessel size or weight can sometimes indicate its longevity. Perhaps it is not surprising that some pots in ethnographic contexts can remain in use for up to 60 years. These tend to be big storage vessel pots where there is low movement and the nature of their use means that they are not as liable to be damaged or broken, as would a small pot that has been carried around frequently. Arrowheads are shot at often moving targets from some distance and it may be that in the context of the hunt, or in dense undergrowth, it is simply more likely that these objects will be lost or not recovered, than is that case, say, for a scraper which is used in a handle and less likely to be mislaid because of the context and manner of its use. Other problems occur with the nature of the material; old wooden objects might be thrown on the fire, old antler objects can be scavenged and completely eaten by dogs. All these things are fairly complicated, but at least the biases are there, and archaeologists are working from the objects and the types that are present on the site back to what might have been there originally.

Missing objects

The significance accorded to the presence and absence and relative quantities of different artefacts on a site is thus an act of interpretation informed by considering a range of possibilities. Occasionally one gets a glimpse of what is missing. For the Egyptian eastern desert site of Mons Claudianus, Maxfield and Peacock (2001: 399) quote evidence from the ostraca (jottings on sherds) showing that some types not yet found during excavations would have existed on the site. Objects missing from the excavation but referred to in the written evidence include a lancet, an axe, chisels, spears, adzes, and wedges, the latter particularly notable since this is a quarry site. Generally tools and wedges have very poor representation compared to the purpose of the site, but it could be that these objects were not left in ancient times at the quarry site where the archaeological trenches were dug, because they could be taken back to the main Roman site and recycled or they could have been abandoned in the residential area. Added to this, iron is still a useful commodity and local Bedouin may well have long since found and made good use of any iron objects that were once on the surface of this site. Thus the following interpretations are all possible reasons for their absence; not present at the location of the archaeological trenches but likely present in the vicinity; not present because of recycling practices in antiquity; not present because such objects would be scavenged throughout antiquity up to the present time.

Deliberate deposition

In contrast, structured deposition and deliberate burial of items favour their archaeological retrieval. Bronze Age hoards arise from a variety of scenarios: scrap hoards, collecting objects together ready for recycling; items buried in the ground for safety, or offerings deliberately left in the ground with no intention of recovery. Other objects such as beakers and urns enter the ground whole, as grave furniture or cremation containers. All of these factors mean that these deliberate burials give us more complete objects, and more sets of objects together, than we would otherwise find. However, there are some objects which will simply never get into the archaeological record, or very rarely, because of either the material of which they are made or the nature of the site. For example, in temperate regions perishable organic materials rarely survive, with the exception of bone and antler.

Value as replaceability and personally significant object associations

Pens as the disposable ubiquitous biros are cheap and readily available: they are used until the ink runs out and then they are thrown away or they are lost. People frequently have several pens in different places, and they are often lent or passed on in an ad hoc way. They are common enough that they are not cared for because they are easy to replace. In contrast, a refillable and more expensive pen that was given as a present engraved with the recipient's name would be kept and carefully used. It might also have a much longer use-life because it was refillable. If it was lent at all, it might be lent only rarely and briefly. If it was lost, people would go back and try and find it. Its status and use would be different than that of the 'biro' pen even though both fulfil the same function.

The value and role of an object will affect how often it enters the archaeological record. In our own world, we routinely lose coins; however if we have something very valuable, if it is lost, we quite often go back, retrace our steps to try and find it. We would not do the same for a penny or cent. So the value that we place on an object affects how frequently that object will enter the archaeological record. Other value systems will also apply.

An object which starts off as one person's personal possession of some value can be venerated several generations or more later as an ancestral object. It becomes more important with time. The reverse is also possible. An object that was very expensive when it was created, for example a high-quality watch, may have been passed down and inherited by children, but if it becomes broken or unfashionable it might become a toy or discarded. Objects themselves sometimes transcend one person's lifetime and they can also change their usage, even within a short space of time. All of this makes for a wonderfully complicated archaeological record, but one that is, none the less, difficult to unpick.

It is difficult to take account of the possibilities for sentimental and personal attachments to objects. It would be very easy to think of heirlooms as valuable objects, but value can be social as well as economic. Objects act as souvenirs and mementoes of people and places or a task. A couple of modern examples make the point. A woman might have her grandmother's cast-iron pastry bowl because it is a good useful object, which was not going to be thrown away after the owner's death and reminds her of its original owner using it. An older woman might have her great-grandfather's anvil. Since he was a blacksmith it has been passed on down into the family as a very personal and originally very sentimental object signifying his profession. It now props open a shed door! Although it could be used for its original purpose, it has not been used for smithing for 50 years or more. We could add to this list the intrinsically valuable jewellery or the antique clock that is much more often thought of as heirloom material, but we should not neglect the role of the still useful object or the sentimental attachments to highly functional as well as eco-nomically valuable items.

Archaeological examples of social concepts of value

Social concepts of value are about more than economics, and occasionally the archae-ological record can demonstrate this. Some menhirs can be shown by the decorative patterns on them to have been broken and taken to two different places. In one case, a menhir fragment formed part of a chamber tomb at Gavrinis, with the adjoin-ing fragment reused in a passage grave, La Table des Marchaund (Le Rue 1984, in Bradley 2002: 36–7).

It is also possible to examine the Bronze Age metalwork deposited in the River Thames with a view to the state in which it was abandoned – after production, in a usable condition, after some form of destruction, after a sequence of use and recy-cling, whether it was deposited as a residue or a fragment, a damaged object or complete object; and in this way to study the range of different processes which contributed to those archaeological depositions (Bradley 2002: 56).

Examples can be found in prehistoric pottery (Bradley 2002: 57) where it can be found that a pot itself was valued, since care was taken to mend it when it broke, despite this being difficult. Grooved ware (Bronze Age, UK) pots, in particular, are repaired more often than other vessels. The classic chronological sequence of an artefact coming into fashion and then going out of fashion can be plotted as some measure of frequency against time to give a clear increase then maintenance in the numbers found, followed by a clear decrease. This distinctive pattern is not observed for some prehistoric British pottery types according to their radiocarbon dates. Bradley

(2002) has, interestingly, sought to explain this discrepancy, not by some fault in the chronological sequencing or in the radiocarbon dating samples, but instead with our concepts of what these chronological styles are doing. In particular, Bradley has posited that some ceramic vessels could have been in use for considerable periods of time and, thus, the radiocarbon determinations made on their depositional contexts date their *deposition* rather than their *manufacture*. All of these issues could explain why some of these objects appear to be very worn or, in some cases, incomplete.

Summary of factors affecting what goes into the archaeological record

There are two sets of biases in the archaeological record: those from the living context of the past and those of preservation. These affect objects of different types and different materials in varied ways, rendering straightforward counts and comparisons problematic.

- Object usability and longevity of function affect quantities of objects entering the record.
- The relative quantities of different objects entering the archaeological record are affected by biases which result from whether the use or context of use of an object make it inherently more likely that it might be left behind or mislaid (e.g. losing arrowheads during hunting).
- The cultural notions of curation, expediency, and efficiency affect the degree of modifications and longevity of use.
- Size ranges, where an object can be too big to transport easily, or so small it is not worth collecting and moving, will bias the objects entering the archaeological record.
- The potential to recycle (e.g. metal) or consume (e.g. wood on a fire) the material so that it does not feature in the archaeological record depends upon the material's qualities and cultural practices.
- The rarity and social value of an object or its ability to be easily replaced affect relative quantities of objects.
- There are often complex social object biographies which may mean that some objects are retained for changed social purposes or have their physical state altered before they are deposited, and/or are deliberately deposited.
- Objects which are placed whole in highly recognisable monuments are discovered relatively easily compared to those entering the archaeological record as single objects off site.
- The chemical and biological preservation rates vary for different materials. On an acid site, there will be very little bone and antler. On a wet, arid, or very cold site, organic materials may be preserved whereas these are usually missing from sites in temperate regions.

The biases are complex, but they are not incomprehensible. However, they are difficult to quantify, and some of these discussions are very much part of the 1970s and 1980s debates where archaeology was losing its innocence and questioning its previous assumptions. The archaeological record is composed of objects which have different use lives and different life histories. These have entered the record in very different ways and in different numbers. Furthermore, objects in their primary archaeological contexts can be disturbed and redeposited in the past before ever being discovered by an archaeologist.

Reading the archaeological record

This chapter has looked at artefact biographies as examples of how bias in the archaeological record occurs and why that bias is interesting to us and also necessary for us to understand in order to make correct interpretations. All of the accumulated pieces of information can be seen as leading to progressively building layers of meaning into the past. However, there are different ways of arriving at these meanings. As theoretical archaeology has shown, there are different questions to be asked: at one level, description is a necessity, and the establishment of regional sequences and geographical and chronological frameworks are crucial. But beyond this again there are the big questions to address – what changed, how did it change, and why did it change? An object which has rich associations due to secure archaeologically defined contexts can be linked to other objects and is more often datable. It can give some of the best detailed information and is crucial to establishing some of those links. This information is largely derived from excavation. There is, none the less, a role for low-grade information on a much broader scale. The diversity of ways in which artefacts are discovered and leave the depositional context has advantages since different discovery methods have different strengths and weaknesses and can be seen as complementary in some respects.

Excavation is very particular in where it finds archaeological artefacts. Survey can provide instead a broad sweep. The plough has, unfortunately for site preservation, but fortunately for the recovery of information, done the damage for the archaeologist and brought to the surface objects all of which could never have been excavated and recorded in one person's lifetime. Excavation favours large sites, but off-site activity and much smaller scale sites are harder to identify. So too, metal detecting finds have provided pieces of information to fit into the data patterns. All these contribute to a study of objects of the past. Initiatives such as the Portable Antiquities scheme in the UK have sought to encourage people to report finding objects to local museums, so that at least somebody will have a note of such objects' existence and the potential is there for them to contribute to these broad-scale archaeological questions. It seems strange to consider big issues in archaeology and then discuss such small pieces of information with, in many respects, such low-grade contextual data, but none the less they are part of the jigsaw puzzle. The archaeological record is always going to be incomplete, and so these different aspects create a mosaic framework which offers the greatest richness of texture and difference, in order to create the best possible means of collecting data about the material culture of the past and, thus, of studying that past.

Starting from an individual object and going on to the archaeological context and then more widely associated archaeological finds is not the end of the story, because with all artefact studies there are other methods and techniques which are used to augment the information available. Dating and phasing are key concerns and have led to important concepts. A *terminus post quem* uses objects within a context to estimate the date *on or after* which the layer was deposited, whereas a *terminus ante quem* is used where a set of layers or features are cut through by later features. The later features give a date *before which* those earlier layers must have been in place (Barker 1979: 194). Archaeologists use the term 'residual' to describe objects which come from much earlier periods, which they believe have inadvertently entered more recent strata. Thus there is material that has remained perhaps in plough soil or perhaps in general debris that has been reincorporated by chance when a feature is dug and backfilled in a later period. Where objects of flint are found in late contexts, such as a post-Roman cemetery, they are assumed to be residual and only minimal information is presented in the excavation report (Haughton and Powlesland 1999). However, this concept of residuality has been responsible for one of the biggest oversights of archaeological endeavours.

It is very easy to think that anything from a context which does not 'fit' with the most recent period is there by chance and is residual. This is not necessarily the case. In particular lithic artefacts found, for example, on Iron Age or Roman sites have typically been seen as *having* to be residual rather than *possibly* the product of flint working in those periods. This idea is now being challenged (Young and Humphrey 1999, Rosen 1997, and for Bronze Age reuse of earlier types see also Edmonds 1995). It is sometimes difficult to recognise these later lithic examples because they do not have formal tool shapes in the way that marks out artefacts from earlier periods. However it is quite clear now that the concept of residuality employed in archaeological interpretation has masked the continuation of flint working practices into the Iron Age and historic periods.

It is also possible on some sites to see that ancient people have picked up objects from a past that is distant to their own present, perhaps as curiosities or talismans, and have used them within their own society. A good example is Anglo-Saxon graves, where amulets of barbed and tanged arrowheads, or small fossils or pot sherds, were seen to be part of a fairly widespread phenomenon of using objects from the past (Meaney 1981, Echardt and Williams 2003). At Stix and Leaves Pueblo in North America as well as Pueblo-period arrowheads there are also examples of arrowheads from basketmaker III period and from middle and late Archaic and basketmaker II types. All these seem to be part of a collecting of earlier projectile points which is witnessed on other Pueblo sites. Up to 25 per cent of the material from the context was not residual, but was from an earlier period (B. Bradley 2000a, 2000b). Similar finds of earlier arrowheads at later sites also occur in Wallace Ruin, identified as an outlier, Pueblo II period site. These earlier arrowheads are not reused and made into new arrowheads. If they are remanufactured at all, it is perhaps for use as ornaments. Since contemporary Pueblo people collect old projectile points for use in rituals, the archaeological examples would seem to echo this practice. These objects are not 'residual' but have at least two past cultural contexts and complex object biographies.

Bradley (1997, 2000, 2002) has recently discussed the use of objects and monuments from the past in Europe. It is not easy to distinguish between items which are residual and those which have been picked up and deliberately collected and used within a past society, as part of their understanding of the past or their collecting of trinkets and talismans, perhaps for magical properties (Eckhardt and Williams 2003). In this way, both in prehistory and in more recent times, it is obvious that societies have taken a great interest in the past depending on their own contemporary social contexts. The concept of residuality needs to be carefully used.

The above discussion also questions the use of the term *in situ*. This term is used to imply that an object has not been reworked by secondary natural processes. Yet it has also been employed to imply that an object is in its original context, meaning where it was used. Given the complexity of issues inherent in modern ideas about complex object biographies and the range of possibilities inherent in figure 3.1, such a usage is now untenable and confusing. For example a quern, reused and incorporated into a wall, is in situ in the wall since it is in the place it was put in its last cultural context.

It is scarcely surprising that the archaeological endeavour of trying to use types and objects from, in some cases, millennia previously to look at the past activities and aspirations of individuals and societies is a difficult endeavour. That does not mean to say that ignorance or difficulties have ever stopped archaeological debate, nor indeed should they ever. But it does mean that the social and pragmatic factors affecting the formation processes of the archaeological record should be a key concern of any artefact analyses.

As much as the way objects *enter* the extant archaeological record can be picked apart for bias, so too the manner in which objects are *discovered* and become part of the known archaeological record is varied and produces its own set of biases. There are many more objects from large burial mounds which survived to be easily identified and dug by antiquarians than exist from more modest and ephemeral features such as disk barrows. There are more complete objects and associated sets of objects from eras when such goods were deliberately deposited. There are phases of prehistory which are object-rich and settlement-poor and vice versa. Practices such as hoard deposition inevitably lead to more object with object associations. Person–object relationships are much better known from eras when individuals were buried with goods. Metal detectorist finds have in recent years added immeasurably to the known archaeological record of this material category though not all have contextual information. The broad-scale information available from plough zone surveys provides a useful contrast to the detail from excavation, but it contains its own biases. Some periods and site types may be much easier to recognise than others: for example a Roman villa with robust and varied pottery, tile, and stone fragments should provide obvious remains in the plough zone whereas the plough may disturb a Neolithic house and bring to the surface small numbers of flint artefacts and friable ceramics which will not survive one winter of frosts. However, there is evidence of how artefacts move in the soil, and the interpretative possibilities for such ploughed remains (Gaffney et al. 1985, Yorston et al. 1990). Even excavated remains can come from projects with very different purposes, with consequent variation in analysis and, as importantly, publication and dissemination (e.g. the so-called 'grey literature' of filed reports from developer-funded excavations: Bradley 2006). Broad-scale artefact analyses are as affected by the variation in the discovery of the archaeological record as they are by its formation.

Chapter 2 explained the processing of finds and figure 3.1 represents these activities as part of an object's current cultural context. Our society chooses to promote certain objects from the past and selects research agendas (Shanks and Tilley 1987). Not everyone necessarily conceives object biographies as an ongoing process. That is why I have chosen to view this as the concept of 'extended object biographies' since not only is our current society using these objects and extending their object biographies but our cultural context may not be the object's last one: after all, it is intended in museum and archive aspirations that the objects should outlive us.

4   Making sense of artefacts

Layers of meaning and inference

In the last chapter, figure 3.1 demonstrated the complexity of patterning in past cultural life and in the archaeological record. Archaeology as a discipline has complex and fragmentary datasets and has developed strong tools to aid in the creation of ideas, and the analysis of data. There are four key tools to make sense of archaeological artefacts: typology, ethnographic analysis, experimentation, and scientific technical analyses. Typology has been a key theme since the origins of artefact studies. Ethnographic analogy has served to aid interpretation using generalised data or specific analogies. Experiments can test out technical details or be used to explore concepts. Together ethnographic work and experimental archaeology integrate and borrow from one another to form the powerful field of actualistic studies. They can elucidate how objects are made or used, the formation of the archaeological record, and the role which artefacts fill in societies. They can enable us to understand pragmatic and social symbolism in objects in ways that would be difficult to do from the archaeological fragmentary pieces alone. In particular, experimental archaeology deals with factual data collection, demonstration, technological investigations, artefact performance, recovery methods, taphonomic processes (post-depositional effects), and scientific method but can also be used to explore conceptual issues. Scientific techniques of analysis are the fourth tool. As science has developed since the beginnings of the discipline of archaeology, so a lot of those scientific endeavours have focused on the objects themselves. The study of the surfaces and the study of the composition of the materials is a basic division, but the dating, characterising (and thus the provenancing) of components or whole artefacts, the styles of technologies and their functions, and in some cases, the destruction and deterioration of artefacts, have all benefited from scientific analysis.

The order in which these tools of analysis are discussed reflects the way in which they have been developed. Typology has been fundamental to archaeology as a discipline and can be both servant and tyrant. Ethnographic analogy and experimental archaeology, the other actualistic, i.e. real-life, study, has been used from very early on. As science has developed so archaeology has benefited from it and brought different techniques to bear on problems. Scientific analyses typically allow objects to be dated and components identified. Not all objects yield the same kinds of information or the same quantities of information and one purpose of this chapter is to pick apart the ways in which archaeologists are able to apply typology, ethnographic data, experimental evidence, and scientific analyses to artefact studies.

Typology

Variables, attributes, and systems

Typology was introduced in the previous chapter but deserves a more critical look at who draws the boundaries and why typologies have evolved, been revised, and even been revolutionised by changes in time and purpose. What most people mean when they commonly use the term 'typologies' is the space/time grid (see Chapter 5), the use of common types that are widely understood for particular chronological or geographical markers, or some combination of those two. Despite the availability of radiocarbon dating, it is impractical for most projects to have more than a handful of dates undertaken. Therefore, typology is still used because it is a relatively cheap and effective method of obtaining fairly precise dates.

Adams and Adams (1991: xvi) make the interesting comment that typological classifications are not wholly objective and they refreshingly address the two parameters of typology – fitness for the research question and practical communication – which lie at the heart of good typological use in archaeology. Primarily, typologies are tools serving a purpose, but purpose depends upon the research questions asked and so it follows that no one typology will serve all purposes. Different typologies will take attributes (i.e. features of an object such as colour, shape, size, style of decoration) and use different combinations of these to create divisions. It would be impossible to use an exhaustive list of different attributes, so they are used selectively, hierarchically, and polythetically to create a system that suits the researcher's purpose. On the one hand they serve as tools for comparison and communication and are at their best when everyone uses the same system and deals with common terms in similar ways. This can be in direct conflict with the need to use a typology to answer a research question, where the question may require a new typology, or the modification of an existing one (Bisson 2000), or a re-examination of what the variations described as 'types' are measuring (Tomášková 2005). Several typologies may be useful and objects can be classified pragmatically into several schemas, using different attributes to address varied questions. Typology is also about numbers. The classic typological issue is how many classes to create (splitting), versus how much variation to allow within the boundary of one 'type' (lumping). It makes little sense to have five hundred 'types' for a thousand objects, nor to have two for ten thousand.

The majority of classification systems used in archaeology are identified most closely by objects typifying a polythetic set of characteristics, but the boundaries between one class and another can be grades rather than strong distinctions. If someone has trouble deciding whether something is falling into one category or the other, then it has more to do with the typological categories than any real distinction between those two tools: the divisions are artificially categorising gradations into classes. Different attributes will also have different places in the hierarchy, so within a polythetic definition it might be that certain attributes will more clearly mark out the class boundaries than will other attributes. All of these factors make for quite complicated mental concepts when sorting into categories. More sophisticated treatments of attributes and classification systems are sometimes required. For example, when trying to classify pottery, attributes could be divided up to assess fabric, forming techniques, form, decoration, and firing. Adams and Adams (1991: 99–142) give an example based on medieval Nubian typology. Large subdivisions were constructed using methods of construction and fabric as the determining characteristics.

As an example of how objects with which we are all familiar can be classified in many different ways according to the precedence given to particular attributes, think about watches. The gross classification could be into pocket watches and wrist watches. Wrist watches could have major subdivisions based on the technology of a digital battery, motion energy, and winding springs. Within the latter, distinctions could be made on the basis of whether the face had roman numerals, all of the numbers present, some numbers present, or no number present but just markers. The types could also be defined by the shape of the watch face. There could be a typology based on the size of the face or size of the strap or simply a measurement of these variables. All of these different aspects might give elements of gender interests, fashions, relative values, and might also indicate, in the case of some of the very technically complex watches, the particular interests of their users. Whilst the first and perhaps the most long-lived type concepts are of intuitive, obvious distinction, other attributes could be used for subdivisions. Types are, therefore, about levels of perception and classification is a system of types which gives precedence to some attributes.

There is a difference between a classification or a set of types in a system and the sorting of objects into a typology (Adams and Adams 1991: 47). It might be that a typology has been designed by somebody who is not then doing the sorting. That is where the issue of communication is so important. If things are not described well as a system, then it will be difficult for another person to use the typology to assign objects into the types consistently. On the other hand, if each type is exhaustively defined, the system might be too cumbersome for another person to use. There is, thus, a consensus that emerges of types which are used as a common language by archaeologists over large areas, and types which are more esoteric or more particularistic to a research question or a research field. Each has its purpose, but the former is a fundamental basis of archaeological progression as a communication tool.

Although it might be an ideal situation if every type in use in archaeology had a full description establishing the key features which define it, in practice, this is just not the case. When types are defined, they may be assigned names which are evocative of the material in question (Adams and Adams 1991: 31). 'Caenta black on white' or 'Mimbres black on white' are terms describing particular styles of pottery (Gilman et al. 1994). This is rather different from giving a code or number. One is an instant mnemonic. In archaeological systems, it is important that the typologies can categorise most if not all items. In practice, most archaeologists use terms such as 'undiagnostic fragment' or 'debitage' as catch-all categories to include everything that cannot otherwise be assigned into one of their more formally defined categories. Though not ideal, this is a pragmatic step taken by most artefact analysers.

Many people have concerned themselves with how we go about creating typologies and sorting materials and the need to go beyond 'typing' to investigate meaning (Adams and Adams 1991, Banning 2000: 36–57, Chilton 1999b, Kvamme et al. 1996, Redman 1973, Read and Russell 1996, Rouse 1960, Whallon 1972, Willis 1997). Each has tried to visualise the steps in the process. All show that there was a great deal of complexity of thought behind typologies. Nobody would devise all of their typological notions from scratch. Everyone is influenced by the typologies that already exist. In particular, as individual archaeologists go on the path towards becoming artefact analysts, they learn the craft traditions of their subject including the typologies, sometimes in explicit, formally taught sessions but more often by doing and by absorbing the implicit concepts. Each field of artefact specialisation develops its own never-ending process of learning and adjustment, which builds on the work that has been done before. With all of this complexity, it is not surprising that specialists tend to adopt one particular field of material, for example ceramics, as their main area, and then, within that, a geographical and chronological period or set of periods. It is also complicated for that knowledge to be passed on to somebody else.

Statistics and computing

Adams and Adams (1991: 108) show that pottery numbers can be significant: in their case, 150,000 sherds were recovered and recorded into a system in a typical season at a Near Eastern site and after a number of years there are now well over a million sherds recorded into one typological system. Counting, weighing, and providing the statistics for those types is not inherently going to tell us something about the people. It is a further layer of interpretation to interpret these statistics, and there is specific literature for archaeologists on the use and presentation of numerical data (Banning 2000, Baxter 2001, Drennan 1996, Fletcher and Lock 1991). However, there would be no numerical data comparisons without typologies: they create the groups which can be quantified or measured for comparative purposes. Where many artefacts show little difference, statistics may be necessary. As examples, the treatment of American northeast versus southwest pottery classifications is completely different, the southwest having a more varied pottery tradition and a much richer set of objects recovered than the the northeast, where statistical analysis is the only means of differentiating similar types (cited in Adams and Adams 1991: 229). So where there are strong intuitive types which yield good results there is no need to have a statistical analysis to try and create types.

There have been moves to place typology on a more objective footing. The algorithms of numerical taxonomy begun by Sneath and Sokal (1962) culminated in a whole series of computer programmes which were grouped together under the heading of 'cluster analysis'. Though the idea was to use computers to create groupings, computers create exactly the same problems as archaeological classifiers: endless splitting into groups with little variation or lumping material together with greater variation in each group, and issues of how to select the particular attributes to which precedence should be given. Thus, in practice, a computer is simply forcing analysts to externalise some of the judgements that are made implicitly by them when creating the old-fashioned set of typologies. Thus seriation is one aspect of typology and it is possible to use a computer to help produce this. But also a frequency seriation can use traditionally produced types and look at the dates (or relative sequence) in which they occur, and in what quantities, to arrive at the classic battleship graph. This typically shows how a style, for example of pottery, begins in a minor way, then becomes very prevalent and more numerous and so the battleship has width, and then gradually tails off again as the next fashion in particular ceramic styles comes in. Statistics and computers are useful tools, but they are adjuncts to what goes on in the minds of archaeologists; they do not replace it by something that is truly objective. A more modern trend has been to accept that intuitive typologies have a place, as do computer analyses, but that explicit recounting of steps can combine these two approaches (e.g. Read and Russell 1996). Computers are excellent for handling large datasets and for analysing trends and patterns within the data or simply to find particular records.

Analyst's versus maker's typologies

To return to the starting point of purpose, two terms contrast – the typological mindset of the person who was making or using the pieces versus the purpose of an archaeologist in creating a typology. These are emic and etic (D.E. Arnold 1971, P.J. Arnold 1999, Washburn and Petitto 1993). If a typology has emic meaning, it is assumed that the makers would have similarly been able to distinguish or categorise the differences between those types. The same is not true of etic meaning, which is very much a typology imposed for external purposes on to the data, irrespective of any categories that the original producing society would have. To return to the point of different hierarchies and different purposes on a grander scale, the individual types may well then be used to make up seriated culture classification sequences. A classic example is Pueblo I, II, III, IV, and V in the Pecos chronology created by Kidder (1915, 1917, Kidder and Kidder 1917). This is still useful and thus fulfils the objective of typology which is to serve a purpose.

Typologies bearing little relation to the maker's perceptions have been criticised (Healey 1994, Roux 1989). Braun (1983) suggests that even the most common objects found – pots – were not designed to have archaeologists study their forms and temper and decoration (though these are important variables for performance), nor were they designed as the sherds in which they are so often typed. They were designed as whole implements, as tools to be used and function in different ways. At the time he was writing the concept of a pot as a tool was subsumed beneath the information that could be obtained from sherds.

Materiality

Because of the differences inherent in the different raw materials, there are typological variations between the different materials. The number of potential variables in ceramic analysis is far larger because, as well as variations in the raw material, the shapes that can be made in clay are endless, and likewise the style of decoration. In contrast, there is inherently less variation possible in lithics: the main one is shape and, to some extent, the raw material. There is also a difference because the bulk of most ceramic assemblages comprise sherds rather than whole pots as originally made. Contrast this with flaked stone assemblages where there is a much higher proportion of stone tools which are, in fact, as complete as they were left by the people who made them but where a substantial proportion of the assemblage may be waste flakes known as 'debitage' rather than the intended usable products. In some ways, a pottery typology has to be based on a type for sherds because that is how they are found. If all pots were found as whole entities, we would have a rather different and perhaps less problematic typological system. If the classification system uses decoration but that decoration is characteristically on one part of the pot, and pots are normally found as broken sherds, then a substantial number of sherds would look plain even if they had once come from a decorated pot. It is only those decorated sherds that will be classifiable into the correct place. A further problem is that some diagnostic attributes cannot be easily identified. Some aspects of common archaeological understanding, such as some typologies of the clays used to form the pots, require microscopes and other equipment not commonly available in the field base.

It is also true that function in both lithics and ceramics is inherently guessed by the typologist. Early on in the history of archaeology there was the 'stone axe', and the 'storage jar', but it was not until fairly recent times with the advent of residue and wear trace analyses that one has actually been able to demonstrate those purposes. For the most part it is the shape, context, and perhaps associated evidence that have allowed those functional purposes to be surmised. A stone axe mimics the shape of a steel one and it is assumed the two have a similar function. If pottery types are not functional ones, in some ways they are serving an archaeological purpose rather than fulfilling an emic one.

However, form itself can be very much determined by limitations of the raw material being used and by the desired functional qualities of the edge and so, in many areas, the form will remain similar despite the period and region being geographically distinct. The field of 'cultural' typology tends to best suit the periods when there were definite styles because here the typologies are recognising and dividing up not just the functional form but a stylistic variation which has a regional and a chronological fashion, such as the varieties of barbed and tanged arrowheads. Conversely, minimally retouched pieces or ad hoc usage of fortuitously shaped stone tools do not lend themselves to these kinds of formal classification systems (Healy 1994).

Problems

The classic lumping versus splitting issue is typified by the so called Typological Debate (Adams and Adams 1991: 265) in America where hundreds of projectile types defined in the 1920s and 1930s are still being used. It is the classification of basic types giving the space/time grid that are still of most use. Others have rightly used experimental evidence to criticise the over-creation of typologies: for example Flenniken and Raymond (1986) showed that experimental sequences of projectile points over their use life created several different recognised types in a formal framework of Great Basin projectile point typologies.

One of the most cogent discussions of the problems with typology has been advanced by Karsten and Knarrström (2003: 14–18). They point out the basic paradox, which is that typologies not only search for similarities but also seek to point out dissimilarities. They give examples where professional consensus does not exist, either through time or according to individuals. Moreover, sorting into predetermined categories can stifle attempts to see different groupings and result in tautology. In this way, what was once a useful tool can result, when it is pursued blindly, in the stagnation of research initiatives. The key issue lies in knowing when variation is regional but contemporary, rather than chronological, and in assigning archaeological time spans to particular chronological differences. In particular, they point out that in their example, the Mesolithic of Sweden, flint dominates as the typing material; elsewhere and for other periods, this would be metal or pottery, and so quite often typological studies of one category of material objects which shape classification systems are subsequently applied to other materials for which there is little evidence, or for which no change is discernible. What is really required to control the typological quagmires is a more holistic perspective.

The concept of an artefact is one which develops over a person's lifetime. People become habituated to particular shapes. Archaeology typically presents typologies as whole objects, but in practice many objects are fragments but with sufficient form remaining to suggest the complete object. Interestingly, psychological research has shown that an adult is far more likely to take into account a fragmentary object's original shape in the naming and classifying of that object than is a child. This means that a portion of a cup is identified by an adult as a 'cup', rather than a piece of pottery or a flat disk or triangle, which is more likely to have been the child's straightforward identification of what it is now rather than what it once was. There are quite complicated psychological processes going on in the standing in of a fragment of something for what it is a fragment of – the whole object (Gutheil et al. 2004) – and such mental processes are part of practising archaeological typology.

Ethnoarchaeology and analogy

The use of other living cultures via anthropological and ethnographic studies is the methodology which, above all others, has been used to make sense of archaeological artefacts and is pervasive throughout archaeological interpretations (Arthur and Weedman 2005, Audouze 1992, Binford 1978, Coudart 1992, David and Kramer

2001, Gosden 1999, Gould 1978, 1980, Hodder 1983, Kramer 1979, Lemonnier 1986, Moore 1986, Orme 1981, Porr 1999, Sillitoe 1988). Archaeologists use the term 'ethnographic' to refer to data taken from other societies. Most often these are societies with a simpler level of technology and, in this way alone, perhaps more suitable as comparative material for studying technologically simpler societies from the past. There are areas of the world where it is still possible to do such ethnoar-chaeology (e.g. Africa, Atherton 1983; Asia, Allchin 1994, Griffin and Solheim 1988–89; Australia, Meehan and Jones 1988). In practice all societies are complex and much can also be learnt from examining one's own society.

The basic methodology is, thus, analogy: something that is perceived in one culture can be used as a point of comparison for something similar in another culture. There is always the problem that some analogies are predicated upon very similar circumstances or upon different circumstances combining inadvertently to create a similarity which, in fact, has no real basis in truth.

Ethnoarchaeology, as a term, is reserved for those examples where archaeologists themselves have gone out to collect the data. This is because the data is then pertinent to archaeological issues. How is ethnoarchaeology undertaken, what data are gathered and what purpose do they serve? The problem archaeologists face is that they have their own world-view both as individuals, perhaps affected by their sex and age, and also as members of their own society. This gives them one highly personal world-view. However, the society that they are studying obviously holds a different worldview, and so it is difficult for archaeologists to step outside their own precon-ceived ideas and notions. Thus, objects or roles of which they have no particular experience, and values and systems of meaning, could be elucidated by using ethnographic data. This is the best-case scenario – where ethnographic data create a wealth of different ideas about objects and about their relationships to people and to material culture – but what happens in practice?

One major concern is that, far from enlarging the experience by which objects come to be interpreted, and the relationships between material culture and people revealed, ethnoarchaeological data actually limit those because only practices which remain can be seen and others may have no modern counterpart (e.g. O'Connell 1995). In this way, ethnographic data have been perceived as a possible limiting factor. However, using data from other societies is bound to give a wider perspective than solely relying on the practices in one's own society. Ethnographic data, at the very least, open up alternative explanations, but on what grounds should analogies be judged? The issues are also clouded because the person who records the ethno-graphic data, whoever they are and whenever they have done it, brings their own world-view to that particular aspect of recording. If some of the ethnographic accounts are historical, then we can imagine that a Victorian with a colonial per-spective might have had a very different idea of what to record, and the value placed on what was recorded. Furthermore, it is obvious that some things were not written down because they were so obvious to the recorder. Since it is absolutely impossible for somebody to record everything, then those choices would have limited what we can now use that historical ethnographic account for. Gender bias in recording is also a key concern. Often the gender of the ethnographer is male and it may have been that they were not permitted contact with the women, or that they themselves perceived the women's activities as of a lesser status and did not record them. In either event, the ethnographic record can be very biased.

A further problem of these ethnographic accounts is that often long-term data are required, because short-term circumstances may vary. It also takes time to gain the trust of informants and participants in this sort of endeavour. Ethnographic accounts where the observers spent a number of years with their subjects are often much more rich because the observer has become immersed in the material culture and people that they are studying.

It is common to think of ethnoarchaeology and ethnographic studies as being done somewhere else, often in what might be considered harsh marginal environments, for example studies of the Arctic peoples or the !Kung San in southern parts of Africa, or western desert Australian Aborigines. Much archaeology takes place in temperate zones and yet there is relatively little temperate zone ethnographic data, for historical reasons. The 'marginal' areas are unsuited to farming and so traditional lifestyles have persisted. In practice there is another underused resource for ethnographic data, and that is the craft traditions and societies in the developed world. Much can be learnt by studying ourselves, and archaeologists have examined modern material culture and how we use and dispose of it, in order to understand some of those processes in a generic sense (Gould and Schiffer 1981). Thus, ethnographic archaeology can come from a variety of sources. The problem is that people have grown disenchanted with the sorts of uses to which ethnographic analogies were put. In particular, sixteenth-century worldviews were often enlightened and transformed (Orme 1981) with reference to the societies that were being discovered and which were then used as alternative ideas for viewing and envisaging that past. However, the evolutionary perspective that was prevalent in the late nineteenth century meant that some comparisons implied that those societies were somehow lesser than western societies. It also implied that there was progressive evolution and that only some parts of the world had progressed, which is very offensive to modern-day thinking. It is scarcely surprising that ethnographic analogy was questioned. However, some seminal papers tried to discuss ways of making aspects of that analogical reasoning more robust and secure (Ascher 1961b).

The concerns of new archaeology made explicit use of analogy (e.g. Binford 1967, Gould 1980, Orme 1973, 1974, 1981). Yellen (1977) tried to put forward different ways in which ethnographic analogies could be used for general models or particular problems, either as a positive means of getting together a range of ideas, or, in what he termed a spoiler approach, as a means of showing that there were alternatives demonstrating that an archaeological interpretation need not hold true. He pointed out that there was also, at that stage, an underused resource of using ethnographic data to test out archaeological methodologies. That has been addressed much more in the intervening years (Binford 1978, 2001, Hodder 1983). None the less, there are still questions about ethnographic analogies which come down to two issues.

The first is particularist, where one ethnographic example is used with a particular archaeological case. The obvious question is why this should be relevant since there is a wealth of ethnographic data making it relatively easy to find an ethnographic case that might support an archaeological interpretation. Such analogies are certainly not proof, but how robust are they? Some ideas hold that such analogies are in some way strengthened if other similarities of environment, group organisation, technologies, or subsistence strategies exist between the two, but why any of those would really lead one to consider the argument more robust is perhaps rather less clear. It is always going to be the case that the particular ethnographic interpretation might be the wrong archaeological one. The second issue is the more generalist uses of ethnography. Unfortunately, these too have their problems since generalisations mask the variation and it is often the variations which are of most interest.

As the above discussion shows, it is not easy to get away from ethnographic data, but nor is it straightforward to use it. Setting down relational arguments and reasoning to substantiate why an ethnographic example might be relevant to the archaeological one is always useful. In this way, ethnographic work can suggest other evidence that the archaeologist could look for, not so much to prove a hypothesis but to seek other evidence to the contrary. Relational arguments show a more contextualised approach to ethnographic data in archaeology. It has been cogently argued that analogy is a relevant, useful archaeological methodology and that, despite the misgivings, there is no sense in not using the ethnographic data and working with analogical reasoning (Gould and Watson 1982, Roux 1999, Wylie 1985, 1989).

Key examples show what can be done using this technique. However, some of the best results have come from 'connected ethnographies'. In places such as Australia and North America, there may be living descendants with folk memories or personal memories of the kinds of activities that might have been going on in a relatively recent past. A classic example would be Spector's (1993) account of an awl found at a relatively recent site in America. Local indigenous informants and ethnographic accounts from the area were able to suggest meanings for some objects. In this way, the decorative handle of a small awl could be read as the work history and the growing cultural status of a woman in her tribe. However, such connected ethnographies are rare and, where they do exist, they may also have their own biases. For example, Australian ethnographies have shown a highly gendered society where both activity spheres and ritual meanings go along gendered paths (Bell 1998): thus it may be that a reading of objects in that society, even in the fairly recent past, needs a gendered ethnography in order to make sense of the objects. The vast majority of artefacts from the past have no obvious connected ethnographies

An excellent use of ethnoarchaeology is where there are living members of a group who can tap into their communal expert knowledge in a way that no modern counterparts can easily replicate. One North American Indian, Ishi, the last Yahi (Heizer and Kroeber 1979), was living in a decreasing traditional society and finally, as the last member of his tribe, he sadly gave himself up in 1910. Expecting to be killed, he was instead taken to a museum and spent his last five years interacting with the curators and public there. There is a paper on Yahi archery detailing his bows and hunting techniques (Pope 1918) and also his flint working (Nelson 1916). Here was somebody who could quickly produce an arrowhead in the skilled traditions of his society; and who could also tell us how he dealt with mistakes and even with getting a chip of flint out of his eye. There are some very pragmatic issues in the extant accounts and there are also some less tangible aspects, for example a study of his songs including one for flint (Nettl 1965). If such a person existed today, we would have a new set of questions to ask of them, but now even fewer people traditionally use stone tools (e.g. Brandt and Weedman 1997). Instead, the actualistic studies of this material category now tend to be done by experimental work, rather than by ethnographic studies, with a few notable exceptions (Clark 1965, Pétrequin and Pétrequin 2000, and Pétrequin et al. 1995, Thery et al. 1990).

There is also an ethical dimension to ethnoarchaeology which is very pragmatic and is much the same as one would set up for encountering any new group of people where one has to try out relationships and establish whom one can trust and whom one cannot, and perhaps some of the reasons why people say and do things differently. Much ethnoarchaeology deals with very paticularist matters which, at best, are nosy questions from a visitor and, at worst, can be intrusive and unwelcome, perhaps causing a loss of status or affecting relationships from which the participants might suffer long after the ethnoarchaeologist has gone home: they are not neutral objective observations but have their own experiences (Barley 1983, Golde 1986, Skibo 1999, Neupert and Longacre 1994). As with any fieldwork study in another culture, whether it is an excavation or this kind of activity, sensitivity to the participants and gaining mutual trust are crucial aspects to good ethnoarchaeological fieldwork in societies other than one's own, but, as stated previously, one's own society has many aspects in microcosm that are worth investigating to give insights into the archaeological record.

Ethnographic usage therefore encounters the following issues: gender bias, historical bias, lack of relevant details, examples mainly confined to extreme environments, studies most often based on relatively short fieldwork periods, and informant bias. None of these issues stops the use of ethnographic data but they do require it to be used carefully. There are useful detailed surveys of material culture (e.g. Osgood 1940), and good examples of ethnographic analogy and the reconstruction of prehistoric artefact use (Owen and Porr 1999, Van Gijn and Raemakaekers 1999). Some ethnoarchaeology looks at the formation of the archaeological record (e.g. Binford 1978). More recently, some projects have emphasised the roles of objects in social contexts and considered aspects of symbolism (e.g. Sillitoe 1998), some look at the use of symbols (e.g. Hodder 1983), and some take the *chaîne opératoire* approach (Lemonnier 1986). All these studies show that no matter what theoretical paradigm is adopted, analogies from observations of our own or other societies are a key feature of artefact studies. General texts also offer ways of seeing issues such as craft and trade (Helms 1988, 1993).

Furthermore, there is now a sense that people act as agents and that material culture is a meaningfully constituted material remnant of social differences and attitudes. For a long time, there has been a debate in historical archaeological periods, whereby the objects and the material remains can contradict what is said in the writings of a society. Often in such societies one has to examine carefully who is doing the writing and with what purpose, because not everybody has a voice and not everybody tells the truth. In the same way, anthropologists or ethnoarchaeologists study a community with which they can have a dialogue, and might well believe that they have the truth, but what people do and what they say can sometimes differ in the present. Sometimes such differences could be malicious and deliberate, or perhaps an attempt by informants to improve their status by not admitting to certain things, or saying what they believe the anthropologist or ethnoarchaeologist wants to hear – a question of politeness and pleasing a guest and visitor. Thus, even with ethnoarchaeology the word and the thing remain as a debate and one which an ethnoarchaeologist still has to establish as being in synchrony.

Experimental archaeology

It is scarcely surprising that ethnographic approaches and experimental ones often are closely allied and use each other's data, (e.g. Anderson 1999, Porr 1999, Gosselain and Livingstone-Smith 1995, Tringham 1978, White et al. 1977) since both can be classed as 'actualistic' studies, able to give tangible data on practical matters. The early antiquarians had a curiosity about how objects worked. In some cases they had a clear sense of the purpose it might have served from the object shape and its similarity to existing objects. They were also living in an age where explorers were returning from different areas of the world with accounts of peoples with simpler technologies. At that point in time, there might be very simplistic assumptions made about the relevant level of society and notions of progression, which we would find today colonialist, if not racist. None the less, they had contacts with societies that were not industrial. Their age in particular was concerned with technological advances and it is perhaps not surprising that many of the early experiments were very simple ones on manufacture and use.

Occasionally, people working on prehistoric objects did come into close contact with relevant techniques still being used, and people such as Sir John Evans (1897) wrote about those who were practising some form of experimental archaeology and the replication of arrowheads. Pitt-Rivers (1875 reprinted in Myers 1906: 36) makes it clear that he tried to make some implements of stone and that he learnt the technique from the more experienced Mr Evans (later Sir John): he also reproduced bone and antler shovels and picks to test out his theory of how these had been used in flint-mining (cited in Coles 1979: 18). Thus, at least two key figures in the development of archaeology were practising experimental archaeology in the nineteenth century as a means of understanding artefacts. There were still, at that point, gun flint industries in Europe and certainly some budding archaeologists would have been able to see some flint knapping by skilled craftspeople. Occasionally, experiments were published in some detail, and more ambitious projects were undertaken, such as a replica Viking boat (Coles 1979: 22).

Other inspirations for experiments were found from excavated objects, perhaps only in fragments, or from ground plans; for example, boats, houses, and tombs have all been constructed using ground plans from archaeological excavations. In all these examples, one common thread recurs – people learnt by actually doing something. They thought of things that they had not previously considered and they found solutions, which suggested other signs to look for in the archaeological record, and so the process augmented the link between evidence and interpretation.

It is this refinement of an idea, a hypothesis, which is at the heart of Popper's (1959) ideas about scientific experiments. Using this philosophy, an experiment never proves positively that something has occurred in the way that the experiment has shown but it does demonstrate a possibility. In fact, as much can be learnt from something that does not work as from a successful outcome. In this way hypotheses or ideas are brought to material reality, tested out in practice, refined and perhaps tested again, in a circle which closes down some avenues of exploration and opens up others. Actualistic studies can be a very powerful tool because they create the opportunity for the archaeologist to look at the material remains of an activity, and to see what traces would survive underground and their relative location and then to think through what would survive in particular soil conditions on an archaeological version of the same site.

Although its origins go back to 1956 and earlier (Anderson 2002b: 11), experimental archaeology came into its own with the creation of two key books, both written by John Coles, in the 1970s. The first of these, *Archaeology by Experiment* (1973), includes several sections specifically addressing artefacts from boats to small-scale objects for craft work and subsistence tasks. *Experimental Archaeology* (1979) contains a very useful section on the discovery and exploration of this form of investigating artefacts, and there are other and more recent overviews (Ascher 1961a, Callaghan 1999, Hurcombe 2004a, Shimada 2005, Weiner and Dreshsel 2002). Although many experiments involving artefacts are highly individualistic, there are some key themes. One is that in the 1970s a number of different, large-scale experimental archaeology projects and other initiatives began: at Butser, UK (Reynolds 1974, 1976, 1979) and at Lejre, Denmark (Hansen 1977, Snyder 2002), major centres were created, and a raft of reconstruction projects ran because of particular key figures such as Callaghan in America and the De Haas father and son in Holland (Anderson 2002a: 23, 2002b).

The interest in experiments seems to have been partly a reaction against typologies in which objects were merely labelled, and partly a desire to identify their roles in the past by finding possibilities and eliminating others in the classic experimental endeavour. All branches of scientific archaeology use experimental work and so in artefact research there are pertinent taphonomic and conservation studies, as well as the more obvious ones of technology, function and longevity. These ideas have contributed to interpretations of individual artefacts, of associations of artefacts, and of whole cultures. There are multiple layers of meaning which can be discerned from experimental archaeology. There are also some caveats and drawbacks. Quite often it would be ideal to perform more experiments, but these tend to be rather like an iceberg – the part that is the active experiment is the area above water and a great deal more planning and research activities go on before and then after the event. Records and standardised recording procedures should be a part of all good experimental work, allowing others to replicate the same procedures.

However, there are practical constraints. One drawback of experimental archaeology is that many useful experiments are done by interested amateurs each year, but these go largely unreported. Good-quality reporting of archaeological experiments is something that should be encouraged (Outram 2005). A good experiment will have clearly stated aims, consideration of which variables are held constant and which are allowed to vary, will understand which methodologies are more appropriate – those of the laboratory or those of realistic, full-scale experiments – and will have given a great deal of thought to the recording methods and the eventual presentation of those results. Many experiments are undertaken for demonstration purposes: these are rarely written up. The growth in interest in experimental archaeology has spawned a whole series of different publications, for example the recent EuroREA journal, the German publications *Experimentelle Archäologie in Deutschland* and *Experimentelle Archäologie in Europa Bilanz* and the *Bulletin of Primitive Technology* published in America.

Many experiments need to run for a number of years to collect good data. There are the long-term earthwork projects which have objects buried as part of the experiment. For example, Jewell's (1963) long-term burial and earthwork experiments were envisaged as running for 128 years and the most recent phases have been covered by Bell et al. (1996). It is easy to think of more objects that could have been buried as part of these experiments, and further issues which they could have addressed, but these are the inevitable benefits of hindsight, and the experiments as designed show foresight and are providing very useful information.

It can be difficult to find people with suitable skills to make some of the objects common in prehistory. For example flint knapping expertise is rare. It is also difficult to precisely replicate conditions such as wind force for repeated outdoor or realistic experiments. Sometimes compromises have to be made and experiments are scaled down and conducted in the laboratory so that they are safer or so that the experiments are better able to control one or more of the different variables. Some of the projects that were set up in the 1970s with the growth in experimental archaeology have tried to get around these problems by looking at experimental work in a very holistic way, so there were buildings, animals, objects, and structures to mimic the known structures, features, and ways of life of a particular time period. For example, Butser was conceived as investigating an Iron Age farm complete with animals, relevant crops, and relevant technologies. These sorts of more holistic experiments have their own problems. It is difficult, without state funding, to know that the experiment will run for a sufficient number of years to have the right information recorded, and the directors of such centres tend to be exceptional people who are interested in both an academic aspect of archaeology and highly practical matters, as well as having superb organisational skills to run a thriving centre.

One contribution of experimental experiential archaeology is to promote an interest in archaeology and artefacts. Such public archaeology centres can provide a strong research message, offer educational value, and be very enjoyable. Figure 4.1 shows three images representing different interactions at Lejre: a visiting family is completing a simple manufacturing task; a volunteer interpreter staying on site is dressed in costume and mending his shoes with appropriate materials; a school party is chopping logs with an axe, lighting fires, and paddling logboats. All are completely absorbed in their activities. Experiential archaeology has its own unique presentational value but it is not necessarily research. At Lejre in Denmark however, because it is a research centre as well as a public centre, there is the chance to collect

Figure 4.1   Visitors engage with archaeological issues at Lejre (*a*) by family involvement, (*b*) by staying as a costumed volunteer in one of the villages, and (*c*) by school visits.

Source: author

information on the longevity of logboats, the durability and repair needs of clothing, and many other issues. Such places also offer access to experienced staff and serve as a resource for researchers doing more particularistic experiments, who want to tap into resources available only at these places. It is encouraging that large centres such as Lejre still want applications from scholars to go and perform their experiments there and give grants for this purpose.

Experiments can be very simple but have profound effects. There was a suggestion that some of the quartzite stone tools found on scarp slopes of soft sediments in Pakistan were caused by natural fractures as they fell down the profile. A simple experiment throwing many similar stones down the hillside demonstrated that this was highly unlikely (Hurcombe 2004b). Coles's (1962, 1979: 198–9) famous experiment to test swords and shields showed that shields made of hardened leather were more effective at deflecting blows from Bronze Age swords than were their thin sheet-bronze counterparts.

Many modern techniques use experimentally determined reference collections against which they can compare archaeological samples. This is true for all use wear functional analyses, whether it is on bone, stone, ceramic, or metal tools (Hurcombe 1992, Juel Jensen 1994, Moss 1983, Van Gijn 1990, Rots et al. 2006, Semenov 1964, Longo and Skakun 2007). Similar experiments have also been used as proof-of-techniques and to create the reference materials for residue analysis of pot sherds, and the identification of plant materials on tool edges and the like (Briuer 1976, Torrence and Barton 2006). Experiments also offer reference data on utility indices for carcasses (Outram and Rowley-Conwy 1998).

It might be thought that experimental archaeology was confined mainly to technologies and to the tangible, but this is not the case (Hurcombe 2004a). There are imaginative experiments which have looked at, for example, chimpanzee stone tool use (e.g. Schick et al. 1999), experiments in taphonomy and artefact movement (Schick 1986, Hurcombe 2004b), experiments reconstructing whole boats to assess performance (Coates 1989), consideration of the process of transferring knowledge and information (Washburn 2001), experiments in the designing of stone circles (Barnatt and Herring 1986) and even bone flute musical experiments (Lawson 1999). The idea of using experimental reconstructions to look at the musical tuning frameworks of bone flutes is an excellent example of the extension of archaeology by experiment into all aspects of archaeology. There are also collections of papers on particular topics (Stone and Planel 1999, Ingersoll et al. 1977, Mathieu 2002, Harding 1999, Amick and Mauldin 1989, Anderson 1999, Reynolds 1974). Experiments have also been used to test the efficacy of methods (e.g. see Newcomer et al. 1986, Hurcombe 1988, Bamforth 1988, Moss 1987, Unrath et al. 1986 and Keeley and Newcomer 1977). Experiments can aid interpretation by giving comparative data, for example use wear of stone tools or pots, or provide quantitative data, for example on the amount of meat and other resources from different animals. They can evaluate different archaeological study techniques for the most efficient way to recover data, for example residue extraction techniques. In almost every branch of artefact analyses, there are experiments which form a database for proponents and analysts to use. Without these, it would be difficult to envisage present-day artefact studies. They have been a backbone to the advancement of knowledge about artefacts. This method is widespread and wide-ranging in artefact studies and through its presentational aspects, which tend to be the best known, it is also serving to educate the public about artefacts. A lot of archaeologists are doing artefact studies by experimentation and it is forming a very powerful technique for advancing these studies.

Scientific analysis

As discussed in the previous section, there are certain key questions that archaeologists want to know – what, when, where, how, what for, and why? and *how* do we know the answers to these questions? In these areas, scientific analyses tend to be about collecting evidence and so they can, at their best, contribute to explanatory ideas addressing 'why?' and to an understanding of how we come to the knowledge and understanding that we do. But they are traditionally associated with 'what?' in the sense of an identification of a substance, or a material, or a residue on an object; with 'when?', as dating, and 'where?' as sourcing it to a particular location, usually the source of the raw material. 'What for?' techniques to determine function have been more recent scientific analyses of a very different kind. Thus there are what might be called hard science approaches to some of these questions and there are also ones where there are more subjective interpretations. In all of these scientific analyses, there is a need to understand the underlying principles, and not to lose sight of the purpose of the analysis and the advantages and disadvantages of a particular technique for solving a research question. Some techniques are undoubtedly simpler to use than others, or require equipment that is more readily available. So the key parameters in analytical techniques are how easy (and how cheap) the technique is to apply, whether the necessary equipment is readily available, the kind and size of sample required, and whether a particular material or artefact can withstand that sample being taken from it, or whether a non-destructive technique is available. All such parameters must then be weighed against the quality of the information obtained.

The scientific techniques extend observations beyond those normally perceptible to humans but the results may require specialist standard samples, expertise, or statistical manipulation in order to discern patterns and make identifications. The preparation of samples, or the manipulation of the data gained from samples, may require more time than the readings themselves. Furthermore there are inevitable tensions in sampling procedures. Analyses are expensive in time and/or money so sample numbers are kept down, and conservation requires taking as little of the artefacts as possible for the analytical samples, yet sample homogeneity and representation of the whole object, and population of objects, all need to be addressed. Some kinds of analysis are very expensive or the equipment or expertise is rare. In practice, most of the richer countries have some form of centralised facilities for scientific analysis or the techniques are concentrated in a few universities or museum centres, although there are some marked differences in funding patterns and research initiatives between countries, as Killick explains (2007). He also clarifies slight differences in terminology: in the UK 'archaeometry' tends to imply 'measurement-based' but not biological archaeological sciences, but in the USA the term is interchangeable with 'archaeological sciences'. Archaeological scientific data need to be based around a research issue and not sit as data-rich, information-poor adjuncts to reports (Young and Pollard 2000). Furthermore, some form of planning to identify and provide investigative funding for the development of emerging fields of analysis is advantageous, and in this respect national funding bodies can affect the kind of archaeological scientific investigations undertaken and the standard of these (Killick 2007).

Scientific analyses can be valued in two ways. Some are highly technical and expensive, but offer a very rare opportunity to collect high-grade information. Conversely, others offer a lower grade level of analysis and definition, but with cheaper more readily available techniques that allow widespread application. As with excavation versus survey; both kinds of information, highly specific on a limited number of objects (e.g. ICP-MS see table 4.2), or lower grade on a large number of objects (such as non-flint polished stone axe thin sections, see table 4.3), have their place in archaeological analyses.

Scientific archaeology has its own specialist literature (Brothwell and Pollard 2001, Cronyn 1990, Henderson 2000, Lambert 1997, Parkes 1986, Pollard 1992, Pollard and Heron 1996). Many other general books cover different object categories and analytical issues (e.g. Banning 2000; Ciliberto and Spoto 2000, Tite 2001). Much information is also contained in conference volumes and, in the past, this has been collated as part of national bodies: for example Rescue and the British Archaeological Trust compiled *First Aid for Finds* (Leigh 1972, Watkinson 1987). The reason objects are divided into material categories is that different materials have different limits and possibilities for scientific analysis and they also deteriorate differentially in the ground. Issues of conservation are not specifically addressed here but good overviews exist (Caple 2000, 2001, Cronyn 1990, Ciliberto and Spoto 2000, Mills and White 1994, Watson 1998). However, there is increasing critical reflection on the role of scientific practice in archaeology and the interpretative framework it serves and generates for different questions, materials, and periods (Bayley 1998, Jones 2004, Killick 1996, 2007, Kingery 1996a, 1996b, O'Brien 1998, Peacock 1998, Tite 1996, 1999, Sillar and Tite 2000, Wylie 1992, 1997).

Scientific techniques of analysis for artefacts have really come about from developments in other subjects. Much has been made in recent years of the developments in residue analyses for functional characterisations and, in particular, the use of these on stone and ceramic materials. Thus, even within a highly technical field, there is fashion and development of new techniques. These reveal new possibilities and, as the science changes, the applications relevant to archaeology develop. For example, there is now a machine which will characterise thin sections automatically, giving high definition of relative compositions and specific point analyses (Knappett et al. forthcoming). The branch of materials science developed for engineering and related fields is highly technical, and archaeology has often benefited as an adjunct to the developments in this field. In contrast, residue analysis seems to have been much more of a development for archaeologists, but this has been possible only because of improvements in the replication of fragments of DNA and increasingly finely tuned processes which allow smaller amounts of material to be analysed in a way that was inconceivable even ten or fifteen years ago.

Three broad discipline groups can be defined: materials science, biomolecular archaeology, and dating techniques. A person who undertakes biomolecular archaeology would likely be based in a chemistry or biochemistry facility, whereas materials approaches might be based in engineering or, in some cases, in archaeology departments. Dating, as a specialised technique, is concentrated in dedicated laboratories. The historiographical elements of the subjects' development influence the way in which archaeological work is now carried out and its possibilities.

Many different science domains contribute to archaeological science. These comprise the biology and biochemistry fields, including genetics, immunology and haematology, and the fields of chemistry, mineralogy, geology, and physics, as well as materials science and tribology (the science of wear). Archaeology deploys a full range of sciences in pursuit of its research goals, but these different disciplines are not necessarily fully conversant with one another and there are some problems over the further dispersal of the archaeological drive in science down to these highly specialist activities. One way of envisaging the analytical techniques spectrum is to see that there are families of techniques associated with particular kinds of very basic questions. One way of answering the question 'what?', and to some extent 'where?', is to state the composition of an object, and by this one normally means the chemical elements making up a substance and the relative quantities of these. However, there are differences even within this. Molecules are combinations of two or more elements into a unit, but elements making up a specific chemical formula may themselves combine in regular but different ways to create different molecular arrangements, for example crystalline minerals and complex biomolecules. Compound molecules formed from different elements behave differently according to their structures as well as their overall composition. To know the element composition of something is not necessarily to know how it will behave if it is identified solely at the level of a building block, rather than the structure made out of the blocks. Thus, it may be more important to be able to identify the actual substance, and for that one needs specific kinds of techniques. Structural analyses of these molecular arrangements thus provide a more specific answer to the archaeological question 'what is this?'. In these descriptions, 'composition' could mean the elements, or the structures of biomolecules or minerals. Both are useful aspects of the information available from analysis and provide both characterisation (the description of components, which may consequently lead to provenance data, that is where the substance originated) and the performance characteristics of the substance.

It would be impossible to undertake an exhaustive study of all of the different possibilities of scientific analysis, so what this section aims to do is to introduce key techniques succinctly by themes. Tables 4.1–4.5 at the end of the chapter provide summary statements and specific information on a suite of different techniques grouped thematically as microscopy (table 4.1), element composition analyses (table 4.2), mineralogical analytical techniques for inorganic crystalline compounds (table 4.3), dating techniques (table 4.4), and biological sample identification and functional analyses (gross morphology, histology and biomolecular analysis of organic compounds, wear studies, various blood residue analyses, phytolith and starch grain analysis) (table 4.5). In Part II later, each material chapter contains a table summarising the analytical techniques used to answer a standard set of archaeological questions (Tables 7.1, 8.1, 9.1, 10.1). These tables allow comparison of different suites of techniques and their application to different materials because the various techniques do not work equally well across all materials and there are some obvious gaps. Reliability of the different techniques can be an issue. Some studies have compared and integrated results across different techniques (Hein et al. 2002) or examined the effectiveness of a technique (Arnold et al. 1991, 1999) but most projects are conducted as stand-alone studies.

Some comments for non-specialists

Some aspects of elements are of interest for sourcing. These are quite often not the gross major elements which tend to lead to identifications of the actual materials; instead these very small trace elements, so called, tend to be those which distinguish one source from another, and so, by looking at some of the smallest amounts of particular, much rarer elements, one is often more likely to be able to distinguish between different sources. Some elements also have different isotopes (small variations in the number of particles making up the nucleus). These internal variations in element compositions are sometimes radioactive and decay in standardised ways by emitting radioactive particles, changing into other isotopes of the same element or other elements. The measurements of either the radioactivity or the relative proportions of different elements or different isotopes of elements can therefore be used in dating processes. The equipment and processes to analyse samples inevitably involve other elements as their physical housing, and the means of transforming, collecting, and measuring the subsequent effects. Furthermore the 92 natural elements all behave in different ways. Therefore it is not surprising that no one method can give equal accuracy and precision for qualitative and quantitative information on all 92 elements. All of the techniques have strengths and weaknesses which are outlined in table 4.2. The major elements may be similar but there could be more variation in the minor and trace elements to help define different groups. It is then a further step to analyse raw material samples collected from sources for ores, clays, or rocks and draw comparisons with archaeological samples to identify sources. This process could require analytical results to be statistically manipulated (Baxter and Buck 2000). The 'provenance postulate' requires that the measurable variation within a source has to be less than the variation from different sources for provenance to be determined ('provenience' is used in North America as meaning 'archaeological context' whereas 'provenance' is reserved to describe the 'source location') (Neff 2000). Where the natural sources are numerous, more of the natural samples will be required and in practice groupings of artefact samples, though statistically valid, may remain unprovenanced. The isotope variations of one element can also assist in provenancing, notably lead isotopes (Gale and Stos-Gale 2000). Other uses of element analysis include the identification of pigments for colouration or other treatment effects.

Crystalline inorganic structures can be analysed to identify the minerals to answer the question 'what?', but much of the archaeological use of these techniques is ultimately addressing the questions 'what groups?' and 'from where?'. Metal ores and products, and natural or added inclusions in pottery, and crystalline rocks can all be identified using mineralogical techniques. Most inclusions in pottery are quartz grains, and these are rarely distinctive of a particular geological source although there may be differences in size and shape of quartz grains suggesting groupings of fabric types. Coarse wares with larger exotic inclusions offer the best chance of identifying a geological source for the pottery raw material(s). Table 4.3 outlines the commonest methods which use relatively cheap equipment, and more sophisticated methods which are more rarely applied and used to address specific questions. However, the biggest issue in this field is that many rocks used for flaked stone tools are very fine and homogeneous (for example cryptocrystalline flints and cherts or amorphous obsidian). The quality that makes them suitable for knapping is also the reason why they cannot be easily identified by their mineralogy using the simpler petrographic techniques. That is why the polished axe thin-sectioning programme is conducted for non-flint rock axes and why there is no simple technique for sourcing flint, the main rock used for European knapped stone tools and many polished axes.

Much has been written about dating methods in archaeology and the advantages or problems of different methods. These are summarised and evaluated in table 4.4 but it is worth noting that relatively few of the commonest techniques such as radiocarbon dating are applied directly to artefacts and that the most frequent finds, pot sherds and flints, are often impossible to date accurately via a scientific technique. In practice it is other material from the same context as the artefacts to which the scientific technique is usually applied. Tables 7.1, 8.1, 9.1 and 10.1 try to make such distinctions clear. However, a trend is emerging for radiocarbon dating to be undertaken on trace samples and this has just begun to make the dating of organic residues on ceramics and even flint look as if this will become part of the future of artefact dating.

Biomolecular residues offer special opportunities for analytical techniques (table 4.5). In particular, sub-cellular structures, for example phytoliths (which are silica cell bodies) and starch grains, have particular shapes and can be distinguished to particular species. Thus, biology contributes to residue identifications, either on the surfaces of objects or from samples taken from archaeological strata. Sometimes histological structures can be identified. Blood residues can be identified and, if recrystallised in appropriate ways, can give specific crystals whose shape identifies the species. Likewise, multi-cellular biological structures can, even if they are just a small fragment, identify the substance from which an object is made if this is in doubt. Occasionally, structures from plant or animal tissues can be identified as residues on objects or as residues in the soil, perhaps surviving as charcoal for example from a burning phase. To this must be added a much more recent development which is based around genetics. DNA analyses and variations of these have recently become much more widespread in archaeology because the techniques have improved the ways of amplifying the small residues that are left on archaeological samples to obtain enough of the replicated material to then perform a normal biological analysis. Until this amplification technique was accomplished, it was much more difficult for archaeologists to use this technique because they simply did not have enough of the DNA surviving to run normal biological tests for this. Other complex body proteins, for example blood, can be used to form the basis of immuno-assay: this simply means that there is an immunological response and, if samples are processed with a known species, then the variety of reactions against these show the bodies' defence against other species, versus one's own. Hence, the analysis is based on immunological responses of a biological body.

Other techniques focus on surface physical and chemical changes. The surface chemical changes, rather like the genetic material, have relied upon recent developments which allow much smaller sample sizes to be accurately analysed. This has meant that archaeological samples have been brought into reach of this technique, notably by the work of Evershed and colleagues (Evershed et al. 1991, 1992, 1997a, 1997b, 1999, 2001), who have successfully analysed and performed experiments showing that chemicals survive in the body of pots and on the surface of them, according to the use or treatment of the pot. There are also surface chemical changes possible because of the object lying in a buried environment or because of certain treatments during active manufacturing, shaping, or hardening phases, so that a piece of metal will have a different crystalline structure at the surface, depending upon particular kinds of treatment during manufacture (see Chapter 10).

The chemical reactions at the interface of an object can sometimes create a layer of affected material which increases through time. It is this basic principle which allows obsidian hydration dating to work. Surface physical changes can be seen on a range of materials, although the causes of these vary. These can be due to deliberate human acts in the past such as manufacturing or use, or inadvertent human acts in the present such as ploughing, or excavation, or result from animal trampling, natural damage from frost, rock falls, or stream movement. Some of these may obscure other aspects of the surface physical changes.

Functional analysis can proceed by identification of residues at the chemical or morphological level or by wear traces. Often the residues are located in an area of wear. Wear analysis makes use of a range of features including edge scars, rounding, smoothing, striations, and residues. The traces can reveal some phases of the object biography from manufacture, hafting, use, reuse, and post-depositional factors. Varying microscopy allows the 'artefact-as-site' concept to develop, with wear and residues running alongside one another.

In all these techniques, certain kinds of methods abound. Invariably microscopy, at some scale, is useful. This can range from a stereo microscope going up to ×60 or even ×100, to incident or transmitted light microscopy, going up to ×500, and scanning electron microscopy which has the greatest magnifications possible. Scanning electron microscopes also routinely have attached to them the EDAX facility which allows element composition to be obtained in a fairly straightforward way. For compound structures, or for other genetic or chemical changes or residues, one instead needs to switch up to a range of techniques which look at the element composition and structure of an object. However, it is still true that thin section analysis (the grinding down of a mineral structure so that light can be shone straight through it with reflective qualities then allowing the discernment of different minerals) is one of the most widely used and productive applications of an analytical technique to archaeological problems. In many cases, the identification of chemical residues and genetic residues are the most complex because the amount of material is so small and the techniques in chemistry may require several different analyses to be run in order to make a secure identification of particular kinds of chemicals, or the degradation products of particular kinds of chemicals. With histological structures, sub-cellular structures, or surface physical changes, archaeological identifications are possible only with reference to a reference collection of known samples. The process is visual and, even where a distinctive structure can be seen, unless there is a similar one in the reference collection, no identification can be suggested. Furthermore, if there are similarities between the sample and the reference material the conclusions drawn will depend upon the ability to use a wide reference collection to rule out other interpretations; the match may otherwise hold true for a range of possibilities. Thus, all of these structure and surface structure techniques rely on good-quality and wide-ranging samples within published work or a physical reference collection.

Reference collections are also crucial to the identification of sources, whether it is by trace element analysis or by mineralogical analysis, so that the nearest likely source can be ascertained. If these techniques are performed in isolation, then they can say what the substance is, i.e. they can describe it, but they cannot attribute it to a source, either definitively or as 'most likely', without this comparative database being available. There are some basic truths such as this hidden within the complex web of individual scientific techniques. It is certainly true that most analyses cannot be undertaken by novices or those without knowledge of their own sub-discipline areas. However, it is equally true though not so often appreciated, that archaeological problems require an archaeological mindset and often a purely scientific analysis will not take sufficient account of the archaeological problems. That is why all of these techniques need their basic principles, their advantages and disadvantages, to be understood by those interested in artefact studies. Not because they will ever use all of them, but because they are a range of techniques available at a specialist level to those excavating sites or studying them from the point of view of material culture.

The best scientific analyses projects are undertaken with good reference materials, clear taphonomic tests to demonstrate that the techniques work on the kinds of deposits in question, and with clear archaeologically defined research goals taking account of the problems inherent in the techniques. Archaeological science is not a magic wand with which to solve archaeological problems. It is a tool like any other where the best use comes in the hands of somebody who has thought about their project and has done their homework thoroughly and has at least a modicum of relevant experience and has accrued other relevant specialisms and taken appropriate advice. One problem with the perception of science that is particularly troubling is the notion that it is objective, whereas archaeological evidence is subjective. If the science is applied to archaeological evidence and it too is subjective, then in practice no knowledge is divorced from the social context and selections which are part of the world-view, the discipline view and the contemporary view of the research endeavour. In this way, biases of sample selection, of research question, of funding sources, of qualified scientists and interests in archaeological techniques, are all part of the normal social paradigm within which all science is undertaken (Dunbar 1995 and Kuhn 1962).

The brief review of techniques and their domains presented here should not mask the fact that there are gaping holes in some of the analyses possible for particular materials. Some categories of material have several prospects for dating and analysis whilst others have few or none. For example techniques easily applied to source and date flint are lacking. Such techniques would revolutionise aspects of the study of this material.

Overview

The ordering of this chapter has tried to reflect the frequency with which different methods and techniques are used in artefact studies. All archaeological studies make use of typologies in some form or another and these have been refined and adapted to serve different purposes. They are definitely servants rather than tyrants. Ethnographic analogy and ethnoarchaeology may not be mentioned specifically in interpretations of artefacts, but in many cases research of this nature underpins conceptual and pragmatic considerations and is endemic in the way we approach artefact studies. To a lesser extent, this is true also of experimental archaeology, the other actualistic study. The two are intertwined. The rarest tools are the scientific analyses. Most archaeological artefact assemblages are examined by an individual looking at features by eye at the macroscopic level. The next most frequent are those which involve relatively low-scale technologies and, in particular, low-power microscopes, some of which require the object to have been prepared as a thin section or a polished section. The other scientific techniques are far less frequently applied. This is not to say that those interested in artefact studies should not be aware of them and know which techniques might best solve archaeological problems.

In science, a little goes a long way, especially because mostly the scientific techniques need to be applied in a highly selective way for cost-effectiveness and because such analyses tend to relate to broad-scale questions, often research questions, rather than common site report issues. Thus, the scientific studies will often cross-cut individual excavations or surveys and use a selection of material available on a broad scale in the repositories – the museums or storage facilities. There is a sliding scale of the way methods and techniques are used within archaeology, but each contributes substantially to the overall aspects of the study of artefacts as material culture.

Table 4.1 General microscopy facilities and techniques

Summary: Microscopy is the most widely used technical aid and is frequently used as part of or before any other technique of analysis.

Hand lens or pocket microscope: Many geological identifications, or quick assessments of surface corrosion, wear or covering (e.g. slips, glazing), can be made in the field using a small hand lens with magnifications of up to $10\times$ or, more rarely, $30\times$. They give a limited field of view (especially at higher magnifications) but are pillbox-sized and highly portable. 'Lighted pocket microscopes' can give up to $100\times$, but their very restricted field of view at this magnification makes them difficult to use for archaeological purposes. However, versions that go up to $30\times$ can be portable (box-shaped and about half a paperback in size) with batteries and bulbs readily replaceable, and at US\$12–30 they are inexpensive. $10\times$ is useful for scanning, while $30\times$ enables more specific identifications e.g. for pottery paste and slip identifications. Modern digital cameras, with macro lens and a tripod to aid detailed photography, can complement the use of such equipment. Some identifications will rely on higher magnifications or thin section work but the benefit of hand lens and 'pocket microscopes' is that they can process material in bulk in the field, with more selective complementary work at higher magnifications where necessary.

Low-magnification light microscopes. Models usually range up to about $50\times$ or even $100\times$. Some have stereoscopic vision, which is useful for viewing irregular surfaces. Most tend to use incident (i.e. reflected) light although transmitted light is available. Camera attachments can be used but these lose any stereo optical effect.

High-magnification light microscopes. Models usually range from $50\times$ to $400/500\times$ but some can go up to $1000\times$ (N.B. for the latter, the surface viewed must be very flat as this magnification uses an oil immersion system to avoid light having to pass through air between the specimen and the lens). Stereoscopic vision is not possible at higher magnifications. It is possible to use either transmitted light (i.e., the light shines through the specimen, usually either as a mounted small fragment or a polished thin-section) or incident/reflected light (i.e., the polished or natural object surface is viewed); some microscopes allow both. The working distance between lens and specimen can be very small, making it difficult to examine irregular or concave surfaces. Many models do not have more than 10 cm between stage and lens, which makes it impossible to examine larger objects but special models can be obtained with either an inverted stage or a long arm suspending the optics over a much lower platform so that specimens of any size can be viewed. As magnifications increase, the depth of field decreases; this is not a problem for flat thin sections, but microscopic irregularities in a natural surface result in less of the surface being in focus at one time. Digital camera systems are available.

Scanning electron microscopes (SEM). These are useful for high magnification (up to $50,000\times$) and do not have the limited depth of field (i.e. the amount of the surface in focus) associated with light microscopes. Many also have an ED-XRD element analysis facility which can analyse particular points on the surface. Most samples need to be coated with carbon or gold and stuck on to a mount since the sample will be in a vacuum chamber. The stage size is usually small (it can be <1–2 cm diameter) so in practice surface peels or small fragments as samples are needed. The equipment is used by many disciplines though not many archaeological organisations have their own.

Sources: Author, Jennifer Moody, Carl Knappett, Gill Juleff, José Iriarte (pers. comm.), José-Yacamán and Ascencio 2000; Killick 1996; Olsen 1988: Tite 1992.

Table 4.2 Element composition analyses

Summary: No technique analyses all elements at any concentration equally effectively, and particular difficulties occur with elements with lighter atomic weights which include most of those making up organic particles. Element analyses in the techniques described below are most often confined to inorganic substances but see also biomolecular analyses used in tandem with other techniques. Currently the complementary techniques of ICP-MS and ICP-AES are the most widely used, although the capacity to combine high-resolution images in an SEM with more problematic element analyses from XRF serves some needs better.

Glossary: H, Hydrogen; He, Helium; C, Carbon; N, Nitrogen; O, Oxygen; Fe, Iron; Ne, Neon; Ar, Argon; S, Sulphur; Cl, Chlorine; Si, Silica; Cs, Caesium; Lu, Lutetium; Os, Osmium; Th, Thorium; U, Uranium.

Mass spectrometry. This loose term is now more specifically known as thermal ionisation mass spectrometry (TIMS). It uses a few milligrams of a solid or powdered sample; this is vaporised, with elements turning into charged particles which magnetic fields then divide into groups identifying the elements. The technique is useful for studying pottery and sourcing (especially for lead because this element has great natural isotopic variation from different sources). TIMS gives higher precision than ICP-MS but is slower and more expensive.

OES: Optical emission spectroscopy, sometimes known as ICP or ICPS. OES as a term was superseded in the 1990s by the more specific terms ICP-OES or ICP-AES to distinguish it from ICP-MS. From the 1980s the technique was gradually replaced by AAS but in 1990s developments in techniques led to ICP-AES gaining popularity for large-scale work where liquid samples were readily obtainable. Sensitivity of 100 ppm and an accuracy to within 7–10%.

ICP-OES, ICP-AES: Inductively coupled plasma, optical (or atomic) emission spectroscopy. Multiple samples, each of 50 mg of dissolved powdered sample, are subjected to a high-temperature plasma field which causes the samples to emit light across a spectrum, the intensity of which varies according to the relative quantity of elements. The entire spectrum and its intensity can be measured simultaneously (more expensive), or as a sequence of different measurements of each element. The technique is useful for measuring major or trace elements in one process. It is widely available but not all equipment has the expensive high-sensitivity features. ICP-AES: Sensitivity 0.5–100 ppb; accuracy to within 3–5%.

ICP-MS (LA-ICP-MS). The plasma breaks the sample (50 mg of powdered sample dissolved, as for ICP-OES, but a smaller amount may be sufficient provided this is representative of the whole) into charged ions which can be detected via a linked mass spectrometer which counts the atoms identifying and quantifying them. The technique is useful for measuring major or trace elements in one process, with a wider range of elements covered than in ICP-OES and with a sensitivity comparable to NAA. However, some major elements cannot be assayed (H, He, C, N, O, Fe, Ne, and Ar), and others are difficult in practice (e.g. lighter elements are measured but with less accuracy, and S, Cl, and Si are problematic because of interference from atmospheric molecules) and with sensitivity comparable to NAA results. It can measure more elements simultaneously and with greater sensitivity then can ICP-AES low-grade equipment, and has the advantage of analysing isotopes, though with greater difficulty than element analysis. New developments using Laser Ablation (LA-ICP-MS) can investigate entire small objects leaving only a crater (a few tens of micrometres across) on the surface. Furthermore a new method of measurement, a magnetic sector multi-collector (ICP-MS-MS) offers the greatest current precision for some elements and has been used for lead isotope measurements. ICP-MS is widely available. ICP-MS: sensitivity 50–1000 ppt; accuracy to within 0.1–1.0%; LA-ICP-MS: Sensitivity 1–100 ppm; accuracy to within 5–10%.

Table 4.2   continued

AAS: Atomic Absorption Spectrometry. Dissolved samples of 10 mg to 1g are used. A flame or an electrically heated graphite furnace fragments the sample into atoms. Light beams characteristic of different elements are shone into the sample which absorbs the light in proportion to the amount of that element present in the sample. It is possible to analyse several elements at a time if a suitable lamp is used, or if each element is measured in turn. AAS is useful for extremely precise measurements of major trace elements. Lamps are available for 65 elements but these do not include C, N, O, S, Cs, Lu, Os, Th, U, or other radioactive elements, noble gases, or halogens. AAS is rarely available. AAS-flame: sensitivity 1–10 ppm, accuracy $\pm$ 1–5%; AAS-graphite furnace, sensitivity 1–10 ppb, accuracy $\pm$ 1–5%.

XRF: X-ray fluorescence spectrometry including wavelength dispersive XRF, WD-XRF and energy dispersive ED-XRF, EDXA, EDAX and the electron probe microanalyser/ microprobe, EPMA. Samples can be a surface 1 mm^2 to 4 cm^2 or 100 mg to 2 g of powder. The sample is excited with either X-rays or electrons, resulting in fluorescence, the colour of which can be used to identify many elements, with the intensity giving their relative quantity. WD-XRF can give accurate quantitative data on > than fifteen elements but requires pellets of powdered sample, whereas ED-XRF is not so sensitive to trace elements but has the distinct archaeological advantage that it can be undertaken in an SEM so that an exact area of a surface can be 'seen' and then a specific part analysed, although elements lighter than sodium are not registered, and the sample size is limited to the stage dimensions which can be only 1–2 cm in diameter. Samples for SEM work may need to be coated with gold or carbon for best results. EPMA is a variation which allows the surface to be scanned and analysed so that elements can be mapped. Increasingly sensitive machines are likely to allow further developments in this field. Samples are usually unaltered and can be reused for other techniques, but some may show alterations of colour or mechanical properties. ED-XRF attachments to SEMs are relatively common but most SEMs have a small stage size and operate in a vacuum requiring the sample to be firmly fixed. It is widely available as part of SEM analysis.

PIXE: Particle or proton induced X-ray emission analysis. Powdered samples of c. 1 mm are used. These are bombarded with protons to excite the atoms but otherwise the technique is similar to XRF, with the advantage that it gives more precise readings for trace elements. PIXE is rarely available.

NAA: Neutron activation analysis. Powdered samples of 10–100 mg are turned into radioactive isotopes of their elements by bombardment in a nuclear reactor. The isotopes emit radiation in proportion to the original amount of the elements present, so elements can be identified and quantified using comparisons with standards. The technique is accurate and precise with high sensitivity. Usually a selection of more than twenty elements are chosen to characterise a sample. The isotopes vary in the rate at which they decay and can be measured, so samples need to be analysed after irradiation and up to several weeks later. Many elements can be analysed together and results can be statistically analysed. The technique is rarely available as a research reactor is required for at least the initial part of the analysis.

Table 4.2 continued

XPS: X-ray photoelectron spectroscopy XPS or electron spectroscopy for chemical analysis (ESCA). Samples are 1 mg of powder or a cut section 1–5 mm thick. These are bombarded with X-rays and the binding energy needed to release electrons of different elements can be analysed and quantified. The technique is suitable for major or minor elements but also useful for analysing elements of up to 10 atomic weight except for H and He. It is possible to do a series of analyses whilst abrading down through a short depth of surface.

Sources: author; Barclay 2001; Baxter and Jackson 2001; Brothwell and Pollard 2001; Carter et al. 2006; Ciliberto and Spoto 2000; Gale and Stos-Gale 2000; Hancock 2000; Henderson 1989, 2000; Hein et al. 2002; Lambert 1997, 2005; Moens et al. 2000; Neff 2000; Parkes 1986; Pollard 1992; Pollard and Heron 1996; Spoto and Ciliberto 2000; Tite 2001; Whitbread 2001;Williams-Thorpe 1995; Wilson and Pollard 2001; Young and Pollard 2000.

Table 4.3 Mineralogical and petrographical analytical techniques for inorganic crystalline compounds

Summary: Mineralogical analysis using thin sections is the most widely applied of all archaeological identification techniques since it is well documented and widely available. It is useful for the identification of crystalline rocks (and therefore not used to source flint or chert which are cryptocrystalline) and natural or added crystalline particles in sherds. Since ceramics, ground and polished stone objects, and building stones constitute a major portion of all archaeological finds, thin section studies are frequently able to distinguish groups and allow rock identifications. The sourcing of such groupings requires the mineralogical components to be tied in to specific geological outcrops, and needs both adequately sourced geological samples for comparison, and natural sources that are mineralogically distinctive to a specific area. Textural analysis can give information on the size sorting and roundedness of grains (e.g. by ice, wind, or water) aiding the distinction of groups or the sourcing of natural or added inclusions in pots. Polished sections of metals can provide information on the technologies employed via the state of the crystalline structure within the metal. Other forms of mineralogical analyses are much more rarely applied.

Thin sections (also called petrological or petrographical sections). A sample ca. 10 × 20 mm mounted on a glass slide and ground down to 0.03 mm thickness is placed under a transmitted light microscope (200×) where size, shape, colour and refraction, and extinction properties under plain and polarised light source can identify minerals and the shape and arrangement of these within the material. This technique is useful for identifying macro-crystalline rock samples, and similar small particles forming natural or added inclusions in ceramics apart from clay particles which are so small that they are visible only as an amorphous ground mass. The technique is commonly available: samples can be filed for reference.

Polished sections. Sections 15 × 20 mm and often set in resin show the distribution and shape of minerals and crystals: sometimes metallurgical polished sections are etched to show weaknesses in structure or differences in crystal lattices. Polished sections are useful for identifying techniques of working for finished metal objects and for analysing slags and smelting remains, and are occasionally used for mineralogical analyses of sherds. The technique is readily available; samples can be filed for reference though metal sections may require repolishing owing to corrosion.

Textural analysis (of minerals). Texture refers to the size and shape of mineral particles (e.g. their relative rounding or angularity) as seen on a polished or ground section c. 15 × 20 mm. Analysis may be carried out semi-automatically by computerised image analysis, and is usually undertaken only for ceramic sherds which have only common minerals as inclusions. This can be useful in identifying groupings of fabric types where inclusions vary little. The technique is commonly available; samples are the same as for thin or polished sections.

Table 4.3 continued

HMA: Heavy mineral analysis of sherds. Minerals with a density of >2.89 are extracted, usually from a c. 20–30 g crushed sample floated in a liquid with a high specific gravity: at least 250 grains are required. HMA is most often undertaken when petrological analysis reveals little differentiation between numerous sources but trace minerals may be source specific. HMA is rare but available, and involves dangerous chemicals.

FTIR: Infra-red absorption spectrometry, Fourier transform. The samples used are 2–5 mg of powder of the whole substance or particular components, and c. 1 mg examined in pellet form. An infra-red beam excites the molecules causing them to vibrate at different frequencies according to the atomic groups in the sample. Since different amounts of the infra-red beam are absorbed where the sample vibration frequency and infra-red light frequency match the atomic groups present, the amount of absorption at different wavelengths indicates the quantities of atomic groups. The technique is useful for identifying poorly crystallised minerals in addition to well-crystallised ones (see XRD). The technique is rarely available, and rarer than XRD.

Mössbauer spectroscopy. Gamma rays from a standard source can be absorbed by similar nuclei in a sample, with the degree of absorption indicating the composition of the sample. However, this effect works only for a handful of elements, but these include one of the most common, iron. The technique can indicate which kinds of ions of iron are present and the mineral compounds in which it is combined, but it is generally now used for giving information on firing temperatures via refiring samples and determining at which temperature the absorption spectra change. The technique is rarely available.

XRD: X-ray diffraction. The samples used are 2–20 mg (usually 10 mg) of powdered minerals or ceramic. These are bombarded with X-rays which are reflected according to the crystal lattices of the minerals, i.e. diffracted, and therefore only well-crystallised structures will respond to the technique. Diffraction patterns are discerned by comparison with known mineral patterns and if equipment, sample size, and quality allow, may reveal relative quantities of different minerals. XRD is useful for distinguishing some high-temperature ceramics and pottery pigments, and can give information on firing temperature in some cases.

Sources: Author; Barclay 2001; Brothwell and Pollard 2001; Ciliberto and Spoto 2000; Henderson 1989, 2000; Kempe and Harvey 1983; Lambert 1997, 2005; Lindahl and Stilborg 1995; Parkes 1986; Peacock 1967, 1968; Pollard 1992; Pollard and Heron 1996; Scott 1991; Tite 2001; Whitbread 2001; Wilson and Pollard 2001; Young and Pollard 2000.

Table 4.4 Scientific dating techniques directly applied to artefacts

Summary: In theory all organic objects less than fifty thousand years old can be dated using AMS radiocarbon dating although some of the object will be lost and the measuring errors and calibration to calendrical dates will give a range which may prove too large to be useful. Sometimes it may be simpler to use other objects to date the context. There are no specific scientific means of dating metal, and only flint that has been burnt can be dated by TL. Other radioactive or trapped particle techniques require measurements of background doses to calibrate results and even then the margins of error may lead to the date range obtained being too large to be useful. Movable ceramics are not generally scientifically datable but organic remains on them, e.g. soot deposits on cooking vessels, can be dated using radiocarbon. Fired clay structures can be dated using archaeomagnetism, provided there is a curve of the variations in the magnetic field through time available for the region. Thus the most frequently found objects, i.e. unburnt flint or chert artefact, and sherds of pottery, are not usually directly datable, but are more frequently dated either by scientific dating techniques applied to their context or by stratigraphic and typological associations.

Table 4.4 continued

Accelerator Mass Spectrometry Radiocarbon dating (AMS). This technique measures relative proportions of different isotopes of carbon in a very small sample, which can then be calibrated using a calibration curve to give a range or set of ranges of the likely date. It is particularly useful for dating organic artefacts since the sample required is so small (milligrams) but in practice it is used only on individually important objects whose contexts cannot be dated by other means. Its application is likely to widen as technological improvements lead to lower analytical costs. Biomolecular analyses now offer the prospects of isolating suitable organic substances for AMS dating from residues extracted from sherds (see also biomolecular analyses). The date range of AMS is notionally from 500 to 50,000 years ago but the upper end of the range is problematic owing to measuring errors, and more recent time periods tend to have other better dating techniques.

Other radioactive elements dating techniques. Most of these are applied not to artefacts but to geological layers, with some exceptions such as **Fission track dating**. This technique normally measures the age of volcanic rocks in which their radioactive particle clocks were reset by the geological heat event which created the rock. Anthropogenically heated obsidian tools will also have had their radioactive clocks reset and thus can be dated by this technique. The radioactive decay of naturally occurring uranium creates stresses in the matrix which can be revealed as 'fission-tracks' by etching the surface of glassy materials such as obsidian. The number of tracks relates to the amount of radioactive ^{238}U present which in turn can give a date if the sample is then bombarded in a nuclear reactor and the new fission tracks compared to those present before. Application of this technique requires access to a nuclear reactor and considerable expertise to interpret observations correctly. It is thus rarely applied to artefacts, and in practice its application is mainly to date the geological events of volcanic activity which are deposited as ash particles especially since its main date range is 10,000 to >1,000,000 years ago, though some artefacts as young as two thousand years have been successfully dated. In some cases obsidian has been provenanced using this technique where the age of the eruption which formed the obsidian can identify the source.

Thermoluminescence (TL). Crystalline minerals trap within their structural lattice electrons originating from the object itself, from external sources of its post-depositional context, or from naturally occurring radiation. When the object sample (crushed material from flint, or grains of quartz or zircon from pottery) is heated these electrons are released, setting its 'clock' back to zero. Thus this technique dates only heated objects, usually ceramics or flint. A sample from which the outer 2 mm have been removed is heated up to 500°C, and the amount of light released is plotted as a 'glow curve'. This is compared with the glow curve of a second sample subjected in the lab to a known dose of radiation. In addition, an annual dose must be calculated using information from the surrounding soil and its background radiation and that of the material itself. This may require a measurement of the background radiation in the soil for several months or the estimation of radioactivity on particular types of grains, and collection of samples of burial soil. To give a date, the two sample curves need to be compared with one another and with the annual dose and these will always be accompanied by error estimates based on weightings of different factors pertinent to that sample and its local burial conditions. Multiple samples are usually necessary. Such analyses require considerable expertise to arrive at a date and are usually reserved for crucial cases (such as the earliest use of ceramics in a region) or for corroboration with other dating techniques. Date ranges owing due to the internal radioactivity differences and saturation points for different minerals. For pottery, the range goes back from recent times (e.g. for dating architectural fired clay in a cathedral) to the earliest ceramics, and for flint back to 500,000 years.

Table 4.4 continued

NB: Optical Dating (OD) or Optically Stimulated Luminescence (OSL) are basically similar to TL dating, but rely on different ways of measuring the trapped charge, and are mainly used on sediments rather than objects.

Electron Spin Resonance (ESR). Although this can be applied to shell and tooth enamel, the latter samples tend to be non-artefactual remains, whilst the possibilities for dating ceramics and burnt flint overlap with TL, which is usually the method chosen as trials suggest that the error of ESR is greater (see Bartoll and Ikeya 1997). There has been some discussion of using the technique to identify heat treatment in flint artefacts (Robins et al. 1978 cited in Aitken 1990). ESR of Fe^{3+} has been used to provenance obsidian.

Amino Acid Racemisation. The technique is applied to protein molecules present in bone, teeth, and shell, but racemisation rates are strongly influenced by local burial conditions and the samples are usually non-artefactual. Racemisation is a change in the optical activity of a substance due to the precise configuration of the amino acid, which, like radioactive decay, changes over time, but which ceases when a point of equilibrium between different forms is reached.

Dendrochronology. This technique uses tree-ring growth sequences (by measuring the tree-rings on a cross-section) to give dates of the *wood growth* (not the date when the wood was used or deposited). Calendar dates of these sequences can be obtained by comparison with a known dated master sequence. The technique is especially useful for dating structures where many large timbers remain so that there is a long sequence of ring growths to compare against master sequences specific to different species, especially, oak, pine, fir, and cedar depending upon geographic region and climatic condition. Date range depends upon the length of the master curves, with the European oak chronology currently extending back to 8480 BC, whereas the North American pine and fir sequences extend to 300 BC. New work will extend the range of dates and species. On occasion tree-ring analysis has been able to show trade in timber by matching to a master curve in a different region.

Hydration/diffusion. Measurement of the thickness (likely to be 0.001–0.05 mm i.e. 1–50 μm) of the hydrated surface layer of obsidian can give age estimates. Although this was commonly performed under optical microscopy (up to 1000×) this method of measuring is unreliable, and Secondary Ion Mass Spectrometry, which measures the depth of diffusion of hydrogen ions, has been shown to be much more accurate. Thus, for reliable and accurate results, specialised equipment for defining and measuring the hydration layer and experience are necessary. The rate of hydration is not constant because it is a diffusion process and slows with time, and the burial context, especially temperature, will also affect the rate of hydration. The technique is useful for relative dating or, where either locally comparable dated samples are available to produce a curve or one has been produced by establishing experimentally the rate of hydration for the type of obsidian at the relevant burial temperature. The burial temperature may need to be measured by leaving a device in the context for a year. Error rates in measuring may give ranges of several hundred years on sample dates only a few millennia old. The date range is theoretically 1,000,000 – 200 BP though chemical corrosion may affect the earlier range by destroying the hydration layer, and recent dates depend upon the rate of the hydration process in different regions so that in practice dates up to 100,000 BP may be more realistic.

Archaeomagnetism (NB different from **palaeomagnetism** of sediments, which is on a geological timescale). The magnetic field in a region varies in declination and inclination over time. Fired clay will take up a weak magnetisation, which is a snapshot of the magnetic field of the time. In this way fired clay objects which have not moved (e.g. ovens, hearths,

Table 4.4   continued

kilns) can have their remnant magnetism recorded. A date is obtained by reference to a calibration curve compiled either from magnetism readings of similar structures of known date or from lake sediments dated by radiocarbon or other means. These must be from the region, and, where the changes are pronounced, more precise dates may be possible, such as the American Southwest. In some cases 'displaced material' (e.g. fired bricks and tiles which are characteristically stacked in a kiln) can have their inclination alone measured once they have been moved. Despite no evidence for declination these objects can sometimes be successfully used for dating purposes. More recent studies have tried to use magnetic intensity alone but with less accuracy.

Sources: Aitken 1990; Ambrose 1993, 2001; Baillie 1995; Bartoll and Ikeya 1997; Bellot-Gurlet et al. 1999; Buford Price 2005; Chataigner et al. 2003; Duttine et al. 2003; Freter 1993; Gowlett and Hedges 1986; Grün 2001; Guibert et al. 1998; Kuniholm 2001; Kuzmin et al. 2001; Latham 2001; Liritzis 2006; Michels 1986; Pettitt 2005; Pike and Pettitt 2005; Riciputi et al. 2002; Ridings 1996; Roque et al. 2002; Roque et al. 2004; Sternberg 2001; Stott et al. 2003; Taylor 2001; Troja and Roberts 2000; Wintle 1996.

Table 4.5   Biological sample identification and functional analyses

Substances such as resins, waxes, fats, and oils can be chemically analysed and variously give information on function, sealants, fuel sources, or hafting methods. Sometimes small fragments of morphologically distinct residues survive on stone or ceramic surfaces or as mineralised deposits on metalwork, so these kinds of analyses overlap with some of the functional analysis techniques: that is why this section groups these sets of analyses together.

Biological sample summary: Distinctive tissue remains e.g. wooden objects, fibres, and bone, antler, ivory, or horn may be distinguished via the gross morphology of distinctive tissues seen in a variety of thin sections or as closely observed patterns on an original artefact. The more robust and larger objects (wood, bone, antler) tend to be most easily identified with the naked eye or limited microscopy whereas more fragile and smaller tissues (e.g. bast (inner bark) fibres, hairs, feathers) may require higher magnifications and access to a wide reference collection of known species or tissues in order for identifications to be secure. On occasion the residue is not morphologically distinct but the substance can be identified using chemical analysis, or a range of immunological and reagent responses. Residues can be identified as deposits in their own right during fieldwork but are more frequently discovered as a result of specific sampling programmes (e.g. on ceramics) or as microscopic traces on the surfaces of artefacts (e.g. stone tools) which is why this set of analyses links with functional studies.

Functional analysis summary: all studies require comparative reference collections of known function or substance and investigations into taphonomic effects. Functional studies of stone tools are the most common and can take a low magnification approach (up to $100\times$, useful for a range of coarse and fine-grained lithics) on the basis of scarring, striations, rounding, and polish where the use-action is identified and use-materials can be determined as broad categories of hard, medium soft, soft or a high magnification (typically $100–400\times$ incident light microscopy used on finer grained lithics) giving use-action and potentially more specific use-material categories, and also using high magnification identification of residues from the surface of stone tools e.g. starch grains, phytoliths, or other histologically identifiable tissues, and more problematically blood residue analysis using a variety of confirmation methods and immunological specific reactions. Fine-grained and unpatinated flint tools offer the best opportunities for microwear whereas coarser grained materials are best studied using the low-magnification or residue approach. Either way, post-depositional effects must be carefully considered. High-magnification techniques require more time but can give more specific data whereas the low-magnification approach is quicker and more objects can be assessed, making it useful for a broader-scale research question. In contrast functional studies of ceramics are less frequent and fall into three main areas: surface wear, carbon deposition, and residue absorption. Wear and soot deposits viewed with the naked eye or low magnifications can identify ranges of functions and in some instances cooking information, such as distance from fire. However the analysis of the absorbed residues can give very specific information on the substances absorbed by the pot. Chemical analyses need information on both the chemical elements present and the structures of the bonds between them in order

Table 4.5   continued

---

to identify the compounds in the sample, but even then, these compounds need to be understood as the degraded products of the original substance. Wear studies can also be applied to bone, antler, shell, or metal tools, and wear and residue studies can also be used on ground stone tools. All functional studies require comparative known data to aid interpretation and need to consider alternative effects of manufacture and post-depositional processes.

Biological sample identification using gross morphology and histology. These can use macroscopic features or incident light microscopy of particles or fragments, or employ transverse, radial, and longitudinal sections. The latter are typically useful for wood identification to species and some natural fibre identification to species or tissue type. The equipment is readily available (microscopes up to $20 \times$ magnification are sufficient), and some useful identification manuals exist for wood, animal hair, and plant fibres, and there is some collected information on the identification of other substances such as bone, antler, ivory, and horn, but expertise and reference collections are rarer for less frequently found materials. In addition some domesticated fibre products may have changed through time. If samples are mounted on slides appropriately, they can be filed.

Sources: Author; Anderson 1980; Anderson-Gerfaud 1986; Barber 1991: ch. 1; Bonnichsen et al. 2001; Briuer 1976; Brose 1975; Catling and Grayson 1998; Forest Products Research Laboratory 1953; Gordon and Keating 2001; Hather 2000; Hurcombe 1986; 1992; Jagiella 1987; Korbe-Grohne 1988; Krzyszkowska 1990; MacGregor 1985; Penniman 1984; Reed 1972; Ryder 1987; Ryder and Gabra-Sanders 1987; Schweingruber 1976; Tomlinson 1985; Wildman 1954.

Biomolecular analysis of organic compounds via the linked techniques of Gas Chromatography-Mass Spectrometry (GC-MS), or Gas Chromatography-Combustion-Isotope Ratio Mass Spectrometry (GC-C-IRMS), also High Temperature Gas Chromatography Mass Spectrometry (HT-GC/MS). Lipid compounds (animal fats, plant oils, waxes, resins) and deterioration products are trapped in the pores of ceramics or stones and can be extracted (via cleaned, crushed, and dissolved destructive 2 g samples usually for ceramics, or via a chemical solvent for stone tools – though the technique is not often applied to lithics) and interpreted as sealants, hafting traces, or the remains of substances associated with use as containers or tools. Although originally the proportions of different fatty acids (degradation products of lipids) were measured directly, work has shown that these vary with post-depositional contexts so now the lipids are extracted. The process requires the extracted sample (either from the interior of the sherd or pot or from a visible residue on the surface) to be chemically treated to break the complex compounds down into those most suited to the two- or threefold analytical techniques. The first is gas chromatography, which separates the sample into its chemical compounds (largely according to their boiling points so GC normally takes place under a programme of rising temperatures) with quantitative data provided via comparison with internal standards added at the extraction stage. The GC products are then measured in a mass spectrometer that is physically linked to the GC equipment: this bombards the sample with electrons so that degradation products are formed, which are then quantified as products with different atomic masses. There are mathematical relationships in atomic mass according to the structures of organic chemistry and different staged degradation products according to the placement of double or single bonds between atoms. In this way both the structural and element composition are assessed, which allows the specific compounds of the derivatised products to be identified. Identification is made statistically by computer, which compares the sample readings' peaks as a 'fingerprint' with libraries of readings from known compounds. The concept of biological marker compounds is important as part of the understanding of the compounds that once existed compared to those which remain in the sample after post-depositional processes and which are analysed. The GC-CIRMS process (the third of the linked analytical techniques) requires the GC to be linked to a combustion interface which oxidises carbon atoms into CO_2 which is channelled into the IRMS to measure

Table 4.5 continued

___

the isotope composition of the carbon as the $^{13}C/^{12}C$ fraction (termed $\delta^{13}C$). The values of this isotopic ratio vary between different plant and animal groups and their compounds, allowing the origin of the archaeological sample to be given. Furthermore this aspect of the analysis can give high-precision data on only 50–100 ng of compounds. HT/GC/MS uses high temperatures to improve the range of lipids to be analysed in a single sample run, allowing highly detailed profile readings, increasing the chance of a specific identification over one based on fatty acid identifications alone. (These techniques have also allowed the isolation of specific compounds for AMS ^{14}C dating.) The level of chemical knowledge required is advanced, and because of the need for comparative databanks the technique has been advanced in relatively few centres which can build up high levels of expertise.

___

Sources: Beck et al. 1989; Beck and Borromeo 1990; Bergen et al. 1997; Buzon et al. 2005; Charters et al. 1993a, 1993b; Connan 1999; Copley et al. 2005; Dudd and Evershed 1998; Dudd et al. 1998; Evershed 2000; Evershed and Tuross 1996; Evershed et al. 1991, 1992, 1997a, 1997b, 1999, 2001; Gernaey et al. 2001; Heron and Evershed 1993; Heron et al. 1991a, 1991b; Heron and Pollard 1988; Hyland et al. 1990; Jahren et al. 1997; Lambert 1997; Mottram et al. 1999; Newman et al. 1993; Patrick et al. 1985; Raven et al. 1997; Regert et al. 1998, 1999; Robinson et al. 1987; Skibo 1992; Smith and Wilson 2001; Stott et al. 2003; Tuross and Dillehay 1995; Tuross et al. 1996.

Use wear studies, also known as functional analysis, traceology, and, for higher magnification techniques, microwear. These kinds of techniques rest on studies of surface wear (known as tribology in materials science) and are most commonly applied to chipped stone tools where a range of fine-grained lithics including flint, obsidian, chert, and quartz have been studied. However, bone or antler, ground and polished stone, metal and ceramic artefacts can all be studied in the same way. Many such studies also incorporate residue analyses since surface depressions and steps can sometimes reveal residues in association with wear traces or in positions indicative of hafting. Macroscopic and microscopic fractures, pitting, striations (scratches), and smoothing ('polish') can be used to compare unknown archaeological wear patterns with known ethnographic or experimental wear patterns to arrive at an indication of 'function'. This can include hafting traces but most commonly identifies the action, material, and sometimes the duration of use. It is much harder to say that a tool was unused since short use times or very soft materials can leave no recognisable traces. The effects of manufacturing and post-depositional processes must also be assessed before arriving at an interpretation.

The low-power approach (employing up to $40\times$ or $100\times$ magnification) uses striations, edge scarring and attrition, plus smoothing or glossing to assess the functions and most often grades the material worked as a series of hardness categories such as 'soft', 'medium', 'hard', with a clear sense of what materials fall into these groupings: e.g. meat would be soft, and bone would be hard. The high power or microwear approach uses magnifications of up to at least $200\times$ and sometimes $400/500\times$. Some studies use an SEM for even greater magnification. Phase contrast microscopes can enhance the visibility of minute changes in the surface but are not essential to the basic technique. Incident light microscopes are generally available but both comparative collections and analyst expertise are also required, and the techniques can be time-consuming and need to be reserved for specific research questions. The technique has developed some understanding of wear formation processes but this is by no means definitive and ways to make the analyses more objective have been assessed (e.g. computer expert systems, measurements, or element analyses). Both high- and low-power use wear techniques have conducted blind tests with varying results which have generally advanced understanding and demonstrated some good results but have also highlighted problem areas of undiagnostic wear. The technique provides interpretations of function based on wear and should state where results are ambiguous or impossible. Normally, analyses focuses on a particular research question as methods of analysis can be time-consuming. Where the

Table 4.5 continued

---

technique has been applied to multiple assemblages over time, holistic cultural information on function is now available and results contribute to major archaeological debates such as the origins of agriculture.

The equipment is available in most labs, and there are some good detailed publications with clear descriptions and plentiful photos, but individual analysts still need to gain expertise by practical examination of wear traces and access to good experimental reference collections. Research into residues sometimes visible on tool surfaces requires additional practical knowledge of protocols and access to reference collections.

Sources: Akerman et al. 2002; Anderson 1980; Bamforth 1988; Bamforth et al. 1990; Choyke and Bartosiewicz 2001; Christensen et al. 1992; Derndarsky and Ocklind 2001; Van den Dries 1998; Evans and Donahue 2005; Fullagar 1991, 1993, 1998; Fullagar and Field 1997; Van Gijn 1989, 1998a, 1998b, 1998c, 2005, 2006, Van Gijn and Houkes 2006; Van Gijn et al. 2006; Grace 1989; Hayden 1979; Hurcombe 1985, 1988, 1992; Kamminga 1982; Keeley 1980; Keeley and Newcomer 1977; Kienlin and Ottaway 1998; Knutsson 1988; LeMoine 1997; Longo and Skakun 2006; López Varela et al. 2002; Moss 1983; Nieuwenhuis 2002; Odell 1994; Odell and Odell-Vereecken 1980; Owen and Unrath 1986; Phillips 1998; Plisson and van Gijn 1989; Rice 1990; Roberts and Ottaway 2003; Semenov 1964; Skibo 1992; Sussman 1988; Tringham et al. 1974; Unrath et al. 1986; Vaughan 1985; Yerkes and Kardulias 1996.

Blood residues, Enzyme Linked Immunoabsorbent Assay (ELISA), Radioactive Immuno-Assay (RIA), crystallisation, dot blot, (DNA) and erythrocyte morphology. Loy (1983) suggested that blood crystal shapes grown from residues extracted from stone tools could be identified to species level but this particular method has proved impossible for others to replicate. Similarly the use of chemstrips (e.g. hemastix) to ascertain the presence of blood residues has caused much discussion since there are possibilities of false positive results although the use of an additional special solution can improve results (Fullagar et al. 1996). Dot blots can be used to give an indication of relative strengths of any residues. However, other techniques, such as ELISA and RIA, which rely on identifying proteins indicating the presence of blood can be sensitive, and more reliable if strict protocols are observed: whilst they identify blood residues, identifying species of origin is a more problematic issue. In many cases the chemical preservation of residues may be too poor for any identification to be reliable, as shown by various taphonomic experiments and comparative tests evaluating different methods. Crossover immuno-electrophoresis (CIEP) has problems because of the cross-reactivity (i.e. more than one species can give a positive reaction) of polyclonal antibodies (i.e the commercially manufactured antibodies used to test the residue) although monoclonal antibodies (reacting more specifically with one species because of the way they are produced) could circumvent this problem, but few of relevance to archaeology are manufactured. 'Dot blot' samples dropped on to nitrocellulose membranes can test for proteins present in blood alone, or in blood and other fluids such as saliva, sweat, and tears. The technique can therefore give a positive result when these other fluids, but not blood, are present so the technique is used as an adjunct to other methods and does not give species of origin. A new line of approach is using the shape of erythrocytes (a kind of blood cell) visible in apparent blood residues: shapes have been documented and experiments on the taphonomic changes in shape are being conducted. The most reliable identifications will be those where several techniques agree, where possibilities of contamination have been reduced or removed, and where comparative soil samples give background checks for generalised reactivity. In addition, whole tool extractions should be avoided in favour of sampling areas where specific 'blood plaque' residues of interest have been observed microscopically (e.g. in areas of wear or with other residues such as hair or erythrocytes). However, the issue is really dependent upon the archaeological question. If use wear examination shows traces of use and a residue whose appearance resembles that of blood, such methods as a combination of chemstrips and dot blot assays can support the identification of these as blood traces as a part of a functionally meaningful pattern

Table 4.5 continued

---

of evidence, but it is a different question to identify the species. For the most part, questions about the exploitation of different species are answered by palaeoeconomic data from preserved bones assemblages from sites rather than linking one tool with a specific species. Particular situations such as very early hunting sites, or special artefacts such as a 'surgeon's knife' may make any residues worth identifying to species if possible, though cuts from the user's hands etc. may always be difficult to rule out. Current DNA studies are working with smaller amounts of ancient DNA, and protocols for preventing modern contamination and testing for this and soil contamination have improved. Despite this most DNA work has been carried out on samples from bones or plants and not from residues of these left on tools or containers, although further improvements in procedures could bring this technique into wider use for stone tool residue identification.

Sources: Akerman et al. 2002; Brown 2001; Castoldi 1981; Cattaneo et al. 1993, 1994; Custer et al. 1988; Downs and Lowenstein 1995; Eisele et al. 1995; Fiedel 1996; Fullagar et al. 1996; Garling 1998; Gurfinkel and Franklin 1988; Hortolá 1992, 2001a, 2001b, 2002; Hyland et al. 1990; Kooyman et al. 1992, 2001; Loy 1983, 1998; Loy and Dixon 1998; Loy and Hardy 1992; Loy and Matthaei 1994; Loy and Wood 1989; Marlar et al. 2002; Newman and Julig 1989; Newman et al. 1996, 1997, 1998; Petraglia et al. 1996; Quarino and Kobilinsky 1988; Shanks et al. 2001; Smith and Wilson 2001; Tuross et al. 1996; Wallis and O'Connor 1998; Yohe et al. 1991.

Phytoliths and starch grain analysis. These plant microfossil techniques are grouped together because they use similar extraction techniques and have similar taphonomic issues. Phytoliths are silica bodies formed within plant cells. Phytoliths occur in many types of plants and are diagnostic to the family, genus, and sometimes species level. In the past it was thought that phytoliths were mainly produced in Poaceae (formerly Gramineae), but there are now one-to-one correlations for a huge number of plant taxa including other herbs than Poaceae, e.g sedges and many trees. Phytoliths on stone tool edges in association with wear may aid in the identification of siliceous plants as the worked material and the shapes of the phytoliths may allow some species to be ruled out or indicate others. Likewise starch granules need not be specific to one species, though some are, but in any event exist in different sets of sizes and shapes for some root and seed crops, or in other plant parts. For several crops (e.g. maize, manioc, taro) starch grains identify plant taxa to the species level. Starch grains have distinctive extinction crosses when viewed under cross-polarised light and are usually described by overall morphology, the position and shape of the hilum (botanical centre of the grain) and its fissures, the number and characteristics of pressure facets, and the presence or absence of lamellae. Occasionally raphides (calcium oxalate crystals) can also be observed. Phytoliths and starch grains are long-lived plant parts which can survive in sediments as well as on tool edges and it is as part of soil samples that they are typically analysed, where there is growing evidence for the complementary contribution of phytoliths and starch grain analysis to investigate environments and site usage, though statistical analysis and other image analysis techniques may aid in interpreting the results. Where phytoliths and starch grains are seen on tool edges, ideally sediment samples also need to be analysed so that background presence from sediments can be ruled out. Extractions from tools need to be from known areas of the tool, so that residues associated with use wear are distinguished from those present as part of hafting or background material. The residues can be extracted by ultra-clean water pipetted on to the surface, agitated, then removed (with the procedure repeated if necessary), or by suspending the relevant part of a tool in an ultrasonic tank. A whole tool extraction can be performed using ultrasonic methods after various spot test extractions. The resulting solutions can then be further concentrated (e.g. by centrifuge) before viewing on a slide mount at typically 200–500× and sometimes 1000× magnification. Reference collections are required, and these are developing rapidly, being built up for different environments, with work in Central and South America and South and East Asia and Australia being especially fruitful and in particular raising the profile of a range of starchy tubers and plants as food sources. The

Table 4.5 continued

technique has been applied to a variety of rocks and both chipped and ground stone tools especially grinding stones. As with all residue analyses, alternative explanations and post-depositional effects must be evaluated. Taphonomic experiments have indicated limited movement in soil deposits and the preferential survival of material caught in cracks on the surface of tools. Ethnographic and archaeological data have suggested a range of alternative cultural sources of residues, such as bark as a wrapping to protect a stone edge during transport, or starchy material as part of binding media.

Suitable mounted samples can be stored though it is the published descriptions and images which are accumulating as reference material.

Sources: Akerman et al. 2002; Anderson 1980; Anderson-Gerfaud 1986; Atchison and Fullagar 1998; Banks and Greenwood 1975; Barton et al. 1998; Fullagar 1993, 1998; Fullagar and Field 1997; Fullagar et al. 1998, 2006; Haslam 2004; Iriarte et al. 2004; Kealhofer et al. 1999; Lentfer et al. 2002; Loy et al. 1992; Pearsall et al. 2004; Perry 2005; Piperno 2006; Piperno and Holst 1998; Piperno et al. 2000, 2004; Powers et al. 1989; Reichart 1913; Therin 1998; Therin et al. 1997; Torrence et al. 2004; Torrence and Barton 2006.

5   Changing perspectives

What, where, and sequences of change

The preceding chapters have covered a large tract of archaeological concepts and alluded to changing perceptions and research agendas throughout the history of archaeology. It is now time to delve into the histories and the paradigm shifts which have both bedevilled and enabled the subject. Artefact studies alongside other forms of archaeological evidence have been affected by paradigm shifts which can be grouped into five major phases as in figure 5.1. An individual studying archaeology does not have to be a proponent of culture history, a functionalist, a processualist or a post-processualist to avoid descending into a schizophrenic nightmare. Why then are the different aspects of archaeological paradigms so often seen as mutually exclusive that post-processualism has also been termed anti-processualism? (e.g. see Wylie 1992). The answer lies partly in the way paradigm shifts occur: a way of thinking becomes fashionable and the novel adaptive phase gives way to dogma and blind adherence. Gradually, too many people become dissatisfied with the excesses of the paradigm. As its flaws or limits become more obvious, what once allowed new insights becomes a straitjacket, and so a few (brave, loud, idealistic, angry, persuasive) individuals propose a novel agenda, and so a paradigm shifts. In part at least, this is a reaction to what has gone before, but the shift is not some objective movement of scientific knowledge (Popper 1957) but a Kuhnian social revolution (Kuhn 1962) perpetuated by the 'subjective' researchers who actually do the 'objective' science (Becher 1989). It becomes the new fashion and many adopt the new paradigm; with time there is again some dissatisfaction and the agenda moves on again. In practice, key features of the old paradigms are not rejected, despite the antagonistic posturing, but retained as I have tried to show in figure 5.1. The old paradigm is not falsified but superseded by one considered more productive. Each paradigm has met key research agendas which were crucial to its age. A series of such paradigm shifts has occurred in archaeology and in each shift research has focused on new questions and approaches although the agenda is not always clear cut (Yoffee and Sherratt 1993). For example, processualists use culture history's concept of social assemblages. Post-processualists use aspects of middle-range theory. Other authors have presented overviews of archaeological theory (Johnson 1999) and the history of the subject (Trigger 1989). The focus here is on how the paradigm shifts have affected artefact and material culture studies.

PARADIGM SHIFTS THROUGH TIME →				
Paradigm 3 age system	Culture history	Functionalism	New archaeology Processual archaeology	Post-processual archaeology Interpretative archaeology
Key interpretative aims *Object sequences*	*Peoples in time and place*	*Tasks, actions, environments*	*Behaviour, formation processes, rigour, social archaeology*	*Thoughts, symbolism, pluralism*

Key questions

	3 age system	Culture history	Functionalism	New archaeology Processual archaeology	Post-processual archaeology Interpretative archaeology
What	●	⬤	●	●	●
When	⬤ relative	⬤ relative	●	⬤ radiocarbon dating	●
Where	●	⬤	●	●	●
How	○	● technologies	⬤ technologies	⬤ behaviour, formation processes	⬤ concepts, agency
Who		● peoples	● skill levels	⬤ hierarchies, subgroups, specialists	⬤ gender, age, mindsets
What for (function)	○		⬤	●	●
What thoughts					⬤ symbolism, perceptions, cognition
How evidence and theories obtained			●	⬤	●
Why changes occurred	● progress	● progress, contact	● needs: environment interactions	⬤ cause: effect interacting factors	⬤ conceptual links
Explanatory frameworks	progression	diffusion, invasion	function, utility, pragmatics	behaviour, social reactions and interactions	cognition, perception, pluralism

○ *incorporated*   ● *considered*   ⬤ *strongly emphasised*

Figure 5.1 Key questions and explanatory frameworks of archaeological paradigm shifts through time

Source: author

The early antiquarians placed objects at the heart of archaeology. Boucher de Perthes, Pengelly, and others contributed to the establishment of the 'antiquity of man' by demonstrating that worked stone tools lay in the same contexts as the bones of animals that were now extinct; both were subject to uniformitarian geological principles which could be seen in the present to act over an immense timescale (Trigger 1989: 72–94). In 1859, three disciplines, archaeology, geology, and Darwin's evolutionary biology, all contributed to the overthrowing of Archbishop Ussher's 4004 BC date of creation based on biblical genealogies. This left a vast sweep of time going back into the remote past without a framework. How was such a time span to be measured or divided up in some way? The objects that antiquarians had been collecting held the key to the first phasing of a history of people at a time before historical records gave dates.

Pitt-Rivers was a highly influential figure in the 1870s, promoting principles of artefact classification as the succession of ideas and revealing '*the connexion that has existed in former times between distant countries, either by the spread of race, or culture, or by means of commerce*' (1875 reprinted in Myers 1906: 15). His work and that of Sir John Evans left a series of figures which visually demonstrate the key interpretative conclusions from such classifications: broad chronological phasing based on similarities between objects and progressive changes in these, set against geographical locations. A diagram showing changes in the material and design details of 'axes' exemplifies this approach (figure 5.2: Pitt-Rivers 1875 reprinted in Myers 1906: pl. II). Sequential interpretations based on similarities in object form and designs had become a tool for a space/time framework based around objects (e.g. Pitt-Rivers 1867 reprinted in Myers 1906: pl. XII, Pitt-Rivers 1875 reprinted in Myers 1906: pl. III) and designs on them, for example the change in designs on coins (Evans 1864, reproduced in Pitt-Rivers 1867, reprinted in Myers 1906: pl. XXI). Whilst some of the details of typologies in some of these figures can now be questioned, they epitomise the key early treatment of objects and the need to order them. Antiquarians knew that the objects were the key to understanding sequences and relationships. '*Progress is like a game of dominoes – like fits on to like*' (Pitt-Rivers 1875 reprinted in Myers 1906: 19), but they also perceived that knowledge of those sequences and their orders was going to be open to revision and overall be a cumulative process. Much of the cultural and chronological frameworks of current archaeology still rest on the accumulated understandings of object sequences in time and space.

Typological sequences as chronological frameworks, though associated with an earlier phase of archaeological endeavour, are not dead but remain part of ongoing useful research initiatives even in well-studied areas. For example Betancourt (1985) published a volume on Cretan Minoan pottery which has served as an introduction to the broad Minoan ceramics sequence to anyone working in the field. It uses information from a variety of sites but even such a book must select examples rather than present an exhaustive list. Frequently authors take a pragmatic approach and use not necessarily the best examples from an exhaustive list of sites but those with which they are familiar or which are accessible. Furthermore in many areas of the world there are many different nationalities contributing to the archaeology of the region with a multitude of projects all at different stages of publication with multiple

	FLINT.				BRONZE.						
	Side Tool	Tongue Shaped	Oval.	Celt	Convex & Flat Surfaces	Stop	Flange	Stop & Flange	Overlapping Flange	Bronze Socket	Iron Socket
Early Palæolithic	✚	✚	✚								
Late Palæolithic	▮		▮	▮							
Early Neolithic				✚							
Late Neolithic				✚							
Early Bronze				▮	✚						
Late Bronze					✚	✚	✚	✚	✚	✚	
Iron Period											✚
Australian				▮	✚						
American				✚	✚		✚				

✚ Denotes common Occurrence   ▮ Rare or Doubtful

Figure 5.2 Broad chronological sequences constructed via changes in the material and form of one item, 'axes'

Source: Pitt-Rivers 1875, reprinted in Myers 1906: plate II

authors. As archaeological data accumulate, it becomes more difficult for any one person to present a complete overview. Books which have proved a useful resource and synthesis gradually become out of date. Chronologies developed initially from one site may be found not to be representative of the entire region – for example the Knossos-based chronology established by Evans (1905) has since been used, amplified or adapted by different authors according to their needs – and what was once an established pattern and communication tool becomes split into different variations which are not mutually understood. In these cases a return to the original and more recent key deposits, with new publications, may be necessary. Hence Macgillivray (1998) has published fuller pottery descriptions of key phases from the Old Palace period at Knossos, and Momigliano (2007) has prepared a further volume revisiting all of the ceramics phases at the site in their own right rather than as an imposed chronological sequence for all sites in the region. The original artefactual material from Knossos is being mined for new information over a hundred years later and is still crucial to establishing site phases from which to draw regional comparisons.

The next key paradigm shift was to group objects into sets which recurred and to explain these sets as cultures. Though the idea was considered by several authors it was more formally established by Kossinna writing about German origins in 1911 (Trigger 1989: 162–3). Recurring sets of artefacts as archaeological cultures, whose differences and boundaries might then be attributed to ethnic groups, allowed earlier twentieth-century archaeologists to write culture histories. Though some of these ideas became political tools for Nazi Germany (Bettina Arnold 1990), there were also broad histories of peoples, with monumental works such as Childe's (1925) *The Dawn of European Civilisation* being published. The latter was in its sixth edition 28 years later in 1957, so such ideas and the 'histories' or space/time frameworks contained within them, were clearly seen as useful for a long time and the concept of groups of recurring objects signifying social groups is still with us. To move from the individual descriptions of sometimes broken fragments of objects to whole objects, to sets of objects that occur together, is to move upwards through a hierarchy most clearly expressed by Deetz (1967): he explained artefacts' contributions to sub-assemblages and assemblages, and whole archaeological cultures made up of different kinds of toolkits used in different kinds of sites. He incorporated more functionalist approaches into his hierarchy by using the concept of toolkits and site functions differing *within* a culture according to behaviour. The term 'behaviour' is very much associated with a new school of thought which sought to move the focus away from 'object as cultures' to objects as the material remains of human activity.

Daring to ask why and trying to be objective

The next major shift was towards processual or New Archaeology but there was an important initiative in the 1950s which prepared the ground for this. Environmental and subsistence issues were seen as highly influential (Clark 1952) and gave rise to a functionalist perspective (Trigger 1989: 244–88) according to which the ancient people were affected or constrained by environmental issues: the objects making up cultures were just a part of a body of data which had to include palaeoeconomic and environmental evidence. However, the concept of economy and environment embraced many aspects of material culture: trade, crafts, and technologies, and the exploitation of resources for food and materials via strategies which used particular tools were all seen as interacting systems (Clark 1952). Furthermore, the labelled 'types' sitting on museum shelves were also being questioned using experimental and ethnographic data as a means of getting more pragmatic information from objects and the contexts of their use (Binford 1967, Coles 1962, 1973). The questioning of which forms of variation were attributable to identity, and which to functional behaviour or other causes, was central to a whole new set of discussions of artefact variability (Binford and Binford 1968, Binford 1972). This came to be seen in broad terms as 'New Archaeology' or 'processual' archaeology. Artefacts were envisioned as acting within the influence of three factors interacting in all cultures; technomic (pragmatic or functional aspects relating to what the society needed from the environment and the manner in which these needs were met), sociotechnic (dealing with social organisation), and ideotechnic (incorporating the ideas and belief systems): an individual artefact could be most strongly affected by any one of these but could be influenced by all three (Binford 1962). A stone knife could fulfil a pragmatic function, be made from imported stone and signal social relations and contacts, whilst the handle and manner of binding might signal an ethnic group or the status of an individual or be decorated with a symbol relating to a belief or perform a ritual act with which it was then associated.

Processual archaeology wanted to answer more ambitious, esoteric questions than the culture histories approach: it investigated the processes of change rather than merely documenting it. New Archaeology (which broadly developed into processual archaeology) was less interested in more challenging goals but above all stressed 'scientific' procedures borrowed from the philosopher of science Sir Karl Popper (1959) whereby hypotheses had to be testable, though success could only prove a possibility, while failure could offer disproof or suggest modifications to the hypothesis. Ideas of objectivity and rigour could be seen as methodological issues embraced by New Archaeology, with generalised statements being more of a feature of processual archaeology. In practice, both have been amalgamated under the general headline of processualism and were novel for the then-ambitious aims of investigating social processes and seeking explanation. While culture history had dealt with factual lists and sequences of change which could be explained only by diffusion of ideas or movement of people, it had no real explanation for internal changes. Processualism, more than any previous paradigm, stressed that a diversity of social questions could be addressed. Its proponents dared to ask why things changed and as a consequence how such changes had come about, not just by looking at external influences but by internal processes within the society itself. Systems theory (Clarke 1968, Salmon 1978, Ploux 1991) broke down complex cultural phenomena into integrated themes such as trade and exchange, technology, subsistence, and art and ritual: the objects could be framed in relation to how the raw materials were obtained, how they were made, and the nature of their use for economic and highly social purposes. In particular processual archaeology emphasised the role of objects within a society rather than as definitions of it, and in consequence how those objects entered the archaeological record, and the building of bridging arguments, known as 'middle range theory' which linked the activities-in-life with the archaeological cultural assemblage patterns that resulted. The explanatory framework and goals moved as well as the methods of investigation.

This paradigm also saw a major shift: no longer were interpretations of evidence taken at face value. The means of building inferences from objects and their contexts was more overtly discussed (e.g. analogy, Binford 1967) and in particular there was extensive reflection on and examination of the creation of the archaeological record, site formation processes and taphonomic (non-cultural) modifications. In particular, middle range theory sought to link the social interpretations which were now the goal of archaeology with the material correlates which formed its evidence base, via robust bridging arguments. All of these benefited from two other developments; firstly, the actualistic studies which used anthropology, ethnography, and experimental work (as discussed in Chapter 4) and, secondly, the availability of evidence from scientific techniques of analysis and computers and statistics as tools to make sense of these data.

David and Kramer (2001: 37–8) rightly select the work of Binford and Hodder as exemplars of two different schools of thought on how to use ethnographic data. Binford was concerned with verification and the relationship between the observed archaeological record and the activities which create that record, whereas Hodder was not so much concerned with verification as with seeing each case in its cultural context, and analysing structures and layers of social behaviour. The former favours quantitative approaches as well as qualitative where possible, and the latter always focuses on qualitative and contextualised approaches. In practice, there are many different schools of thought and even these authors have developed their ideas over time. Ethnographic archaeology is a broad field with many different approaches being adopted. The natural science approach, whilst accepting that there is individual variation, none the less still seeks generalising principles which could be applied cross-culturally. Thus ethnographic data has contributed greatly to middle range theory and understanding how objects enter the archaeological record in different situations. In some cases, researchers favour the reformulation of these principles as almost law-like statements. Processual archaeology stresses quantification and objective evidence. The approach is none the less interested in the dynamics of culture change and the causes and effects of these, and is not concerned with static entities.

Studies of artefacts were opening out and taking the subject in new directions, but there is always a downside and a counter-reaction. The drive for objectivity in data studies and techniques of analysis, with the idea of law-like generalisations, could make such studies seem to reduce material culture to soulless numbers and facts with little attention paid to symbolic meanings. It was against these aspects of processualist approaches that post-processualism was born.

Asking why but accepting subjectivity and individuality

Post-processualism was a series of different reactions against the prevailing paradigm which incorporated many different critiques. However a central theme was to emphasise that people were not just reactors to events but were able to manipulate situations: they were able to use symbols and identities in different ways and to convey meanings. In recent years such ideas have been termed 'agency', a concept discussed further below, which has a strong sense of the individual as an actor in social networks. Post-processualism, or 'interpretative archaeology', allowed for many different ways of interpreting the evidence to exist including feminist and indigenous perspectives (Hodder 2005). Allowing subjectivity was not equated with giving all theories, however derived, equal weight: there was instead some sense that interpretations would be weighed and judged into a best-fit pattern even if multiple possibilities were still acknowledged. It seems as though there is more common material between the two approaches than might be recognised at first sight. Certainly the processual school of archaeology, whilst seeking to be as objective as possible, is in no sense claiming to be devoid of subjectivity; whilst the post-processual school has perhaps recognised that it does not, nor can it ever, enter the minds of past people. No one school of thought is going to allow the impossible, which is to truly know what went on in the past and what people thought about what went on.

In contrast to an approach influenced by the natural sciences, those influenced by the social sciences looked at levels of different concepts. Objects stand for other things (semiotics) (e.g. Hodder 1987) and can offer structured meanings, but recent thinking has stressed that the significance of artefacts will always vary depending upon the meaning that they are assigned in a particular culture. The way in which they are perceived (Thomas 2006) and become categorised or 'objectified', used as metaphors, and are consumed or used by that society, changes the meaning and the experience of objects (Tilley 2002, 2006, Miller 1985, 1987, 2006) and Miller in particular has explored issues of material culture (e.g. Miller 1995, 1998). Style was explored as a concept rather than a descriptive system and authors have revisited their own ideas on this (Sackett 1977, 1990, Wiessner 1984, Wobst 1978, 1999). This willingness to be reflective characterises the paradigm. Post-processual approaches are multiple and have varied over time. A key legacy is the deconstruction of the practice of archaeology (Shanks and Tilley 1987) since the recognition that archaeology was not a neutral endeavour was crucial. The post-processual school opened up a Pandora's box of perspectives that were missing from the testable hypotheses of New Archaeology, though they were present in some of the anthropological work of the processual school. There is explicit recognition that a researcher brings their own worldview to their studies. Gender issues, colonialism, the idea of symbolic capital (the cultural symbolism of past material culture valued in the present), the appropriation of past material culture or symbols from it, and the ownership or repatriation rights over this material by their original cultural owners are all part of a postmodern pluralism. Some of the separate fields have also developed along their own paths. For example, archaeologists' debate on the cultural rights to objects, and the treatment of them, has moved on in tandem with initiatives to curb the illegal trade in antiquities (Brodie et al. 2001, Robson et al. 2006, Vitelli 1996). In the field of gender archaeology, once women in archaeology were discussed, gender issues including queer archaeology followed, along with interests in children and mothering (see case study below). Post-processualism has enriched the debates on material culture because of its willingness to open up such perspectives to scrutiny.

Some aspects appear less enduring. Though it is accepted that practice is an important part of social structure (Bourdieu 1977) the polarised dualities which some used as structuring principles are less convincing. Many recent overviews question the simplistic dichotomies of object–subject, animate–inanimate and the simplistic reading of material culture as text, instead drawing out the symbiotic relationships between people and objects (Knappett 2005a). Renfrew and others have become much more interested in cognitive archaeology and the thought processes that lie behind past actions and practices, sometimes known as an archaeology of mind (Renfrew 1994, Renfrew and Zubrow 1994, Mithen 1996). More recently, this school of thought has dealt with material engagement theory and explored concepts of materiality and the manner in which people as individuals engage with the material world and use it for symbolic storage and as a means of creating social value (DeMarrais et al. 2004, Malafouris 2004, Renfrew 1998, 2001, 2004).

Objects materialise thoughts, and in the study of material culture the paradigm shifts have seen 'technology' transformed from the documentation of a process to a discourse on the conceptualisation of technology (Chilton 1999a, Costin 1999, 2005, Dobres 1999, Knöpfli 1997, Lemonnier 1976, 1986, 1989, 1993, van de Leeuw 1993), the selection of technologies as social choices (Loney 2000, Sargent and Friedel 1986, Stark 1999, Schlanger 1991) and signals of ethnicity (Sterner 1989), and the way in which people viewed technologies (Ingold 1990, Jones 2001, Roux 1990, Wright 1993).

The changes outlined here offer sweeping overviews of processes which are by no means homogenous or synchronous. Much of the literature on the theoretical issues involved is densely written and little would qualify as light reading. The simplest means of looking at what changes the processual to post-processual paradigm shift has wrought is perhaps to present two case studies. The first looks at the influence of education on a value system for objects from another culture and the other examines the ways in which studies of polished stone axes have followed paradigm trends where agendas have changed considerably.

Social influences from the past

A major phenomenon of the veneration of a particular period and region of the past was the British early eighteenth-century fashion for sending young men from upper-class families on a tour of Europe, as a means of finishing their education (Scott 2003). A key component of that education was the classical literature of Greece and Rome. Thus, it was only natural when young men went abroad for them to visit classical ruins and to take an interest in objects of art from these periods. Because of their wealth, many could afford to purchase some objects as works of art (often statuary) and bring them back to Britain where they would be displayed in great opulence in some of the main country houses of the time. Sometimes these works were exchanged, or sold to the newly formed British Museum where they formed the basis of a national collection. Britain's love affair with the ancient Greek and Roman past influenced architecture as well as putting objects from this past inside the houses of the great and wealthy. It lent them an air of sophistication and increased their status (Scott 2003). The accepted educational curriculum and fashion thus come to play a part in the value placed on objects and those which were collected or singled out for special treatment.

Changing interests within polished stone axe studies

Polished stone axes are a good example of the changes wrought by the move away from culture history. Instead of the battle axe culture and the space/time framework of different types of polished stones, Clark, in his classic 1965 paper about the traffic in stone axes and adze blades, was able both to show a European perspective on these objects and also to incorporate ethnographic information into a wide-ranging archaeological discussion of this one artefact class. In true functionalist perspective, the range of uses for an axe was considered by using the ethnographic evidence. Clough and Cummins's (1979) volume on stone axe studies had reports on experiments and ethnographic examples as well as typologies and surveys. There were also collective results from the petrography of such artefacts which for Britain gave 'trend surface diagrams' linking sources of rock to quantities of stone axes as some form of distribution maps, though such maps can now be seen as problematic. The eclectic nature of the contributions to this volume and others such as Wright's (1977) *Stone Tools as Cultural Markers* can be seen as a measure of the changes that were taking place in the study of artefacts resulting from the major shift in paradigm to processualism.

An innovative study of axes (Bradley and Edmonds 1993) looked at both the production and exchange of stone axes, but focused not on the details alone but on the interpretation of those, and, in particular, using fieldwork evidence from the archaeological source at Great Langdale, UK, and scientific data, examined the earlier and later significance of the so-called axe trade. In particular they used scientific data to suggest that several rock outcrops were identical and that the selection of extreme locations for extraction activities could be attributed to social concepts of value rather than technical differences. This is a book which combines solid fieldwork and data with a more theoretical approach and has at its heart the understanding rather than the documentation of this phenomenon. Pétrequin and Pétrequin (2000) have undertaken a detailed study of polished stone adze production in modern Papua New Guinea which incorporates rock extraction, technologies of manufacture, hafting practices, and usage, with all of these documented socially, and with the symbolic aspects recorded alongside technical detail (Thery et al. 1990). It is a classic example of the development of the *chaîne opératoire* approach, combining a sequence of actions set firmly in their social context with the wealth of data all fully documented. The modern concern with the symbolism of artefacts is exemplified by Brumm's (2004) discussion of Australian stone axes which links different kinds of evidence to suggest the strong relationship between the raw materials and ancient cosmological and symbolic systems. All these polished stone axe studies ally theoretical insights with substantial data collection. In contrast, Strassburg's (1998) concern with the symbolic looked at the meaning behind some of the variation in polished stone axes and was a self-consciously postmodernist endeavour, offering a deconstruction of some of the terminologies and associations of this genre of artefact.

Lastly, now that we are much more concerned with the manner in which finds enter the archaeological record and the things that happened to them as part of that last cultural act of deposition, Larsson's (2000) article is a good example. He looked at a cache of Neolithic axes from Sweden which seemed to have been deliberately transformed by fire before they were deposited. The article goes on to consider colour changes and the act of transformation or destruction and the difference in perception between those two key tenets – were these axes destroyed or were they transformed? The two, although both possibly resulting in the fire damage which we can see, hold very different conceptual meanings.

Gender and age

The 1980s onwards has seen the field of women, gender, and children develop rapidly. Some of the issues show strengths and weaknesses in the approaches taken to material culture interpretation. Thanks to the wealth of writing in recent years biological sex is now distinguished from the social construct of gender, and studies have moved on from talking about 'women' (Dahlberg 1981, Ehrenberg 1989) to the discussion of gender (Gero and Conkey 1991, Claassen 1992, Hayden 1992, Du Cros and Smith 1993, Pyburn 2004, Wright 1996, Nelson 1997) and queer archaeology (Dowson 2000, Matthews 2000). Though gender is recognised as a social construct, it does have biological sex as its starting point, and as such it is coloured by 'reproductive potential'. As Rega points out, 'gender without at least the referent of biological sex wouldn't be gender; it would be something else' (2000: 238), but there is another referent because 'variation in age is crucial to understanding gender' (Claassen and Joyce 1997: 4). Greater emphasis is being given to age as children, mothering, and families are entering the discussions (Baxter 2005, Beausang 2000, Sofaer Derevenski 1997, 2000b, Kamp 2001, Lillehammer 1996, Moore and Scott 1997, Rega 1997, Wilkie 2003). Gender develops at the level of the individual and their life, as well as being a construct of the social whole. From our perspective gender constructs might appear to be in stasis within a community and period but it is lived in a state of dynamic equilibrium within the whole society across generations. A key theme is perception. How might individuals within a society perceive gender and age and how do we perceive them? To an archaeologist, material culture is an obvious category of evidence, but it is also featuring more frequently in historical and classical studies showing different ways of looking at the issue (Donald and Hurcombe 2000a, 2000b, 2000c).

Material culture is a key means of signalling gender and age categories within a society alongside, and sometimes in contradiction to, sexual bodily characteristics. The most obvious method of signalling gender with goods is via body adornment, but gender is not just about appearance of the individual, it is about the actions of the individual and the social contexts in which these are performed. The involvement of an individual in food collection and processing, in the production and use of artefacts, and performance of reproductive, nurturing, and ritual activities will all contribute to the perception of that individual within their community. The places in which these acts are performed, and the other individuals who watch or participate, are also important. Within this complex web of individual behaviour there is a plethora of opportunities to convey 'gender' to the other members of the community because gender is performed as lives are lived, not limited to the expression of sexuality. If archaeologists are looking for gender constructs, then they should look at the level of the everyday tasks as well as body adornment. Thus gendered crafts and technologies have emerged as key material culture themes (Brysting Damm 2000, Costin 1996, Hendon 1997, Hurcombe 2000a, Senior 2000, Wright 1996) with specific case studies in lithics (Bird 1993, Gero 1991, Gorman 1995, Owen 2000), ceramics (Mitchell 1992, Wright 1991), metal (Sofaer Derevenski 2000a), and weaving (Hamann 1997). The problem is in perceiving when an activity is exclusively or primarily gender-specific and placing that activity within its social milieu. There are also now discussions of the role of children's labour in crafts, or the role of toys in the archaeological record (Greenfield 2000, Haagen 1994, Park 1998). Material culture of clothing and adornment and its association with skeletal evidence is a particularly rich source of gendered material culture evidence (Wicker and Arnold 1999) showing the gendering of both children and adults (Albrethson and Brinch Petersen 1976, Rega 1997, 2000). Modes of dress also construct gender and subdivisions within the life-cycle (Stig-Sørenson 1991, 1997) and the portrayal of the body likewise (Alberti 2001, Rice 1981). Skeletal evidence can physically show gendered task-related differences (Molleson 1994). Ethnographic evidence and historical data both offer a crucial link in gendering past behaviours. Although older ethnographic texts undoubtedly have the problem of being mostly written by men, they do offer a starting point. There are also notable instances where women have been the focus of ethnographic studies (Mason 1895). Investigating distant prehistoric communities without either historical or ethnographic accounts presents a challenge (Dobres 1995, Hayden 1992). Given this potentially problematic starting point, it is even more important to do something which is a mark of good archaeology: the separation of evidence from interpretation (Hurcombe 1995). One of the features of the gendering of archaeology over recent years is the demonstration of overt and implicit bias in fieldwork, data interpretations, and presentation, with the contention that objective science is a myth (Gero 1996, Jones and Pay 1990, Wylie 1997).

A key concern is that when archaeologists document difference they too often try to ally the variations to *relative* status. A household has a great deal of material culture which reflects different activities. Some of these conform to broad gendered patterning and individual interests. As an example take items that might be in a modern household. There is his climbing gear and woodworking tools and her volleyball kit and sewing machine, but the masonry equipment and angle grinder are hers and the fine framed needlework pictures are his by inheritance from a female relative. The jewellery broadly reflects their gender in style but it is also different in quantity. She has more and the items are generally smaller, spanning a variety of periods since some are inherited; he has less (by weight or number) but has the single most expensive item which is contemporary. If archaeologists were to excavate the material culture of this household they would see differences, and some would be due to gender, but disentangling the gender of owner or producer, or user or wearer, would not be straightforward let alone the roles and status conveyed by the items. Some of the production equipment would be the most costly in monetary terms, but the items that are valued most are those which have personal meaning. If all this material was preserved and conveniently associated with bodies there might be an attempt to explain the 'anomalies'. In much the same way as Conkey and Spector (1984) reported the differing interpretation of grinding equipment in female versus male graves, as user versus producer, so very different interpretations of the material culture outlined above could be advanced. There would be clear differences, but it is the interpretation of these and their relative status that would be open to bias. The material culture would not be the same but it would be a mistake to interpret that difference as inequality. This exemplifies a key point when gendering material culture. If we seek gender in the past then it is indeed likely to be expressed by differences in material culture but these may be difficult to unravel. It is going to be difficult to disentangle maker, owner and user and to see cases with both cultural 'norms' and social blurring of the generalised pattern. Yet to recognise the latter is to reveal something interesting – new categories; or simply to discover that individuals stretch boundaries. However, it is an altogether separate and much more problematic step of archaeological inference to assign relative status to the gender differences.

However, where there are good associated data, some interesting social conclusions can be drawn. For example, where colonist and non-colonist material cultures differ, some insights into their interactions can be seen (van Dommelen 2006, Given

2004, Lyons and Papadopoulos 2002) along with the way in which indigenous objects alter in meanings (Thomas 1991) or where material culture from gendered graves shows intermarriage (Lyons 2000).

Given that gender and age are key structuring principles in all societies, the freedom to consider these aspects and to see many different ways in which such subjects can be addressed is refreshing and enabling. The developments in this field more than any other have been part of a fundamental shift in material culture studies.

Multi-faceted perspectives

Objects are not 'static facts' but interact with people. As much as people are in a constant state of flux, so the artefacts, as material cultures, are also ever changing, with the ability to reinforce, reinvent, and renegotiate social relationships between people. Material culture can embody and help form social relationships: the acts of making, using, transforming, and depositing objects can transform people's relationships. Furthermore, material culture objects are integral to human cultures, certainly from the Upper Palaeolithic and arguably from much earlier, and, in some senses, they also form a part of primate cultures (Chilton 1999a: 1, Shanks and Tilley 1987, McGrew 1992).

The key to all of these issues is to understand that, in a modern view of material culture, objects constitute as well as reflect relationships. Or to put it another way, material culture helps make culture in an active sense. Wobst (1999) carries this one stage further by referring to human artefacts as material interferences or interventions, since they have the intention to change something or to prevent a change occurring. Communication by other means is open to humans, for example speech and gesture, but objects are tangible ways in which people can interfere with the status quo. Wobst argues that change is, in effect, necessary for the same message to be communicated, since, if the same means are used all the time, they will not necessarily be read in the same way, or will not be as overt (Wobst 1999: 130–1).

Bourdieu (1977) stands out because, as a philosopher, he was interested in the focus on practice. Not just what people say they are going to do, but the act of doing it, colours thinking and in this respect there are certain points in common with the idea that objects have animacy and are in some sense alive. The act of doing something is an important part of the creation of material culture and the use of something and the practice of an activity all have social consequences. That is why material culture studies can help us understand and read archaeological past societies – what people did – and give some indications of what they thought and, in some cases, how changes to those systems of thought and systems of practice arose. The latter aspect is at the heart of the concept of agency.

Although different authors vary in their use of the term 'agency', the concept centres on how meanings and change occur at the level of the actions of individuals (although not necessarily the actions of any one specific individual) and groups and their effect on material culture (Dobres 2000, Dobres and Hoffman 1999, Dobres and Robb 2000, Gell 1998, Hoskins 2006, Johnson 1989). Recent work on agency has concentrated on putting these concepts into practice (Dobres and Robb 2005, Dornan 2002, Gosden 2005, Joyce and Lopiparo 2005, Owoc 2005).

The key modern perspective on material culture is encapsulated in the play on words in 'thinking through material culture' (Knappett 2005a). In particular, objects can have animacy, agency, and personhood. They can be used as thinking aids and, in this sense, they have their own animacy, and it is not a simple dichotomy between person and thing but rather an interplay between them. Objects become part of our thought systems and, in turn, colour and channel those thought systems, possibly in particular routes or in new directions where there is a breakthrough. Animacy implies that things have a life of their own and in some ways this is true of objects even though this would seem to be counter-intuitive. This is because the object lends itself to particular pathways or activities and it is certainly true that objects do have a life of their own, sometimes outlasting their maker or their user, and sometimes shaping cultural icons and metaphors.

Here, it is worth explaining that some of the systems of language for social interpretations of material culture can use specific terms from semiotics or rhetoric. These can seem rather unfamiliar to archaeologists. If one wishes to express a similarity, then in rhetorical terms this might be a metaphor; in semiotics it would be an icon. If the relationship is contiguous alongside, then it could be an index in semiotics, or a metonym in rhetoric. Likewise, the terms 'symbol' and 'synecdoche' might mean similar things, where there is a part to whole relationship, rather than it being similar or alongside, the one perhaps signifying or standing for the other. Actor network theory (ANT) is a way of looking at technologies and society which arose in sociological studies of technology; again it sees people and things not as mutually exclusive but as more fluid concepts each of which has agency (Knappett 2005a: 75). Some of the modern discussions of material culture are peppered with such terms used in quite specific ways, but it is important to realise, as well, that some terms are used slightly differently by different authors. For example, Gell (1998) used the term 'art and agency' in a particular way, but that does not mean to say that others have followed that particular reading. It is not helpful to endlessly define terms; the essence of these approaches is a more conscious examination of the interplay between object and person and the way in which an object can be taken at face value, or have one set of facts known about it, but can embody so much more.

Other important aspects of developments in material culture studies include the multi-disciplinarity of thinking (Knappett 2005a, Tilley et al. 2006) and the establishment of the *Journal of Material Culture*. The pages of this journal are an interesting juxtaposition of different approaches, materials and knowledge systems all brought to bear to unpick aspects of material culture. For example, historical period studies offer a rich contextualisation and the chance to test out new approaches (Karklins 2000). Although many disciplines contribute to material culture studies, archaeological research relies upon it to a unique exent. There are two recent works which pursue different approaches for the student of material culture studies: *Handbook of Material Culture* (Tilley et al. 2006) and a five-book series covering some of the origins of material culture studies and its revival (Buchli 2004). The latter assembles an impressive range of key articles through time.

There is one last concept, affordance, which is useful although it is in its infancy in archaeological discussions (Gibson 1986: 127–43, Knappett 2005a: 45–58, Knappett 2005c). It is a complementary *interaction* of animals with their environment, and a complex perception by a person (subjective) of what is afforded by something (objective physical properties). Affordance rests upon the knowledge, which can be visually perceived, of how materials and shapes behave on the basis of previous knowledge and experience. At its simplest this could be what an object lends itself to doing: not its role in the environment, nor in a manufactured object what it was created for, but what it will physically support or what it can be used to make happen. Physical constraints such as objects which are graspable, portable or movable all offer different possibilities. In many respects, the concept of affordance underpins some of the discussions of materiality in Chapter 6 because physical material properties will allow or exclude doing something. The object shape can also determine whether something is useful for a particular purpose. There is a consequence both of materiality and also of the shaping of the object: for example, a book can be used to prop up an uneven table – it was not designed for that purpose, but can be used in that way. A stack of paper will do just as well, a wedge of wood would also serve this purpose; but a hollow tube of paper is unlikely to have sufficient strength and so the shape and the nature of the object, rather than its material per se, have some interplay with this concept of affordance. Although he did not use the term affordance, this understanding is inherent in discussions of material science and material culture by Kingery (1996a and 1996b). Though they are not articulated in other discussions, I contend that personal knowledge and skill, both learned in a cultural context, are also involved in the perception of affordance. If a watertight container is wanted, a gourd affords a suitable shape, substance, and material. Rushes can be woven into a watertight container but only if the person looking at the plants has the knowledge of this as a possibility and access to the physical skill to weave such a basket. A concept of affordance, incorporating personal knowledge and skill, also simultaneously explains why no classification system will ever work perfectly and why the function of some ancient objects is not known to us. The same object can offer many possibilities for use, and there are uses for which we have no perception of affordance because our society does not need them and indeed has no knowledge of them.

Affordance can be envisaged as one aspect of the wider field of materiality. Another is cross-material relationships which are being explored via skeuomorphism, the copying of one object in a different raw material which makes visual reference back to the original (Harrison 2003, Hurcombe forthcoming, Knappett 2002). Materiality is the social relationships between materials and people: it is becoming a major approach within material culture studies, explored further in Chapter 6. In general, archaeologists know more about the physical properties of materials and technical aspects of object manufacture than they understand about their affordances or actual function, despite recognising the importance that the performance of a task can have for artefact meaning and symbolism.

Overview

The development of artefact and material culture studies can be seen from the very beginnings of archaeology, but it went through certain transformations up until the 1960s, flourished along particular routes in the 1970s, and then came into its own, partly with the provision of post-processual archaeologies, in the 1980s. The way in which objects, minds, and animacy interplay with one another, and cognitive archaeology, both show current concerns with understanding the thought processes that objects engender in humans. Objects are the especial concern of archaeology, but historical subjects, geography, anthropology, and sociology all contribute to a more multidisciplinary advancement of material culture interests.

In all of this rich discussion there are many different references and approaches, but, pulling them all together, one can say that the relationship between a material, its cultural modification into either a usable object or the detritus from that process and its subsequent reshaping, reuse, deposition, survival, or change because of post-depositional processes, in part relies upon its materiality and on physical limits, but also in part, relies upon what people did with that object, their purposes for creating it and what social practices it documents for us to discover. Function is changeable and mediated through social relations (Graves-Brown 2000, Ingold 2000), but for historical reasons a discussion of function is incorrectly identified as referring back to the 'functionalist' paradigm of the early to middle part of the twentieth century. Functional determinism, especially, has since been categorically rejected, thus to talk of properties and functions can seem a retrogressive step, but discussions of materiality in material culture must move beyond such historical prejudices. For archaeological artefacts, the difficulty lies in finding ways of reading that evidence and that is what all of these ideas about social aspects of material culture are about – an increasing sophistication of how to read information from objects. However there is no one magic formula. If there were, material culture studies would be both much easier and also more boring. The complexity and the difficulty are what make it so interesting.

Part II

Materials and materiality

6   Materiality

Materiality and matter reality

Material culture exists in five senses' worth of glorious three-dimensional full colour. The written accounts of material culture, which form the primary medium for academic discussion, are inevitably limited because there is no way to smell, taste, or hear material culture. Images of objects can convey textures visually but, having already lost one dimension, most illustrations are then reduced further by losing colour. These losses reduce the perception of materials as material culture. Materials behave in certain ways constrained by their physical properties and they also have colours, textures, sounds, smells, and tastes. Furthermore, any material used in material culture has a source which will form an important aspect of its social character and its behaviour as a material. Geological resources (clays, minerals, rocks) come from specific places in a landscape. Plant resources have a generic habitat and appearance according to species, a specific location and qualities related to their individual growing conditions there, as well as qualities dependent upon age and season. They may be deliberately planted or managed resources. Many of these same issues also apply to animals which can in addition directly interact with people. It is possible for an individual or community to personally know a plant, animal, or mineral resource and to have a relationship with it and for there to be a social history related to a resource. Materials also have different life spans and respond differently to deliberate attempts to destroy them. The permanence or transience of a material or its capacity to be recycled into something else may be an important aspect of its social perception. All of the above characteristics are facets of materiality but they can also amount to a personality for an individual material resource. Materiality thus encompasses the material source and human relationships with it, the perception of that material with all five interacting senses through time, and the behaviour (sic) of objects made from it. All these also affect how an object is studied by archaeologists.

Part II is organised by major material categories because this made best sense of the issues of materiality, that is the sense of the resource and its material qualities, the past crafts of transforming materials into material culture, and the present craft of studying artefacts as items of past material culture. Each material chapter tries to convey a sense of materiality by combining practical information, conveying a sense of the sumptuous richness and diversity, and creating a sense of the possibilities, whilst retaining a clear structure and an evaluation of the archaeological study of that category of material. Alternative categorisations such as those outlined below did not stand up to close scrutiny but require some discussion.

One way of grouping technologies is to use the terms 'reductive' and 'transformative'. 'Reductive' means that, when shaped, the material is diminished: pieces removed cannot be put back. The most obvious example is wood – once it is chipped, the chip cannot be replaced. By this definition reductive technologies would also include stone, bone, antler, ivory, and horn. In contrast, 'transformative' materials are those which are irreversibly changed by fire or chemical process, for example, firing clay to produce ceramics and reducing ores to metals by smelting. Neither process can be reversed. 'Additive' describes technologies such as textiles and basketry, where the material is added cumulatively to make the product. These terms, especially 'reductive' and 'transformative', have a useful general coherence and have become part of an accepted way of looking at materials. However, a closer look shows that there are not such clear cut boundaries between these different technologies. It is possible to transform chemically and by heat materials such as wood which can be bent using steam; antler and bone can also be slightly bent by such methods or have the mineral component chemically leached out, leaving more flexible materials. Charring wood carefully (for example for a spear tip) will harden it, and careful charring and scoring of an antler allows it to be snapped by a sharp blow. Chemical methods can irreversibly alter the qualities of hides and turn them into tanned leather. Plant fibres can be rendered down by hot, caustic solutions. Even stone, a seemingly obvious 'reductive' material, can be irreversibly transformed by the subtle use of heat in order to improve its knapping qualities but decrease its elastic properties (see Chapter 8). Furthermore, stone artefacts are often just the functional edge of an item that is composed of several different materials. Archaeologists frequently consider and classify the one element that has survived in a composite tool. Does this make the tool as a whole part of 'additive' technology? In a way it is a composite additive tool with replacement and adjustment possible, but the individual stone blade component is reductive. Even seemingly obvious additive technologies such as basketry can be viewed differently by seeing baskets not as a product 'made' to a mental template but as something 'grown' (Ingold 2000) where the individual plant elements forming the coil material for a basket might be whole but constrained into a shape using other modified plant elements which have been 'reduced'. Again, this example shows a composite hybrid which cannot easily be slotted into just one of the tripartite division of technologies as reductive, transformative, and additive.

Reductive, additive, and transformative technologies have no simple correlation with the performance qualities of the materials as brittle, resilient, or flexible. Brittle-reductive could describe flaked stone, whereas resilient-reductive would better describe wood, bone, antler, ivory, and horn. Brittle-transformative could describe ceramic fired clay, whereas resilient-transformative could describe metal tools. Flexible-additive could cover cordage, textiles, and some baskets, though tougher basketry items using round wood or split wood could also be described as resilient-additive. Hide products, depending upon the method of preparation, could be flexible or resilient, and their technology could be reductive or additive or a combination of both e.g. a plyed cord (additive) prepared from strips of hide (reductive). The range of possibilities is simply too great for these kinds of simple divisions to be a useful means of ordering a suite of artefact discussions. However, all materials have a source and it is more logical to use major source categories as an organising principle.

Materials and their materiality are more complex than commonly believed and that is why so much space in the ensuing chapters has been devoted to images of different materials and to describing what kinds of attributes those materials have and the ways in which they can be worked. This is not about technological pedantry but about material possibilities and materiality.

Just as gender is a social construct based around biological sex, so material culture is a social construct based on the physical properties of materials and how these can be obtained and formed into artefacts. To deny the physical differences between sets of materials is to go against nature and to create false divisions for objects from the past. Furthermore, if materials are organised by themes of function instead, then this requires there to be a sound basis for assigning function and for at least broad functional themes to hold true across all sorts of different periods and different regional traditions to facilitate comparisons. This is quite simply not the case. It also suggests that 'function' exists as a separate utilitarian factor when in fact it is intimately linked with many others such as style and design (Conkey 2006) and social relations (MacKenzie 1998). 'Function' is not a single utilitarian concept but a complex web of pragmatic possibility or affordance (Gibson 1986, Knappett 2005c), conceptual plan, and social role. Firstly, material culture technologies vary with time, creating and opening up different opportunities and possibilities. The same function could be served by different materials using different technologies and have different social resonances. Secondly, and perhaps more importantly, there is no sound and widely available basis for determining even the pragmatic function of an object. Functional analysis is possible on a wide range of the materials covered in this book but the technique is not widely applied. When the results of such studies are available they show that the functional terms can be completely wrong. Frequently, a systematic examination of a range of pieces from an assemblage has found a mismatch between items that are described as tools versus other items: some of the latter are used, but are just not sufficiently finely shaped for archaeologists to recognise them as implements. Moreover, items which have traditionally been described by functional terms such as 'knives', 'arrowheads' or 'milk jugs' were not necessarily used for that purpose (Nieuwenhuis 2002: 107–14, Yerkes and Gaertner 1997: 64, Craig et al. 2003). In all of the ensuing chapters, whether it is for stone, bone, or ceramic items, it is obvious that we do not fully understand artefacts and the way they could potentially be used. The functional names assigned to types can be wrong and are often no more than guesses. Given this, it is hard to envisage a valid functionally themed set of discussions. Nor do we always have a clear understanding of the processes of forming those materials into usable objects and the ways in which the material, the manner of obtaining that material, the colour and physical resistance properties of the material, might lend opportunities for expressing particular beliefs or symbolising particular things. The modern world is just too divorced from these kinds of materials. That is why the concept of materiality advanced here stresses dealing with the physical reality of the processing and use of objects and the symbolism that can be inherent in those processes and functions.

The concept of materiality has been used by recent authors in different ways, some rooted very much in the nature of the materials (e.g. Parker Pearson et al. 2006, Jones 2004 and comments) and some focusing on the way humans have mentally engaged with materials (DeMarrais et al. 2004, Graves-Brown 2000, Meskell 2005, Miller 2005, Tilley 2004). The roots of concepts of materiality must be based on the realities of dealing with the physical matter which forms the raw materials for material culture. That is why the range of materials has been divided into four gross categories with some sub-sections. The four materials chapters that follow have been grouped according to gross sets and then have deliberately been ordered to make a point about which materials might have been in use first and might have been the most important. So the first one is organics because wood, and to some extent hides and fibres, might have been the first kinds of materials used, not flaked stone. A stick for digging up roots and tubers opens up a resource that cannot readily be exploited by digging with hands alone. Though chimpanzees use unmodified rocks and anvil stones for cracking tough nuts, they also *shape* a stick for termite fishing (McGrew 1992). Stone edges can be used to cut meat, but people also have teeth for that purpose; some of the earliest stone tools were used to work wood and to work other materials (Keeley and Toth 1981), in other words, the *raison d'être* for the modified flaked stone traditions might be the fact that our ancestors were *already* exploiting organic materials. Hence, organic materials are ordered first. In addition, though organic finds are not frequent, they form the majority of all material culture items, and even today in modern homes most furnishings, clothing, and objects are in these materials. Their under-representation in the archaeological record is no excuse for ignoring them. Furthermore, though they contain the greatest variety of materials within their global heading, the kinds of problems encountered and some of the technologies are very similar. That is why there are not separate chapters for bone, antler, ivory, horn, shell, wood, and plants. Stone is second because of its longevity as an exploited material and its durability, then ceramics (including a small discussion of glazes and glass) and lastly metals since these are the most recently exploited major category of materials.

Experiencing materials in the modern world

If experiencing materials as material culture is part of a worldview, what does the modern world reveal about our understanding of the materials which were commonly used in the past? If we examine a modern person's concept of the material and their experience of it, then what follows is revealing. Metals are largely experienced in the modern world as cutlery, jewellery, pots and pans, white goods, nails and screws; they are predominantly high-quality steels and, unless people have done metalwork at school or have a particular interest, then they, personally, will have no understanding and little experience of the processes of reducing raw materials to metals and of then working those up. Even in school metalworking classes, it is the finished metals that are worked: these are not produced from ores.

Many of the processes of working materials involve heat, but a modern person rarely processes materials with heat any more except in cooking, and even here practical skills can be in decline (Sutton 2006). Increasingly, people have little personal experience of fires as they live in centrally heated (and often hearthless) homes, with gardens inappropriate for bonfires. Many people growing up today will have experienced fire mainly as barbecues. Therefore the way in which colours in a fire can be read as ranges of temperatures, which in turn will make certain processes possible, is not within many people's direct experience.

Ceramics are still widespread. People understand mugs, teapots, and other common types, and perhaps have experienced earthenwares as flowerpots, and high-fired porcelain as fine tableware, but again there is no sense of process. Even where people have taken pottery classes or have experienced making pots at school, the material is provided ready-mixed. There is no sense of extracting that material from the natural resources, putting other things with it to make up something which is then transformed by fire. Instead, people are given a ready-made raw material which has already been highly processed, and their experience of firing will be to put it in an electrically controlled, time- and temperature-managed kiln. The other item discussed under ceramics is glass. Our modern concept of glass is of a very clear material used for drinking vessels, vases, and bottles, or as high-quality window glass, or toughened glass on car windscreens and on buildings. It is not rare in our society, but modern glass is a highly developed product, and perceptions from the modern world are unlikely to match with the qualities of glass which would have stood out in the past. Instead, in the past glass might have been experienced as a rarity, able to capture light, to have translucency and give the wonderful possibility of jewel-like colours standing out against other much less intense colours and textures.

Most people's experience of stone is limited to decorative jewellery, ashtrays, bowls and similar vessels, and perhaps decorative hearthstones and fireplaces, and walls in the garden or rockeries. But they themselves will not normally have produced that material, and, whilst they may have built walls or paths in the garden, they are unlikely to have ever used stone to make other things, or to know intimately its knapping qualities, fracture abilities, and performance as an edge and as a grinding surface. Some of the most decorative large-scale stonework will have been seen by most people when they visit a bank or hotel foyer, rather than any other place.

So far as organic materials are concerned, wood is probably the material with which people today are the most familiar. It is in our houses as floorboards, doors, and chopping boards (though these are going out of fashion) and most people still have wooden furniture, but they could not necessarily describe what species it is, the method of working it, or why a particular species was chosen, nor indeed what the tree looked like or where it grew. Textiles are bought in shops as plain weaves, slightly decorative weaves, or knitwear, and the raw materials are usually wool, cotton, linen or, increasingly, synthetic 'fleeces'. There is little sense of process for the plant-based fibres (e.g. the retting process for producing linen from flax plants) or of the variety of other possible plant-fibre sources such as tree-bast fibres, since the latter are not commercially viable in the modern world and thus not within the experience of most people. Likewise with baskets: these in the modern world conjure up images of wicker and willow or split cane because the former are still (just) commercially viable and the latter are imported as a cheaper product from East Asia, even though this material is alien to temperate climates. Rush or grass are not so well known as basketry materials. Modern people do not understand the use of a basket as an everyday container, because we have plastic bags, nor would they understand that a basket can be watertight, because we have other containers to do that. Nor necessarily would they understand the strength of a basket. The strongest basket in most modern households is perhaps a wicker log basket, yet baskets can be made which act as ship's fenders or large cages.

Hide and furs takes on completely different connotations in our own societies. In many respects they are seen as 'forbidden' because of the politics of animal rights. Most people's experience of 'hide' might be a sheepskin rug, a leather coat, or a leather bag; these are all highly processed to make them very flexible and there is no way most people would have experienced these processes nor experienced other ways of rendering the materials. Even leather shoes rarely have stiff leather soles and most people have never seen a leather bottle as a rigid object, though they may have seen Spanish-style soft hide *botijos*. Perhaps the nearest they have come to skin as a hard rigid material is when buying rawhide dog chews for a pet.

Of the hard animal materials, ivory is completely forbidden as an item that encourages the poaching of an endangered species, although some antique pieces might survive in a modern house. Some people might perhaps have had antler toggles or bone toggles on a duffel coat, although these are increasingly of wood or plastic. The handle of a corkscrew might be of antler, or the handle of cutlery might be of bone, although these are now old-fashioned items. Similarly, a generation ago horn might have been experienced as a flexible 'shoe horn' although even then it need not have been appreciated that it can be translucent when it is finely worked and forms a good shape for a container or funnel. Perhaps the best-known category of hard animal materials today is shell, because of people collecting them on a beach. They might experience the raw material, but they do not necessarily see it as useful because they have never had to put those uses into practice.

This long litany might seem to labour the point, but none the less it is fundamental to the concept of materiality. If we, as archaeologists, want to understand materiality, then we need to understand the materials, their properties, and where they come from, and see the kinds of relationships and symbolism that might be inherent in all of that operational chain of raw material sourcing, production, use, and deposition. There are concepts that are not well known to us because of our own limited experience with these materials in the modern world. Colour is something that we underrate continually as archaeologists. Phillip Larkin wrote 'sun destroys the interest of what's happening in the shade' (1964: 21), meaning that intense sunlight will blind the eye so that events in the shadows cannot be perceived. That is what strong colour does to muted colour variations and to textures. In our own world, we have material culture with vibrant, strong hues of colour in many shades; there are very shiny surfaces, and completely transparent materials. All of these would have been so rare for most of the periods studied by archaeologists. My contention is that we have trouble perceiving subtle colours and textural patterns in the material culture of the past, in the way that ancient people would have perceived them, because we are blinded by present-day expectations. Nor do we see translucency, sparkle, and shine as special when these are commonplace today. In a world where colour was not readily available except as flowers, then the ability to dye materials, even with fugitive, transient dyes, or the ability to make objects from intensely colourful materials such as the blues of faience and lapis lazuli, the variegated green of malachite, the deep rust reds of carnelian heated stones, or the intense yellow, orange, or red and translucency of amber, would have been truly exceptional.

In all of these ways, I think we underrate the symbols and the uses of colour in the past, and we consistently underrate the subtle use of colour, such as different intensities of brown in a stone, or flecking, or the ability to weave a texture alteration and pattern into a mat or a basket, the play of different lines, features, and flecks in wood. We do not see them because, to allude again to Larkin, our eyes have been blinded by the sun of colour into ignoring the interest of what is happening in the shade, as texture or muted colour. Archaeologists are just beginning to appreciate some of these colour issues and related symbolism (Boivin and Owoc 2004, DeBoer 2005, Gage et al. 1999, Jones and MacGregor 2002, Lynch 1998, Young 2006) which can amount to cosmological relationships (e.g. Charles et al. 2004 and Saunders 2004 on American cultures and Taçon 2004 for an Australian example). Likewise, archaeologists are just beginning to explore acoustic qualities (Scarre and Lawson 2006), and light and visual issues as well as textural and other senses (Cummings 2002, Dawson et al. 2007, Hurcombe 2007, Lawson 2006, Lazzari 2003, MacGregor 1999). The post-processual agenda places materials and material culture firmly within a sensory view of the world where old Cartesian dualities are inappropriate because object, mind, and body are seen as interacting in complex ways. There is also an increasing sense of materiality in general (e.g. Tilley 2004, Parker Pearson et al. 2006, Ingold 2007, Knappett 2007) and of materiality reflecting permanence and transience and the way in which certain animals and combinations of material are associated with the living and the dead (Parker Pearson and Ramilisonina 1998). The act of extracting material may be important, especially where this creates a strong colour marker. When chalk is dug, a gleaming white surface appears and small objects can be carved from it, or massive ones by patterning the landscape with exposures of chalk. Some sense of the materiality aspects of extraction from the ground is inherent in Topping and Lynott's (2005) discussion on mines. There are also tantalising hints of materiality issues in some historical period material culture work, for example Brauner (2000) on glass, ceramics, and their reuse, and Russell (2000) on the use of particular kinds of colours as currently poorly understood aspects of African-American spirituality. There is also a wealth of meaning in beads (Sciama and Eicher 1998). These examples are all materials which survive well in the archaeological record. Less tangible, but none the less perceptible in the ethnographic record, there are the symbolic relationships that might exist with natural materials and animals and plants, for example the significance of hides and skulls as representations of animals, or perhaps as important items in their own right (Davis and Payne 1993, Piggott 1962), or for trees as religious objects (Shutova 2006, Rival 1998). The way in which organic materials are used in the past is linked to qualities which are not always about their practical usage but may relate instead to symbolism and social ideas (for wood species Coles 1998; for ivory McGhee 1977, and for bone amongst other materials White 1989a, 1989b, and 1992). Indeed, the use of symbolism via colour and ochre has been traced back 92,000 years in Israel (Hovers et al. 2003). Furthermore, the sensuality of material culture and the relationships between different senses' perceptions have recently been addressed as a concept of intersensorality (Howes 2006), though Ingold (2000: 268) convincingly argues that the idea of five separate senses can be seen as a contemporary social construct of perception. Furthermore, there are now explorations of sensory perception and material culture in anthropology, museum studies, and other fields which have much to offer an interdisciplinary debate on this cross-cutting topic (Bataille and Sontag 2001, Berger 1972, Classen 1997, 2005, Classen et al. 1994, Edwards et al. 2006, Grimshaw 2001, Hetherington 2003, Howes 1991, Paterson 2005, Serematakis 1996, Stahl 2002, Rodaway 1994). It is clear that sensory social constructions differ across societies (Ingold 2000: 160, Classen and Howes 2006: 199–200).

My concern with the ensuing materials chapters is to try to convey some sense of these issues of materiality to an audience that may themselves not be familiar with or have personal experience of them. That is why the discussion of each kind of raw material is opened with a series of images of objects made from the set of materials contained within the chapter to give overall impressions of the qualities and the range of products that can be made with these materials, hopefully conveying not just a visual sense but a visual reminder of texture, a sense of warmth, resonance, acoustic qualities, and smell.

Illustrating materiality

Archaeological researchers and lecturers spend a lot of their time providing illustrations as a communication tool. My department is lucky in having two gifted and highly experienced illustrators and we have collectively invested considerable effort in illustrating this book. Many are experiments but I had a vision of how the illustrations should work. One archaeological book that was very influential was *Symbols of Power at the Time of Stonehenge* (Clarke et al. 1985). It was produced to accompany an exhibition and used stunning colour illustrations. It linked the present in with the past by using photographs of modern badges of insignia, and other contemporary symbols of fashion (punk hair styles), role (traffic warden), and status (chief constable) and startlingly showed some modern replica metalwork which shone. The latter altered forever my perception of patinated bronzework. These illustrations conveyed not just technical information but a sense of the materiality of the objects. One non-archaeological book was also influential. When I was researching material culture and practical issues in the 1980s for a PhD on the use wear of stone tools, the 'survival' volumes were useful as one of the best sets of detailed information on how to do certain processes (hide and fibre preparation, rope-making, etc.). Though it was still difficult to do something based solely on the information they contained, they conveyed more practical information than many ethnographic accounts. Furthermore, knowing what was possible often helped make sense of material culture patterns. For the most part such books were illustrated in black and white (e.g. McGee's 1978 wonderfully titled *No Need to Die*) except where colour was deemed crucial, such as aiding the identification of plants that can kill (in Wiseman's 1986 *SAS Survival Handbook*). The basic problems were twofold and inherent in all experiment-based investigations, namely, 'how to' knowledge and 'practice makes perfect' physical experience. In undertaking the experiments these aspects improved but something invaluable, and not in these books, was gained: a physical appreciation of these materials, their performance characteristics at different stages of working, the sound, feel, and smell of them being worked, and the look and qualities (weight, texture, sound) of the finished objects. It was not until after my PhD that I came across a different kind of survival book which better conveyed my experience of materials. This was Ray Mears's (1990) *The Survival Handbook*. The illustrations were partly in colour and conceptually the book was not about 'survival' as 'not dying' but was revealed in the subtitle, *A Practical Guide to Woodcraft and Woodlore*. He has since gone on to produce more books and television programmes which he presents as the concept of 'bushcraft', which term better captures the artistry with which practical needs are met. His DVDs offer some of the best means of understanding natural materials available to archaeologists and include small skills clips that are not part of the broadcast programmes. The appreciation of skills which are not merely about subsistence survival but about artistry in the use of natural materials is a theme of which archaeologists should be well aware. It is often the elegance and artistry with which artefacts are made which allows them to be read as material culture.

Archaeologists need at some level to be materials experts. Students and researchers need to observe closely, make deductions, and form interpretations based on physical evidence as well as theoretical awareness. Theories lead to particular questions which in turn link to targeted data collection, but for material culture this is still a physical activity and knowledge-set. The researcher who cannot separate stone and bone, or recognize struck flint from frost damage, will make misleading interpretations. That is why some illustrations focus on key ways of reading information such as the textural details of a sherd wall, and the natural and cultural features of flint.

Many books on materials or artefacts have very dry images of drawn disembodied hands as 'how to' diagrams, or line illustrations of artefacts as used in excavation reports and as the objects are found (incomplete, degraded). Such images are truthful and factual but they depersonalise the production of material culture which in real life always involves people and societies. This should not be read as a lack of support for technical archaeological illustration. Modern publishing and digital cameras make the use of photographs possible in a way which would have been impossibly expensive in the past, but measured line drawings are crucial for cross-comparisons of forms and technologies, and in many respects convey more information than a photograph because they encode technical information. Flake scar patterns on flint are clear from drawings, but in a photograph lighting these clearly over a whole surface is more difficult, which is why the figures showing flake features, flake terminations, and knapping issues are drawings not photographs. The convention of drawing a pot as if a quarter section were missing (Chapter 9) allows the interior and exterior surface decoration to be portrayed as well as the profile, giving one very condensed set of information. Several photographs could still not convey the same information. Even in the age of digital cameras such issues mean that archaeological illustration is still a valuable exercise and it is one on which I and others have spent months of our lives.

Despite this, I have deliberately tried to minimise these kinds of 'dry' illustrations and instead have tried to include some more contextualised images of people, processes, and objects (such as weaving in Uzbekistan). Where details can be shown only by a close-up, the maker's hands provide the scale and a more personalised image. We have also taken photographs of modern, replica, and archaeological pieces together so that the contrasts are clear and the vibrancy of the materials in their original state (such as amber) and qualities of the objects made from them resonate from the page. This is all the more crucial because in the modern world people often have no experience of flaked stonework or what bone and antler look and feel like when fresh. Some of the 'dry' microscope images also leap off the page when they are in colour (e.g. pot thin sections).

The illustrations to Chapters 7–10 form a major contribution to the way in which the message of this book is conveyed, and certainly the energy expended in their production was not invested just to make them look pretty but rather to bring out their qualities. However, the fact that some are visually attractive is part of the message. Some materials have stunning qualities and those are just the visual ones, let alone the ones experienced through sound, smell, texture and taste. Many of the illustrations are composites from a range of sources addressing one issue or showing diversity. There are over two hundred separate images illustrating the next four chapters and these go some way towards conveying a sense of materiality that underlies my approach to archaeological artefacts as material culture. Unashamedly, the illustrations are collectively designed to appeal to more senses than the visual, and to create some kind of a reaction. That is what happens with real materials as material culture and that is the essence of the concept of materiality advanced here.

7 Organic materials and artefacts

So many materials, so little surviving

Organic materials are the most frequent category of material culture in life, but the least well known from their archaeological remains because they are so vulnerable to both chemical and biological attack. The opening images, figures 7.1–5, set the tone for a set of material culture which is around us, but with which we are no longer in touch, in some cases literally, in other cases in terms of the knowledge of the plant or animal and its landscape setting or production technologies (Chapter 6). The wooden objects in 7.1 and the basketry objects in figure 7.2 form an interesting contrast. On the one hand, we think of tree products as wood for structural timber, as a rigid material (for example floorboards) and perhaps also for small things such as handles, but we do not think of them in terms of a flexible material, for example the use of roots, bark, and wood as basketry and cordage materials and as cloth from bast (inner bark) fibres (see figure 7.14a). However, a brief review of the items on figure 7.1 shows the variety of ways in which wood can be used. The small item, top right, is a wooden turned vessel that is a unit of measure for capers in Malta. In the detail images a range of uses and technologies are depicted: the spears (figure 7.1a) are fire-hardened ones from Papua New Guinea – the pronged one is for hunting food while the viciously pointed fire-hardened tip on the right is for stylised warfare, where the technology is designed not to kill but to wound, so that honour is served and the wound heals; the comb (figure 7.1b) is there to show that wood can form composite items – the teeth are made of individually shaped slivers of wood, finely bound together, whilst the whole object is socially important as a courting comb from India (Nagar and Misra 1994); figure 7.1c shows a robust cup roughly hewn out of solid wood. Wood is usually thought of as a hard but insulating material, well-suited to making structures, furniture, and solid containers. Gardeners will also be familiar with smaller roundwood as 'bean poles' and wicker fencing.

In contrast, the overriding impression of the cordage, basketry, and textile materials in figure 7.2 is of resilient, flexible containers and baskets, soft fabrics, and stout strapping, but, more unusually, there are pieces of clothing, for example the plaited rush footwear (bottom left). The archaeological items are pieces of prehistoric fabric from Robenhausen, Switzerland, made by basketry-style twining technique (figure

7.2a), flexible cordage (7.2b), and a variety of different kinds of textile fragments, (7.2c). Figure 7.3 shows the uses of hair, hide, and other animal products as warm and soft skins, furs, cordage, belts, and straps, and as tougher items such as a sheath and a shield, and as a resonant material forming a drum. Figures 7.3a–c are designed to show different qualities that are not so apparent in our modern world. There is brain-tanned buckskin (figure 7.3a) to show how soft and flexible this hide material is and the finishing stone used to whiten it and raise the nap. In direct contrast there is the solid and yet not brittle flask (figure 7.3b) made out of dried raw hide, a state in which hide is rarely seen in our own society. It is a good material for carrying gunpowder because it neither conducts heat well nor makes a spark on contact with other materials. These are all qualities of hide which are hidden from our everyday experience of them as a material. Furthermore, we are unlikely to use hide in its thickest forms and rarely make objects of hide as stiff as possible; thus (c) shows a detail of the thickness of the hide shield.

If figures 7.1–3 are taken together, they all show a great diversity in hardness and usage of the different materials, as either individual pieces or composite pieces with other materials. In particular, the photograph of hide objects conveys warmth, and all have a similar range of tonal colours. In figures 7.1 and 7.2, several colleagues commented that the pieces on the left of each image drew their eye with the one signifying 'Africa' and the other signifying 'South America'. Even a small amount of decoration, colour, and figurative art is enough to draw attention and be used to give a (false) visual cue to what is otherwise a set of eclectic cultural material. The coloured and figurative symbols and styles of decoration are much more easily read in these images than are the materials themselves: colour and strong pattern draw the eye, especially where subtle textural pattern and small variations in tone are relatively unfamiliar in the viewer's own society. Broad surfaces of wood, hide, basketry, or textile all offer a place on which any design in relief or contrasting shades will stand out visually. In contrast, but often at the same time, these sets of organic materials also dominate as enclosing containers, clothes, and coverings: they offer protection and cushioning to things inside them from damage, the elements, and unwanted attention.

In comparison, figures 7.4 and 7.5 give examples of some of the hard animal-based materials – bone, antler, ivory, horn, and shells. These objects are constrained by the natural shapes in which they occur and by the anisotropic nature of the material, that is their properties vary in different planes. Antler, ivory, horn, and most bones occur as elongated round shapes. Pieces such as ivory, horn, or long bones are also hollow, or have material of a different density in their centre. These features all restrict the possible size and shape of the objects made from them. They can range in colour from browns and fawns to rich creams and sparkling whites, with possibilities for taking a smooth polish in horn (when the material might also be translucent), bone, and ivory. Shell colours are more variable but also offer strong whites as well as pearlised shine and iridescence. The hardest materials in this group can be used as points and edge tools, but the whole group can be used as decorative elements, as containers, or as fittings or handles connecting to other material elements of culture.

Finally, we do not normally consider substances as artefacts, but they are involved in the processing of other items of material culture and many come from the raw materials above. Fats, oils, waxes, resins, tannins, pigments, and dyes can be used to colour, preserve, waterproof, soften, mend, and fix other materials to form cultural items. Thus organic materials as a category cover a very wide range of naturally occurring materials. The manner of treatment of any of these can transform their performance properties giving yet more variation. It is scarcely surprising that organic materials dominate the material culture repertoire of societies, but because of their vulnerability in the ground, and the degraded state in which they are commonly found, they are not accorded the prominence in archaeological studies which they deserve. This discussion tries to redress this imbalance and stresses that these are living-based resources which exist in particular landscape settings.

Raw material properties and characteristics

This chapter is organised by groups of technologically and functionally linked items which often cross-cut raw material sources. There are four broad groupings; firstly the harder animal products of ivory, bone, antler, horn, and shell, secondly wood as timber and roundwood, thirdly hide, and fourthly, cordage, basketry, and textiles. The latter includes animal sinew, wool and hair, soft plants, willow and other very young wood growth, tree fibres, and bark. These are grouped together firstly because the technologies in turning fibres into fabric apply to fibres of both plant and animal origin and secondly because cordage–basketry–textiles are a contiguous group of technologies. Woven textiles, nets, and some basketwork use cordage and some of the earliest textiles are twined like basketry or use looped netting. Hair, wool, processed fibre, or whole plants can all be worked up using a similar technology after the initial collection process. Therefore, the main difference is the manner of extraction of the raw material. Since organic materials are living, the first point in discussing their materiality raises questions of life or death. Some organic resources are available only after death, or collecting them results in death. Others can be harvested or collected with no harm to the living. If we accord significance to places in the landscape for stone or metal exploitation, then the landscape setting and personal interaction with living objects should surely offer more intimate opportunities for living plant/animal–person interactions. The intimate relations of husbanding these resources and the social symbolism of the character of animals and plants surely present significant aspects of their materiality very early on in our past.

Figures 7.6 and 7.7 show the diversity of resources available from living things, and also some of the constraints. These were put together because much of the potential for the use of animal and plant products is not well understood because they are not prevalent in the modern world; for example, particular bones on the skeleton are used because they have round cross-sections, or D-shaped cross-sections, or, in the case of a scapula, form a wide blade-like natural beginning point. Some bone elements have particularly thick or strong bone structure. However, there are other issues to take into account. Antlers can be collected in season when shed, or taken off a hunted animal. Depending upon the species, the age and sex of the deer may affect the quality, size, and precise arrangement of the antler and there may be a season when the antler is at its best. Close familiarity may allow wool or hair to be plucked or groomed from a living animal or collected from areas frequented by them in the moulting season. A hide is available only on death, and figure 7.6 tries to show the other products available from one animal once it is killed. There will even be a season to take pelts in order to avoid larvae holes in the skins. The age of the animal may be important. If very fine hide is required, young animals may provide this. Thus collecting animal materials raises issues of husbandry of resources, the state of the desired raw materials, and the seasonality of some aspects of the resource. It is inconceivable that the interplay between the different raw material products and the food resources available from one animal were not interwoven (McGregor 1998). In different periods there might be both farmed and wild animal resources to be mentally mapped in time and space against current and future needs.

For plant products, a small valley on the fringes of Exeter University campus (figure 7.7) exemplifies the diverse resources able to supply basketry, cordage, and textile materials, as well as wood. Further details of plants which have useful properties, but which are very poorly understood for such in the modern world, are given in figure 7.8: flag iris (Iris pseudacorus), cat tail or reedmace (Typha sp.), club rush (Scirpus lacustris; in North America tule, i.e. Scirpus acutus is used). See also the very much smaller soft rush (Juncus effusus), stinging nettle (Urtica dioica), and the inner bark from the shoots of trees such as lime (Tilia), willow (Salix), and ash (Fraxinus) in Europe, and for North America some of the same or related species (e.g. Stewart 1977, 1984). Each of these species has both a general habitat and a specific place where an individual plant grows. Thus figure 7.7 is just a part of my mental map of where certain plant resources can be found near my working area, but it is supplemented by detailed mental snapshots of where to find the tallest or strongest stands of a particular species, a particular size or straightness of willow stems, or a particular angle of branch and tree that might fit a hafting arrangement. There is also a mental plan, looking years ahead, of when certain resources can be taken again. All of these species have a season when the resource is at its best or is easiest to extract. For example Typha, Iris and Scirpus can be cut in early summer after the plants are fully grown but with plenty of good weather ahead for drying them before storage. Bast fibre from shoots and trees is best obtained in late spring and early summer as the bark will peel easily then, whereas cutting the same trees for basketry could be done in the autumn when the tree is moving resources down into the roots (Hurcombe 2000a). In periods when many people in a community would need similar resources there might have been a clear sense of who could harvest particular stands of plants, or a way of marking a tree to be used by a particular person for a special purpose. The regrowth from previously cut plant stands and the scars on trees from harvesting bark, resin, or a flitch of wood (Turner et al. 2000, Rhoads 1992) might all have been visual cues to communal or individual access to those resources.

Such time and space maps, interweaving management cycles, and the intimacy of knowledge about and interaction with plant and animal resources would have been important aspects of their materiality and symbolism, as explored later. In a more materialistic way, each individual organic material has variation by sex, age, species, and growing conditions. Some specific issues are presented here for the major groups of materials but it is worth drawing attention to the wider range of other organic products which affect artefact production. Figure 7.7 points out pine as a source of resin, but fruit trees are also useful in this respect. Such trees can be scored or have small sections of bark removed to encourage more resin to slowly exude (Abbott 2004: 42). If resin-rich logs are burnt slowly the tar can collect in the bottom of a vessel. Resins and tars, especially birch bark tar, can be used for adhesive fixings, mending, and waterproofing and even as a sticky substance for entangling birds (Aveling and Heron 1998, 1999, Beck and Borromeo 1990, Brzeziński and Piotrowski 1997, Charters et al. 1993a, 1993b, Connan and Nissenbaum 2003, Gianno 1990 and Langenheim 2003, Nagar and Misra 1994: 178, Newman and Serpico 2000). Fixings of manufactured pitch are used in the Middle Palaeolithic and late Middle Pleistocene (Koller et al. 2001, Mazza et al. 2006). Plants also provide charcoal for pyrotechnology, woodash for caustic solutions, wood smoke for curing food and hides, tannins from bark for curing hides, and vegetable oils (liquid at room temperature) and fats as lubricants and waterproofing (Serpico and White 2000a, 2000b) as well as poisons for arrows and medicines (Pole et al. 2004). Straw can be a craft commodity (Anderson et al. 2006) and plants can be used as dyes (Tomlinson 1985) or as coatings for ceramics (Diallo et al. 1995, Heron and Pollard 1988). Animals likewise produce more than the obvious skin, bone, antler, horn, hide, hair, fur, or feathers. We often forget that animals can provide important sources of oils and fats (e.g. Nicholson 2005, Mulville and Outram 2005), and there is also beeswax (Brown 1995, Crane 1983: 240–6). Bees can be managed or taken from the wild and their wax has a range of uses as a sealant and adhesive. It is possible to use just resin or tar to fix tools in place, but a mixture of 50 per cent resin and beeswax makes a very effective hafting material, and fillers such as charcoal can reduce some of the rigidity or plasticity of resin and beeswax respectively. From the Bronze Age onwards wax is used for the casting technique termed lost wax (see Chapter 10). Hooves and horns can also be boiled down to make glue whilst milk can be used as coating for ceramics; blood and eggs are useful as binding agents; urine (which when stale becomes ammonia) is useful for degreasing and whitening hides; and brains can be used in tanning hides. There are also other special uses of organic materials, for example as perfumes (Mattingley 1990), hide as parchment (Read 1972), and papyrus as paper (Leech and Tait 2000).

Taken altogether there is a very wide range of organic materials available for use in the production of material culture. Their use as food products would be closely interwoven with the need for raw materials for crafts and the whole would provide a rich knowledge-base for social issues of symbolism and materiality.

Bone, antler, ivory, and horn

Figures 7.9 and 7.10 show comparative structures and shapes of teeth and ivory, of bone, antler and horn. They are placed in this order because ivory is the most brittle and hardest, with horn being at the other end of the scale (MacGregor 1976, Penniman 1984, Ramseyer 2001). However there are quite fundamental differences between the properties of bone, antler, ivory and horn. Ivory is the densest of all with bone, then antler following. Similarly shaped pieces of bone, antler, ivory, and horn would have different degrees of translucency, density, and flexibility. Horn is the most flexible of all, followed by antler, bone, then ivory. Horn is also translucent, although very finely worked ivory can sometimes have this quality. Bone, antler, and ivory can gleam white or shades of cream and their crystalline structure can make an object appear almost sparkly. Although this is difficult to convey with a photograph, some sense of what freshly made objects in these materials might look like can be seen in figures 7.4, 7.9 and 7.10. With all objects of bone, antler, ivory, and horn, the maker would have been aware of the difference in the cross-grain versus along-the-grain structural qualities of the material, and objects found in the archaeological record should always be envisaged from different angles, so that the lie of the material in the original animal product can be established. The visible grain can be distinctive of a particular species, as seen in the example of the ivory croquet balls in figure 7.9, where the distinctive circular criss-crossing patterns are typical of elephant ivory (Penniman 1984: plate 1). It also reveals the small inset section in the centre, which has a different alignment of the same pattern. This is where the maker had to take account of the fact that the tusk is hollow and patch in another piece of ivory. Understanding such small details allows the correct identification of the material to be made in archaeological finds and also gives some insight into the cultural versus pragmatic choices made during manufacture.

These materials vary in their properties and in their availability. They come in a variety of shapes and sizes, according to species, but also, for bone, the density depends upon the body part, because the stresses in the body are differently spread across the bones and this is reflected in their structure. Figure 7.6 identifies the bones most commonly used for craft purposes. These are mostly long bones because they give the greatest length of material; they can also, depending upon the body part and species, be round or D-shaped in profile which is useful. Ribs make good spatulas and polishers, and scapulae can be used as shovels, but are also used for objects requiring thin flat bone. Fibulae are suited to making awls, and both fibulae and metapodials have rounded ends which can serve as self-made handles. Bones such as metapodials have a groove down the middle which makes it easy to deepen this groove and split the bone down the centreline. In such ways the bone shapes lend themselves to particular kinds of uses, some of which are illustrated in figure 7.4. The awl in the photo is made on a split metapodial. For bone, as well as the differences in shape, there are two types – dense and cancellous, or spongy, bone. Dense bone forms a layer around cancellous bone, but the thickness of the denser material depends upon the protection it is designed to give (cranium and ribs) or stress it has to take (long bones carrying body weight in motion). Many bones are hollow inside: for example, see the sawn transverse and longitudinal sections in figure 7.9 showing the natural flat surface and thickness of dense bone, which made these skeletal elements attractive for making tools such as points, awls, and needles. The high density of bone means that it is not such a good shock absorber as antler, but it is less brittle than other mineralised tissues, such as tooth enamel (Scheinsohn and Ferretti 1997).

Antler also varies in shape by species. Red deer antlers, for example, have a major brow tine at right angles to the main shaft, a bay or trey tine, sometimes also known as bez and trez, and an area at the top called a crown, which radiates out several points. Thus red deer antlers present the opportunity to have a long straight shaft and, if desired, a point at right angles to it. This is the classic shape for antler picks, as used to make massive monuments such as the Neolithic henge at Avebury, UK. Caribou also provide long antlers. Flat shapes are available from animals such as elk in Europe or moose in North America. Fallow deer and reindeer have combinations of flat and arching long tines in their antlers. The age and diet of the animal can affect the density of the antler, and as an animal matures it can also have more complex arrangements of tines. The corona is the interface between pedicle and antler and a slightly flared coronet appears at the bottom of the antler. It is the presence or absence of these that allow some antler pieces to be determined as cut or shed antler if the end is preserved. Different species and sexes shed their antlers at different times of the year. Antler is dense: it has a similar mineral composition to bone and is similarly anisotropic. It has two advantages over bone – antlers are grown by the animal annually, and antler has a higher tensile strength. The latter quality makes it less likely to split under impact. This is why its use as a shock absorber sleeve between polished stone axe and wooden haft is not surprising, and why it has also been used to make barbed points for hunting, and as a soft hammer for making stone tools. Antler can come in very heavy, dense units and has also been used for mattock-like implements, and as narrow slivers for other items such as combs and needles. These make use of the fact that, although the centre of antler is spongy and less dense, the outer area can be very much more compact (see cross-section in figure 7.10). With care, it is possible to distinguish the spongy material contained within antlers from that seen in bone. Both have the problem that that the spongy material is not very useful and, as fragments, would be chewed up (dogs can chew antler away completely) and would leave few traces in the archaeological record as the debris from manufacture.

Ivory too, comes in different shapes depending upon the animal. It is possible to identify different kinds of ivory materials (see Krzyszkowska 1990, Penniman 1984). The most obvious is elephant ivory, which has very distinctive patterns (see figure 7.9 and above) and is the longest of the tooth materials which are labelled ivory. These also include hippopotamus tooth and tusks of the walrus and narwhal whale. Each of these animals lays down a different pattern of material and has a different internal cavity. Ivory is brittle so it can be chipped or riven to split along longitudinal planes.

Even horn comes in different shapes depending upon the species. Its properties, however, can best be seen by modern explanations of the craft of stick making (Gowan 1991). Horn is not mineralised and hard in the same way that the others are. Instead horn can best be understood as keratin, the same material as fingernails and hooves. As such, it absorbs and can be softened by water. Antlers are not horns and the two should never be confused. The two are structurally very different, can be worked in different ways, and horns are not shed. Horn can be cut and unwrapped from its original cone shape, which is impossible for antler, bone, and ivory. Horn grows as a covering around a bony core and, where horn does not survive on a site, its use as a raw material can still be inferred because of cut marks around the base of the bone cores which grow out from the skull to support the horn structures.

Finally, in cold regions, where there are deer but where wood might be in short supply, antler serves many of the same purposes as wood. Thus the French name for antler, *bois de cervide*, 'wood of deer', makes a great deal of sense.

Shell

There are numerous natural history textbooks on shells and where they may be found (e.g. Mayo 1944, Dance 1974) but Claassen (1998) provides a comprehensive description and assessment of archaeological shells as subsistence, environment, and artefact objects. The most impressive shell objects from the archaeological record are from the larger varieties which come from deeper rivers and the sea. These environments can sustain larger body mass. Smaller shells tend to be used whole for decoration, whereas larger ones can present more opportunities for use as composite items or for modification into tools or shaped, decorative items. As a calcium-based mineral, shell is brittle but is still suitable for some purposes. Large trumpet-like shells can be 'blown' to produce a sound (as depicted on a seal, Karali 1999: 102) and some of the larger varieties may have been capable of giving very resonant calls (Skeates 1991). Other qualities of molluscs may be significant aspects of their materiality. Some are hallucinogenic (Glowacki 2005) and, for the shell used to temper some forms of pottery in the British Neolithic, it seems that choice of temper could be a material reference to the sea and used to symbolise a particular relationship with the dead involving the sea (Parker Pearson et al. 2006).

Wood

Each tree species has its own qualities which may suit particular purposes because of the structure of its wood, bark or bast, growing patterns (size, shape, regeneration), branching habits or chemicals (resins, tannins, etc.). Although we like to think we understand wood, it has properties unfamiliar to most people and has considerable variation by species and further divisions by age and size. Some of the names associated with woodland management and wooden artefact production use terms in particular ways. Wood generally refers to poles and brushwood suitable for light structures and fuel, whereas timber is a term usually reserved for very large trunk material. Although 'timber' is more impressive, 'wood', called roundwood by archaeologists, is the most useful material as it is regenerative and comes in a form useful for many jobs without too much preliminary working, for example, as handles or for charcoal production. Within a forest or wood, particular kinds of trees may grow in distinctive patterns. In various wooden shipbuilding technologies, particular angles of trees would have been highly sought after, as these needed to be hewn from trees growing naturally to give the right shaped pieces of timber.

Trees grow by laying down new wood each year from a layer of cells inside the bark called the vascular cambium, which produces sapwood. Eventually the growth here becomes so far removed from the nutrients available in the cambium layer that active growth in that region ceases and it becomes part of the heartwood, as opposed to the living wood or sapwood. The sapwood has the highest water content and thus will shrink more and split during seasoning; this wood also contains nutrients and is thus more attractive to insects and fungal attack than the heartwood. So for structural timbers the sapwood is often removed. The arrangement and patterns of cells forming the wood are diagnostic of a particular genus and sometimes species. Deciduous, broad-leafed trees are said to be hardwoods, whereas evergreen coniferous trees are said to be softwoods, but not all hardwoods are hard and not all softwoods are soft. Qualities such as resilience (ability to flex or withstand shock) and the ability to be burnt easily, or to be worked in particular ways, can all make species selection a choice or a matter of intended use. The term 'ring porous' indicates the burst of growth in spring in trees growing in temperate regions, where many species of hardwood produce very large vessels for the spring growth early in the season and these tail away into smaller vessels which form the rest of the season's growth. This distinctive zoning of large and small wood vessels together forms one year's growth. It is these patterns which mark out the annual rings counted by dendrochronologists. The late wood contains many more fibres and it is this wood that is strongest. The term 'diffuse porous' is used to describe woods which do not have such a strong distinction between early and late wood and the size of the cell structures. The transverse connections between parts of the wood are called medullary rays. The structures of the wood and the growing conditions of a tree in relation to the others around it are all factors that will influence the shape of wood available to be used and the manner in which it may be worked.

Figure 7.12 shows four useful trees from temperate climates with sections from different angles to show the patterns of annual growth and features such as medullary rays. Oak (*Quercus* spp.) is ring porous with large, distinctive medullary rays. On the transverse face, there are very long rays and, between these, stripes of pores formed by late wood. On the radial face, broad sheaves of rays are exposed giving a characteristic quartered pattern of oak. Elm (*Ulmus* spp.) is ring porous with small medullary rays and has a characteristic wavy appearance of the pores in the late wood, visible in both transverse and tangential faces, whereas these are seen as flecks in the radial face. Ash (*Fraxinux* spp.) is ring porous but lacking obvious medullary rays. Yew (*Taxus baccata*) has obvious growth rings, but with a gradual transition from early to late wood. The reason that oak is a good structural timber is because of its strength and branching habit (it often forms natural arches which made it useful for cruck construction) and also because of the radial fissures visible in transverse sections (see figure 7.12), which allow it to split radially. Radially split planks do not warp in the same way as tangentially split ones. Thus this particular property affects both technologies and uses. Elm, another hard wood, is frequently used where there is a need to withstand water, for instance it is used for tables and as the paddles of watermills. Ash is a favourite material for handles because of its shock resistance. In general, trees growing in watery areas tend to give water-resistant woods, for example alder is often selected for making buckets. Yew is a very flexible elastic wood, which is why it is particularly favoured for bows, pins, and awls, but it is poisonous to animals, which is partly why it is often grown in enclosed areas such as churchyards. Willow (*Salix* spp.) is also a resilient material (it is still used for cricket bats) and, as young growth, is very flexible and is the material used for making wicker baskets. Other species have flexible withies for example cedar (Stewart 1984: 161–9). Beech is good for turning and has also been used for furniture and spoons. Box (*Buxus sempervirens*) is the strongest and densest wood and can be used to strike flint and detach a flake, and thus soft hammers of wood used in flint knapping are always made of box wood. Because of its dense structure, it is also good for items such as combs and fine, strong, small boxes, as its name implies. Hazel (*Corylus* spp.) is often grown as a coppice wood and, because of its ready regrowth and flexible nature, is used for making hurdles. Other sources state the characteristics of a wider range of trees (e.g Tebbs 1984) and examine the role of timber in a region (e.g. for the Mediterranean, Russell 1982).

Some trees are very difficult to kill and, once felled, will regenerate from a stump. These regeneration practices mean that some species can be managed very effectively by coppicing – cutting the tree down to its base from which it will regenerate. The regrowth is cut when it reaches the desired size and the shoots grow quite densely and so are long and straight. Pollarding is a similar strategy, but with the branches being cut higher from the ground, keeping the regrowth away from browsing animals.

Bark and bast

Bark, for example birch (*Betula* spp) (Gramsch 1992) and cherry bark, can be used for containers but birch bark is an especially flexible material which grows more thickly in colder climates. The thick bark can be carefully peeled off trees to make watertight vessels up to the size of a canoe (McGrail 1987). Bark also floats, and rolled birch bark floats are known from Mesolithic sites such as Tågerup (Karsten and Knarrström 2003: 186). Bark is also suitable as a lid or stopper, especially cork (Oliveira and Oliveira 1991). Corky bark found on the British Neolithic wetland site of Etton would have been brought onto the site, perhaps because of tannins in the bark which can be used for tanning hides or as an aid to dyeing (Taylor 1998). The use of bark need not kill the tree providing it is not removed around all of the circumference, and scarring on trees from the extraction of bark for crafts is one feature of lived-in landscapes (e.g. in Australia, Rhoads 1992, and for Northwest America, Stewart 1984: 113–17, and Turner et al. 2000).

The bast (the inner bark fibres as shown in figure 7.14a) available from some species, notably lime and willow, is especially fine and strong, and can make very fine cordage. For other mostly tropical species, the inner and outer bark can be stripped off whole in the rainy season to make bark cloth, a practice prevalent in areas of the Pacific, in South Asia, and in some areas of Africa (Pole et al. 2004). In North America, the bark of red cedar (*Thuja plicata*) and yellow cedar (*Chamaecyperis nootkatensis*) provides the major raw materials for mats, basketry, and cordage production as well as being beaten to soften it for use as bedding, clothing, and towels (Stewart 1984).

Roots

The young roots of mature trees can be dug out and pulled up in the spring when the sap is in them. With the outer bark removed, the roots can be carefully split to the desired thickness, dried, and stored for use in basketry and cordage. Stewart (1984: 171–7) describes this process for cedar where roots c. 2.5 cm. in diameter are used, but spruce roots and others can be similarly treated.

Hide

Hides can exist as furs and are important because of that quality (e.g. Cameron 1998, for early medieval trade, and Howard-Johnston 1998, for trade in classical antiquity) but, moving back in time, the trade in furs is a strong supposition in the Bronze Age as part of exchanges for metal resources (Coles 1982). In some cases the use of fur or hide can be documented by particular sets of foot bones left in a pattern in the archaeological record in conjunction with the type of animal (e.g. for the late Upper Palaeolithic and Mesolithic, Charles 1997). Much less obvious to modern eyes but evident from the ethnographic record is the use of fish skin (e.g. Hurcombe and Williams 2002, Owen 2000, Reed 2005) and, although we think of wool as one of the standard products from animals, in fact this was not always the woolly material that we see in modern sheep which have been selectively bred for precisely this effect (see Ryder 1969, 1980, 1984b, 1987, 1992). Nor do we commonly consider hair as a useful material but see Fletcher (2000) for Egyptian examples. Large animals produce thicker hides, and it is usually thickest over the neck and shoulder area. Thus in many prehistoric societies, an ox hide would be amongst the thickest and toughest materials available. A softer hide can be made if the fur or hair is removed because the skin is thinner and can be worked from both sides. A raw hide can be allowed to dry into a shape which it will then hold. Hide expands when wet and can be used as a tight binding which will shrink on drying and make the binding tighter still. Raw hide will become stiff as it dries unless it is worked. The shield in figure 7.3 has been produced by soaking and hammering raw hide against a wooden mould, and then allowing it to dry and impregnating it with wax (Coles 1962). Different species also give slightly different qualities, affecting for instance the choice of materials for clothing and kayaking (Oakes 1987 and Pauksztat 2005). Thus the raw material qualities vary considerably depending upon the animal and treatment of the skin. The method of preparation will vary depending upon the desired use (e.g. Otak 2005, Pedersen 2005, Petrussen 2005, also Klokkernes and Sharma 2005). Perhaps the most thought-provoking find of recent years has been the Ice Man (a prehistoric man preserved in the Alpine ice discovered in 1991). His clothes and equipment reveal the use of hides and skins which are both finely worked and finished and show a range of different animals and skin preparation techniques used for different purposes (Groenman-Van Waateringe 1993).

Cordage, basketry, and textiles

In the modern world, very few of the items in figure 7.18 would be understood as a set of materials and a set of technologies. By far the most common are those made of wicker. However, cordage, basketry, and textiles can be made from whole plants, split plants, wood or bark, bast fibres of plants or trees, animal hair or wool, or some combination of these as often there are two different elements. For each community the landscape setting will present different plants, trees, and animals from which to make the cordage, containers, clothing, bedding, and tools which are a feature of this group of organic material culture items.

Archaeological study strategies

Bone, antler, ivory, and horn

If the soil is acidic, bones, antler, and shell will not survive although otherwise their mineral component makes them relatively robust. The bones of young animals are generally weaker and do not survive as well as adult bones, but equally, because they are weaker, they are not so often used for manufacturing implements. Where bone artefacts are found, it is useful to look for marks indicating how the item was made or used. With antler, the same technique can be applied except that antlers acquire some patterns of wear during their use by the animal, for browsing or for fighting, and these have to be ruled out before establishing whether a wear pattern is from a different kind of cultural purpose (Olsen 1989). Similarly, there needs to be an understanding of different elements of the assemblage for different purposes, for example fragmentation where fat might be the desired end product (Outram et al. 2005). Studies of very ancient bones focus on the identification of cut marks (Blumenschine et al. 1996) and taphonomic experiments on the deterioration and transport of bone (Andrews 1995). Bone and antler wear studies have become more commonplace (Choyke and Bartosiewicz 2001) and are showing that, as with flint, where functional assumptions are tested by use wear, there is not always a correlation between the typological name and the true range of functions of the object (Mobley-Tanaka and Griffitts 1997). Ivory can be identified to species (see above) but more surprisingly a recent study of red deer canines identified species, age, and sex which was especially useful because these were made into Upper Palaeolithic beads (D'Errico and Vanhaeren 2002). Horn is by comparison very poorly studied, but this can be explained by its poor survival since, unlike the other materials in this category, it has no minerals (Millard 2001).

Studies of bone and antler tools now incorporate investigation of the curation of bone (Bíró 2003, Emery 2001) and the social and symbolic nature of bone (Russell 2001a, 2001b; Smirnova 2001, Sidéra 2001). Issues such as craft specialisation and gender (James 2001, Spector 1993, McGhee 1977) are all on the research agenda, and the use of deer canines, including imitations in the Palaeolithic carefully carved to resemble real teeth (White 1989a, 1989b, 1992, and Choyke 2001) suggest that the teeth could have been important symbols.

Shell

Shells that are used as decorative items tend to be singled out, but investigators of most sites regard shell as subsistence evidence with some possibilities for dating or establishing seasonality of collection (e.g. Shackleton and Elderfield 1990). Claassen (1998: 199–203) draws attention to the basic problem of recognising shell tools when the only modification can be mistaken for accidental damage, and identifies the need to look for patterns of damage in amongst the 'subsistence' assemblage. Though it would be useful to be able to source shells chemically to their environment, a number of factors have to be taken into account, and in practice it is usually the species habitat as opposed to the location of the archaeological find spot which has provided evidence of trade and exchange in shells. As more comparative analyses are done, this situation will improve (Claassen 1998: 212–18).

Wood

Experiments play a crucial role in demonstrating technological possibilities for making implements in different periods using appropriate tools (e.g. McGrail 1982, McNabb 1989). A variety of different techniques of wood analysis are available. Cut radial, transverse, and longitudinal sections from wood can be used to identify the species of origin, although this is more difficult to do from whole objects. This is most interesting where there are carved prehistoric wooden figures with hints of a pattern in the species selected for creating these possible 'characters' linking with ancient Norse mythological links between trees and gods (e.g. Coles 1990, 1998). The lie of the piece in a tree can also be constructed using the features of the wood grain revealing details of the selection of wood from within the tree. Dendrochronology can be used for dating large individual timbers, especially where there are many from one site so that the individual pieces can contribute to the creation of master dendrochronology curves for the whole site, but it is possible to use dendrochronology for more than dating. It can also elucidate woodland management practices such as coppicing by looking at the number of years' growth before cutting. The technique does not work well for wood species where rings are frequently missing or where false rings are prevalent, or where tree rings are unclear or show little variation. In practice dendrochronology is applied to only a few species suitable for the technique which are used for large timbers in areas where either wetsite structures below ground (such as wharves and piles) or dry site structures (such as roof beams) offer better preservation conditions. There are also biases because there are periods and sites where deliberate depositions occur in wet places, for example Bronze Age Europe, and the Windover site in Florida (Coles and Coles 1989: 173–97). AMS radiocarbon dating opened up the possibility of dating smaller wooden artefacts. With the increasing numbers of wet sites and a better understanding of the objects and structures found within them, it has been possible to investigate novel techniques, for example examining woodworking toolmarks (Sands 1997). More recently, the advances in genetic analysis have opened up the possibility of the genetic identification of tree species (Deguilloux et al. 2006).

Perhaps the greatest problem in finding wooden artefacts lies in the combustibility of the material. Old objects thrown on the fire will never survive. However, occasionally such objects are charred rather than consumed, thus improving their survival chances. What is more problematic is recognising as such the thin ephemeral remains of small objects during excavation. There is a bias against small-sized objects of material culture and, where these are preserved by chance in the middle of a normal temperate site with no organic remains, it can be difficult to spot the potential object in time for it to survive the excavation process.

Hide

It is possible to use the pattern of hide skin follicles to identify species of origin, and microscopic studies can reveal specific processing technologies such as the creation of true leather which is a chemical alteration of the hide (Procter 1903, Reed 1972, Woodroffe 1949). The microscopic fibres can be examined to determine species of origin if they are not too degraded (e.g. Van Driel-Murray 2002, Bonnichsen et al. 2001, Korbe-Grohne 1988, Meeks and Cartwright 2005). With advances in genetic analysis, identification of species may yet be possible on very small fragments. Use wear traces can document that hide working was taking place (Mansur-Franchomme 1983) but, perhaps most interestingly, a detailed wear study (Hayden 1990) of Middle and Upper Palaeolithic hideworking tools, by using comparisons with ethnographic data, was able to suggest that the Upper Palaeolithic tools characterised very fine hide working to produce high-quality items.

Cordage, basketry, and textiles

The evidence for these technologies in the archaeological record is dispersed, and suffers from being published as small sections in site reports. There are also few archaeologists who specialise in analysing these sets of material because they are so rare. This also leaves the finds isolated as often the more material that is seen the more the connections between them can be understood and odd aspects of design or technologies become clear. Cold climates, dry climates, and wet sites have all helped to preserve, in small patches, such finds but the best accounts are where a specialist has brought these scattered finds together to make comparisons (e.g. Bender-Jørgensen 1992). In dry regions, more collective assemblages exist, and from these we can gain a sense of what is missing from so much of the rest (e.g. Hays-Gilpin 2000).

The identification of species, anatomical part, and technology are all basic archaeological data. Many of the problems of these related sets of craft activities is that they start off with fibres produced in a variety of ways from parts of plants or animals which are then combined using basketry, plaiting, or weaving techniques. Where materials are found, the fibre-type or species may be able to identify microscopically (e.g. Jakes et al. 1994, Wildman 1954, Ryder and Gabra-Sanders 1987, Raheel 1994, Gordon and Keating 2001, and see Chapter 4) but it can be difficult to identify a small degraded fragment (possibly also affected by conservation treatment) that is only one part of something larger. There must also be comparative reference material, which is why identifications are often merely to generic terms such as 'bast' or 'grass'. It is also very difficult to describe adequately the great variety of effects it is possible to achieve in these materials. Wendrich (1991, 1999) in particular has tried to solve this problem by creating a descriptive system, a part of which is explained here for cordage in figure 7.15. The way in which individually twisted yarns can then be put together to make plyed and cabled cordage can be recorded accurately using this method. Thus the dispersed finds provide information which is fragmentary, with inherent difficulties caused by the very manufacturing processes under study.

Sophisticated devices for weaving, such as looms, are composed of individually very simple wooden elements (figures 7.19 and 7.20). If they were found as fragments, these would not necessarily be recognised as fragments of a loom. When wooden items are preserved at a site, many of the pieces cannot be interpreted (e.g. Louwe Koojimans and Kooistra 2006), most likely because the tasks which they fulfilled or the implements of which they formed a part are so little known in the modern world. Thus, we cannot often use tools to get at the technologies of weaving. However, there is also a case for reassigning categories such as 'points' from hunting to basketry and fibre production tools, and needles from sewing to netting and looped fabric work (Owen 1997, 1998, 1999). There are increasing interests in these kinds of technologies from people engaged in use wear analysis because of the enigmatic plant working traces seen on archaeological stone tools (Van Gijn 1998b, 1998c, Hurcombe 2006, Juel Jensen 1994, Owen 2000). The evidence may well be there, but it may require archaeologists to look very specifically for it and for some categories of tool to have their assumed functions revised.

Techniques of analysis include the beginnings of isotope sourcing of prehistoric willow and tule textiles in North America (Benson et al. 2006), and investigations of the cultivation of fibres (Bradhsaw et al. 1981, Godwin 1967, Pals and Van Dierendonck 1988). However, the pollen evidence for some fibre and basketry species is affected by the poor survival of some species' pollen such as flax; or the species' pollen may be present but interpreted as part of the background environment, disturbance, or weeds (Hurcombe 2000a). Perhaps the growth in the range of palaeoethnobotanical techniques will redress some of these problems (Fritz 2005). However, there are ways of using circumstantial evidence such as looking for cloth making at Akrotiri (Tzachili 1990), which also has insect evidence for a silk cocoon (Panagiotakopulu et al. 1997), and at features which could be a grain storage silo or a vat for dyeing (Sagona 1999). There are also other ways of investigating organic crafts, for example by artwork on pottery, or on frescos, for example the baskets in the frescos at Akrotiri (Beloyianni 2000). Impressions sometimes survive in clay (e.g. Adovasio 1977, Moore et al. 2000: figure 10.4: 282, Owoc 2007). The evidence available can also include pottery skeuomorphs incorporating design elements from textiles and basketry on to ceramics, and a variety of other circumstantial evidence (Henshall 1950, Hurcombe 2000a, Manby 1995, Ortman 2000). Such borrowings between materials are mapping the relationships between objects (Tilley 1999).

In all of the technologies and discussions in the archaeological record, what is lost is the status and social significance of such craft activities. These can be part of ethnoarchaeological studies (Silvestre 1994). In figures 7.16 and 7.19 this Uzbek woman spins (using a spindle whorl), dyes, and weaves her own items and is known locally for her skill as a weaver (for the valued aspects of this craft as evenness of weave and use of colour and pattern see Friedl 1989: 162). Her ground loom dominates the space outside her house and is some seven metres long, yet the archaeological evidence for this would be some very simple pieces of wood, one very distinctive and polished wooden weaving sword, and two widely spaced stake holes that probably would not even be recognised as a pair on excavation. Similarly, the upright loom depicted in figure 7.20 has no below-ground features and few distinctive individual wooden elements, although if inorganic loom weights are used this can be some of the strongest evidence for this kind of craft activity. The backstrap loom, which is tensioned by the waist (figure 7.20b) could need a comb or other implement to tamp down the weave and, if this is made of bone or antler, this might be the surviving element to be recognised rather than any of the other traces. Felt making (figure 7.20c), where wool is trampled, so that the fibres interweave to make large tracts of fabric, would leave no trace in the archaeological record.

Technologies

Bone, antler, ivory, and horn

A variety of sources cover technologies of bone and antler from a range of periods (Gostenčnik 2003, Johnson 1985, MacGregor 1985, MacGregor and Mainman 2001, Ramis and Alcover 2001, Tuohy 2001, Zhilin 2001), covering both whole assemblages, (e.g. Provenzano 2001) and particular finds such as ivory animal carving (Amirkhanov 1998). Given the tough nature of these materials, they are generally assumed to have been worked with a burin (graver) in earlier prehistory. Antler also has a series of grooves, naturally formed on the shaft, and these can sometimes be deepened using burins, or completely new deep grooves can be made into the spongy core. If the antler is then flexed, long splinters can be extracted. This technique is well documented from the Mesolithic site Star Carr (Clark and Thompson 1953). Less well known is the fact that antler can be scored in a ring and then slightly charred, after which a sharp tap will cause it to break at the desired point. Such techniques would have been very useful in an era without metal tools. These materials can all be made easier to work by soaking, but if left for too long the nutrients still present in the materials start to rot and the smell is then very difficult to remove. However it is also possible to flake bone: for example, see the two images in figure 7.11 of a bone flake and a flaked bone heavy-duty cleaver. When sufficiently dense, bone behaves as any other brittle solid, and fracture mechanics principles can be applied to it. In particular, bone and ivory can have dense areas that can be worked very finely and polished to take on a highly lustrous quality. Some bones have natural holes in them because of the position of nerve or blood vessels, whereas a bored hole may be straight-sided or hourglass-shaped (see detail in figure 7.9) depending upon the method used, but either will go straight through the grain and reveal the cross-sectional differences in the antler or bone structure, whereas natural holes carrying nerves and blood vessels have no such profile.

Shell

Shell is quite brittle so groove and snap techniques work well, as do grinding techniques and a variety of drilling methods for boring holes. Where the shell is large enough, flaking is also possible, and Claassen (1998: 197) also lists incising, inlaying, and etching as techniques used in the working of shell in the American Southwest. Roth (in McCarthy 1976: 90) suggests it is best worked when fresh. Some studies have investigated deliberate treatment to affect the raw material properties of shells by immersion in sea water to allow gradual changes in the aragonite crystals, decreasing the solubility, and thus improving the shell's properties for use as adzes (Moir 1990).

Wood

Green (fresh) wood is much easier to work than seasoned (dried) wood (Abbott 1989, 2004, Langsner 1995, McGrail 1982). If large pieces of wood are dried, the outside will dry more quickly than the interior, making splits more likely to occur. Working the wood while it is green not only allows a softer material to be shaped but also reduces the bulk allowing for more even drying. Figure 7.14 shows some of the range of woodworking techniques, from the use of the inner bark for fibre (7.14a) to the use of flexible outer bark for containers leaving scars on the trees (7.14b), or as solid strips of bark for roofing over simple shelters (7.14c), hollowing out the interior wood by adze (7.14d) although this might also have been charred before adzing. In an era without metal tools, this might have been an effective way of hollowing out solid wood vessels (see Mears 1990). There is also a simple but effective turning machine, known as a pole lathe (7.14e). The latter involves a springy branch of wood tied down at one end with the cord passed round a turning pole and operated by tying the other end of the string to a pedal, so that, as the foot presses down rhythmically, the pole pulls back up and the whole operates on a continuous, alternating bow system, like a bow drill. Turning can give spindle shapes but also small vessels (e.g. for medieval vessel turning see Pugsley 2005). Wood can also be carved (7.14f) or split using wooden wedges (7.14g). As figure 14.17g shows, the split is happening in *advance* of the tip of the wedge along the lines of the grain. Traditional methods of felling a tree or removing a flitch of living wood leaving the tree to recover are described by Stewart for North American cedar (1984: 29–103). Felled large trunks can be processed in a number of ways but, without metal tools, are most easily worked when they are green by hammering wedges in, forcing the split down the grain into the desired shape. It is possible to halve or quarter a large trunk. If planks are desired, radially split ones, using the centre as one edge and the outside wood as the other, follow a natural pattern, whereas splitting across the grain at a tangent will allow the wood to warp convexly as it dries. Oak barrel staves and items such as cricket bats also take advantage of radially split timber. With metal tools it is possible to saw wood, but different teeth are used to saw green and seasoned wood. Wood can also be steamed and bent into shape (Abbott 1989: 115–23, Stewart 1984: 84–92).

Hide

Although we are familiar with hides, there are different ways of treating them to obtain true leathers, which are chemically altered tanned products, and there are some standard works describing this process (Procter 1922, Reed 1972, Ryder 1970, Stanbolov 1969, Thomson 1998 and Woodroffe 1949). There are excellent ethnographic or recent traditions of hide working documented, for example those of Ethiopia (Brandt and Weedman 1997) and elsewhere (Aten et al. 1955, Bahnson 2005, Drucker 1965, Frank 1998, Hill 1960, Mann 1962). A basic *chaîne opératoire* can be constructed. Freshly killed animals can have the skin removed starting with a cut along the centre of the belly in a medial line which is then taken down the inside of each leg and around the tail and head depending upon the desired parts. The skin can be folded in half, wet sides together, and then transported. If it is not going to be worked immediately, it must be dried (e.g. slow air-drying or by adding salt) to halt decay processes. The hide will need to have excess fat trimmed or scraped off. If the hair or fur is to be removed it can be soaked in a variety of solutions to facilitate loosening the top layer of skin. These processes can use scrapers in a variety of materials. The skin will dry stiff so it must be stretched out and allowed to dry slowly, then rolled up, or moulded into shape and left to dry, or if a soft hide is required it must be worked intermittently during the drying process. Each time a skin gets wet, it will stiffen up, so to permanently soften the hide and loosen the fibres requires the use of chemicals and physical working of the skin (brains, buttermilk, urine, smoke, oils, tannins, ochre, woodash, and sand can all be used as a part of these processes). The final lengthy stage for making a high-quality skin is to curry it by further scraping to loosen and soften the fibres, achieving a good drape.

Cordage, basketry, and textiles

There is excellent coverage of modern and recent basketry craft traditions (Daugherty 1986, Florance 1962, Gabriel and Goymer 1991, Gillooly 1992, Maynard 1989, Peabody Turnbaugh and Turnbaugh 2004, Rogers 1994, Wright 1983). Baskets generally fall into one of two technologies – spiral coil baskets or woven baskets – whether these are made of soft materials such as rush, or tougher materials such as willow withies. There are also techniques such as twining or pairing, which can create very tight joins, but even here basketry may deliberately create open weaves, for example clam baskets, as illustrated in figure 7.1 mid left, or a fishing cran, a unit of measure for herrings (figure 7.18i). Alternatively, the woven elements can be rapped well down (i.e. pushed close together) to create a very strong and smooth structure as in a shopping basket (figure 7.18h). The starting mechanisms can be distinctive, for example the spiral start in figure 7.18b or the star burst effect in figure

7.18e. Netting also has a division into knotless, as demonstrated in figure 7.18c from an Australian aboriginal bag, or knotted netting, as seen in figure 7.18f. The specific aspects of the technology and elements such as the strengthening of a basket side by means of a waling technique are not well appreciated. Such elements can be read however, by practising craftspeople and used to suggest relative purposes for baskets (e.g. Hurcombe and Lemieux 2005).

Cordage and yarns start with a technology which is very simple but time-consuming. Materials can either be rolled against the thigh or twisted by hand, but even a small device, such as a spindle whorl, which is a small fly wheel to help create the twist, will speed things up. I have seen Uzbek women spinning beside the road, or even as they walk (e.g. Dunsmore 1985), because this time-consuming activity requires them to embed it in other aspects of their daily lives. Once spun, the cordage or yarn might be plyed before it is used, but there are then a variety of methods for working it up into larger objects which leave very little trace in the archaeological record and are very difficult to identify (for examples see figures 7.19–20 showing loom types). There are many useful ethnographic accounts of plant use (Densmore 1974, Gustafson 1980, Zola and Gott 1992, Latz 1995, Del Mar 1924, Dunsmore 1985, Grieve 1931, Kuoni 1981, Stewart 1977, Mowat et al. 1992) and good outlines of different techniques of weaving for braids and narrow wares (Carey 2003), sprang (Collingwood 1974), tablet weaving (Collingwood 1982, Andersen 1967) and ply split braiding (Collingwood 1998) but it would be difficult to identify some of these techniques from fragments. Figure 7.17 shows some of these difficulties; (*a*), (*b*), and (*c*) are all different techniques which produce exactly the same narrow band, woven effect, but one is produced via card tablet weaving, one by loop manipulation and the other by ply splitting. Likewise, a woven fabric with one set of passive elements and one active element, will create exactly the same pattern if seen as a fragment, as one where there is one set of multiple active elements as in a braid technique, or one active element as in a knot technique. Sprang is a different technique which is known to have been used for some of the caps and netting found in the Danish Bronze Age (e.g. Hald 1980). The threads are worked over one another by hand, using shaped sticks to hold the work in place, but as the work progresses the mirror image is created at the bottom of the work (figure 7.17g–h.). Again, it is impossible to see that this technique was used, unless sub-stantial amounts of the fabric remain complete. Thus, the fragments that are often all that survives make it difficult to identify precisely what technologies might have been used to create a given effect. Furthermore, knotting, netting, and basketry use very few tools, and an awl and a knife might be the only tools necessary.

Function

Bone, antler, ivory, and horn

There are only just beginning to be good studies of bone, antler, ivory, and horn wear traces and so, in many cases, there are items such as awls or spatulas, or other names which suggest a function but which can go no further. The literature on wear and modification of bone is steadily growing, giving more specific information on function (e.g. Antipina 2001, Hannus et al. 1997, Choyke and Bartosiewicz 2001, van Gijn 2005, 2006, Jensen 2001, Luik et al. 2005, Lyman et al. 1998). Bone has a slightly rough surface texture, so care must be taken when trying to look for manufacturing or wear traces on archaeological bones because natural soil processes can affect the surface. The properties of bone and its fortuitous shapes are useful for making skates and sledge runners (McGregor 1976) but there are also more enigmatic implements such as 'bubble ended tools' (Griffitts and Bonsall 2001), and particular pieces (e.g. Olsen's thong smoothers 2001). Dice and gaming pieces are also traditionally made with bone and, from the Upper Palaeolithic onwards, there are decorative carvings and figures. Flat surfaces such as rib bones are also used for engraving. Furthermore it is now known that very early examples of flaked bone tools exist, for example flaked bone Acheulean hand axes (Mussi 1995: 33–35 and see Freeman 1983, Hannus 1997). Figure 7.11 shows both a flaked bone sharp tool and a heavy-duty cleaver. The corresponding wear can be examined under the SEM (figure 7.11).

In many cases composite objects of bone and antler employ the individual elements to make best use of their different properties. Antler and bone composite combs deploy the bone to form a plate holding together the antler tines. Excellent overviews stress the slight differences in performance of these materials which are known to be part of past exploitation strategies in bone and antler in comb manufacture (McGregor 1985, McGregor and Currey 1983). These kinds of property-based choices are made and found worldwide (Scheinson and Ferretti 1995, Riddler 2003). The shock-absorbing qualities of antler make it a good choice for a sleeve to cushion stone axes in their wooden hafts in the circum-Alpine region in the Neolithic (Bocquet 1994), and it is also ideal for use as projectile points (Pokines 1998) or as picks (Cluttonbrock 1984), hoes (Bagshawe 1949), and maceheads (Simpson 1996). There is variation even within different types of antler. Modern flint knappers have in their tool kits elk as the densest antler soft hammer, but also other forms of antler. They would not use bone in the same way. Some archaeological soft hammers have been found, notably the early Palaeolithic one at Boxgrove, England (Pitts and Roberts 1997: 296, figure 54). Ivory is dense and is an excellent material for seals and fine carvings (Hayward 1990, Gelvin-Reymiller et al. 2006, Krzyszkowska and Morkot 2000, LeMoine and Darwent 1998). Its use for decoration or carved artwork dwarfs its occasional other usage. Horn survives least well in archaeological contexts and is a very rare find. It can be found in dry areas, such as Egypt, but most archaeological finds of horn come from Roman and medieval contexts, or later. However it is has undoubtedly been worked earlier because the Palaeolithic Venus engraving from Laussel, France, clearly depicts a horn being held (Bahn and Vertut 1988: 99, figure 67), and there are Bronze Age burials in waterlogged deposits in Denmark with horn combs preserved, a replica of which is shown in figure 7.4. Horns make very good vessels for drinking or for pouring because they are naturally funnel-shaped, which is why they have also been used as powder horns, also illustrated in figure 7.4.

Shell

Shells can be used whole for decoration, or their natural shapes lend themselves to usage as scoops, scrapers, and spoons. Where there is a good size and range of shapes available, shells can be used for a much wider variety of purposes. In Aegean pre-history they are used as trumpets, scoops, lamps, beads, pendants, polishers, spatulae, maceheads, buttons, bracelets, figurines, vessels, and spools and are also depicted as imagery on pottery and on seals (Karali 1999). In Australia, shell was also used for chisels, knives, balers, water holders, and fish hooks (McCarthy 1976: 90–3, O'Connor and Veth 2005). Claassen (1998: 201) also lists shell net mesh gauges, handles, spindle whorls, and adzes. Egg shells can also be used, for example ostrich egg shells in Egypt (Phillips 2000). In addition, shells are known to be traded large distances and can be used as an exchange unit (Cribb 1986).

Claassen (1998: 203–12) gives an excellent review of shell symbolism, for example for fertility, colour, and various forms of well-being. In the Americas, shells have been seen as part of the materialisation of power (Bayman 2002) and in Europe there are copies of shells in other materials: for example there is a limestone carving imitating a Miocene marine gastropod from Neolithic Malta (Oakley 1965a, plate 1), and Skeates (1991) has suggested that their use as trumpets may have been allied to their use as symbols via an exploration of Triton's Trumpet, which he describes as a Neolithic symbol based around a large shell. The use of shells as beads in the Palaeolithic has attracted particular attention (Vanhaeren et al. 2006, and Vanhaeren and D'Errico 2006). They looked at Upper Palaeolithic Aurignacian beads of all kinds, including a large number of shell beads, characterised them and used the evidence to suggest ethnic groupings for the Aurignacian in Europe. It is clear that shells can be a richly symbolic set of material culture items.

Wood

In most regions wood was a ubiquitous material and would have formed a major component of any society's material constructions and artefacts. In areas with good preservation conditions, such as the circum-Alpine region in prehistory, there is extensive evidence for the use of this material in many different ways. Figure 7.13 shows a diagram of a prehistoric house annotated to justify the archaeological evidence for each of the features described, from the wooden shingles of the roof to the structure of the building and its flooring. The use of wood reveals specific choices in many different societies, for example in Chacoan society (Windes and McKenna 2001), Palaeolithic Europe (Nadel et al. 2006), and Neolithic Europe (Banghard 2000). Many authors have investigated the character of wood for broad uses: for trackways and associated wooden finds (Coles et al. 1978, Coles et al. 1973, and Orme and Coles 1983); for domestic wooden artefacts and household items (Earwood 1993 and Waly 1999); for a range of wooden objects, and also nets and other plant material fragments (Burov 1998, Coles 1992); for the use of wood by ancient Egyptians (Gale et al. 2000); for wooden figures (Coles 1990, Van der Sanden and Capelle 2001); for wheels (Sleeswyk 1987); for boats (McGrail 1987, 2002), and for various other purposes (Taylor 1992, Lillie et al. 2005, Pryor 1998, 2001, Schledermann 1996). The other key use of wood is as fuel, relevant here especially because of the role of wood or charcoal in many artefact manufacturing processes but most obviously in ceramic production and metallurgy (Tillman 1978, Tillman et al. 1981).

Wood undoubtedly has a social identity and can be a prestige item (Evans 1989, Croes 1997, Lentz et al. 2005). There are studies of sites where the selection of species for the manufacture of wooden artefacts might have been for the symbolism attached to particular species as much as for properties of the raw material (e.g. in Japan, Noshiro et al. 1992, and in Europe, Coles 1998), and birch bark found as packing material in Scandinavian passage graves may likewise have contributed to the symbolism of the site (Dehn and Hansen 2006). There are new ways of seeing trees as part of tree cultures with characters of their own based on their habits, performance, and biographies. As such they have places in the landscape, hearts, minds, and myths of societies (Hagender 2001, 2005, Jones and Cloke 2002, Muir 2005).

Hide

The archaeological finds and significance of industries associated with hide vary considerably in different regions and periods, with the Sudan (Ryder 1984a) and *The Mary Rose*, an English Tudor flagship (Ryder 1984c) as particularly rich examples. Also notable are Roman leather working (Gansser-Burckhardt 1942), Iron Age Hallstatt (Ryder 1990) and the Iron Age leather found on some of the bog bodies of Europe, including caps and capes and cordage (Fischer n.d), Egyptian leather working (Van Driel-Murray 2000), and hides for Bronze Age shields (Waddell 1998). More unusually, one of the uses of a fleece can be to trap gold in streams (Ryder 1991), and, on the basis of an insight from a pottery skeuomorph, it is suggested that there are spoons of hide (Manby 1995). Furthermore, there are images of so-called ox hide ingots, suggesting that, in much the same way as the fur trade in Canada resulted in pelts which could be counted and graded to serve as units for barter, so too ox hide metal ingots were used as units of currency (Briard 1976).

Cordage, basketry, and textiles

Cordage, basketry, and textiles provide containers (for transport, storage, or cooking), clothing, nets, ties, matting, and bedding. There are studies of archaeological baskets (e.g. early Holocene Californian basketry, Connolly et al. 1995; prehistoric basketry from Texas, McGregor 1992; Mesolithic Russian material, Burov 1998), and of cordage (Hurley 1979, Earwood 1998) as well as fabrics using a variety of twined, net, or woven technology (Adams 1977, Adovasio 1977, Andersen 1987, Barber 1991, 1994, Bennike et al. 1986, Broholm and Hald 1948, Pétrequin and Pétrequin 1988, Soffer et al. 2001, Wendrich 1991, 1998, 2000). Nets and hair nets also exist (e.g. Burov 1998, Gramsch 1992: 70, Lee 2005) and it is surmised that net hunting may have been significant in the Ice Age (Pringle 1997, Lupo and Schmitt 2002). Where a site has suitable preservation conditions the recovered objects include all of the above plus organic materials used for hafting (Bocquet 1994). There are also broad surveys bringing together disparate archaeological finds of textiles (Bender-Jørgensen 1986, 1992, Vogelsang-Eastwood 2000, Harris 1999, Henshall 1950, Médart 2000, Wild 1970, 1988). Within these collections of assemblages there is sufficient information to start looking at stylistic characteristics and social identity in basketry (Bernick 1998, Evans 1989, Rimantiene 1992) and clothing (Buijs 2005, Heckman 2005, Rodman and Lopez 2005). Clothing can identify gender in social (Stig-Sørenson 1997) and physical ways (e.g the textile menstrual belts found on Anasazi sites, Hays-Gilpin 2000), and can be envisaged as a second skin mediating a border between the body and the outside world (Warnier 2006).

At the moment, little attention is paid to the potential symbolism of cordage, basketry, and woven products, although broad ethnographic surveys show good examples of the range of designs and symbols that can be placed on such items and literally woven into them (see Barber 1991). There is significance in the sets of numbers of elements needed for basketry and textile weaves. Contemporary ethnographic surveys (Kent 1983, Stevenson 1974, West 1989) also show a cultural dimension that is expressed through these technologies, but, specifically, there are woven messages and repeated designs which symbolise imbued information (Boetzkes and Lüth 1991, Harvey 1996, Paine 1990, 1994), and that is without allowing for the extra layers of meaning and cultural information that could have been provided by natural dyes, for which there is plenty of ethnographic evidence (e.g. Balfour-Paul 1997, Hall et al. 1984, Wickens 1983). The manner of production also needs close attention because there are ethnographic studies which show the symbolism inherent in the linked but separate traditions of looping versus knotting (Küchler 2002, MacKenzie 1998).

Organic material culture is redolent with opportunities for symbolism. That is why in this chapter, despite its archaeological rarity, its ethnographic ubiquity is taken as a reason for devoting substantial amounts of space to it. Much circumstantial evidence can be generated by combining archaeological and ethnographic data.

Overview

With the exception of the organic hard mineral materials, organic material culture is rare. It has its own *chaînes opératoires*, usable lives vary, and containers and clothing can be handed on to others or have their use change as they become worn. They are also valued items which can be treated in particular ways and placed in the ground in special contexts. We are fortunate that some of those contexts, such as caves, bogs, and mountain shrines, aid their preservation, but organic material culture is not generally recovered from surveys and excavations. Occasionally commercial exploitation of other resources brings to light bog finds, but it is usually the bodies which attract attention and the remaining elements of material culture are recovered as an adjunct to these. Would mechanical peat reclamation notice nets? Size and rigidity

Table 7.1 Techniques of analysis used to address key questions for organic artefacts

ORGANICS	What is it made from?	What is the character of the material and can it be grouped?	Where did the raw material(s) come from?	How was it made?	When was it made? Or when was it deposited?	Was it used? What for?
	Identification	Characterisation	Sourcing/provenance	Technology	Direct dating	Function
Bone, antler, ivory, horn *Frequent*	By eye usually to establish material and in many cases species	Irrelevant	Some species may not exist in the region and could use isotope analysis to examine broad regions of origin	Macroscopic features on surface	AMS ^{14}C possible, dates growth of material	Usually based on shape but macro- and microscopic wear traces can be used
Shell *Occasional*	By eye to establish species	Irrelevant	Some species identifications show object is far from species' nearest natural environment	Macroscopic features on surface	AMS ^{14}C possible, dates growth of shell	Usually based on shape though potentially macro- and microscopic wear traces can be used
Hides, furs, hair, leathers *Rare*	By eye or microscope to species or species group; other techniques may show chemical treatments used to process skins	Where species identification not possible may still be able to establish sets of material by similarity of physical features	Some species may not exist in the region	Macroscopic features for garment production etc. and microscopic fibre study and chemical analysis for processing treatments	AMS ^{14}C possible	Usually based on shape though potentially macro- and microscopic wear traces can be used

Basketry/cordage Fibres, textiles *Rare*	By eye or microscope to give major category e.g. bast fibres or species	Where species identification not possible may still be able to establish sets of material by similarity of physical features	Some species identification may show far from natural occurrence e.g. silk	Macroscopic features	AMS ^{14}C possible	Usually based on shape though potentially macro- and microscopic wear traces can be used
Wood *Rare*	By eye or microscope to species; may also determine timber v. roundwood	Where species identification not possible may still be able to establish sets of material by similarity of physical features	Some species may not exist in the region or dendro sequence may show timber was grown elsewhere	Macroscopic features	^{14}C possible but dates growth of wood, dendrochronology possible on large sets of timbers but likewise dates wood growth	Usually based on shape though potentially macro- and microscopic wear traces can be used

do affect the inadvertent recovery of organic objects. This is equally true of excavations in temperate areas. Ephemeral carbonised remains of a net, or a textile fragment as part of black organic matter in the base of a ditch would not necessarily be recognised in time to be lifted in a block for careful excavation under laboratory conditions. The digging process favours robust materials which the trowel can glance over and reveal to signal more careful excavation, or objects which a trowel can free from the soil in a stroke. Either of these acts would destroy the organic object in the scenarios above. Thus the old adage that 'you see what you are looking for' is true of the excavation of organic remains.

The preservation of organic artefacts is rare and conservation can be costly (Cronyn 2001, Watson 1998). The one advantage that we do have is that, where such material survives, there is quite often wood, basketry and cordage, and potentially also textiles, all together and so the interaction between these can sometimes be seen. Nowhere is this clearer than in one of the most important finds of the last century, Ötzi the Chalcolithic Ice Man from the Alps (Barfield 1994, Von den Driesch and Peters 1995, Egg et al. 1993, Fleckinger and Steiner 2003 and Goedecker-Ciolek 1993, Höpfel et al. 1992, Spindler et al. 1995, Sulzenbacher 2002, Winiger 1995). His clothes and equipment are thought to be a minimalist set of gear to survive and yet his material culture has a diverse range of species and technologies. There are seven articles of clothing and twenty pieces of equipment (tools, weapons, containers, cordage, firemaking kit), which together utilise seventeen different species of plants (whole plants, shredded plants, bast fibres, bark, split wood, round wood as twining, stitching, handles, and stiffening) and eight species of mammals as containers, cordage, and clothing (hide and fur, stitching, cordage, and many composite items such as the bearskin-soled shoes with twining cordage to keep in the grass insulating material). Handled tools were also present, featuring the few elements which would normally survive – one flint knife element, and one copper axe element. This gives an overwhelming impression of what is missing from most sites: undoubtedly we underestimate the range of use of organic materials as containers and clothing (Fienup-Riordan 2005, Kuoni 1981). So where does that leave us? Dating organic objects is not usually a problem because of radiocarbon dating, and there are also techniques for identifying species which genetic signatures may yet improve further, whilst sourcing is usually as much about species identification and the location of the nearest natural habitat as about any more sophisticated analysis (table 7.1). Overall, it is the survival of the finds and the ways that we think about organic material culture that really limit this field. The challenge is to be more imaginative in our examination of inorganic materials and archaeological features, thinking through the evidence which they might offer on organic material culture.

The richest current and future source of evidence for organic material culture is the ethnographic record and contemporary craft traditions; it is these that show us the possibilities of what might have been there in most temperate sites. In the future, it is possible that wear traces from inorganic materials and microscopic traces will play a greater role in the general archaeological evidence trail for the use of organic materials. However, rare preservations of sets of organic remains from unusual or biased contexts will stimulate debate on the role that these aspects of material culture played. There will be steadily accumulating evidence from a range of sites in cold, dry, or very wet conditions which will allow us windows into these all-important technologies, which would once have been the majority of the material culture record but which for us are very much the minority.

8 Stone materials and artefacts

So many artefacts, but how many are tools?

Stone is the most durable element of the archaeological record, which brings with it particular advantages and disadvantages. There are three major divisions within lithic artefacts; firstly flaked stones, commonly made from chert or flint, but also from other types of stone; secondly, polished, pecked, and ground stones, ranging from polished stone axes to beads and colourful stones that can be finely carved to very rough grinding stone materials; thirdly, building stonework, which covers a range of materials from local unmodified stones to dressed and polished fine stonework for more prestigious buildings. Stone finds are plentiful, but the study of lithic artefacts is unusual because the by-products can far outnumber the intended item, creating a special set of evidence for the sequences and contexts of production, modification, and discard. In particular, because of its durability and its reductive technological processes, stone artefacts, especially flaked stone ones, have lent themselves to the *chaîne opératoire* approach. That is also true for querns and polished stone items where the initial manufacture involves flaking, and can also be true of the building stones, but pecking, polishing, and grinding leave minimal traces because the pieces removed at any one time are so small that they can be blown away or incorporated into other deposits: grooved polishing slabs or pecking stones may form the best traces of such activities. Furthermore, extraction sites for building stones may leave few traces because continued exploitation may destroy evidence of the first exploitation at such sites.

Each of the major categories of stone artefacts has its own analytical strengths. The range of the materials can be seen in figures 8.1–3. These cover flaked stone in a variety of finished forms and nodules of the raw material (figure 8.1) from beach cobbles to fine grained flints with thick cortex, distinctive flint such as the grey striped material from Krzemionki, Poland, to jaspers and fine grained volcanic tuffs which can be knapped. Some hafted pieces are also included to make the point that many of these artefact types are in fact just one component of composite items of equipment. In contrast, there is the polished stone work (figure 8.2) for smooth edged tools, axes, adzes, chisels, shaft hole implements, and erratics such as the stone balls shown, and, for overtly decorative purposes, beads, bracelets, figures, and pendants where the colour, translucency, or special features, such as the electrostatic charge of amber, might have marked out such materials. If stone is polished it makes an even edge, but it also brings out some of the natural flecks and grains in the raw material and, in most cases, a polished stone item is aesthetically more appealing than a non-polished item. Some tools of polished stone may be polished only on the working edge to save time, particularly when the material is especially hard to polish (such as flint). The category of polished, ground, and carved stones covers a diverse range of materials – from amber with its translucency and startling colours to the neutral tones of gritty or otherwise rough materials, useful for grinding surfaces, to rocks which can be pecked or knapped into shape and which will then firstly take a polished edge and secondly perform well as an edge tool in an appropriate hafting. Adams (2002) covers all of the diverse objects within 'ground stone tools'. There are abraders, smoothing and polishing tools versus the grinding slabs and quern stones. There are also percussion tools and what she describes as hafted percussion tools, which include not just the obvious axes and adzes but also picks or mauls where there is ore extraction, or objects which might have functioned to till the earth such as mattocks or hoes. Some items within this general category also have a boring through the centre. Examples are shaft hole implements, also called battleaxes. Smaller ground stone items include awls, disks for spinning tools, settings for the bases of fire or other drills, and the polished stone spheres or other erratic types, which are usually seen as high-status objects. There are also polished stones that survive well in the soil and polished stones which deteriorate rapidly: for example the shale button and bracelet fragments in figure 8.2 show the tendency of shale to fragment after deposition.

Contrast the images so far (figures 8.1–2) with the images of slate, roofing tiles, and some selected decorative items of building stone (figure 8.3). Most of the examples shown are soft enough to be easily carved, or are striking in colour. Some are tesserae, small shaped fragments which make up durable and decorative mosaics. The range of grinding equipment (saddle quern, rotary querns, pestle and mortar) is not so attractive because, for functional reasons, these are large objects made from rough-textured rocks. Figure 8.3 shows two basic quern types – rotary querns and saddle querns, as they are called in Europe. There are also manos and metate which are the terms used in North America. Manos, or rubbers, are the upper stones, whilst the saddle querns, or metates, are the lower querns. As illustrated here, European ones tend to be adequately described by the term 'saddle', whereas metates have a slight lip which ensures that the material being ground falls back into the centre. This does not mean that the others had design problems, because for the most part the settings of these implements are lost and a cloth or a hide spread underneath could easily be used to catch extraneous material, or they may have had other perishable settings. The rotary querns may have had holes for handles, and they may have had hoppers of organic materials which have not survived. Those without any handle hole at all could have had a band around them to attach the handle (Beloe 1892) as shown in Figure 8.3. The other main types are pestles and mortars. The small tub-like stone in figure 8.3 is an example of a different kind of upper stone, from the Bulgarian Neolithic, which may have served much more as a pestle than as a rubber. Also, even rotary querns have different shapes and sizes depending upon regional and period-based styles. The upper stone on the right is a Hunsbury type, or a beehive quern, made of millstone grit, whereas the one in the centre is a lava stone from the Mayen quarries in Germany. Such stones were widespread in the Roman period. Thus there were a variety of styles even within something which is broadly understood as a set of classes.

Some examples of the ways in which large-scale stonework, some natural and some shaped, can be used in stone buildings are also presented in figures 8.3–4. In periods without metal tools, pecking, chipping, and especially flaking would have been the only ways to work solid materials which didn't have natural cleavage planes. Those which did have natural linear cleavage planes could be used in different ways, for example, slate shaped into roofing material. Fragments of roofing, walling, and decorative stonework are often picked up on surveys as the artefactual evidence of buildings. Figure 8.4 gives contrasting examples of stonework using a variety of buildings. There are examples of carved stone at Exeter cathedral and the detailed carving of lions above the gate to the Palace of Mycenae. It is not by chance that all of these features are illustrated by buildings which would have been prestigious in their region and intended to be long-lived. To some extent in contrast, the Anazasi Cliff Palace dwellings in North America show instead extensive ranges of buildings in stone for a whole community but intended for short-term occupancy. The detail (8.4a) from a southern English church shows how soft carvable limestone can be used in combination with shaped flint to provide decoration known as flushwork, while on the right local raw flint nodules are used for the rest of the walls. Carefully faced walls can be seen in the kiva illustrated (figure 8.4c) which typifies the way stone can be used as facing material, with rough edges and rubble forming the interior of the wall. The archaeological record of the use of building stone tends to be entirely based on the product or extraction site. In the latter case, the key problem is that, if it is a good stone source, it will have been extensively extracted in later periods, thus largely removing earlier evidence. However, buildings can be composites of many different materials, and rubble walls can have smooth facings of mud or plaster. Plaster is made by pulverising particular kinds of mineral and can be painted (see figure 8.3). The material offers special opportunities but is relatively rare compared to the other categories addressed here where the material can be ubiquitous and form a large proportion of the finds from a site. However, on sites where it is common, the sourcing of plaster materials (e.g. Gale et al. 1988 on Mycenaean gypsum) and studies of fresco styles are important (e.g. for Thera's Minoan frescos, Palyvou 2005, Sherratt 2000). Rocks and minerals also contribute to the artefact record as paints. Ochre is used in other processes such as hide working (Sagona 1999, Audouin and Plisson 1982).

In summary, stones provide materials for building, and can be used as hammers or grinding slabs, or as decorative pieces. They can also provide sharp edges suited to a variety of subsistence tasks but, as importantly, serve as tools to make other implements. In this crucial way, before metal is available, stone underpins the ability to make material culture. Most communities use different materials for different purposes. The way in which people obtained this heavy and crucial set of materials gives social as well as technical information to archaeologists. The qualities of these different stones are highly varied and part of the materiality of stone.

Raw material properties and characteristics

Rocks are widely available but particular qualities are sought out for the different properties outlined above. Buildings can be made from rounded rubble but hard, durable material with a tendency to fracture in planes to make oblong shapes is easier to stack. Whilst many stones will polish through wear, grinding stones need to retain a rough surface even as they are worn down. Soft, fine-grained rocks are good for carving. Distinctive colours or patterns within rock, or its appearance when polished, can all make the material suitable for decorative building or carving work. The challenge here may have been to find unflawed blocks large enough for the intended purpose. Good stone for flaking, in contrast, must have conchoidal fracture, i.e. be fine-grained or amorphous with no preferred fracture lines. Thus external blows determine the flaking, not predetermined cleavage lines, inconsistencies in the matrix, or flaws. Rocks with conchoidal fracture include obsidian (a volcanically formed glass), flint, chert, quartzite, and basalt.

For pecked or polished implements, natural stones which are close to the intended shape will save time: oval beach pebbles can be reshaped into stone axes by polishing and minimal amounts of pecking. Stones soft enough to polish easily but which can also be knapped allow a quick reduction to the approximate shape and similarly reduce the polishing time, especially when skilled flint knappers can make such rough-outs very accurately.

Building stones can include pillars and columns which are very attractive, such as those in purple from Mons Porphyry (Egyptian desert), which were valued by the Roman emperors because of the purple colour of the stone which was of symbolic significance in their social context. The granite from Mons Claudianus (Egyptian desert) (Maxfield and Peacock 2001) could have been valued because of the qualities of sparkle within the raw material, which was flecked white and black with some veins. Certainly the siting of these quarries in the remote Eastern Desert of Egypt required supply routes for the quarries which could be maintained only with imperial levels of support and access to resources. This alone could have marked the rock as special, reserved for those at the highest levels of the contemporary society. Tesserae, used to make mosaics in the Roman period, are made from a variety of different colours of stone, in whites, blacks, and browns, to form geometric or realistic designs and sometimes can be found individually. At a more mundane level, cobblestones on roads or the floor of houses, and pivot stones, door jambs, lintels, and the like may be made of suitably fracturing rocks, or the local material that is to hand; but, in prestigious buildings, polished marble or granite may be found, the harder and more attractive stones being placed where they will catch the eye and be most noticeable. The selection of stone balances the difficulties and costs of transporting heavy material over a distance against the desired properties of the stone. Slate is a durable roofing material which is relatively lightweight because it can be riven so finely. Some examples are illustrated in figure 8.3 where the character of the holes and the shape of the tiles can give rough dating information.

Stones are also useful for their ability to withstand heat as hearthstones or firestones. The latter are found as fire-cracked rocks, used by heating them directly in the fire, quickly washing off the ash and then putting them into a container with the liquid to be heated. These can be very effective, but brittle rocks are not suitable for this practice because the quick change in temperature fractures them. Fire is useful in two ways in stoneworking. Fire can be used to crack large boulders or fracture off large pieces of rock from a cliff face, both of which may ease extraction. There is also evidence that fire can be used to transform the flaking qualities of some kinds of flints and cherts and other siliceous, flakable stone. For example, since the 1960s and 1970s, it has been known that heat can be used to improve, in some respects, the knapping qualities of flint (e.g. Crabtree and Butler, 1964, Collins and Fenwick 1974, Hester 1972, Luedtke 1992, Mandeville 1973, 1983, Patterson 1981, 1995, Purdy and Clark 1971, 1979, Schindler et al. 1982) and there is some resurgence of interest in this (e.g. Kelterborn 2002). The practice seems to have been a particular strategy in some periods, e.g. the Mesolithic (Price et al. 1982). Although there have been some improvements in the methods of recognising heat treatment, this is still a very subtle effect (Melcher and Zimmerman 1977, Olausson and Larsson 1982, Rapp et al. 1999). Heat pre-treatment improves the effects of the flint and should not be confused with heat damage (crazed surfaces with pot-lid fractures or other heat spalls, figure 8.12b). Both can be deliberate (e.g. Larsson 2000) and in some cases represent a cultural phenomena, for example the burnt mounds and fire-cracked rocks believed to have been used in cooking or producing steam for saunas (Buckley 1990, Barfield and Hodder 1987, Hodges 1955, House and Smith 1975, and Lovick 1983).

Many more subtle cultural alterations of stone exist in the archaeological record than are commonly appreciated. Within all the categories of stone artefacts, it is easier to recognise the well-shaped from the roughly shaped and the exotic import within a background spread of local natural stone. Furthermore it is much easier to identify a complete piece than a fragment.

The flaking qualities of rocks vary, with glassy brittle materials such as obsidian flaking more easily for fine work than tougher conchoidally fracturing rocks such as quartzites. The two most common flaked stone materials are flint and chert. Both are siliceous rocks found within other sedimentary rocks. The silica replaces part of the parent rock, to form a nodule of flint or chert within it (Mason 1978). The shapes of these nodules vary greatly because of this. But because the silica replaces material in sedimentary rocks, there are sometimes fossils and impurities within the nodules. The purer the parent rock, the purer, fine-grained, and even the siliceous nodule will be. Thus, in very pure forms of limestone, called chalk, there is flint, but less pure forms of limestone may well have chert deposits instead. At this point, it is obvious that the terms 'chert' and 'flint' are loose descriptions. In Britain, archaeologists use 'flint' to describe the purer, finer, better knapping-quality material originating from chalk. The coarser, more opaque varieties are usually termed 'chert'. In North America, almost all such rocks are called chert. In Britain, some local varieties termed 'chert' are in fact, greensand cherts. Some materials which are knappable and called cherts are jaspers. Thus the nomenclature in different areas of the world and between geologists and archaeologists varies.

Flint and chert nodules vary in their internal colours, in flecks and textures, and in the nature of the outer cortical surface. This can vary in thickness and in the distinctiveness of the boundary between cortex and interior. These features vary even at one source. The variation in such features can be described but is usually difficult to attribute to a specific location although a good local knowledge of the geological sources can give an indication of the local possibilities.

Stones can be found in two different contexts; primary geological contexts where the rocks were formed, and secondary geological contexts where a natural process (e.g. glaciers or rivers) has moved material and laid down deposits. It is misleading to see maps of raw material sources which indicate only the primary flaked stone deposits because in many areas (e.g. Saville 1997 on gravel flint exploitation in Scotland) it is the secondary geological contexts which are exploited, and all the available sources which need to be taken into account in order to interpret past choices of material exploitation. Figure 8.5 shows a range of different sources and extraction sites. There are chalk cliffs showing flint nodules as dark dots laid down in seams. Flint is formed via the gradual replacement of the chalk with silica. In consequence, some flints will incorporate fossils or other features present in the original chalk. Flint nodules come in a variety of sizes and shapes. Some are too small for working and some have too much cortex within the flint rather than only on the outside. In contrast, secondary deposits can be seen as glacial clay tills, as in the area of the UK northeast of Hull. The fast-eroding clay cliffs contain within them a variety of glacial erratic cobbles, including flint, which are deposited onto the beach by wave action forming shoals of pebbles. Sta Nychia on Melos (Greek Cyclades) is a primary geological source of high-quality obsidian. Large areas of the hillside (figure 8.5d) are covered in artefacts as the waste from knapping rough-outs which were then taken away (Torrence 1986: 164–217). At such sites, errors of manufacture or natural flaws cause partly finished items to be left in place. That is what is illustrated in a millstone quarrying site to the west of Sheffield, UK, and in the 18-metre pillar left at the site of Mons Claudianus, a Roman gneiss quarry in the Eastern Desert of Egypt. These show what is possible in the way of archaeological evidence of extraction. Where knapped stone or large-scale workings are found, the durability means that, provided more modern and recent extraction has not removed all traces, there will be debris to be found and the selection and knapping sequence can be documented. That is not so easily the case where there is no extraction. For example, at Anazasi Cliff Palace site there is no debris in the form of flakes and chips, because the material has been pecked into shape from naturally available blocks of rock. Occasionally, sites such as Cliff Palace have hammer stone spalls (small flakes which occasionally break off the hammer stone itself) as the remnant of the activity, so the archaeological evidence can comprise not the product itself but the tool that was used to work the product.

Finally, it is important to consider the contexts of stone resource exploitation, not just as the social organisation of an activity but in terms of the social symbols possible within the colours of the stone, journey to a source, physical setting of the source or access issues, and of course the durability of the stone or its acoustic properties or other special qualities. The role it plays in symbolic or mythological connections may be a part of source exploitation (Taçon 1991): getting stone from a source need not be a utilitarian task. Amber can be studied for its role in trade, styles of objects, and contexts (Beck 1985, Beck et al. 2003, Beck and Shennan 1990, Gimbutas 1985), but ancient writers and traditional Latvian songs both allude to its connections with the sun (Olcott 1985 and Vīķis-Freibergs 1985). The materiality of stone encompasses both its physical qualities and its source characteristics.

Archaeological study strategies

Some stone objects receive much more archaeological attention than others. Though beads, stone vessels, and stone statuary all attract attention, polished stone axes are the most ubiquitous and perhaps the best studied range within polished stonework because they are easily recognised, long-collected, and approached in a diverse range of study types (see Chapter 5 and below). Many objects of polished stone can be sourced and studied for manufacturing and stylistic traits. New techniques allow the identification of some stones such as jet (Allason-Jones and Jones 2001), and the social role stones played is being emphasised (Sheridan and Davis 1998). Even for building stone analysis, whilst there are classic works (Davey 1961), more modern work has emphasised social aspects such as the evidence from town walls for the use of various materials in different periods and information on the associated stone industries (Creighton and Higham 2005: 121–5).

Although there is a wealth of evidence and discussion on the sourcing and significance of polished stone axes, these have interestingly shown that new information is still possible. At one of the most famous sites of manufacture in Britain, in the Lake District at Langdale, scientific analysis of the rock quality shows that the rock chosen for extraction came from an area that was very high up and was perhaps quite dangerous and an extreme place to work, even though slightly lower down there was rock with the same physical characteristics (Bradley 1990a, Bradley and Edmonds 1988, 1993, Bradley et al. 1992, Bradley and Suthren 1990, Bradley and Ford 1986). It seems that there was an element of limited access or daring in the exploitation of particular sources. This conclusion would not have been possible without scientific analysis because it could have been argued that there was some material quality which was particularly sought after from the upper source. The scientific analysis was able to show definitively that there was a highly social explanation for a particular archaeological pattern. Other studies have also shown a more social dimension considering the politics of supply and the social context of manufacture (Clarys and Quartermaine 1989, Cleghorn 1986, Clough and Cummins 1988, Cooney 1989, Kars et al. 1992, Pétrequin and Pétrequin 2000, Thirault 2005, Toth et al. 1992). All of these are being woven into much more social interpretations of stone axe manufacture and exchange practices. Analysts of some of the ethnographic examples are also considering ownership, longevity, and disaggregating the manufacturing processes to show which parts are conducted by specialists versus which parts are considered more general, and which parts are most personal to the end user. For example the angle and lengths of the haft and the design of the haft binding can be an indication of personal and tribal preferences (Pétrequin and Pétrequin 2000, Toth et al. 1992). Furthermore, there are examples of stone axes as hoards, or being deliberately destroyed, or being found in particular places which indicate that the contexts of their deposition are also an aspect of their social life and meanings (Cooney 1998, Larsson 2000).

Ground stone tools for grinding other materials are perhaps a particularly difficult class for archaeologists to study. As figure 8.3 shows, querns tend to be unwieldy items. In the present, they create storage and labelling problems. The very fact that they are suitable as grinding stones means that they have rough surfaces and their shapes and the fragments that they break into often make writing directly on the object difficult and tying on a label problematic. Provenance information can thus be lost even where it was once known. They are also items that may be noticed during ploughing and can be brought in to museums with only vague provenance details (field, parish) or have details of their secondary context in walls or as gate props. Finds of grinding stones in context can give very social information, and there are studies of this genre (e.g. Harsema 1979, Langdon 2004, Moritz 1958, Watts 2002 on grinding and milling equipment), while the rock materials can lend themselves to petrographic sourcing (e.g. Peacock 1980 on Roman millstones). Interestingly, different kinds of rotary quern can occur within one settlement, suggesting either that there are differences in status between those who had access to imported materials and those who used more local products, or that they performed their tasks in slightly different ways. It could be that different varieties might be better for rough grinding versus fine milling. Such studies are rare and it is difficult to envisage archaeological experiments accurately replicating long years of wear. In this case, actualistic studies would be better carried out in ethnographic contexts rather than experimental ones. But it also shows how little we truly know about their function and it seems there are likely to have been misidentifications; for example Adams (2002: 134) documents some objects labelled as disk mortars which have traces of soot around the basin and one which appears to have some form of handle, which could alternatively be explained as oil burning lamps, although of a very simple kind. Furthermore, mortars can exist in the landscape, in the form of natural rocks (Adams 2002: 134). As a category, the ground and pecked stone tools are by far the least well appreciated and studied of a range of items produced in these kinds of raw materials.

By far the most prolific evidence is of knapped stone. There are good general accounts of flaked stone technologies and the general methods of study (Andrefski 1998, 2000, 2001, Edmonds 2001) as well as strong traditions in knapping experiments (Johnson 1978). Typologies and studies for different periods and regions have been built up, often over several generations. Classic types defined in the 1920s are still being used, although the broad categories are used more than specific sub-types (e.g. burins, Burkitt 1920, and discoidal polished knives, Clark 1929). For both general terminology of knapped stones and classic Palaeolithic types, the French traditions based around their rich sites have formed the basis for studies elsewhere (Bordaz 1970, Demars and Laurent 1989, Inizan et al. 1992 and 1999 to name but a few in a longstanding tradition). There are overviews and detailed studies for other regions (for Britain, Edmonds 1995, Green 1980, Waddington 2005; for North America, Kooyman 2000; for Australia, McCarthy 1976, Holdaway and Stern 2004). Some sites have been used to stand out as examples and lend their names to major cultural terms, for example La Gravette (Lacorre 1960) for the Upper Palaeolithic Gravettian, but other work for the period and region would need to be consulted (e.g. Amirkhanov 1998 for the Eastern Gravettian). The classic excavation reports continue (e.g. Leakey and Roe 1995) but many projects now take a broad geographical approach to an issue, using lithic scatters to examine landscape or ecological issues (Allen 1995, Kuhn 1995, Odell 1996b, Schofield 2000). General theoretical discussions (Carr 1994, Henry and Odell 1989, Ashton and David 1994) provide snapshots of contemporary thinking.

Concerns with the earliest stone tools continue to be a feature of lithic studies (Schick and Toth 1993, Gibson and Ingold 1993, Milliken and Cook 2001) and there is now research on more unusual deposits or tools (Scott-Jackson 2000 on early artefacts from clay with flint deposits, in Britain, and Willoughby 1987 on battered spheroids in Africa). The origins of artefact groups have also been reassessed across large geographical regions (e.g. Shea 2006). As part of the development of knowledge of particular periods, there is increasing awareness of the use of flint in more recent periods. It has long been understood that the gun industry (a gun flint is visible in figure 8.11e) required flints (e.g. Forrest 1983, Kenmotsu 2000), while there is an increasing interest in the neglected role of flint in the later Bronze Age and Iron Age (van Gijn and Niekus 2001, Rosen 1997, Young and Humphry 1999).

Even though modern societies with traditions of knapped stone are very rare, some ethnographic work is still possible (Toth et al. 1992) and ethnographic analogies and reconstructions are still fundamental aspects of lithic analysis (Owen and Porr 1999). These in turn inform experimental work. Experimenting with flint has been part of the subject from the very earliest periods (e.g. see Johnson 1978) and continues to be widely applied as part of understanding technologies and technical choices (Amick and Mauldin 1989, Bosson 2001, Hurcombe 1993, Shea et al. 2001), for wear analyses (e.g. Keeley 1980), and for investigations into the formation and retrieval of the archaeological record and distinguishing natural and cultural transformations (e.g. Bowers et al. 1983, McBrearty et al. 1998, Schick 1986, including also patination and post-depositional damage: Rottländer 1975, Lautridou et al. 1986, Sieveking and Clayton 1986).

The technological understanding developed with practical flint knapping expertise (Crabtree 1972) has continued. Modern knappers (Brandt and Weedman 1997) may not know the complex mathematics behind flake fracture (Cotterell and Kamminga 1987) but neither did their prehistoric counterparts. Detailed technological studies have become part of the modern suite of analytical studies (e.g. Ahler and Geib 2000 on Folsom point design) and it has become standard practice to investigate aspects of the reduction sequences and strategies present on a site (Bradley 1975, Van Peer 1995), to detail the variation in raw materials, and to give overviews of the quantities of different formal tool types (Hiscock 2002, Shott 2001) and debitage categories (Andrefski 2001). Refitting studies (Hofman and Enloe 1992) can identify knapping sequences and also the intended piece that has been taken away from the site. This can be very useful cultural information and can give insights into the intent and technological style. Reduction sequences, sometimes combined with refitting, allow the *chaîne opératoire* approach to be developed (e.g. Giria and Bradley 1998). It is not surprising that this approach, investigating the chain of operations as a sequence allied to locations and organisation, was developed within flaked stone tool studies which offer this evidence so clearly.

Some aspects of stone artefact studies have only been touched on here, for example the phenomenon of Neolithic flint mines (e.g. Russell, M., 2000, Sieveking and Newcomer 1986) and frequently a combination of studies offers detailed information. For example, a combination of use wear analysis and refitting led to some very specific interpretations of the numbers of people at a short-term site and the precise activities with which they were mainly engaged (Cahen and Keeley 1980).

Function is the reason why stone tools were created but it remains one of the most problematic areas. The techniques exist but they are specialist and still quite rarely applied. Wherever functional studies have been carried out to any extent, they have inevitably led to revision, firstly by extending the notion of what can be identified as a used tool and detailing features to recognise these, and secondly showing the inaccuracies in function-linked names for types (e.g. Niewenhuis 2002, Salls 1985, Juel Jensen 1994, Van Gijn 1990). We also do not, in a modern way, understand the qualities of a stone edge, which is a fundamental failing in a raft of studies. That is not to say that much has not been achieved; it has, and good overviews exist (Odell 2000b, 2001, Longo and Skakun 2006).

Odell (2000a, 2001) has written two substantial papers evaluating development in lithic research which cover a vast array of literature. There are paradigm shifts and minor revolutions in lithic studies, for example the work of Torrence (1983, 1986, 1989a, 1989b, 1989c), which was characterised by looking at stone tools as elements of time management, as well as the more traditional production and exchange of stone tools. Exploitation evidence continues to reveal social information (e.g. Barber et al. 1999, Ericson and Purdy 1984) and even in the long-established technique of thin section analyses there are new contributions (Curran et al. 2001). However, there is still a quest for a usable way of sourcing flint and finer-grained lithic materials (e.g. Pretola 2001), but there is still no commonly available technique for this. Likewise, although heated flint can be dated using TL, there is still no method for directly dating the majority of flint tools as they are found. However, there has been and continues to be growing awareness of heat pre-treatment, some effects of which can be so subtle as to be almost impossible to detect in the archaeological record without a great deal of experience and knowledge of particular features (e.g. Lea 2005). Researchers have started to recognise unskilled flint knapping and, where there is also three-dimensional recording and evidence for structures the location of individual knappers, or locations of styles of flint knapping, can be established. In some cases, this has led to the identification of children's flint knapping (e.g. Finlay 1997, Fischer 1989, Grimm 2000, Pigeot 1990) and to studies of how bead knappers develop their skills (Kenoyer et al. 1994, Roux et al. 1995).

One of the most fundamental rethinkings of the archaeological record, because of a change brought about by scientific analysis, is the example of the Cahokian acquisition pattern. This eastern woodland prehistoric cultural development in the USA has long been seen as a political and economic power within the region and amongst the elite goods there are stone pipes and figurines made from a red stone.

It had been thought that this was from a source of Arkansas bauxite; however, Emerson and Hughes (2000) showed, using a combination of X-ray defraction, sequential acid dissolution, and ICPMS, that the source was in fact made from locally available flint clays. Alongside other evidence, this fits a more distinctive pattern which suggests that the Cahokian society exploited resources chiefly in the northern Ozark highlands. Thus, the science has suggested a reassessment of the sphere of influence and role of Cahokian trade and contacts in the region.

Likewise scientific analysis established an important point in Israel. By using the quantities of a beryllium isotope in flint artefacts from different layers in the prehistoric caves of Tabun and Qesem, Verri et al. (2005) were able to show that the Acheulo-Yabrudian cultural artefacts from four hundred thousand to two hundred thousand years ago contained very small amounts of beryllium, consistent with flint obtained from a substantial depth of more than 2 metres. Thus it would seem to be evidence for a form of flint extraction which was highly targeted even at this early date.

Technologies

Stone provides the evidence for more than two million years of tool making. However, stone tools need not be the earliest form of material culture, just the most durable and recognisable remnants of early artefact use. This chapter focuses on common finds and those aspects of stoneworking which are least well understood. Soft stones can be carved with stone or metal chisels and, if there are metal saws, they can also be sawn. The simplest stone technologies are those of pecking, polishing, and grinding where low skill can achieve reasonable-quality finished objects, but finer flint knapping technologies are highly skilled crafts. One of the commonest means of working stone in the past, knapping, is also the least known in the modern world, and that is why it is emphasised here.

The key techniques for working these stones are pecking and chipping – with a chisel in periods of metal, but otherwise with a hammer stone – and, if perforations are required, the use of borers or drills. For some bead works, these must be very fine and great care must be taken to hold the bead steady and maintain the line through the stone. In some examples, the style of the hole can indicate the manner in which it was drilled: for example some holes have what are known as hourglass profiles, that is, they are drilled through from both sides and worn down gradually from the centre, creating a very distinctive profile. Occasionally, objects may be drilled from just one side, in which case it is a sloping surface. However, other kinds of drills, such as that used by Sloper (1989) (figure 8.6), spin around a central point and, thus, a circular ring is worn down with a plug of stone removed. Such techniques give much straighter bore profiles and may, for the purposes of hafting, be more desirable. In any event, the drilling of a hole will weaken a stone considerably. There are various ways of drilling, ranging from a simple bow drill to a more robust example where the object is held stationary on the ground, with a tree, or other solid surface, used as the other fixing point, so that a more robust action can be used on the drill. With all of these, there is a balance between the accuracy with which the hole needs to be drilled and the rapidity with which it can be drilled.

Some kinds of rocks will require special care. Objects made out of such rocks as shale require careful selection of the raw material so that the stresses and strains that occur during manufacture will utilise the grain and flat planes. If worked against the grain, the object is more likely to fracture in manufacture or use.

Stone was also used to make containers, noticeably the very finely made vessels from Egypt (Aston 1994), and all forms and sizes of figures and statues (Aston et al. 2000). Ancient Egyptians used stone for a range of products from gemstones to building stones, with supporting pictorial evidence for some of the technologies involved. One of the most intriguing aspects is how the interior of these very fine vessels were hollowed out (Hester and Heitzer 1981, Odell et al. 1996), since these stone vessels were made in periods without metal tools. As an example of how a polished soft stone object can be made, Sloper's (1989) experiment in the manufacture of a Bronze Age-style shale cup shows that it is possible to achieve a very fine product using very simple tools as shown in figure 8.6, and Stocks (1993) has described experimental methods using particular kinds of twist-reverse-twist drills (TRDs) versus a bow drill. Interestingly, although the latter is quicker, it is more likely to result in breakage. Furthermore, he has also experimented with bead making (Stocks 1989). Stones can be used as they are to make very attractive beads, but they can also be heated to improve the colour, as exemplified by both modern ethnographic studies and earlier Indus bead industries (Kenoyer 1986, Kenoyer et al. 1991, 1994). There are also more general accounts of the social implications of beads and bead makers (e.g. Sciama and Eicher 1998).

Flaking technology

Pieces of flint or chert are interpreted by examining the patterning of ripple marks, striking platform location and angle, ventral and dorsal surfaces, the presence and location of cortex, the type of termination, the direction of the dorsal scars and the presence of any retouch or fine shaping after flake removal. Cores are likewise assessed on the flake feature characteristics, the angle of the platform, and the direction of the blows of previous removals. That is why all technology books describe such flake features and why labelled diagrams indicating what they look like are crucial. But, ultimately, the typologies used will depend upon the period and region and local work done previously, and, in many respects, the precise observations and classification of the material depends entirely upon the research questions. For example, it is pointless to classify material into how much cortex is present unless it is assumed that there are knapping variations with only some sections of the chaîne opératoire present – and perhaps these differ across different source materials, or in different areas of the site. Likewise, statistical examination of length/breadth ratios may be pointless unless it is expected that these will show, via a general trend that has already been established, a particular range: for example for Britain length/breadth ratios of flakes may indicate broad phasings in prehistory. However, there are often pointless statistics available, which aid neither interpretation nor description. Basic and commonly accepted typologies and counts of material into these types do, however, facilitate comparisons with other sites in the region and are usually an unwritten standard of archaeological recording (see fuller discussion in Andrefski 2005).

Stone tool drawings are one of the most effective ways of communicating information about a stone (figure 8.9). The styles which dictate the rendering of features visible on the real object into a schematic diagram, which has measured accuracy, makes very clear subtle features difficult to photograph in one shot. The ventral face is the result of the fracture that detached that particular flake and reveals information on this flaking event. There are features which show the bulb of percussion formed when a cone crack propagates through the raw material detaching the flake. As it does so, the force expands out from the point at which it was struck and that is why, rather like ripples in a pond when a stone is thrown in, there are ripple marks on a stone flake. Sometimes there are also stress fissures at right angles to these ripple marks and, occasionally, near the cone of percussion there will be a small, feather-like flake scar called an eraillure or bulbar scar. All of these features allow the point at which the blow was struck to be determined and the flake to be orientated. The dorsal face, or the back of a flake, contains information on the history of previous flaking events on the nodule or core before the present flake was removed. There are the intersecting scars of previous flake removals. The direction of the ripple marks of these gives some indication of the manner of working of the core and the history of previous removals, prior to this flake coming off. That is why it is worth recording them accurately on technical drawings. Fine-grained materials will show these sorts of features more frequently than coarser-grained material such as quartzite, where the ripple marks can be quite coarse features, but there will be a number of stress fissures.

The reason why flaked stone is so useful is predictive flaking. The material does not have any preferred fracture lines and so the place at which the nodule is struck and the choices of direction and force made by the flint knapper determine the shape that comes off. That would not be true of slate, where the raw material has a tendency to fracture in particular planes, because of the way it is laid down as a rock. Figure 8.7 shows the key important features of such flaking. The angle between the platform and the face must be less than 90° in order to detach a flake. The blow must also strike near the edge. Crucially, the shape of the face immediately below that striking blow will determine the shape of the flake detached. That is the most poorly understood issue within flaking technology. Thus, where there are no features present, a conchoidal or shell-like flake results. If there is a slight ridge, then the flake will follow that slight ridge, which may be straight down, or, if the ridges go at angles, then the flake that results will have to follow those angles. This is because the flake fracture propagates partly by reflected waves of compression that come back from the face of the piece. That is why a skilled flint knapper can determine the shape of the pieces. It is also why, if a particular shape of flake is desired (unless a nodule happens to have the right characteristics on the raw surface), the knapper has to make it have those key characteristics. This is the secret behind making a good blade core – setting up a long ridge from which to take off long, characteristic, blade-like flakes. This short discussion has covered only the basic essentials. For more detail see Bradley et al. (1989), Lord (1993), and Whittaker (1994).

Other examples of the knapper's choices lie in the kinds of object used to deliver the force to detach the flake, along with the direction and the manner of contact. Figure 8.8 shows five key ways in which flakes may be detached: firstly, using hard hammer percussion, in this case a small stone; secondly, using soft hammer percussion, here a piece of elk antler, but other soft hammers of different antlers and boxwood are visible in the same photograph. Thirdly, a blow can be very precisely directed using a punch which is then struck with another soft hammer. In the case of the image shown, the flint knapper has the core held securely between his knees. Fourthly, small flakes may also be pushed off by hand, called pressure flaking. In the image shown, the knapper is removing flakes from the face that is turned into her palm, with a covering holding the material in place and protecting her hand. Lastly, larger flakes can also be pushed off, but these require some implement that will allow greater force to be delivered, using more of the body. Here, an example is shown of a chest press, where a person can lean weight on to a core held in a small device at their feet. All of these techniques result in slightly different forces and give subtle variations in the manner of flakes detached. Certainly the softer hammers and the pressure flaking give more refined ways of working material.

Flake terminations provide one way of seeing people's mistakes. Most flakes detached will have a very fine termination when seen in side view, so that they feather into the surface and tail off at the end of the flake. Where the blow is not correctly delivered or there is a flaw in the raw material, a hinge fracture, a step fracture, or a plunging fracture can result. The plunging fracture may take away the bottom of the core, whereas a hinge fracture or step fracture may create a problematic lump on the core face, which will hinder the satisfactory removal of subsequent flakes in that area. Knapping is about a *sequence* of actions because the legacy of previous flake removals affects the core face and all later removals. Sometimes cores will show where other flakes have been directed, perhaps from another direction, in order to get rid of these problem areas. Flakes with these problems can be found as discarded items.

Some long blades or long flakes may be deliberately snapped, in order to make them a better shape for fitting in a haft, or for some other intention. Others, as they fall away from the core, may have a small amount of retouch, known as spontaneous retouch. Otherwise, these raw flakes that come off a core can be worked down further, i.e. retouched, using some of the finer techniques of knapping, and very finely shaped material can result. This finer working allows very regular and distinctive shapes to be created, for example the highly shaped types shown in figure 8.11. These are both an asset and a problem in flaked stone research. Such distinctive shapes, once described, allow other similar pieces to be assigned with some confidence to the same category, that is, named in the same way, by somebody else on another site. This is positive in that it facilitates communication. The problem is that such highly shaped types usually form the minority of an assemblage yet attract most of the attention and many have assumed functional names that are complete misnomers. Objects which to us seem like points, for example the Dalton point shown in figure 8.11, were sometimes used as knives (Yerkes and Gaertner 1997). Furthermore these are just the very well shaped pieces. Many unremarkable and unretouched flakes are potentially useful because they have sharp or blunt edges and shapes which suit particular purposes. It is very difficult to spot such edges without careful and painstaking examination. This means that, in many cases, formal retouched tool typologies are really one small subset of the full range of tools that were used in a society. This obvious point is not one that is generally appreciated by non-specialists.

Furthermore, tools can be reused, either by recycling, or by resharpening, or simply being picked up perhaps hundreds if not thousands of years later and being used as objects which have already been humanly formed. Use itself may be quite a complicated process (Hurcombe 1994). It is these complex processes which give us the most value, since those are the cultural choices.

Distinguishing natural effects

In flaked stone analysis, natural processes need to be distinguished from intentional, artefactual processes. Key aspects of these are illustrated in figure 8.12, and there are also excellent accounts and illustrations in the European literature of the problems of distinguishing natural from intentional damage (e.g. Beuker 1983, 1990, Petersen 1993). Chemical processes in the ground can react gradually with the flint to create a white patina, or a glossy patina. These can be entirely natural, but a glossy patina will prevent the formation of a white patina, whereas a white patina can have a glossy patina formed over it. The beginning stages of a white patination produce an optical effect which can appear speckled or bluish in tone. Flint is never blue, but it is occasionally described as such because of this patina effect. Likewise, small fossils may feature in the flint. In some cases these have undoubtedly been seen as a feature of the flint by the maker and incorporated into some aspect of the design (Oakley 1965a, 1965b). The patination may however be affected by the fossils within and flecks within the natural raw material, giving a very spotty appearance, as can be seen in figure 8.12c. Furthermore, both heat and cold can also damage the surface (figure 8.12a and b). Heat results in myriad small cracks over the surface known as crazing and small pot-lid fractures. If there is iron present, there may also be some reddening, but this depends upon the original colour and chemistry of the flint and is not always found. In contrast, frost damage creates pitting which is in the form of much larger concave hollows, some of which have a curved linear fracture in the centre of them. Alternatively, frost damage can be columnar and, where it is very regular, a novice might mistake it for a blade core.

It is small important details of observation like this that allow the characteristics that were intentional on the part of the maker to be distinguished from those which are post-depositional, or simply part of the natural flaws and processes of the formation of the flint or the geological processes which have acted on it since.

Function

Because stone endures, it is made to work and manipulate other objects, or it is made into items for display and lasting significance. Its durability may be an important part of its usage in funerary monuments (Parker Pearson et al. 2006). However, that is not to say that stones are not still components of a largely organic material culture assemblage. Quite often, the manner and style of hafting renders them more effective tools. This is something that is frequently forgotten and needs further work (Rots et al. 2006). Furthermore, only highly shaped pieces are usually defined as 'tools' whereas simple flakes can form effective tools. The issue is one of recognition and perception; for example, an obtuse edge can be a functional one (Crabtree 1972). Where wear traces have been studied, these have shown problems in the recognition of unretouched flakes used as tools and in tools used for task-related sets of activities (Van Gijn 1990, Hurcombe 1994). Wear traces can be studied at different levels to examine a suite of alterations and residues (see Chapter 4). Figure 8.13 deliberately shows obsidian wear and residue traces since one problem is that some functional studies are thought to rely on 'polishes' alone. In fact they use a wide range of surface changes. Obsidian is already a highly reflective material, so this suite of images shows textural surface alterations, striations or scratches, and small flake scars which taken together can distinguish different materials. Residues can exist as shapes on a surface or can be the subject of starch grain, phytoliths, or chemical analysis all of which have their own strengths and weaknesses (see Chapter 4). Use wear studies themselves have several different aspects (see Chapter 4) and the large scale and long tradition of such work in Russia (Semenov 1964, Phillips 1988) has enabled broad interpretations to be made. The low-power approach commonly used in North America has also led to some very large-scale deductions (Odell 1996a, Tomášková 2000). Because of some very detailed microwear recording, there is also a sound tradition of a self-critical approach to use wear studies (e.g. Odell and Odell-Vereecken 1980, Sala 1986). Whole sites have been studied in detail (Lewenstein 1987), or particular post-depositional effects (e.g. Lancaster 1986, investigating wind action), and papers have focused on a particular set of functions (e.g. Juel Jensen 1994) on plant working. Work in Europe using the microwear approach is starting to come of age and produce a broader sweep, particularly where there are well-established laboratories which have acted as a centre for the work (van Gijn et al. 2006, van Gijn and Houkes 2006 on flint and ground stone tools). The variety of information can also be seen in collected volumes (e.g. Anderson et al. 1993a, 1993b, Longo and Skakun 2006). Wear traces give functional, technological, and post-depositional information, but this form of study is time-consuming. However, shape alone is a poor determinant of function. Use wear analysis continues to be thought-provoking in its interpretations (e.g. Gräslund et al. 1990), since people still experiment with the manner of damage and processes (Derndarsky and Ocklind 2001), and continue experimenting in using computerisation to facilitate the interpretative decision-making processes (Van den Dries 1998). Further work on DNA recovered from stone tools has been conducted on ethnographic (Kimura 2001) and experimental examples (Shanks et al. 2001).

The situation for understanding flaked stone function is mirrored in ground stone analysis. It is worrying to come across whole classes of artefacts which have not been recognised in terms of their purpose. Adams (2002) shows what is missing from the range of ground stone types considered and recognised within the archaeological record, an example being a type she describes as hide processing stones (Adams 2002: 96), which in some cases would be quite difficult to recognise archaeologically. Although they might be picked up as traces of working, they would not necessarily be studied or accorded any other kinds of analysis. In figure 7.3a the buckskin has been whitened and the nap raised by the white soft stone, used as a colouring and finishing tool.

Grinding equipment is often assumed to be primarily for subsistence tasks but an item might have served more than one purpose, as recent use wear and residue studies have demonstrated (Dubreuil 2004, 2006, Fullagar and Field 1997, Fullagar et al. 1996, 1998, 2006, Hamon 2003, 2004, 2005, Hamon and Samzun 2004, and Orozco-Kohler 2000, and for mortar and pestle use see Campbell 2002). Such studies are beginning to provide a social dimension to these objects, and research has shed light on both subsistence practice changes and the social origins of cooking and dining (Wright 1994, 2000, Adams 2002: chapters 2 and 3). Grinding stones and the early origins of plant processing development are becoming an adjunct to studies of the development of hunting techniques. Traditionally studied as evidence of trade and contact, in recent years they have been the subject of much richer and more mature studies, with many more social dimensions. Rotary querns can be shown to have changes in style and fashion, although they present their own problems, since an object which could have a usable life of eighty years or more is not going to reflect short-term fashions. The decorated quern stones from Ireland and Wales (Griffiths 1951, Caulfield 1977) show that, whilst these objects might be connected with the 'daily grind', they were also worthy of decoration and there is evidence of them being dowry items and of being passed on from mothers to daughters. The durability of these stone items does mean that they will also see reuse. Items can be used as weights, as fragments in buildings even when they are broken, or they can serve multiple purposes, forming a pitted surface for holding, for example, bow drills or other items.

Other objects which are not often considered in an assessment of function are honestones (e.g. Crosby and Mitchell 1987) and touchstones (Moore and Oddy 1985), and there are also objects made of chalk and soft rock carved as symbols (e.g. an engraved chalk plaque, Varndell 1999).

Overview

Table 8.1 gives an overview of what can be done and how it can be done for most of the key questions asked of lithic raw materials by archaeologists. There are glaring omissions. There is no technique available for sourcing flint and chert, which are amongst the commonest of flaked stone tool materials. Neither is there a direct way of dating them, unless they have been burnt, nor is there a direct way of dating polished and ground stones, or indeed building stones – all these largely have other methods of dating but the single most useful and revolutionary invention in lithic analyses would probably be a method of independently dating flaked stone artefacts.

In general, the character of the archaeological record can involve large amounts of waste at extraction sites and so the reductive nature of the material and its

Table 8.1 Techniques of analysis for stone artefacts

| STONE | What is it made from? | What is the character of the material and can it be grouped? | Where did the raw material(s) come from? | How was it made? | When was it made? Or when was it deposited? | Was it used? What for? |
	Identification	Characterisation	Sourcing/provenance	Technology	Direct dating	Function
Flint/chert *Very frequent*	By eye and fracture qualities	By eye using colour, inclusions, cortex features	No specific technique though chemical trace elements may give possibilities and for some areas physical features matched against good reference collections may aid sourcing	By eye using fracture features on surface	No technique	Macro- and microscopic wear traces; residue analysis (phytoliths, starch grains, tissue types, blood, mineral traces, resin traces)
Obsidian *Occasional*	By eye and fracture qualities	By eye using colour, inclusions, cortex features; rarely applied but can use trace elements or remnant magnetism	Trace elements can give sources but requires reference set from sources and for these to be distinguishable	By eye using fracture features on surface	Fission track or hydration dating possible but latter requires comparative data to calibrate	Macro- and microscopic wear traces; residue analysis (phytoliths, starch grains, tissue types, blood, mineral traces, resin traces)
Polished/ground stones, querns, mortars *Frequent*	Macro- or microscopic mineral identifications, e.g. thin sections	By eye or microscope mineral identifications	Sometimes possible by eye or microscope mineral identifications but requires reference set from sources	By eye using surface features	No technique	Potentially same as above

Table 8.1 continued

STONE	What is it made from?	What is the character of the material and can it be grouped?	Where did the raw material(s) come from?	How was it made?	When was it made? Or when was it deposited?	Was it used? What for?
	Identification	Characterisation	Sourcing/provenance	Technology	Direct dating	Function
Burnt flint Occasional	By eye and fracture qualities	Irrelevant	Not normally considered	By eye but heat damage may have destroyed much of these	TL possible but effects of local conditions need to be gauged via dosimetry	Potentially some wear traces might survive but much depends upon the severity of the heat damage
Building stones Frequent	Fracture properties; macro- or microscopic mineral identifications, e.g. thin sections	Largely irrelevant	Sometimes possible by eye or microscope mineral identifications but requires reference set from sources: some fine stones e.g. marble can be sourced via isotopic analyses	By eye using surface features	No technique	Inferred from context or shape

durability, leads to a great sympathy with the *chaîne opératoire* approach, which was in fact developed as part of a repertoire of lithic analysis. Their durability also means that most stones survive most post-depositional processes. But equally, the larger elements amongst them may be reused as walls or in other ways, and spotting that reuse as part of any second cultural context or object biographies can be more challenging. Some stone is altered before it goes into the ground, and that is only just beginning to be recognised as part of structured deposition. In our current cultural context, there are some very uneven treatments of the objects discussed by this chapter. Chance finds are highly biased to those which can be most easily recognised: for example, a barbed and tanged arrow head, or a polished stone axe, or those items which are heavy enough to be noticed when ploughing such as a very large set of building stones, or perhaps a quern stone. Surveys of either natural exposures or agricultural exposures are excellent ways of collecting broad spatial landscape data, and lithic analysis is a key aspect of these sorts of studies. Excavations targeting later periods can largely ignore flaked stones by treating them as inevitably part of reworked material.

Building stone is not very well dealt with, except perhaps for mosaics and highly decorative pieces. Polished stone, amber, and such items tend to be very carefully stored and may well end up on display, whereas the vast majority of flaked stone artefacts will never go on display, except as examples of debitage and flaking strategies. The storage of stone materials presents problems. Flaked stone has the advantage of being relatively small-scale, but for bulky items on many sites hard decisions are made over what is to be kept as samples or examples even before objects come off site or are allowed into a store. All of these factors contribute to the mosaic of information available from the archaeological record, but flint itself has one abiding value – it is durable and it is here to be studied, sometimes for millennia. It is also often a composite element and/or a tool for working other materials. As such, studying archaeological stone tools potentially gives information on the exploitation both of stone and of other perishable materials. The latter is in its infancy but is the field with the greatest potential.

9 Clay (and glass) materials and artefacts

A widely available and highly plastic material

Clay as a raw material has both ubiquity and versatility. It occurs widely and can be used for making objects, from figurines and containers to substantial structures and buildings. It can withstand heat and provide waterproofing. Archaeologists typically think of fired clay, but it may be used unfired. However, with the exception of clay used in structures, it is rare to find such material in the archaeological record unless it has been accidentally fired. As a raw material, clay is dominated by one property above all others, its plasticity. Conversely, it can be transformed into a rigid and brittle material which retains the shape given to it when plastic. The plasticity of the medium allows impressions of other materials to survive on the surface occasionally, but, more importantly, the ease with which the material can be shaped and decorated makes it the most expressive widely surviving aspect of the material culture record. Though clay can be rendered into any shape, for successful firing even shapes are better. Furthermore clay is not one uniform material but varies: clays fire at different temperatures and have different properties. As figure 9.1 shows, fired clay can be decorated in many different ways. It can be used for large storage vessels, cooking pots, fine tablewares and lamps, as well as for bricks and tiles. Once fired, it is brittle and so all of these items can be recovered from the archaeological record as fragments, with those used in situations where they frequently break being amongst the most numerous. From later prehistory onwards, pottery fragments known as sherds are usually the most prolific finds on a site.

In general pots have four main characteristics: shape, manufacturing technology, decoration, and the material itself. The latter is known as a paste comprising the background clay and naturally occurring or added inclusions (temper) within it. The finished pot will also be affected by the method of firing. The key to understanding the central role of pottery in archaeological finds analysis is to realise how much information on the *whole* object can be gleaned from just one surviving fragment of it – a sherd. If placed carefully in the hand and viewed from many different directions, a single sherd can often be seen to have an orientation where the profile makes sense. If this orientation is then used against a reference chart of circles, the diameter of the pot at that point can be determined and the interior versus exterior can also be established. These surfaces and the profile of the sherd can be used to establish the basic shape (or a part of it) represented by the sherd and the surfaces examined for any decoration. The interior and exterior surfaces may also reveal sooting, or some aspect of firing technology. In addition, the broken edges reveal the composition of the pot, its paste (the fine materials) and any aplastic inclusions (these can be natural coarse inclusions and/or deliberately added aplastic inclusions known as temper), and provide information on the kinds of firing temperatures achieved via the porosity and the atmospheric conditions of firing by means of the colours within the sherd wall. It is also possible to distinguish features made when the clay was wet from those made after firing. In an archaeological illustration, the pot is represented by a scale drawing which is rendered as if the pot was looked at sideways on with a quarter cut out (see figure 9.1, mid right). This allows one drawing to convey a shape, a profile, and images of any exterior or interior decoration. Thus a few sherds provide a wealth of technical detail some of which can be conveyed concisely in an archaeological illustration. The paste is not so easily depicted but similar pastes can be identified and a ceramic assemblage can be sorted into the types which exemplify the different pastes, forms, and styles which are a mainstay of the published reports on ceramics.

Clay as an *unfired* raw material is, however, underrepresented in our ideas about people's use of clay in the past. It forms clay tablets and seals. Clay can also be smeared over other materials, such as basketry, to render them more rigid, smoother, tougher or waterproof, or more resistant to insects. For example, in parts of India an above-head-height storage basket smeared with clay and placed on a clay platform is used as a storage bin (Dhavalikar 1994: 42). It is common to see mud brick buildings or adobe constructions in dry areas of the world (see figure 9.2b–d). However, even in temperate climates clay was a well-used and established building material. It was the material that could have been put round a wattle construction to make a watertight wall and could also be combined with chopped straw and stones, to make material which in Britain is known by regional names, such as 'mud and stud', or 'cob' (Sunshine 2006). The key requirement of clay walls in rainy climates is that they have to be kept dry on top and protected from the elements as much as possible, either by a protective wash or by low eaves. Even today, there are substantial clay walls which have their own small roof to prevent rain penetrating downwards and many also have stone footings to protect the wall from rising damp. There are some studies of the decay of unfired architectural clay (McIntosh 1974, 1977), and a case can be made for seeing architectural clay structures as artefacts (Gilman 1987, 1989, Wilshusen 1989, Palyvou 2005, and Sherratt 2000) and as open to benign and intentional destruction (Stevanovic 1997). Clay can also form a sealing layer for below-ground structures, for example storage pits, ponds, or working hollows, and because it can have distinctive colours it can also form flooring or capping layers: there is some evidence for this within round barrows in the British Isles (Lynch 1998). Clay is also useful for any structures which have to withstand heat, such as kilns (see figure 9.6) and ovens (see figure 9.2.c).

Architecture can also use clay as a fired material. Bricks are well known in the archaeological record and their colour, sizes, shapes, and styles can provide broad dating evidence, for example dating Roman, medieval and post-medieval deposits on surveys. Furthermore, bricks can be a prestige building material in periods and regions where most buildings were of wood. Petrographic and NAA studies of bricks from a chapel built around AD 1667 in Maryland, USA, have shown that its bricks were from combined clay sources, whereas other brick structures of the period can be matched to a single local clay source (Armitage et al. 2006). Fired tiles can form roofs, flues such as hypocausts, floors, and walls, for example the colourful buildings in Asia such as those in Samarkand (see figure 9.2a).

Clay as a wonderfully plastic material changes completely when it is fired. If clay is simply dried it hardens but it can be broken down again, recombined with water and then reused. However heating beyond a particular temperature for any clay will result in an irreversible chemical change, where it becomes much more fragile and permanently takes on the shape that it has held as clay. This transformation creates many opportunities for the use of clay as ceramic.

Raw material properties and characteristics

Clay is not just one type of material; different minerals make up the clay body and these can affect features such as its plasticity, openness, and firing (maturing) temperature, that is the point at which it becomes irreversibly altered. The temperature at which this irreversible change takes place can be as low as 415°C but is more usually about 650–700°C. Different clays reach this conversion point at different temperatures, with earthenware clays changing at the lowest temperatures. Clays which fire at these temperatures would, in fact, begin to sag, distort, or melt at higher temperatures.

Clay is made up of particles less than 0.002 mm diameter. Furthermore, these tend to form plate-like particles rather than round ones and so they tend to align and slide over one another especially with water surrounding the particles. Because of its geological nature, clay can be found in two basic ways – within primary geological contexts or in secondary contexts. Primary clays include china clay, whereas secondary clays will have been eroded and redeposited in sedimentary layers elsewhere. Secondary clays tend to have a greater variety of minerals within them. Both are highly weathered mineral materials, often composed chiefly of the most resistant particles, for example, feldspars and granites. Clays will outcrop in different places, common examples being the sides of rivers, streams, or cliffs. This variety of parent material, particle size, and depositional context gives each source highly individual characteristics which affect the way the clay behaves when it is being worked and when it will chemically combine to lose irreversibly the water within it.

Primary clays, such as china clay, tend not to be suitable for hand-building techniques and they also have higher maturing temperatures, making them unsuitable for simple firing techniques. Often, secondary clays are red because of high amounts of iron oxide and these tend to form earthenwares needing only low firing temperatures, but they can also make good-quality structural clay items, such as tiles and bricks. Where secondary clays contain large amounts of organic material deposited alongside the clay, these tend to vitrify and are suitable for firing to the very high temperatures necessary for stonewares. Other forms of clay can withstand much greater temperatures before they start to distort and will become highly vitrified. Such ceramics can be much less porous than the open structure of earthenwares. In general, finer ceramic vessels require clays that will fire at higher temperatures.

At a non-industrial level, clay for ceramics can be dug, dried, crushed, and sieved. Even where the clay source is part of a major industry, once extracted it will still have to be processed before use. Large stones or materials such as roots or leaves that have got into the clay need to be removed. Obviously clay is heavy and the nearest suitable sources tend to be used. A different method is to mix the clay with water and then leave it to settle gradually. Archaeologists call the added non-clay component of ceramics *temper*, although the potting term is *filler*. Temper can improve the forming, firing or performance qualities of the clay. Some clays have natural inclusions which act as temper. If the clay has no natural temper, this may need to be added (see figure 9.7 for a variety of tempers). Sand (quartz) is commonly used. It lessens the risk of cracking in use and can sometimes be seen as rounded particles (see figure 9.7f and g). Flint and chert can occur naturally in clays but they can also be prepared as an additive. They can be calcined: that is, when they are heated above a certain temperature, which varies according to their mineralogy, they change nature and become internally fractured and more brittle. If high firing temperatures are required, then calcined flint is a better material, since this has already been thermally altered so that changes within the flint will not affect the firing, and calcined flint is easier to crush into small particles. Calcium carbonate (limestone, calcite, or shell) can be used for lower firing temperatures, but will undergo chemical reactions at higher temperatures causing either damage to the pot or its complete disintegration. It is also possible to use 'grog', ground-up pottery. Fine organic tempers will improve the plasticity and assist with firing. Coarser organic tempers such as chopped straw reduce shrinkage and improve workability. Some clays also have natural organic inclusions, for example algae and bacteria. Organic temper usually fires out leaving distinctive voids. Occasionally other minerals are deliberately added as surface effects. The mineral mica fuses at about 1000°C and can create a sheen on the surface if a rich layer is applied.

The kind of clay and the use of temper can affect the plasticity of the raw clay, its ability to hold a shape whilst the pot is being formed, the firing qualities, or some aspect of the fired pot's performance in use. In all these ways, potters in the past would have needed to choose suitable materials. In many respects, local clay materials for low-fired earthenwares would have been the most commonly used, but, wherever a particular colour or high firing temperature required, specific clay sources might have been needed: for example there are clay mines (Nicholson and Patterson 1985), and traditional sources of clay, if extracted extensively, will eventually require new sources to be located (e.g. Knappett 1994). The clay may have both technical and social processing needs (Smith 2000).

Archaeological study strategies

There are many overviews of ceramics as a whole or for particular periods (e.g. Freestone and Gaimster 1997, Gibson 2002, Gibson and Woods 1990, Orton et al. 1993, Peacock 1977, Reed 1990, Rice 1987, Rye 1981, Shepard 1985, Velde and Druc 1999), and some classic texts putting forward a particular theme or project (e.g. Arnold 1991, 1985, Barley 1994, Barnett and Hoopes 1995, Cumberpatch and Blinkhorn 1997, Kinnes and Varndell 1995, Van der Leeuw and Pritchard 1984), as well as some shorter overviews (e.g. Knappett 2005b, Bourriau et al. 2000). Other work brings together sets of particular kinds of pots, for example Cleal and MacSween (1999) on grooved ware, O'Riordan and Waddell (1993) for funerary bowls and vases, and Clarke (1970) for beakers. There are also interests in not so much firing temperatures as pyrotechnology across different kinds of material culture production (McDonnell 2001, Rehder 2000). There are now fewer publications specifically on styles of decoration, other than the amassing of disparate finds within one corpus. Where painted designs and decoration are seen as significant, they are investigated in terms of style as agency and innovation (e.g. Hegmon and Kulow 2005) or to question why a pot was decorated at all (David et al. 1988).

Generally assessments of function have emphasised a more social context and tried to assess meanings (Burley 2000, Deal and Silk 1988, Griffiths 1978, Hally 1986, Rice 1990, Rotlander 1990, Smith 1988). For example, the functional variations in Maya spiked vessels might be seen as a cross-over in terms of both style and also meaning (Deal 1982). In the last twenty years, there have been some excellent studies based on mechanical performance and functional aspects of different effects in ceramics and their subsequent usage. These have not been so much on functional analysis as performance, or even information on affordance. More researchers are trying to look at the observed variations which have traditionally been used to characterise and group ceramics, as components of the performance of pots (Braun 1980, 1983, Bronitski and Hamer 1986, Dunnell and Hunt 1990, Ericson et al. 1972, Mabry et al. 1988, O'Brien 1990, Pierce 2005, Schiffer 1988, 1990, Skibo and Schiffer 1987, Skibo et al. 1989, and Young and Stone 1990). Some have investigated this in a very technical way such as by studying thermal conductivity, or ability to withstand thermal shock, but others have concentrated more on a sense of the usability and longevity of different components within an assemblage. Though not all these authors would see their technical studies as contributing to this goal, their collective work now makes it possible to disaggregate the idea of an assemblage as a unified whole and see instead sets of ceramics which might behave and be replaced on very different timescales (Deal 1985, Longacre 1985, Nelson 1991, Schiffer and Skibo 1989, Shott 1996), thus offering very different opportunities for conveying social information and surely affecting the relative quantities of different kinds of ceramics in the archaeological assemblage and the inferences to be made from these. The recent developments in wear and residue studies of ceramics (see Chapter 4) offer further potential to integrate function into wider debates on performance and object biographies.

The longevity of pottery (Freestone 2001) and the ubiquity of clay have long been considered to make it a great social investigative tool, because the assumption is that everybody within a ceramic-using society has pottery or has access to pots. This can, in some instances, be a very minimal access or problematic. Adams and Boling (2000) consider the status and ceramics for planters and slaves on American plantations. Likewise, use-alteration as an indicator of socio-economic status has been the subject of Ethiopian work (Arthur 2002). This absence or paucity is just emerging as a field of study.

Pots can have complex biographies, and some extension to their use-life is implied by certain features such as drilled holes, sometimes seen as a phenomenon and sometimes as an attempt to mend or retain precious ceramics for a social reason (e.g. figure 9.8b and Cleal 1988). The relative importance and economic status of ceramics can also be constructed using historical sources, for example the set of indexed values for economic scaling of English ceramics imported onto the continent of eighteenth- to nineteenth-century North America (Miller 2000). Furthermore, ceramics incorporate other things because of the tempers within them. This sense of the possibilities for incorporating other materials within the fabric of a new pot is alien to the modern world where people are users rather than producers of ceramics. Even pots made at school or in pottery classes will have most often used pre-processed clay. Potters will not have formed the clay from materials that they themselves have prepared and chosen to put together into that vessel. In many periods of prehistory, people would have been intimately involved in what went into the pot, as well as the cultural ideas and shapes that they wanted to make in that material (Stilborg 2001, Woodward 2000, 2002).

None the less, there is an underlying, pragmatic issue with ceramic vessels. They interact with food and storage items very directly and can be envisaged as competing within the general sphere of 'containerisation'. Pots are above all containers and, as Ellis (2006: 235–6) explains, the whole issue of containerisation is one which we are lucky enough not to have to solve personally. This would have been an issue in the past and, although containers can be made of metals, this was a not a practical option for most people until recently. Hides and leather can make good containers and have the advantage of not being breakable, but hide is open to decay and can be eaten away by small infestations. Ceramics instead offer the chance for a relatively hygienic, stable surface, from which animals, pests, and dirt can be excluded, especially where a lid is used as well. Thus, the shapes of vessels have to solve problems of storing liquids and materials or perhaps servings of food (for example the food vessels of the Bronze Age in Europe, Waddell 1998) and of course, as cooking vessels, they must be able to withstand heat. They also act as a safety deposit for items of more precious materials, and some traditions see the pot as the container for the remains of the body and for the goods that go with that body: they enclose the whole safely. In all these ways, ceramics offer innovative and highly practical opportunities for solving containerisation problems.

Pots, however, do not exist in a vacuum. Since the unfired clay is plastic, occasionally ceramics make concrete references to other kinds of materials in the form of skeuomorphs or impressions. These are visual and textural echoes of other materials and objects, and such studies offer different kinds of information from pots and their interaction with other craft spheres, although this field could benefit from a more theorised context (Gibson 2002, Hurcombe 2007, Manby 1995, Owoc 2007).

Non-vessel clay

There are many different ways in which clay can be used. Figurines and spindle whorls of clay can be widespread depending upon the period and region. Clay pipes were ubiquitous on later sites once smoking had become a fashion and, since they are easily broken and discarded, are found frequently. Occasionally the pipe bowls are decorated, making it easier to identify the precise type, but even some semblance of bowl shapes can give chronological information, and clay pipe fragments continue to be important as dating and social evidence (Bradley 2000, Oswald 1975).

Bricks and tiles can provide very important dating evidence (e.g. Bodribb 1987) and adobe and mud-brick architecture can reveal techniques of manufacture and phasings in buildings, because there are structures in such buildings and they can be very complex (La Violette 2000). In figure 9.2b, the Casa Grande surviving adobe wall has turtle-back features showing the method of construction. There is mud-brick architecture all over the Near East across many millennia. In ancient Egypt Kemp (2002) describes the early occurrence of the use of soil to form walls of mud set against organic material acting as structural supports. There are few true mud-brick buildings in the pre-dynastic period in Egypt, but in northern Egypt the advent of mud brick architecture is one sign of a major culture change shortly before the first dynasty. To make effective mud brick does require a mixture of clay with other materials; for example heavy clay would require some addition of sand, and organic materials can act as a binding agent. The evidence for making mud bricks is much more difficult to find. In some cases the bricks were marked before they dried, so that phasing information can be available from differential marking or different sizes of mud brick, although this requires careful excavation techniques as shown in figure 9.2d. The practice of impressing bricks with an official stamp is known from the beginning of the eighteenth dynasty in Egypt (Kemp 2002: 83). The humble brick can be seen as a symbolic or social item: for example magical bricks inscribed with words of protection (Thomas 1964, in Kemp 2000: 84), and Boivin (2004) even gives an example of the use of mud plaster to coincide with concepts of cleanliness and purity in the Indian subcontinent.

The significance of clay as a raw material is underrated by archaeologists because we take it for granted. It generates possibilities for colour in a way that few other materials can match. If the buildings of Samarkand in Central Asia are compared to those in existence in Europe dating from the fifteenth century, they are stunning examples of the use of brick and glazed ceramics to create colourful, impressive buildings. Whilst the European cathedrals may have once been more colourful on the inside, on the outside at least they were more muted in tone. Ceramics offer colour from the earth tones of slips and glazes, and the black versus the white, to the reds and sometimes vibrant oranges of terracotta wares. Thus the colour range of ceramics would initially have been confined to earth tones, but it was possible to play with tonal contrasts on these surfaces. Furthermore, once glazes were available, the colour palette acquired a greater range and vibrancy.

With all of the variations possible in shape, style, and decoration, what role have technological studies filled? It is true that there are more socially orientated studies; study of pottery technology is still important, but in latter years it has tended to be for its social aspects. For example, Roux (1989) studied the potter's wheel and the concept of technical competence, and in particular surveyed what other potters valued in fellow potters' work and knew to be difficult to achieve. These insights from within the craft offered new ways of looking at archaeological data and, indeed, the French tradition of studying technological choice within technological change is very strong (Roux 2003, Lemonnier 1986, 1989, 1993). In particular, researchers are disaggregating aspects of technology, realising that different kinds of traits, found and able to be characterised by us on sherds, travel in different ways in societies. It is more difficult to copy a manufacturing technique than a style of decoration. For example, Neupert (2000) looked at factions within different clay compositions, and Gosselain (2000) looked at linguistic and ethnic groups, with a view to identifying similar manufacturing techniques versus similar forms of decoration and found that it was the fashioning and firing technologies which linked with established ethnic groups.

Technology is being disaggregated, with NAA studies documenting changing sources of clay despite similar technological practices (McClure et al. 2006) and a consideration of the effects of behavioural practices on ceramic composition and the definition of production locations (Carpenter and Feinman 1999). Some of the most interesting aspects of these are coming from actualistic studies based in ethnography and experimentation, where the transmission of decoration styles is demonstrably easier than the transmission of technologies (Gosselain and Livingstone-Smith 1995, Costin 2000). Increasingly, it seems that the application of techniques of analysis is being more selectively applied to more socially orientated research questions (Lindahl and Stilborg 1995). In general, the role of ethnoarchaeology in ceramic studies is very strong (Kramer 1994, Longacre 1991, Longacre and Skibo 1994).

One field where analytical tools have combined with ethnographic cross-cultural studies for a fundamental reassessment is in the estimation of firing temperatures. Discussion has centred on whether sophisticated scientific techniques offer any better results than field-based ones, and whether temperature alone is an adequate distinction when it is firing conditions which are of most interest (Gosselain 1992, Livingstone Smith 2001, Tite 1969, 1995). On the basis of cross-cultural information, it was concluded that firing technologies could be categorised by a number of socially significant facets but could not be simply divided into open versus kiln categories, nor indeed, could the soak time (time at the highest temperature) categorise these two different methods. Also, fuel was found to have no effect on the overall temperature achieved, this being part of a more complex interaction between the manner of the firing, the number of pots fired, and other factors. Even small differences in slightly protected bonfire firings can vary conditions within them significantly, and the classification and treatment of kilns is by no means constrained to simply bonfires and kilns (Blinman and Swink 1997, Rice 1997, Nicholson and Patterson 1989).

Scholars have also looked at the social contexts of ceramic production, notably Wright (1991) with a view to investigating women's labour and making pots, Sillar (2000b) covering a concept of households and communities, Janusek (2005) on ethnic identities, and Hill and Evans (1989) on relating cooking practices to particular crops. Likewise studies of decoration are not confined to style or identifications of substances but look at how these interweave with social and political groups and particular slips and paints (Cecil and Neff 2006, Cotkin et al. 1999). Throughout the production sequence which renders clay into fired ceramic there are also many opportunities for symbolism (e.g. Gosselain 1999).

The quantities of pottery found require statistics to give overviews (Sussman 2000), and there will always be a need for scientific case studies of distinct features, for example the analysis of Roman sherds with a high silver content (Adan-Bayewitz et al. 2006). However, there are also reviews of scientific techniques at particular stages (e.g. Carr 1990, Tite 1992, 1996, 2001, Whitbread 2001). These evaluate the way archaeological science is being used and, whilst there is a value in documentation (Hart et al. 1987), there is also critical reflection in the field (Neff 2001). New analytical methods allow very detailed composition analysis but these need to be strongly linked with more traditional macroscopic analyses (Knappett et al. forthcoming). As the possibilities for residue analysis grow, there is an increasing sense of the sherd-as-site which was first mooted twenty years ago (Hastorf and DeNiro 1985 and see Chapter 4) but again the very specific data are used to best effect on problems defined using more traditional analyses, for example the use of prehistoric pots for processing dairy products (Copley et al. 2005).

The most ubiquitous analytical technique is still petrological analysis, which uses readily available equipment with well-established identification methods (see Chapter 4). Figure 9.12 shows a range of thin sections to indicate the different kinds of inclusions that can be distinguished and the ways in which the shape, rounding, and size sorting of the inclusions can be assessed using a polarising microscope. Firing effects, voids, textural concentration features, and clay mixing effects can also be studied. Thin section techniques show the make-up of the paste and give some information on the manner of processing it and forming the pot. These result in characterising the different pastes and can sometimes indicate the provenance of the raw materials. For a useful overview covering key laboratory methods of analysis see Ellis (2006: table 8.1).

Technologies

Preparation of raw materials

Figure 9.4a shows dried clay, dug from a valley bottom, being crushed on a slab of rock. This crushed clay is then sieved to remove roots, leaves, and extraneous material and any large items. Temper, here in the form of sand, is added in a ratio of about 1:5 or 1:6. This is then gradually mixed with a little water in much the same way as making pastry. The clay must also be kneaded to remove any remaining air trapped within it. If air bubbles stay inside the body of the pot, the air will expand in the kiln, causing the pot to burst apart at that point. Kneading the clay is thus an important aspect of making a pot: there are several techniques, but all require a gradual mixing to be combined with a pushing action to drive air out of the clay. Since clays have different properties, they can be combined to obtain particular effects. Clays can also be refined by levigation, combining them with water and drawing off the finer particles held in suspension. Such techniques produce very fine clay.

Forming

When wet and thus workable, clay may not hold its shape well if it is too wet, so there needs to be a balance between workability and the ability to hold shape. That is why larger coil-built pots are often built up in stages. It is also noticeable that, despite the fact that clay can be formed into any shape, fired vessels tend to be a limited range of shapes. This is in part because it is difficult to dry materials evenly or to fire them evenly where there are sharp changes in the thickness of the clay. Some shapes are also difficult to produce. If, for example, a pot needs to be enclosed at the top then this has to be done gradually if it is built using the coil method, and even on a wheel the final part of the gap will be difficult to close in. One way round these forming problems is to use moulds. These can result in highly decorative, formalised repeat structures, but many moulds are simply an old pot or a basket which acts as a base in which the clay is placed as a lining, or it is upturned and the clay placed over it. The sherd in figure 9.4d has a basket impression on its interior surface because an upturned round basket has been used as the basic forming device with the clay being applied on the outside: the reverse could also be true. Pots with flat bases will also sometimes be formed and turned on mats which may leave traces on the base. These production impressions are different from deliberate impressions intended as decoration. Other manufacturing surface features can be observed. Moulds may leave seams, there may be marks where handles have been added and the clay pressed, or the method of removal of a pot from the wheel may leave a distinctive pattern, as seen in figure 9.4c.

At its simplest level, a pot can be formed by working the clay between two pinching devices. Figure 9.3a shows a thumb and forefinger being used to make a pinch pot, but a paddle and anvil can be tools used to perform much the same function on larger pots. The other highly versatile technique is the coil method (figure 9.3b and c), where the clay is rolled into long pieces which are then added as coils, forming the body wall by increments. The material is then smoothed, either by hand or by using a small implement to draw the clay up and down the vessel wall to make a smooth and uniform shape. Occasionally sherds are found where the fracture has broken along these lines within the clay body: for example figure 9.4b shows inverted 'v' markings which are the physical remnants of a coil technique on this shell-tempered pottery.

Hand-made techniques are perfectly adequate and can produce pots in reasonable numbers, but, where larger markets are available for the intended product, the quickness and uniformity of using a wheel can assist the potter. The wheel is also used for the quality of form it produces, not just for speed of production. Before mechanisation, the method of propulsion of the wheel was the key issue. A kick wheel requires a small wheel for the pot to be formed on, and a linked larger wheel, which acts as a flywheel and can be kicked into motion to keep the pot turning. Two examples of other forms of solution are illustrated in figure 9.3d and e. One is to have an assistant who turns the wheel whilst the potter forms the clay. The other is a large, heavy wheel which is set spinning using a large stick and which, because of its weight, retains its momentum, allowing the potter to sit down quickly and start to shape the clay before the resistance of hands on the clay eventually causes the wheel to slow down too much so that the whole process must be repeated. Wheel-throwing pots can increase the rate of production, but increased production may not make economic sense unless there are large markets and the ability to transport the pots to the markets effectively. A mixture of hand- and wheel-forming techniques may be employed such that the wheel is used not for throwing but for final shaping (Boileau 2005, Roux 2003, Roux and Courty 1998).

Where there are sharp changes in shape, that is carinations, it is sometimes easier to form these separately and then join the two pieces. That is how some necks and rims are formed. Handles are added after forming the pot. Traces indicating the method of manufacture for pinch pots, paddle and anvil, and coil pots can be very difficult to find because of surface treatment. There are some placements which suggest wheel-throwing but, for the most part, the key archaeological evidence of mass production is the large kiln sites, where the advantage is that the source of clay, the styles, and fabrics can all be typed and act as a known reference group and eventually a dating sequence. Sherds found elsewhere in the region can be matched against this and correctly attributed to source and date – for example, the regional ceramic sequence created within the Iron Age Danebury environs programme in the UK (Lisa Brown in Cunliffe 2000: 79–126, and see also Carver 1985 for urban pottery seriation and Hilgeman 2000 for a North American example). Where the industry is large-scale there would be sheds for drying or for storing finished products ready for market. However, drying a pot in preparation for firing is very important, as it needs to be done evenly and obviously in a protected area. This can make small-scale potting a seasonal occupation in temperate climates.

Firing techniques

Firing techniques vary and can create distinctive colour effects forming part of the intended decoration. Other decorative effects are often created before firing (see below). There are good overviews of firing and kiln technologies (Kingery 1997 and Rice 1997) as well as particular examples of distinctive kilns such as the Anazasi trench kilns (Blinman and Swink 1997) and ethnographic accounts of firings (Nicholson and Patterson 1989). Particular choices of technologies and fuels can be social choices as well as technological ones (Sillar 2000a). The essentials are that, if clay is still damp when it is fired, the water inside the clay will turn into steam and the pot will shatter. So pots need to be dried out thoroughly before firing. Successful

Figure 7.1 Wood and tree products as materials and artefacts: from this image, on most temperate sites, only the shells and glass beads (mask) and metal (endpieces of comb; hook of spindle) would survive, but careful excavation might reveal that they once formed part of perishable organic objects. Details: (a) tips of spears from the Highlands of Papua New Guinea, (b) a 'courting' comb from India as an example of wood as a composite material: made from small pieces of wood carefully bound within a set of steel endpieces and with some light charring as a decorative effect, (c) a cup or ladle crudely carved from solid wood

Source: author with thanks to the late Malti Nagar for the courting comb

Figure 7.2 Cordage, basketry, and textiles mostly from plant materials: from this image, on most temperate sites, nothing would survive. Details: (*a*) later prehistoric finely twined fabric from Robenhausen, circum-Alpine region, preserved in wet conditions, (*b*) cordage, and (*c*) various textile fragments preserved in desert conditions

Source: author

Figure 7.3 Hides, skins, hair, and fur as materials and artefacts: from this image, on most temperate sites, only the metal fittings (hide bottle and leather straps) and soft sandstone (used to finish the buckskin) would survive. Details: (*a*) very soft buckskin with its finishing stone, (*b*) a set rawhide decorated powder flask, (*c*) side view of the hide shield

Source: author

Figure 7.4 Bone, antler, ivory, teeth, and horn as materials and artefacts: from this image, on most temperate sites, ivory, bone, and antler would survive (provided the soil was not acidic) but only the metal fittings (powder horn) would survive from the objects of horn

Source: author

Figure 7.5 Shells as materials: a variety of shapes and colours allows the use of whole shells for decoration but some natural shapes are well suited to being used as spoons, scoops, or scrapers: from this image, on temperate sites, the shells would survive (provided the soil was not acidic) and, with careful excavation, the placement of the shells might reveal that they were once decorating a perishable organic object

Source: author

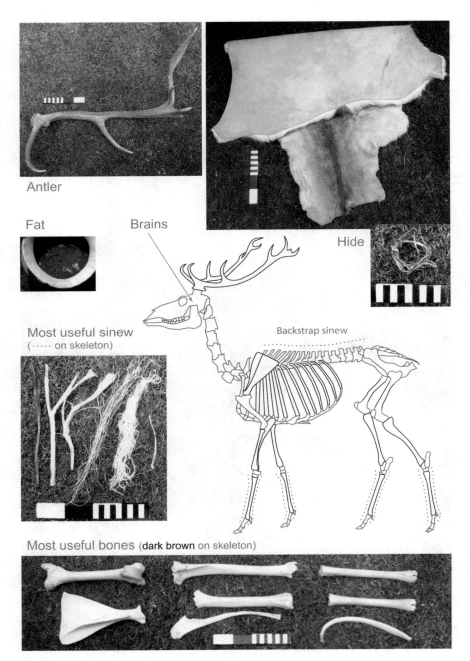

Antler

Fat

Brains

Hide

Most useful sinew
(····· on skeleton)

Backstrap sinew

Most useful bones (**dark brown** on skeleton)

Figure 7.6 One animal as a material resource: an example of a red deer

Source: author

Typha (also
Iris out of
picture)
*Cordage
Basketry*

Willow
*Cordage
Basketry*

Holly
*Cordage
Basketry*

Oak (also
beech, ash)
*Wood
Basketry*

Nettle
*Cordage
Textile*

Bramble
*Cordage
Basketry*

Lime
*Wood
Cordage
Textile*

Pine
*Wood
Resin*

Figure 7.7 Diverse plant raw materials available even in one small valley on Exeter University campus

Source: author

Figure 7.8 Common useful plants from temperate climates whose usage is little known in the modern world: (a) soft rush, Scirpus lacustris and large sedges, Carex sp., (b) Iris, Iris pseudacorus, and cattail, Typha sp., (c) young lime, Tilia, shoots and detail showing bast fibres being stripped; (d) tall stands of nettles, Urtica dioica

Source: author

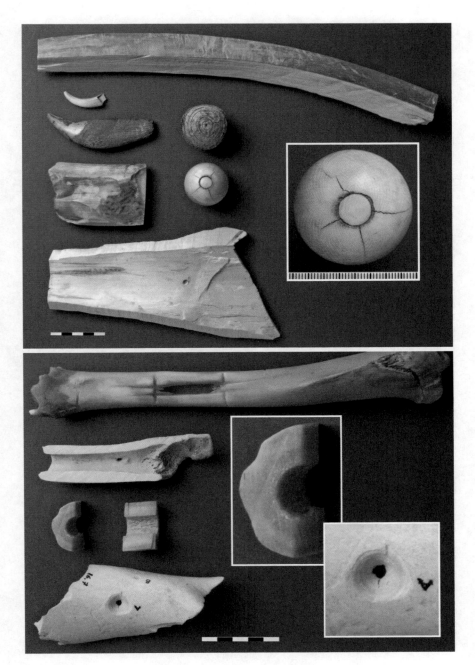

Figure 7.9 The shapes and structures of ivory and teeth, and bone

Source: author

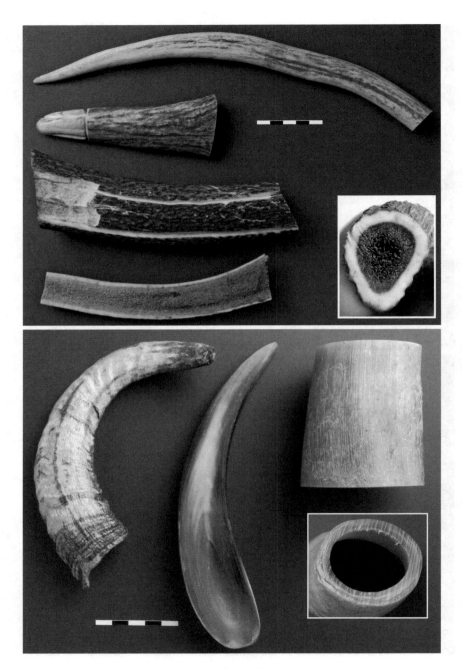

Figure 7.10 The shapes and structures of antler and horn

Source: author

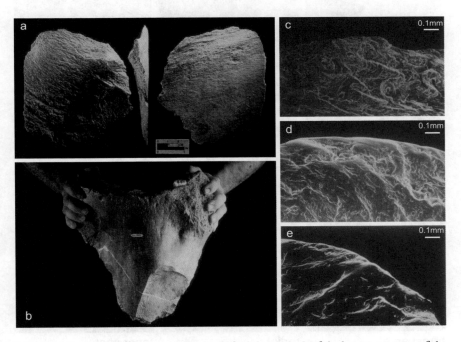

Figure 7.11 Bone tools and wear: (a) green or fresh bone can be flaked, retaining some flake features and providing a sharp edge (flake) or (b) a heavy-duty edge (cleaver); (c) modern flaked fresh elephant bone (SEM image), (d) the same after about ten minutes of cutting meat, (e) a similar wear pattern on one of the Lange/Ferguson site bone flake specimens

Source: Adrien Hannus

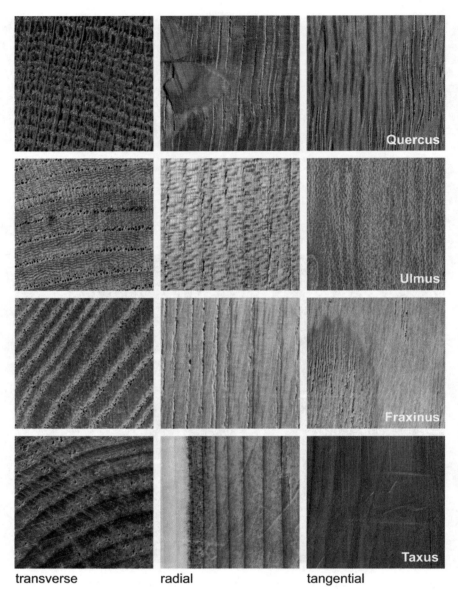

transverse   radial   tangential

Figure 7.12 Wood grain macroscopic characteristics

Source: author

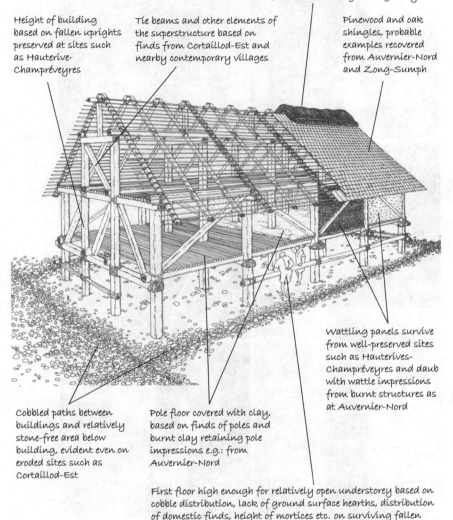

Pollen and macro remains indicate that
relatively little reed fringed the lake
c. 1000 BC, so reed thatching on ridge only

Height of building
based on fallen uprights
preserved at sites such
as Hauterive-
Champréveyres

Tie beams and other elements of
the superstructure based on
finds from Cortaillod-Est and
nearby contemporary villages

Pinewood and oak
shingles, probable
examples recovered
from Auvernier-Nord
and Zong-Sumph

Wattling panels survive
from well-preserved sites
such as Hauterives-
Champréveyres and daub
with wattle impressions
from burnt structures as
at Auvernier-Nord

Cobbled paths between
buildings and relatively
stone-free area below
building, evident even on
eroded sites such as
Cortaillod-Est

Pole floor covered with clay,
based on finds of poles and
burnt clay retaining pole
impressions e.g.: from
Auvernier-Nord

First floor high enough for relatively open understorey based on
cobble distribution, lack of ground surface hearths, distribution
of domestic finds, height of mortices etc. on surviving fallen
uprights and lack of evidence for house walls at ground level:
based on evidence from recent excavations of Neûchatel Late
Bronze Age villages

Figure 7.13 The archaeological evidence for wood used in a house in the circum-Alpine region
based on a reconstruction drawing by Béat Arnold (1990: fig. 69) of a house from Cortailloid-
Est c. 1000 BC

Source: after Coles, B. 1992: 148, fig. 16.1

Figure 7.14 Working wood: (a) the position of the bast fibre layer, (b) scarring on tree from bark removal, (c) bark used to construct a shelter, (d) adzing out solid wood to make a boat, (e) a pole lathe for wood turning, (f) prehistoric carved oak figure from Kingsteignton, UK (340 mm high), (g) splitting wood using a wooden wedge to rive the fibres apart

Source: author, except (f) Royal Albert Memorial Museum and Art Gallery, Exeter, and (g), Caroline Jeffra

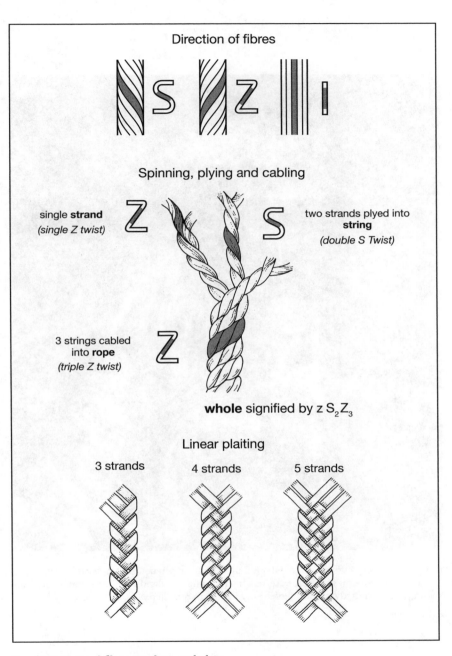

Figure 7.15 Twisted fibres, cordage, and plaits

Source: author with cordage description system based on Wendrich 1991

Figure 7.16 Uzbek craftswoman hand-spinning locally grown cotton. No distaff is used since the prepared and combed fibres are wrapped around her hand and unwound as they are spun up and collected on the spindle ready for her to dye then weave the yarn

Source: author

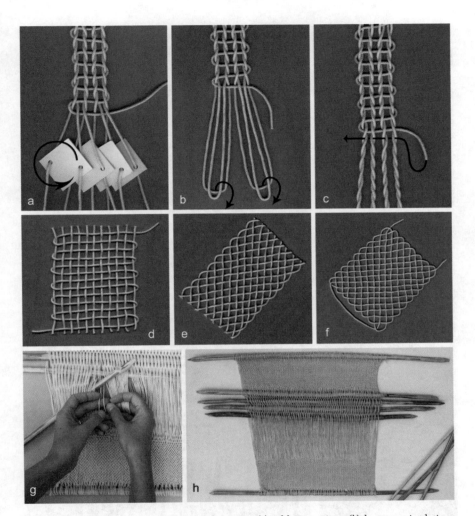

Figure 7.17 A variety of interweaving techniques: (*a*) tablet weaving, (*b*) loop manipulation, and (*c*) ply splitting all give the same woven pattern; likewise fragments of (*d*) woven interlacing with two sets of elements, (*e*) braided oblique interlacing with one set of elements, (*f*) knotted oblique interlacing with a single element would be indistinguishable; (*g*) sprang uses an odd number of warp threads held in place by two rods and as the threads are drawn over one another at the top they are held in place for a couple of rows by other rods, and (*h*) a mirror image of the weave is formed at the base

Source: Jacqui Carey

Figure 7.18 Basketry techniques: (*a*) plain/chequer weave, (*b*) coiled basket with spiral stitch and exposed core, (*c*) looped netting, (*d*) twilled weave, (*e*) coiled basket with lazy squaw stitch with core not visible, (*f*) knotted netting, (*g*) pairing/twining using a set of two weavers so that differences in colours can give alternating effect (1 and 2), or the angling of the pairing in two adjacent rows can be used to create a herringbone effect (3), (*h*) plain wicker and waling (here three rods woven under one and over two) which gives extra strength, (*i*) fitching, a pairing technique often used to hold passive uprights firmly in place especially where these are widely spaced and the work is largely open, as in this herring cran: the uprights are a wood billet, stripped whole withies and halved roundwood

Sources: author, except (*i*), photograph by Peter Montanez, annotations author

Figure 7.19 Uzbek craftswoman weaving on a ground loom with heddle and sheds (a). She sits on a low board which moves with her as the weaving progresses along the entire length of her veranda (b). Although the wooden weaving sword (c) used to beat down the weft would be a recognisable artefact if it survived, the pieces of wood making up the loom are not overly shaped and the ground traces are two stake holes some 7 metres apart
Source: author

a

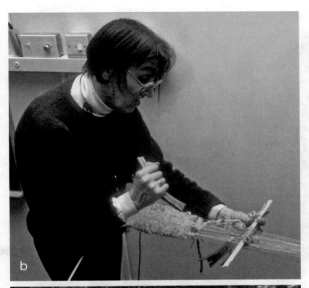

Figure 7.20 Other weaving devices and felt work: (a) upright warp-weighted loom showing a simple frame and groups of warp threads attached to loom weights. The angled view shows the method of raising different sheds using a separation of warp threads at the base with the alternate shed made by adjusting the heddle rod near the top. The most distinctive remnants archaeologically would be the weights, since the wood elements have little specific shaping features if found as individual fragments. (b) A backstrap loom tensioned by hooking the front part over a nail, branch or toe, with the back part round the waist and the body position adjusting the tension. Here, the weft is packed down using an antler comb which is most likely to be the only item to survive. (c) Felt tent being erected: felt strip visible in the foreground

Source: author, except (c), Valerie Maxfield

Figure 8.1 Flaked stone raw materials, artefacts, and hafted tools

Source: author

Figure 8.2 A selection of archaeological and modern polished and pecked stonework: including stone balls, polished axes (some in antler sleeves), an adze, chisel and shafthole implement; shale bracelet rough-out and fragment and button much degraded, modern amber showing reflective qualities and colours and duller amber Anglo-Saxon bead necklace

Source: author

Figure 8.3 Fragments of building stone, plaster, tesserae, and tile plus grinding stones as saddle and rotary querns and a pestle and mortar

Source: author, except pestle and mortar, Bruce Bradley, and handled set of quern stones, redrawn by author after Beloe 1892

Figure 8.4 Architectural stone: (*a*) flint flushwork and freestone from a Suffolk church, (*b*) carved detail of the lion gate at the palace of Myceneae, Greece, (*c*) Anasazi (Ancestral Puebloan) kiva in southwest Colorado, (*d*) carved and massive stonework at Exeter Cathedral, (*e*) a range of cliff dwellings at Cliff Palace, Mesa Verde National Park, southwest Colorado

Source: author, except (*c, e*), Bruce Bradley

Figure 8.5 Stone Sources. Primary and secondary geological contexts are both important sources of stone, e.g. (a) bands of darker flint nodules where they have formed in the parent chalk and are now exposed in sea cliffs and stacks at Beer, Devon, (b) beach deposits of shoals of erratic rocks including flint which have eroded from glacial clay tills forming low and rapidly eroding clay cliffs at Dimlington, northeast England, (c) geological deposits of obsidian nodules densely packed and large enough for knapping at Sty Nychia, Melos, Cyclades, where extensive

areas of the hillside (d) are covered with waste flakes from flaking preforms to take away, (e) shaped but discarded millstones and quarrying debris at the Millstonegrit quarries at Stanage Edge, UK, and (f) working debris and a broken column 18 m long left at the site of Mons Claudianus, a Roman tonalite gneiss quarry in the Eastern Desert of Egypt

Sources: author, except (f), Valerie Maxfield

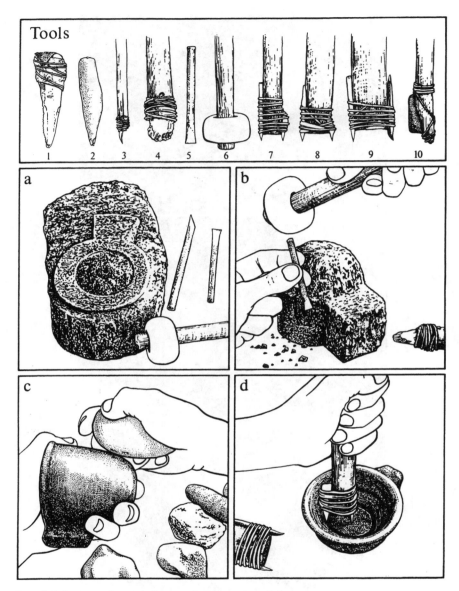

Figure 8.6 Stages in the manufacture of a Bronze Age shale cup

Source: Devon Archaeological Society (Sloper 1989) and Piran Bishop, illustrator

Successful predictive flaking:
- uses angle between platform and face of <90°
- directs blow close to edge
- takes account of the shape of face below the striking point.

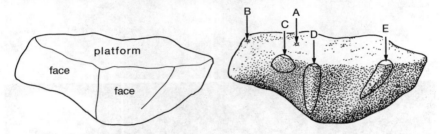

Striking event	Force applied near edge	Platform & face angle	Flake detached	
A	NO	>90°	NO	Herzian cone subsurface flaw
B	YES	>90°	NO	Partial Herzian cone and crushing
C	YES	<90°	YES	Conchoidal (shell) flake resulting from smooth face
D	YES	<90°	YES	Long narrow flake following long ridge on core
E	YES	<90°	YES	Angled flake following angled ridge

Figure 8.7 Predictive flaking: schematic diagram of a flint nodule and striking events to show consequent flakes and damage

Source: author

Figure 8.8 Different methods of applying force to detach flakes: (a) hard hammer percussion flaking, (b) soft hammer percussion flaking using an antler hammer with other wood soft hammers nearby, (c) indirect percussion using an antler punch and boxwood hammer, (d) pressure flaking in the hand, (e) pressure flaking using a chest press

Sources: author, except (b), Bruce Bradley

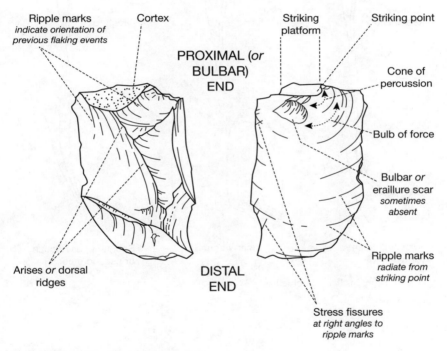

DORSAL FACE
A history of previous flaking events

VENTRAL FACE
Information on this flaking event

Ripple marks
indicate orientation of previous flaking events

Cortex

Striking platform

Striking point

PROXIMAL (or BULBAR) END

Cone of percussion

Bulb of force

Bulbar *or* eraillure scar *sometimes absent*

Arises *or* dorsal ridges

DISTAL END

Ripple marks *radiate from striking point*

Stress fissures *at right angles to ripple marks*

Figure 8.9 Flake drawing to show key features

Source: author

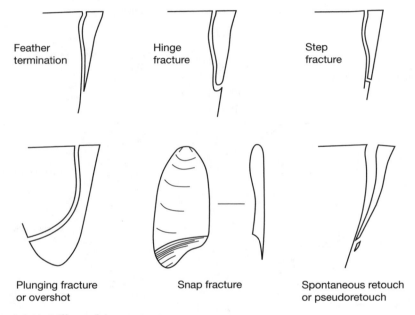

Figure 8.10 Different flake terminations

Source: author

Figure 8.11 A selection of classic flake stone types: (a) Early Archaic Dalton 'point' (also used as a knife), (b) Archaic spear point, (c) Predynastic Gerzian knife, (d) Clovis point, (e) gunflint, (f) mesolithic microliths, (g) early Neolithic leaf-shaped arrowheads, (h) late Neolithic transverse arrowheads, (i) Early Bronze Age barbed and tanged arrowheads, (j) Woodland period Snyder's point, (k) Solutrean laurel leaf

Source: author

frost damage

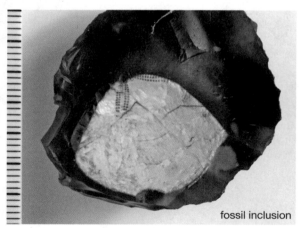

fossil inclusion

Figure 8.12 Effects from natural and cultural processes: (*a*) natural frost damage and fossil inclusions

Source: author

surface crazing
and fractures

reddening

heat damage

whitening and beginning
of calcination

surface crazing

Effects from natural and cultural processes: (b) heat damage

Source: author

fresh fracture

fracture showing penetration
of white patina

2 cm

stained white
patina

white patina

glossy patina over
faint white patina

glossy patina

Effects from natural and cultural processes: (c) patination
Source: author

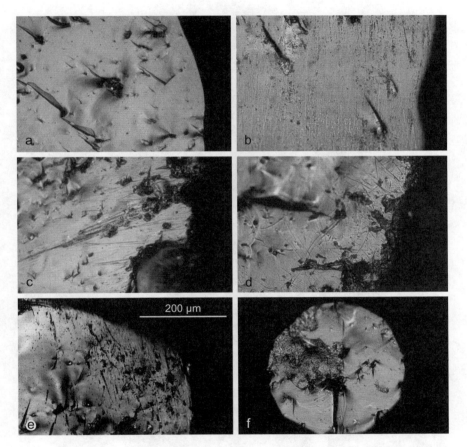

Figure 8.13 Use wear on obsidian tools (all at same scale) used to work different materials: (a) natural flaked surface with crystallites and stress fissures, (b) cereals, (c) wood, (d) hide, (e) bone, (f) residue from meat

Source: author

Figure 9.1 Fired clay as vessels of all shapes and sizes, pipes, bricks, tiles, and sherds
Source: author

Figure 9.2 The structural use of clay: (a) tiled brick buildings in Samarkand, (b) classic Hohokam adobe structures at Casa Grande, southern Arizona, (c) clay ovens, Pakistan (d) mud-brick walls, Uzbekistan and (e) roofed cob wall, Exeter, UK

Sources: author, except (b), Bruce Bradley, (c), Carl Knappett

Figure 9.3 Methods of forming clay vessels: (*a*) a pinch pot, (*b*) adding coils, (*c*) smoothing surfaces, (*d*) stick-turned wheel, (*e*) assistant turns wheel

Sources: (*a*), author, (*b–c*), Bruce Bradley, (*d*), Carl Knappett, (*e*), Bryony Kelly

Figure 9.4 Simple preparation of clay and traces of forming techniques: (*a*) crushed and sieved clay with sand temper to be added, (*b*) traces of coil formation visible in sherd break, (*c*) marks of removal from the wheel on pot base, (*d*) basket impression from use as a mould for forming pot

Source: author

Figure 9.5 'Protected' simple firing sequence: (*a*) a small pit is dug and a fire is lit to dry out the ground, (*b*) the ashes are spread over the base of the pit, (*c*) firewood is laid in the pit and the pots placed on top (*d*) with more combustible material placed around the pots and further material to be added nearby, (*e*) fire is lit, maintained, and (*f*) allowed to burn down to ash when it is covered with soil from the original pit to allow slow and protected cooling

Source: Bruce Bradley

Figure 9.6 Other kilns: (a) clamp kiln where pots are enclosed by the combustible material and then a layer of turves, (b) updraught kiln where pots are fired by stacking them in the upper storey with a separate fire box below ground level (and to the right of this photo)

Sources: (a), Caroline Jeffra, (b), Carl Knappett

Figure 9.7 Sherd breaks as information on firing temperatures and atmospheres, clay and temper effects (all at same scale, ×3), (*a*) earthenware sherd: porous grainy structure on fracture surface, (*b*) stoneware sherd: more vitrified, smoother fracture surface but very fine grainy texture just visible, (*c*) porcelain sherd: highly vitrified, smooth fracture surface, (*d*) orange/yellow profile, fired in an oxidising atmosphere, organics may or may not have been present originally; a mixture of angular fragments visible as inclusions, (*e*) black profile, fired in a reducing atmosphere, organics may or may not have been present originally, very fine quartz particles visible, (*f*) fired in an oxidising atmosphere with a mixture of inclusions, round dark ones likely to be grog, (*g*) angular and rounded mixture of inclusions and light grey internal area, (*h*) a double core margin effect suggesting a complex sequence; fired in a reducing atmosphere, cooled rapidly in air, reduced again with the colour changes having sharp boundaries, (*i*) sherd incompletely oxidised with alignment of shelly temper to the margins and rim formation

Source: author

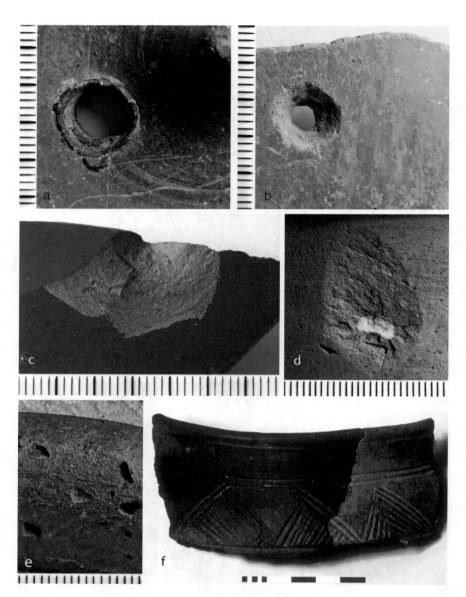

Figure 9.8 Other ceramic effects: (*a*) hole formed in wet clay, (*b*) hole bored in fired clay, (*c*) flake fractures visible on hard and fine sherd, (*d*) spall removed owing to expansion of calcium carbonate inclusion, (*e*) voids can be from fired-out organic material or leached out by soil conditions, (*f*) two refitting sherds showing leaching out of one buried in a different context

Source: author

Figure 9.9 Simple decoration techniques: (a) burnishing, (b) drag, (c) impression, (d) stamp, (e) slip, (f) mould, (g) Pueblo (prehistoric Hopi) Sityaki polychrome with mineral paints, (h) Puerco Pueblo Black-on-Red (red slip, black organic paint), (i) Gila polychrome: white (volcanic ash slip), red (iron oxide slip), black (organic)

Source: author

Figure 9.10 A variety of glazes and effects: (*a*) thinly applied lead-based glaze coloured green by copper, (*b*) thicker green lead glaze, (*c*) brown specks caused by iron, in the yellow lead-based glaze, (*d*) appliqué strips and glaze used in combination, (*e*) iron-rich slip under the lead glaze gives a brown colour to the glaze, (*f*) same sherd in side view clearly showing the glaze as a thin layer of glass except where the glaze has puddled inside the base, (*g*) majolica, (*h*) salt glaze (grey) coloured by underlying slips, e.g. cobalt (blue), (*i*) porcelain, Japanese Omari ware

Source: author

5 cm

Figure 9.11 Glass objects: Roman vessel and sherd, Roman glass gaming pieces and a selection of bead fragments plus Anglo-Saxon blue and amber coloured glass bead necklace (some using millefiori technique) now with a slightly crazed surface texture, whilst the various glass fragments (bottom left) show differing degrees of surface degradation

Source: author

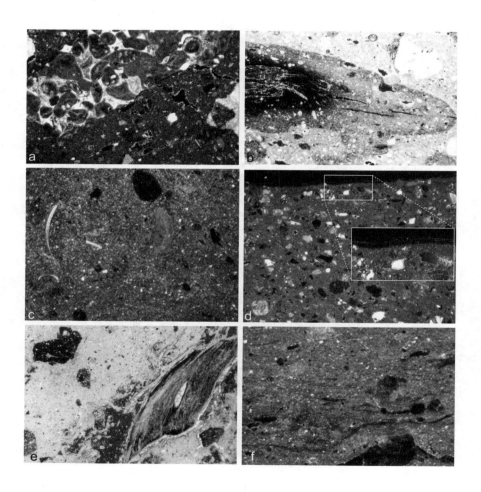

Figure 9.12 Ceramic thin sections (Scale: 4 mm across base of image): (*a*) large inclusion of microfossiliferous limestone (EBA sherd from Kilise Tepe, Turkey, Knappett in press), (*b*) curving inclusions (on left) of shell temper (sherd from Iasos, Turkey, Momigliano and Knappett forthcoming), (*c*) grog (i.e. fired pot, top left) and bone (striated inclusion, right) temper (EBA sherd from Kisile Tepe, Turkey, Knappett in press), (*d*) linear, partly burnt away organic temper (horizontal lines across centre) and a firing effect (darker oval feature across centre) visible microscopically (EBA sherd from Kilise Tepe, Turkey, Knappett in press), (*e*) main body of sherd has many inclusions of angular to sub-angular quartz, feldspars, and other minerals such as epidote plus some foraminifera (spheroidal microfossil, bottom left), with a red slip showing as a fine band lying on top (IA Black-on-Red ware sherd from Kinet Höyük, Turkey (Hodos et al. in press), (f) textural concentration features (these can be clay pellets or mudstones) and a clay mixing (dark narrow banding) feature (sherd from Iasos, Turkey)

Source: Carl Knappett

20 cm

Figure 10.1 Copper and copper alloy tools and weaponry
Source: author

Figure 10.2 Copper, copper alloy, lead and precious metals as jewellery, coinage, fittings, utensils, figurine, and bell; iron and steel edge tools and fittings

Source: author

Figure 10.3 An overview of the key archaeological raw materials for metalwork: native metals, and ores used for smelting

Source: author

Figure 10.4 Gold piece showing hammer marks and burnishing and some lipping at edges

Source: author with thanks to R. van de Noort, 2007

$$CuCO_3.Cu(OH)_2 \rightarrow 2CuO+CO_2+H_2O$$

$$2CuO+CO \rightarrow Cu_2O+CO_2$$

$$Cu_2O+CO \rightarrow 2Cu \text{ (metal) } +CO_2$$

Figure 10.5 Modern copper smelt in a small crucible: (a) crushed malachite, (b) with charcoal added, (c) placed in a charcoal furnace where smelting resulted in small amounts of copper metal according to the chemistry shown

Source: author and Gill Juleff with thanks to Neil Burridge

Figure 10.6 Casting copper and copper alloy: (*a*) casting high-tin bronze in a three-piece ceramic mould, with an unusual wooden mould visible in the foreground, (*b*) tin cast in a sand mould, (*c*) stone moulds with copper and bronze castings on the ground, (*d*) three-piece ceramic mould with vents for air expansion and a funnel effect at the top, (*e*) and (*f*) the bronze and copper casts from an axe mould and the sections through these

Source: (*a*)–(*d*), author, Julia Wiecken and Andrew Young; (*e*)–(*f*), author and Gill Juleff

Figure 10.7 Smelting and forging iron:
processes and archaeological evidence.
Experimental shaft furnace charged
with crushed ore and charcoal reacting
with the chemistry shown to produce
a bloom of metal which would need
to be forged to get rid of impurities
then shaped into the desired form

Source: author and Gill Juleff with thanks
to the Wealdon Iron Research Group

Crushed haematite

Extraction trench

Charcoal

Reduction zone
$$3Fe_2O_3+CO\rightarrow2Fe_3O_4+CO_2$$
$$Fe_3O_4+CO\rightarrow3FeO+CO_2$$
$$FeO+CO\rightarrow Fe \text{ (metal)} +CO_2$$

Combustion zone
$$C+O_2\rightarrow CO_2$$
$$CO_2+C\rightarrow2CO$$

Excavating furnace walls

Bloom

Forge

Hammerscale

Figure 10.8 Smelting iron and producing steel in Sri Lanka: (*a*) hillside furnace extending along the face of hill with the back wall cut into the hillside, (*b*) a front wall of clay with a line of tuyères at the base (*c*) tap slag can be seen running out of the base, (*d*) the resulting bloom of metal cut and polished to show structure, (*e*) forging the bloom on a traditional anvil

Source: Gill Juleff

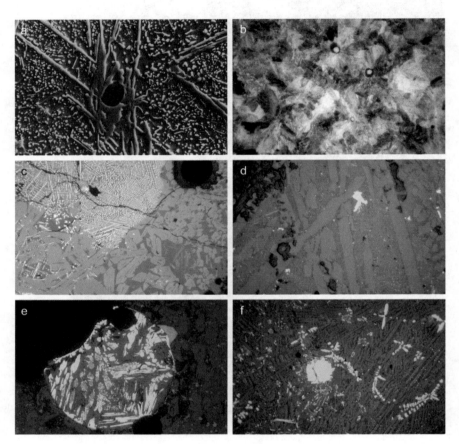

Figure 10.9 Metal sections to show structures: (*a*) crucible steel ingot showing an inclusion within a high-carbon steel (SEM image polished and etched section), (*b*) high-carbon steel showing a fully eutectoid structure (polished and etched), (*c*) iron slag showing typical three phases of dark grey glassy matrix, mid-grey iron silicate, and white dendritic iron oxide (polished 150×), (*d*) copper slag with pyrites inclusions (brassy) (polished 120×), (*e*) copper prill within a slag indicating possible smelting of copper, dark hole is post-depositional corrosion (polished 150×), (*f*) copper ore inclusion within a slag

Source: Gill Juleff

firing is also more likely if the dried pot reaches the firing temperature of the clay gradually and then sustains that temperature for a period known as the 'soak time'. When the clay matures or sinters, the clay particles bond together. This begins at about 415°C, but is a slow process at this temperature. With slightly higher temperatures, the process can be completed more quickly. Many different kinds of kilns and different forms of fuels can be used, but variations in fuels and kiln styles give different temperatures and, as mentioned previously, quick changes in temperature can result in pots fracturing because they cannot withstand the sharp temperature change. That is why kilns which separate the fire from direct contact with the pot are likely to have a lower wastage rate. That is not to say that bonfires cannot be used very successfully to fire pots. With certain modifications, the pots can be protected during some of the most crucial beginning and closing phases of the firing.

The sequence illustrated in figure 9.5 shows a 'protected' bonfire firing. On a still day a small pit is dug and a fire is lit in this; this dries out the ground getting rid of any residual moisture and creates an ash bed on which to lay the firing materials and then the pots themselves for the firing. The soil from the pit is reserved for later use. The bonfire is built up, with the firewood being placed directly around the pots to be fired, and the combustible material is lit. Small amounts of extra firewood will be added, but the main event is the building of the firewood and the pots into one mound, with combustible material at the base. As the combustible material burns away, so the pots start to become exposed. It is at this point that they are most vulnerable and there are various ways of protecting the pots. One way would be to have stacked waster sherds around the outside of the pots to be fired, another way might have been to have had a low turf wall surrounding the pit. If there is strong wind or rain the pots will be too exposed to extremes of temperature and will fracture. As the fire burns slowly down, the pots become more exposed, and can be left to cool overnight in the ashes with the addition of some soil to cover the material. The whole can then be excavated and the pots allowed to cool down slowly the following day. Such a pit firing leaves a very shallow burnt depression in the ground and would be difficult to distinguish from other forms of burning events. It is also likely to be an off-site activity.

The clamp kiln illustrated (figure 9.6) has used a similar technique of lighting a fire to dry out the ground, with the pots then placed on the ash. A small turf wall is built up around the area. Combustible material is placed around the pots and the whole is covered over by the turves. Here, the clamp kiln is being lit from a central hole initially, to draw the fire upwards before it is closed down. The firewood itself forms a structure for the turf to lie up against. The fire is left to burn down and to cool completely. In some cases, the combustible material will have left a void and so there will be some collapse of this form of kiln, but the turves should provide protection against quick changes in temperatures and thermal shock breakage. Such a kiln would leave very little evidence in the ground, other than a burnt shallow depression and again, is likely to be an off-site activity. Before the use of formal kilns, which reach higher temperatures and may have bigger piles of waste material (called wasters), there is very little direct evidence of firing techniques, and the main evidence comes from the sherds themselves.

The Pakistani updraught kiln shown in figure 9.6 has a firing chamber at below ground level and a permanent floor with vents, so that the fire is drawn up into the cylindrical chamber of the kiln. Large waster sherds can be used to protect the pot, as seen in the photograph. The kiln is filled from the top and can use a variety of fuel sources. Such kiln structures have lower wastage rates and can be reused many times. The specific design of these varies. Some have tall chimneys to increase the draught in much the same way as modern chimneys. Other kiln designs draw the heat up and then down over the pots to be fired, and these are known as downdraught kilns, but essentially the key distinction is the separation of the combustible material providing the heat from the pots which are to be fired. In Britain, the Potteries area at Stoke-on-Trent is famous for its bottle-shaped updraught kilns which produced pottery for export to much of the world (Thomas 1971).

Archaeological discoveries of kilns are usually made because of large deposits of waster materials. These are distorted shapes, cracked pots, glaze mistakes, items fusing together. On such sites, the finds trays may well be wheelbarrows – there are vast amounts of wastage material from kilns. However, a sherd can reveal much about the firing conditions if not the precise nature of the kiln, and vitrification is a clue to temperature.

Firing effects

The first firing effect is observed by looking at the porosity of the sherd wall (figure 9.7a–c). With higher temperatures the sherd wall becomes denser: the clay vitrifies. Figure 9.7a–c shows three sherds of earthenware, stoneware, and porcelain all at the same size. The texture of the sherd walls is visibly different as the porosity decreases as the firing temperature increases (although over-firing can also increase the porosity, allowing well-rounded blister-like voids to form). The open texture of the earthenware profile even allows some of the lines from forming the pot to be clearly visible and the pores which make the pot permeable can clearly be seen. Figure 9.7d–i shows sherd profiles with examples of a variety of tempers and firing effects.

The second firing effect is manifested in the colour tones of the interior and exterior of the sherd wall and within the heart of the material. Organic material, if either added by the potter or naturally present in the clay, would begin to burn away at 200°C. The carbon material within the clay on the surface of the pot will burn away first. If the temperature is maintained or increased, carbon within the wall of the pot will also be used. This is important because there are atmospheric firing effects that give different colours according to whether the pots are being heated in an oxidising atmosphere, where oxygen is plentiful, or where oxygen access in the kiln has been limited and thus the burning results in carbon monoxide gasses and creates a reducing atmosphere. In particular, reduced firing gives grey and black tones, whereas oxidised firing gives red and orange tones. This can most clearly be seen in the sequence of sherd profiles shown in figure 9.7d–i. The sherd in 9.7e is very dark: it was fired in a reducing atmosphere and it is likely that organic material was naturally present in the clay. In contrast, 9.7d is a buff-coloured sherd with slightly darker core, indicating an oxidising atmosphere. In some cases, the interior surface of the pot has a different colour from the exterior, or within the sherd wall there is a section with a different colour called the core. The core and the margins of the pot can have a very distinct colour boundary in fine pastes or where sharp changes have taken place in atmospheric conditions; blurred boundaries tend to occur with less fine clays or in pots fired at lower temperatures. In many respects, the oxidation layer on the outside can indicate what happened to the pot at the end of the firing. It may have been removed from the reducing atmosphere of the kiln and left in the open air whilst still warm. In such conditions, the outer area of the pot would become oxidised. If ash partially covered the pot, then an uneven firing effect would result, with those parts of the pot exposed to the air rendered red, but other covered areas would have the grey and black colours of reduced firing conditions. Sometimes quite complicated sequences of colour changes can be observed in the sherd walls (see figure 9.7h for an example). Pots which have reddened external walls, but grey cores, may have been fired in an oxidising atmosphere but for insufficient time for oxidation to penetrate fully throughout the body of the pot, especially if there was originally organic material present in the clay.

Although colour is generally an important guide to firing conditions, it should be noted that, in bonfire firings and some other simple mixed firings where fuel and ceramics are in close proximity, smoke effects can cause dark patches, varying the colour even on the surface of one sherd, as well as whole pots and particular pots within different areas of the fire. It is the ubiquitous iron that usually colours most clays into red or grey tones, depending upon the atmosphere in the kiln. Iron-poor calcareous clays give buff or pink fabrics. However, white clay is exceptional: because of this it was desired for creating fine and pale later ceramics such as china and porcelain. These also required special temper materials which would not colour the pottery, which explains why flint was calcined and crushed in mills to serve the pottery industry (e.g. Cheddleton Mill, UK, Copeland 1972), and with bone likewise added as temper in the production of 'bone china'.

Overview: a sherd as a source of information

The firing qualities, decoration, and inclusions can all be used to characterise particular kinds of pottery and, if supplemented by scientific analyses such as petrological studies, can result in specific sources being identified, thus outlining patterns of exchange and trade. The sherd in the hand is a very important form of archaeological evidence. Where it is combined with contextual information its value increases again and, because pottery is so durable once it is fired, it tends to be a dominant force in studies of material culture and artefacts found on sites. A range of different effects can be seen in figure 9.8. In terms of understanding object biographies it is important to distinguish between the hole made in soft clay and the hole bored into fired clay as part of a separate and subsequent act. Figure 9.8a shows how the wet clay is displaced and forms a rim around the hole, whereas the bored hole (figure 9.8b) has a porous surface and has also worn away the slip coating. Figures 9.8c and d show the conchoidal fracture qualities of a hard and fine-grained sherd which has been damaged on its already broken edge some time after firing, compared with the spall fractured from the pot during the firing process by the uneven expansion from the inclusion within the sherd wall. Figure 9.8e shows the voids on the surface which can occur where organic material has been fired out of the pot, or where a mineral inclusion has been weathered out of the sherd. Figure 9.8f offers a note of caution by showing two refitting sherds which have become very different in appearance simply because they were buried in different post-depositional contexts within the same site. Thus close observation of a sherd reveals information about features from manufacture, usage, and post-depositional effects.

Decoration

Most decoration is effected before firing but it is treated out of the production sequence order here because of the particular ways in which archaeologists have used decoration as a means of distinguishing key types with implications for dating. Styles change quickly through time. It is possible to become familiar with key styles of decoration and pastes, so that broad chronological phasings of different materials can be rapidly achieved by eye. The way in which this works is exemplified by the sherds shown in figures 9.9 (textural and slip effects) and 9.10 (for glaze effects). All of the sherds shown could be given a broad date within a particular region on the basis of their decoration effect or texture. The sherds also convey the sizes and shapes of the original pots, which offer further information as certain forms are very characteristic of chronological and regional types. Although highly specialist knowledge might be necessary to study pottery in detail and give fine detail on phasing, major categories such as majolica, Samian, cord-impressed and salt-glazed wares are readily recognisable and, once the characteristics are outlined, earthenwares, stonewares, and porcelain are likewise distinguishable. In general, a sherd will vary in terms of its colour, hardness, feel, visual texture, inclusions, surface decoration or treatment, slips or glazes and the effects of these, as well as its form. In all these, the textures and features most obvious to a modern-day viewer are the form and colour of the finished vessel, and to some extent, its performance. Finely fired porcelain will ring and has particular tonal qualities. Other earthenware sounds will be familiar to most people as the noise of a flowerpot touching the ground or another object. Some mugs will be stoneware fired. Thus, even in the modern world, people will be aware of differences in ceramics and can be attuned to these, with a little reflection on the technologies and differences involved. Likewise, once outlined, various decoration techniques are distinguishable. Figure 9.9 shows the difference between burnished surfaces, marks made by displacing wet clay by drawing a line versus impressed and stamped decoration, slip-coated surfaces and moulded decoration, and the kind of colours it is possible to achieve using minerals and ash. Figure 9.10 is a contrast because the glazes offer a greater colour range, as discussed below.

Although the Romans made some rare glazed vessels, up until the twelfth century most decoration was a textural alteration formed either by impressing or altering the surface in some way, or by adding a coating of mineral or organically derived paints or slips over the pot. A slip is a high-water-content clay, which is poured or painted on to a dry pot, although dipping is also possible. It is possible to use self-slip made from the same clay as the pot or to use different colours of clay or add pigments to create decorative effects. Occasionally, pot decorating tools can be found, but these can be as simple as a bird bone, a fingernail, or a smooth stone which can be used to polish the surface – this is known as burnishing. Figure 9.9a shows an example of burnishing with linear facets: finer and even similar surface effects are known as polishing. Burnishing and polishing must be done when a pot is leather hard, as it will reach a stage where it is too dry. By creating a compressed outer layer, the permeability of the pot is reduced.

If clay becomes ceramic when it is fired and some of these particles vitrify and fuse together in an irreversible process, so the process of vitrification is also one of becoming glass. That is why clay and glass can be seen as a continuum. The glaze has to vitrify at a lower temperature than the ceramic body but the development of glazes created many more variations in decoration.

Glazes

A glaze is essentially a layer of glass melted onto the surface of a pot. It can be coloured by different additives: one of the first of these used was lead, because it has a low melting temperature of under 1000°C. Lead itself gives a yellowish glaze, but in typical early medieval examples this was coloured green by the addition of copper, as seen in figure 9.10a. Later and finer examples had a more thickly applied glaze and thus a more solid green colouring (figure 9.10b). These sorts of techniques were used on green glazed pots called Tudor greenwares and are still commonly applied. Some of these kinds of glazes were used in combination with appliqué strips, especially on jugs (figure 9.10d). A yellowish lead glaze could also be coloured by specks of iron added to the glaze, giving a brown speckled appearance (figure 9.10c), although some clays which are iron-rich can also give a brown glaze. Where an iron-rich slip is applied underneath a glaze, this can colour the whole glazed area a rich brown (figure 9.10e and f shows in plan and profile the thickly applied glaze with the iron-rich slip applied thinly beneath). Later glazes use other materials such as tin and cobalt, giving multiple colour effects and distinctive general groups such as majolica (figure 9.10g), stonewares with cobalt glazes (figure 9.10h), and in later periods fine porcelains (figure 9.10i).

Glazes have the advantages of making the open pores of earthenware more water-proof, although the use of different clays allows stoneware firing to solve this problem in a different way. In particular, in the fifteenth century double firings were achieved, where the pot was fired to form the finished body (biscuit firing) and after a glaze had been applied a second firing took place. Initially, glazes were simple powders spread onto the surface of the pot, but the biscuit firing allowed a more even application of the glaze, since the porous fired surface absorbed the water of the suspension and allowed a thin, fine coating to be formed. Salt glazing was common in the sixteenth and seventeenth centuries, especially in Germany. This glaze gives a very glossy effect, and takes its name from the addition of salt late in the stages of a firing. The salt vaporised and combined with the clay body, to form a glaze on the surface, but hydrochloric acid fumes were given off during firing. Newer glaze formulas required higher-temperature firings and were developed later.

Glass

Glasses are covered as part of this clay chapter, because by far their most prevalent use and occurrence for most archaeologists is as a glaze in later periods of pottery production. That is not to say that glass is not an important material in its own right. There are some materials which have had to be very summarily treated for reasons of space in this book, and glass is undoubtedly one of them. For those working in periods or areas of the world where glass is a significant material, Henderson (2001 and 2000: 24–108) offers an excellent overview of the range of techniques which can be applied and the issues in glass production and study. These references cover glass as a material and as a glaze to colour or to improve the impermeability of ceramics. However, in many areas of the world and for vast periods of time, glass is a highly specialised find. Figure 9.11 shows some archaeological glass as complete Roman and modern vessels, along with beads and gaming counters, a vessel fragment, and glass fragments in various states of deterioration. The bead necklace is Anglo-Saxon and has some multicoloured beads, showing the millefiori technique where differently coloured rods of glass are fused together, and then used to make beads. The image shown makes clear the special qualities of glass – firstly as something rare in the ancient world because of its translucency. Whilst we live in a world which has many instances of translucent glass, the ability to see through an object or to have light reflected back with sparkle would have been so much rarer in the past and it is difficult to downplay the significance of this for the creation in glass of translucent objects. However, some of the earliest uses of glass are as highly coloured materials for decorative purposes. The key issues of glass materiality are that it is a highly specialist technology and remained a high-status product for much of its history, offering intense colours for decorative items, but also translucency and delicacy.

Glass itself is best understood as a super-cooled liquid: it does move and flow but too slowly for it to be perceptible. There is no particular alignment or structure within it, as there is with a mineral. This lack of order is a characteristic of liquids, and glass can hold in suspension other materials that help to colour it. A few general comments about the production of glass will be offered here. Glass was first made in the Near East around 1700 BC and was primarily reserved for small items of jewellery forming part of very rich sets of material culture. It is primarily composed of silica, to which soda, potash, or lime has been added. Other materials can be added as a flux though these may also have their own history of supply and demand (Shortland et al. 2006). Glassmaking requires high temperatures and the material can then be softened so that it can be moulded into a variety of shapes. The colouring of glass can be deliberate using minerals, but the translucency of glass can be compromised by this and clear glass can also be a desirable feature, which means that mineral impurities from the raw materials may have to be extracted in order to obtain the desired effect. For example, cobalt makes glass blue, copper will add green colours and a dark olive tone is the result of iron impurities. The earlier production of glass was thus highly specialised and its usage was restricted. Because glass finds tend to be quite specialist, there are some themed discussions on key types and periods, for example Brugmann (2004) on Anglo-Saxon beads, Fleming (1997, 1999) on aspects of Roman glass, and discussions on faience (e.g. from Egypt Nicholson and Peltenburg 2000, Henderson 2000; and on isolated finds elsewhere Sheridan 1995).

As with other transformed material industries, compositional analyses of glass are common (e.g. Baxter et al. 2006), and studies of the technologies involved and sources of raw materials are also investigated (e.g. Silvestri et al. 2006). Glass can also be recycled, and some scientific analyses demonstrate this practice in the past (Degryse et al. 2006).

Glass was more widely available from colonial periods onwards and offers different research themes in these more recent periods. Glass was the material for trade beads in the colonial period (Sprague 2000), and bottle glass is a particular find on colonial-period sites (Lawrence 2006). Bottle glass was valued by native peoples for its exceptional knapping qualities. Aboriginal glass knapping is well known (Harrison 2000, 2003), and some modified glass tools in Louisiana have potential as information on African-American knapping (Wilkie 2000). Also, blue beads could have been a culturally significant object for African Americans (Stine et al. 2000). These kinds of approaches addressing very recent periods offer some of the most exciting new developments in such studies.

Function

Function study rests on the properties of clay but takes into account context, content, use wear, and secondary usage. Clay is used for waterproofing, provides containers for transport, storage, cooking, and eating, can be built into ovens, furnaces, and kilns, and may be formed into tools, models and figurines, bricks, tiles, daub, and mud brick. The colour, form, and decoration can all encode social information. Pots to us are overwhelmingly about vessels. However, this use initially may not have been so obvious to prehistoric societies. The earliest fired clay objects are statuettes and figures from Upper Palaeolithic Dolni Vestonice (Vandiver et al. 1989). Ceramics are a transformative technology and it could have been seen as a magical transformation of a material to make objects that were figures and representational art. The adoption of pottery for vessels comes at a much later period, and, although there are aceramic Neolithics and pre-Neolithic ceramics, it tends to be associated strongly with the advent of farming and perhaps a slightly more settled way of life.

Although we see cooking pots as enabling the direct application of heat to raise the temperature of a liquid inside a vessel, this does not seem to have been prevalent in the earliest phases of pottery use: the first use of pots at early ceramic sites is not necessarily for food (Vitelli 1989, Rice 1987, 1990). It is possible to use skin bags or baskets as cooking containers, or employ other forms of cooking which do not need any container. Perhaps cultural traditions of food preparation, cooking techniques and containers are strongly conservative social elements.

In periods when vessels are frequent there can be marked functional divisions. Pots as part of funerary rites or in other ritual contexts offer different information from the pots used and broken in the course of everyday tasks. The shape of a pot offers the most obvious information on function, usually suggesting a broad spectrum of uses. Some forms are simply impossible to use in particular ways – a broad open dish is not suitable for carrying liquid, whereas closed neck shapes are. Roman amphorae are seen as the ubiquitous transport vessels for liquids in their period, the vessels that took those goods around the Roman world. Studies of the performance qualities of different vessels (see above) are allying technical details of form and fabric with potential usage, giving information on the links between technology and function, as cultural choices.

It is easy to lose sight of the other crucial dimension of pot function: what the pots contained. Prior to the 1990s, researchers had looked at the soil that was remaining in pots, or, occasionally, residues such as a fired crust on the outside of a vessel or organic material preserved by metal corrosion, but for the most part the function of pots remained unknown. This is changing thanks to the discovery that the remnants of lipids and proteins can survive in the porous pot walls (Evershed et al. 1991, 1992, 2001, and see Chapter 4). This has been one of the most exciting scientific analyses developments in recent years. These sorts of residue studies based on chemical techniques have been supplemented by use wear studies based on fracture mechanics and by using experimental and ethnographic data as their reference material to investigate the primary function of vessels (e.g. Skibo 1992), and also individual sherds as tools (López Varela et al. 2002). The chemistry can give very definitive answers but it may also mix results. The use wear analysis could be applied more widely and perhaps in a more generalised way. In all of these respects, wear and residue studies on pots have started to come of age and provide more detailed information on the function of ceramics.

There are also other uses or appreciations of clay evident from the Upper Palaeolithic, for example the children's footprints, deliberately impressed into the clay floor at Niaux Cave, France (Bahn and Vertut 1988: figure 3) and the clay bison at Tuc d'Audoubert, France (Bahn and Vertut 1988: figures 61–2 and 120–2). The plastic medium of clay is appreciated for the qualities of being able to be shaped into a form, or to take an impression, but these are in very special places and the clay is serving distinctive purposes. Examples of ceramic vessels set down into benches exist from Akrotiri, Cylcades (Doumas 1983: 53–4 and figs 22–4). This is a good example of how such clay materials would have been used in a living context, as both house walls and benching and creating a permanent environment for these large storage vessels. As mentioned above, sherd fragments can also have a secondary use and be recycled. They can serve as the basis for making other objects such as spindle whorls or as the ostraca of the Roman period, when anything from shopping lists to short notes could be written on scrap sherds of pottery (e.g. Maxfield and Peacock 2006). Both clay and fired clay can be a material for forming artefacts.

Overview

In the great wealth of data available from pottery, it is easy to lose sight of the fact that pots are tools and that clay is used for more than ceramics. The latter is to some extent understandable because the evidence for the unfired use of clay is so much more ephemeral. It is, however, possible to see layers of clay capping barrows (Lynch 1998) and these could have been as much about colour as anything else although raw clay is as likely to be part of the symbolic use of mineral resources as stone (Taçon 2004). Thus, colour might have been quite an important and underrated aspect of raw material selection. One example of excavators trying to take account of unfired clay used for houses, storage facilities, furniture, or features such as ovens or kilns draws attention to the volume of clay that has been used for these purposes and interestingly suggest that the non-ceramic clay and ceramic clay have different sources, tempers, production processes, and different life histories (Tringham and Stevanović 1990: 323). It would be interesting to see other studies evaluating the use of clay as a raw material for non-ceramic use.

As fired material, vessels overshadow brick and tile. There are various studies that have been completed on the breakage rates, depending upon particular functions and the rates at which households use particular different varieties of pots. The manner of their use affects the quality and quantity of ceramics in the archaeological record. In later periods ceramics dominate the finds on excavation sites and field surveys. We are used to seeing whole pots illustrated for particular periods simply because they were deliberately deposited complete in their own right or as containers for other substances or items placed in the ground. The relationship of these buried pots to those which existed in the living context is not always so clear. Furthermore, not all kinds of ceramics survive equally well in the soil. Apart from accidental firing, there is also the problem that there is a bias in the archaeological record towards the survival of those ceramic objects which have been fired at higher temperatures, since these tend to be less porous and therefore less susceptible to damage in the soil. That is especially true of earthenware ceramics from prehistoric contexts, which are then brought to the surface with a plough. These will not survive the frosts of one winter on the surface because water enters the pores and when it freezes expands, fragmenting the pot sherd. Equally the earth tones and small size of prehistoric sherds will not stand out to the untrained eye, whereas whole vessels inadvertently discovered, or colourful pieces, will attract attention. Chance finds of pottery are thus biased. Where systematic surveys have been undertaken, though, ceramics, bricks, and tiles have provided excellent indicators of the date, size, type, function, and status of a site. One of the problems of archaeological ceramics especially, but also structural clay items, is their sheer quantity. They can create statistical and logistical issues for the writing of reports and storage and analysis, let alone processing on site. Table 9.1 shows that pottery studies contain an inherent contradiction: they are key dating evidence on most sites where they exist and yet there is no common and ready scientific technique to date them. Where styles change rapidly and historical sources can tie these in to narrow date ranges it is difficult to see how the stylistic information dating contexts could be improved upon.

Table 9.1 Techniques of analysis used to address key questions for clay artefacts

CLAY	What is it made from?	What is the character of the material and can it be grouped?	Where did the raw material(s) come from?	How was it made?	When was it made? Or when was it deposited?	Was it used? What for?
	Identification	Characterisation	Sourcing/provenance	Technology	Direct dating	Function
Fired clay objects Very frequent	Clays are easily recognisable though more specific identification of the clay chemistry may be necessary for understanding an effect or identifying a source; specific identification of glazes and pigments might involve chemical analyses	Mineral inclusions and size/shapes in thin sections may allow grouping which are not possible by eye: heavy mineral analyses or trace elements in the paste may allow groupings	See left but requires comparative reference collection from known locations and for these to show distinctive characteristics	By eye using macro features; chemical analyses or mineral changes to give information on mixing, forming, decorating and firing conditions	No common technique (though AMS ^{14}C may be possible on adhering soot or organic residues; TL possible but effects of local conditions need to be gauged via dosimetry)	Form gives some limits; potentially macro- and microscopic wear traces; residue analyses (lipids, complex proteins)

In situ fired/baked structural clay *Occasional*	Clays are easily recognisable though more specific identification of the clay chemistry may be necessary for understanding an effect or identifying a source	Irrelevant	Largely irrelevant	By eye using macro features	For fired clay archaeomagnetism is possible but requires regional archaeomagnetic variation through time to be known; TL possible but effects of local conditions need to be gauged via dosimetry: for baked clay organic material within the clay may enable AMS ^{14}C	Macroscopic features
Unfired clay *Occasional* *Frequent as mudbrick*	Clays are easily recognisable though more specific identification of the clay chemistry may be necessary for understanding an effect or identifying a source	Mineral inclusions and size/shapes in thin sections may allow grouping which are not possible by eye: heavy mineral analyses or trace elements in the paste may allow groupings	Potentially see left but requires comparative reference collection from known locations and for these to show distinctive characteristics	By eye using macro features	No technique	Form gives limits

However, dates for undifferentiated material in prehistoric periods would prove useful. Here, the developments in residue studies show that AMS dates from residues may yet offer such a technique though it would not be common or cheap. It is also evident that in many respects the key ceramic scientific analysis is to characterise the paste but not necessarily to source the materials to a particular point in the landscape.

Ellis (2006) gives an excellent account of artefact handling in the field and conservation issues. On-site cleaning should not be invasive or vigorous, and objects cleaned with water should be thoroughly dried to avoid mould growing later. Where calcareous deposits have built up on the surface, it is best if these are cleaned by a trained conservator, as putting sherds in dilute hydrochloric acid will also destroy any calcareous slips or tempers and it is difficult to remove the acid fully. Ellis also stresses the need for a good research design, centred on behaviour and social dimensions, with both numbers and analyses as equally valueless without a research question (Ellis 2006: 245). However, there is a basic set of information normally included in any report: a sherd count and perhaps more complex analyses to record it against form types and paste types. Sherd weights can be an adjunct to this and it may be useful to present the minimum number of vessels or estimated vessel equivalents. Such summaries can facilitate comparisons across sites, periods, and regions.

Pots from the Neolithic onwards have tended to be one of the most prolific sources of archaeological evidence and it is scarcely surprising that they have gained prominence in the way in which cultures are defined. Often it is the pottery that is used as the shorthand for describing a culture, for example the Linear Band Keramik of Neolithic Europe. However, the significance of ceramic evidence to the archaeologist is not just one of convenience for present-day purposes. Pots were often important blank canvases on which to encode cultural and functional style, and so the styles defining archaeological cultures were presumably relevant to the society concerned, because an enormous range of possibilities exists for vessel shapes and forms and decoration styles. Pots vary tremendously in their function and in the stylistic information that they convey for the purposes of individual status, group, or sect affiliations. It is the ultimate plastic medium, and it is because of this that archaeologists can study this rich source of data in the ways that they have done. Interestingly, the scientific analysis of pots using primarily petrographic analysis is relatively low-cost and employs readily available technology and is, in many respects, the archaeological scientific technique most commonly and usefully applied. Consequently, ceramic archaeologists are frequently both effective archaeological theorists and scientists and are able to make rich interpretations derived from a mosaic of data sources. The way in which researchers are now disaggregating aspects of the transmission of technological knowledge versus styles using broad ethnographic field data is an example of the combinations of approaches working well in integrated projects. The richness of the data available from ceramic studies rests on the wealth of possibilities inherent in the operational chain and individual object biographies. Making ceramics has many analogies with baking: the choice of ingredients and sources, the proportions, mixing techniques, shapes formed, manner of decoration and 'cooking methods' all involve technical possibilities but present opportunities at every stage to let people make distinctive personal and cultural recipes to serve both everyday needs and special events.

10 Metal materials and artefacts

Getting an edge and taking a shine

Metals in the modern world are strong, sharp, or shiny. They form a highly recognisable aspect of material culture. With the exception of gold the character of freshly made metalwork is quite different from the state of metal objects emerging from the soil in excavations. The rarity of the resource and the difficulty of manufacture are often considered in the discussion of metal objects. It is the performance and appearance of freshly made metal artefacts which are the key to understanding their role in society, but the earliest usage was for decorative purposes. It is their appearance rather than their edge qualities which first draws them into the cultural sphere. However, for the vast majority of their uses, they are the tools to take an edge and to get a shine. They can look stunning, and their performance in cutting and piercing, once certain aspects of the technology have been mastered, is second to none in terms of the performances of materials for doing those particular tasks. That is why metal superseded stone.

Metals are among the materials that we know best in the modern world, but, as a quick look at figures 10.1 and 10.2 shows their use was more limited in the past: for example, they were not used extensively for structures until the Industrial Revolution. Instead what dominates all kinds of metalwork from archaeological contexts is firstly, edge tools, and, as a sub-section of this, weaponry; secondly, decorative jewellery pieces; thirdly, other forms of utensils, perhaps using sheet metal; and lastly, 'fittings'. In some cases the latter could be seen as decorative, but they are also functional, serving to make a secure fastening device for a textile or leather strap. A metal buckle secures a strap in an adjustable and strong way which might not be possible by tying a knot in the organic material. Metal is also found as various 'units' in the past: as units of raw material, known as ingots or currency bars (e.g. Briard 1976, Budd et al. 1995), and currency, coins, measures, and weights (e.g. Lassen 2000, Pulak 2000, Ruiz-Gálvez 2000). Coinage has its own vast literature and, because of the materiality approach adopted here, coins are not discussed further, other than to note that our modern-day concept of coins as units of change for buying everything is not what would have happened in the earliest use of coinage, where metal coins were of very high denomination and should be seen as a token of extreme wealth wrapped up in one coin. It should also not be forgotten that metal has a particular sound quality: it tinkles, and, when well made to a resonant shape, it can resound in the form of a bell. There are many cultures in the world where sounds play an important part in religion and in warding off evil spirits. The acoustic quality of metal could have been a very distinctive part of the soundscape of the past. There are even early metal musical instruments such as Bronze Age metal horns (lur) from northern Europe (e.g. Coles 1963, 1967), and Hosler (1994, 1995) has demonstrated the importance of sound, colour, and meaning in metalwork in West Mexico. In excavated metal objects colour and sound are both degraded and in any event conservation practices would normally prevent metal being struck to test its sound quality. Figures 10.1 and 10.2 try to convey some sense of the original qualities of metal in the sense of colour and shine, though sound is more problematic.

Figure 10.1 contains a modern replica sword with a riveted handle composed of layers of antler and wood glued together and with a stone inlay; a 10 per cent tin bronze flat axe, with an ash handle, with the blade set with resin and beeswax into a cleft in the wood and bound with sinew; a looped palstave (a socketed metal toolpiece similar to an axe head) set in a multi-component wooden haft with the loop used to tie the head on; a replica copper sheet shield, showing the reinforced rim and the thinness of the metal which has been cut by a sword; archaeological socketed axes (some with loops) and replicas (made by Neil Burridge) of a socketed axe, an unlooped palstave, a ribbed dagger, the Bush Barrow (UK) axe, and an early Bronze Age copper flat axe; also archaeological flat and flanged axes. The whole assemblage presented in figure 10.1 ties in with the dominance in the Bronze Age of metal as weaponry, and the way in which archaeologists have used differences in hafting, flaring of the edge, ribbing features, and socket details to name their types and focus solely on the metal component of objects that would once have been composite. The archaeological bronze has, on the whole, kept its edge well but the replica pieces, despite a slight dulling, show more of the lustre and brilliance of the original material.

The qualities of metal as an edge component are well known, but it has also been useful as sheet metal, notably for cauldrons with waterproof joins and rivets, some decorative items, shields, musical instruments, and horse fittings (e.g. Coles 1962, Waddell 1998: 229–35, 240–2, 296–8). 'Weaponry' can dominate Bronze Age metalwork studies but palstaves (top right), and flat and flanged axes (top left) could have been tools for hedging, working wood, or general-purpose foddering, pulling down branches from trees, and gathering firewood, rather than necessarily weapons of war. There are certainly some items which are about display and status and perhaps the posturing of the potential for war (Harding 2004, Osgood and Monks 2000), but there are many objects whose main daily functions may have been more mundane but which could also have been weapons if the need arose. The sword, the rib dagger, and the shield are, on the other hand, definitely associated with warfare (see Bridgford 1997 for sword use evidence), although aspects of those are more functional than others: certainly a thin metal shield with no backing would prove ineffective, compared to those made from wood or hide or with backings of such materials (Coles 1962). So figure 10.1 encapsulates the dilemma between what is functioning as a tool for a range of purposes, versus what is fulfilling a social purpose and a social aspect of warfare.

Compare figure 10.1 with the images forming 10.2. The top set of objects tries to give some impression of the wealth of purposes served by metal other than as an edge tool. This variety of utensils, decorative and functional items, including fittings as part of composite artefacts, is shown in the top picture. Thus in the top image there are gold rings symbolising marriage in our own society; a gold strip of metal from the Sutton Common Iron Age site (UK); a simple silver bracelet; a bracelet using the different colour properties of brass and copper and an even lighter, high tin bronze to create a pattern; an inlaid silver wire on bidri (an alloy of copper, zinc, and lead) giving a black metal bracelet; a cast bronze goat bell with bent wood collar; a tin-washed copper sieve; a lead ingot; a strip of corroded lead and a corroded spoon-like implement, also of lead; a strip of decorative lead with diamond-shaped impressions stamped in it; a matched pair of Roman fibula bracelets to be worn on either side of a cloak; a bronze spoon and canister; a bronze stopper fitting for a bottle; buckles and a small riveted fitting; various cruciform and round brooches; a long pin; two Anglo-Saxon square-headed, gilded brooches, one incomplete; a cast bronze satyr; a variety of real and replica coins including a large copper-alloy Roman sestertius AD 81, a small shiny silver denarius, circa 205; two replica stamped gold coins of the Iron Age Dobunni, a small token, a silver groat of Henry VI circa 1430, and a silver penny of Ceolwulf I, AD 821–3. Coins conveniently frequently advertise both date and maker, and, with reference material and a clear image, can usually be identified and add to dating evidence. For the rest, styles of shapes and technologies give rough clues to date and cultural affiliation but these can be very approximate and are sometimes impossible. In general, the more embellishment, the easier it is to read stylistic information to give a date.

The lower image shows a typical range of iron objects. By contrast with the others, the darker sheens on modern replica iron and steel work and the rusted fragments of some of the archaeological pieces make these generally duller. These objects are dominated by edge tools, for which iron and steel are good materials, and 'fittings' which use the strength and flexibility of the metal. Fittings are often overlooked as a major use of ironwork. The objects that we find in the ground are of course also denied their hafts or other elements. Some sense of that is retained in these sets of images here. There are modern and archaeological axes, a medieval and replica arrowhead, an Anglo-Saxon spearhead, complete with wood inside the socket, a shield boss, some modern nails, twisted metal, a door hinge, strike-a-light, a set of leather working tools using reworked file steel which is high-grade, a hafted knife with inward curving blade, chisel, archaeological and modern knives and an outward curving knife with a decorative brass-studded wooden handle. This set of images highlights the contrast between the way in which archaeologists normally find metal work as corroded or at the very least dull or patinated material, versus the way those objects would have been in use; this is especially the case for bronze and copper where we find them as patinated green or brown objects with a dull texture, whereas when first made they are vibrant shiny materials in some ways reflecting the shine of gold. When new, copper is pink whereas bronze is 'gold' and tin is 'silver'. Hosler

(1994), Keates (2002), and others have commented on these colour qualities as being significant, in particular perhaps representing or symbolising sun and moon in combination. The one exception is gold, which keeps its lustre, so the Anglo-Saxon square-headed brooches gilded with gold still retain some sense of how they would have been when new. However, lead takes on a white dullish patina and iron becomes heavily corroded and can rust entirely away. In particular in Figure 10.2, bottom right, there are archaeological remnants alongside modern replicas of an axe and a knife respectively.

There are also differences between wrought iron and steel. Steel is a much more forgiving metal: owing to its high tensile strength, it will flex but not break. In this way it keeps its edge better and this metal in particular would be singled out for different kinds of uses where high-performance edge tools were advantageous, for example as swords or chisels. Furthermore, some material can be used specifically to coat other less valuable items or to prevent corrosion. Two examples are given in the images – the square-headed brooches of a copper-alloy base are coated with gold, whereas the copper sieve of sheet metal has a tin wash applied, which would be less susceptible to corrosion during use.

Though metals can preserve adjacent organic materials via their corrosion products, in general we do not understand them as materials which interface with other perishable materials. Each item shown could potentially have interacted with objects of other raw materials, either in the form of wooden handles at its simplest or in the form of pins for textiles and cloaks, such as the set of two Roman fibulae; as the fittings for organic boxes, bottles, and straps; the spatula for ladling other substances and the edge tools for working other materials; even the door fitting of iron would have interacted with wood to make a composite item, and the sieve was used to process and prepare food.

What is more, different kinds of metal have very different starting points; iron ores are generally more widely available than copper or tin deposits but the process of obtaining it requires more technical capabilities in pyrotechnology. The first widespread use of metals gives us the broad chronological phase name 'the Bronze Age' but the raw materials for its production were nowhere near evenly distributed across the regions which used such tools at this time. Metals, above all else, are about inequality. Whereas the raw materials discussed in previous chapters have been generally widespread and ubiquitous, metals (with the exception of iron) are intensely limited in comparison to these other products. That has lead to interesting uses for them and ideas about them, in particular Coles (1982) makes the point that there are vast areas where many metal hoards are found, but with no natural metal resources, thus the metal that is found in these areas represents significant organised amounts of the exchange of goods and materials on a scale not previously documented and possibly not previously seen in the past.

Raw material properties and characteristics

Figure 10.3 gives a brief overview of the raw materials from which archaeological metals commonly arise. The earliest use of metals is as decorative material from native deposits, that is ones where the raw metal occurs naturally in such a pure state that it can be used as it is. In archaeological terms, gold and copper are good examples of native metals. Indeed gold is found only in its native state since it is inert and does not readily combine with other chemicals under natural conditions (though it can be alloyed with other metals, as we shall see). That is why it does not tarnish over the years, and gold objects that have been put into the ground many millennia ago emerge from it still shiny and attractive. Native copper is sometimes found together with other minerals, such as copper sulphides, in igneous basalts and related rocks. The example shown illustrates the spongy dendritic nature of such material although it is dense (see right edge of copper illustrated in figure 10.3) and shows that it has pinkish qualities, even as a raw material. Furthermore both these native materials can be hammered into shape because copper and gold are also ductile metals, soft enough to be hammered into the desired shape, and with the hammering also serving to squeeze out any impurities. Gold is especially ductile and can be hammered into fine gold leaf, and different pieces of raw material can be combined simply by hammering. These properties made such native metals relatively easy to exploit.

Native metals, once recognised, could have been obtained from landscapes where they existed naturally, and worked using nothing more sophisticated than convenient stones as hammers and anvils. In this way wires, copper beads, and the like could have been made (Wertime 1964, Hauptmann et al. 1999). If the starting point is native gold and copper, it is not surprising that technologies were simple and that the objectives were perhaps more connected with the shiny, reflective, bright, colourful materials, as can be seen in figure 10.3, rather than with their abilities to take an edge, in the case of copper. Even a relatively lately exploited metal such as lead can be seen in an area for the first time as an ornament, as in the lead beads in an early Bronze Age Scottish necklace dated several hundred years before lead was more commonly used (Hunter and Davis 1994) and in South Africa both copper and iron were used as ornaments (Miller 2002). Copper is used for the first metal edge tools. In some parts of the world with early metallurgy industries, there is a chalcolithic phase, a Copper Age. Copper as an edge tool is not as good as bronze or iron as it is a softer material, but, none the less, it may have had certain advantages over stone in that it could be resharpened more easily, and was more forgiving as a material and would chip less easily. However, the categorisation of types of metals and an appreciation of their characteristics was neither immediate nor along an inevitable route, but part of a social process termed 'envaluation' whereby new metals or alloys have their roles conceptually crystallised within a society (the term derives from Taylor 1999), and where changes occur as an interplay between the appreciation of performance characteristics and social resistance (Lahiri 1995, Lechtman 1996).

For archaeological purposes, the main metals for edge tools are copper (Cu, melting point 1083°C), tin (Sn, 231°C), which combines with copper to form bronze, and iron (Fe, 1535°C), and for precious metals gold (Au, 1063°C) and silver (Ag, 960°C). Lead (Pb, 327°C) is also important as a soft metal or as part of an alloy added to copper or tin. As the uses of copper grew, so there was not sufficient native copper, and other ways of obtaining copper from different kinds of compounds were introduced. The geochemistry involved in minerals and their formation can be complex, resulting in a variety of different chemical compounds; however, there are a few salient points which illustrate best the key points for archaeology. Figure 10.3 shows both their colourful nature and a rough ordering of these, with the next most obvious sources of metals being the oxides where the metal is combined with oxygen. It is difficult to convey the true sense of these minerals when one of the most important measures is their density, which cannot be conveyed in an illustration. In common with other metal-bearing ores, metal oxides can be very heavy because of the high quantities of metal contained within them. The key archaeologically important oxides of metals are haematite (iron) and cassiterite (tin). Cassiterite can look quite dark, almost leaden in appearance, but still shiny and with some lustre. One of the samples shown is fractured rock, the other is a set of river gravel pieces known as stream tin. Haematite ranges in colour from red to shiny gunmetal grey. Limonite is an iron hydroxide which was an important source of ore in antiquity and is orange or yellow. Oxides tend to be the easiest to smelt and reduce into the metals. However, some metals are not often found as simple oxides. That is why copper oxide, although in practice a good material for smelting, is rarely found because it quickly becomes copper carbonate, for example malachite as illustrated. The reactivity of copper is also the reason why objects often have verdigris, a corrosion layer, tinged green, on the outside. For some complex copper mineral compounds a successful eventual smelt is more likely if the mineral is first roasted to turn the complex mineral compound into copper oxide.

The next easiest minerals to exploit are the colourful carbonates, where the desired metal is combined with CO_3. Carbonates have the advantage that the main chemical combinations are with elements that can be released as gases within the furnace although there are always some impurities. The mineral iron carbonate is siderite with an orange tinge to it, and for copper, malachite, which is green and is also used in jewellery, and azurite, which is blue. Green is very characteristic of copper.

Another set of mineral compounds from which metals can be obtained is the sulphides. These are recognisable, as they tend to be quite shiny minerals. Chalcopyrite contains a high percentage of copper and is typically a brassy yellow with obvious shiny metallic qualities. Galena, lead sulphide, is the main ore of both lead and silver because traces of silver are included as silver sulphides within the main parent mineral. It should be possible not to confuse chalcopyrite with gold, because the gold is much softer and much heavier. However the identification of minerals rests not just on colour and shininess but on cleavage properties and knowledge of the parent rock and of the different ways in which the rock might be combined, and thus there are few archaeologists who would reliably make mineral determinations.

These then, are the very colourful raw materials from which metals are derived, some of which might have been sought after in their own right. For example, haematite can make attractive beads and can also be used to polish and to colour hide work. Malachite has a very distinctive green colouring. The qualities of some of these rocks may have been apparent to people in the past even though they did not know their chemical formulae. Once a society is using metals, prospecting cues are just some of a set of skills which need to be brought to bear. Consequently figure 10.3

has identified gaps and has tried to lay out, in a visual form, the key identifications of different kinds of ores. The above descriptions are really a quick guide to try to show the distinction between these different minerals at a gross level, highlighting those which are most relevant to archaeology, but skate over a lot of detail which would be crucial in reliable, solid identifications. The key point here is how people in the past might have been able to find such mineral deposits and, if they knew that in an area they had already successfully found and used particular kinds and colours and qualities of rock, then it is not inconceivable that they would have looked for those same qualities in other places nearby, once the original sources had run out. Some form of 'prospecting' must have gone on in the past. People would have been looking for certain visual and tactile characteristics, and it is these which have been the focus of this discussion. Certainly the beautiful shininess and the distinctive colours would have acted as cues to suggest that people tried particular kinds of rocks and deposits. If they did not work, then they might have realised that they had made a mistake, but none the less the visual cues would have been the lead in to exploration. There are also particular kinds of plants which will act as a visual cue to sub-surface mineral deposits since, in many cases, these metals are leeched from minerals out into the soil and into streams and watersheds: there will be particular habitats connected with those minerals which are present, encouraging, in some cases, specific plants. To people who are used to exploiting all kinds of natural plant materials, this might have been an important clue.

Archaeological study strategies

Metallurgy, unlike the other fields of study we have discussed, has a significant division between those who study the objects produced and those who study the technologies and the archaeological remnants of metallurgical processes, although this division has been decreasing in recent years. Studies of the Bronze Age have been dominated by typologies of metalwork objects leading to the definitions of phases and descriptions of many types of swords, types of palstaves, and types of spears. In addition, there is another archaeological research theme which pursues the technologies and the manner in which the raw material was extracted and worked. The latter can be pursued at a chemical level rather than an integrated chemical and archaeological analysis. Metallurgy is one of the most studied aspects of material culture and one which is most often studied using scientific analyses.

There is a large range of general surveys of metallurgy, specialising in different places (e.g. Asia: Bisson et al. 2000, Anatolia: Alishan Yener 2000; Egypt: Ogden 2000; Colonial America: Mulholland 1981), as well as more general surveys (e.g. Craddock and Hughes 1985, Craddock 1995, Craddock and Lang 2003, Tylecote 1976, 1986 and 1987, Oddy 1980, Young et al. 1999) and, interestingly, those who have covered metallurgy as part of pyrotechnology (Rehder 2000). Several books focus on the origins of metallurgy, since this has a long tradition as part of chronological phasing (e.g. De Jesus 1980, Greenfield 1999, Killick 2001, and Budd et al. 1992 for the development in Britain) and there is always interest in the first development of particular products: for example the advent of carbon steel is another milestone in metallurgy (Godfrey and Van Nie 2004). There are also general works focusing on particular kinds of metals (e.g. tin: Penhallurick 1986, Bouzek et al. 1989, Yener and Ozbal 1987; copper alloys Coghlan 1975, Dungworth 1997; lead: Rowe 1983; and for Roman copper alloys Çukur and Kunç 1989, and fourth-millennium BC evidence for copper mining in Europe, Cernych 1978, Golden et al. 2001, and Maggi and Pearce 2005). Some areas have rich natural resources for metallurgy and now have well-documented extraction and product evidence set in social context (e.g. for Ireland O'Brien 1994, 1996, 2005, and see Clarke et al. 1985). Classic work has also focused on the production, typology, and distribution of metalwork and the social implications of these (e.g. Rowlands 1976). Some studies have investigated ethnicity using artefact styles and technologies (Larick 1986, 1991). Mining and extraction industries are an obvious topic (Craddock 1989). Methods of working metals have been a key theme and on occasions for good reason: for example sheet metalworking is a particular kind of skill and prestigious objects can be made from it (e.g. the Gundesrup cauldron, Denmark: Berquist and Taylor 1987).

Other typical analyses focus on the use of trace-element analysis to identify sources so that the movement of materials and products can be traced. Copper artefacts of the Copper Inuit have been analysed as a means of investigating the objects that were made from local native copper, versus those from nineteenth-century European smelted copper, allowing social implications to be revealed (Wayman et al. 1985). It is possible to use element analyses such as PIXE to investigate sources of gold (e.g. Guerra and Calligaro 2004), as well as investigating the techniques of working, distribution, and deposition of gold work (e.g. Eogan 1994, Hughes 2000, Smith 1978, Taylor 1980). It is not surprising that gold can also be thought of as a symbolic material with key objects being made from it, for example small boats from Nors, Denmark, where in 1885 a pot was found with about a hundred small boats, 10–17 cm long and with ribs of now decayed bronze which were coated with thin gold foil which has survived (Jørgensen and Vang Petersen 1998: 90–1).

Archaeological studies of iron are dominated by a focus on edge tools (e.g. Tylecote and Gilmore 1986) and production techniques, typically in bloomery smelters (Pleiner 2000), but there is also a rich set of ethnographic information (e.g. Rostoker and Bronson 1990, Schmidt 1997), as well as strong traditions of experimental work (e.g. Norbach 1996, Sim and Ridge 1998). Smithing is less often commented upon (e.g. Ehrenreich 1985). In part, this is explained by the fact that, although smithing is known to have taken place in order to work the iron, it can be harder to find the archaeological evidence for this kind of production activity, because as figure 10.7 shows, the forge can be very itinerant and simply a small pit in the ground with charcoal placed in it and bellows running in from a shallow slot trench. Though anvils can be formally shaped objects, they need not be, and, though there can be traces of hammerscale (the small wafers of oxidised metal knocked off during striking, see figure 10.7), these would corrode and disperse unless the hammering was carried out for a long time at the same place. Where forges are set in more formalised surroundings and there is a stationary smithy, this kind of evidence might be easier to find, but would still require a 'floor' to be recognised archaeologically, and then this to be linked to metalworking traces. Certainly very few smithing floors are known, although the Exmoor Iron Project (UK) has recently discovered one such (Juleff pers. comm.). The scale and style of production in different periods has been the subject of technological and socio-economic studies (e.g. Schrüfer-Kolb 2004, Groenewoudt and Van Nie 1995), and in recent years in particular much has been gained from the study of slags specifically (e.g. Juleff 1998 and the ongoing Exmoor Iron Project).

Interests in experimental work have a very long history in metallurgy (e.g. Cushing 1894, Ottaway 2003, Ottaway and Seibel 1998) and it is a subject well suited to actualistic studies. In areas where traditional techniques have not survived, it is sometimes difficult to get archaeological evidence for the exact nature of the processes and precise arrangements which would have made these industries possible: for example different kinds of bellows and the means of directing the air into different parts of the combustion zone can make the difference between success and failure, but these are rarely documented (though see Šebesta 1992: 55–80). Much practical information is inevitably drawn from ethnographic and contemporary surveys. Fortunately, there are some excellent studies which cover practical details and pay great attention also to the social contexts and symbolism in metalworking (e.g. Brown 1995, Herbert 1984 and 1993, Horne 1994, Keller and Keller 1996, Rowlands and Warnier 1993). It is possible to show a potential effect in a small crucible in an electric kiln but in many cases more realistic full-scale experiments might be required.

There are now also publications discussing the role of metals in generalised social contexts, for example landscape issues (Brück 2001) and general ideas amalgamating different topics about social aspects of metals in society going beyond the analyses (e.g. Ehrenreich 1991, Gordon and Killick 1993, Pare 2000). This is not to say that the scientific analyses are not still investigating the origins of archaeological metal for good reason (e.g. Rapp et al. 2000 on geological sources of artefact copper; Gale 2001 on the sources of copper via scientific analyses in the Mediterranean, and Begemann et al. 2001 showing local and imported technologies versus materials in Sardinia) and more general scientific studies (Craddock 1980). There are also useful field guides to the identification of metal (e.g. Light 2000) and overviews of corrosion processes (McNeil and Selwyn 2001).

Though there has been some interest in the wear analysis of metals (e.g. Bridgford 1997, Gordon 1983, Kienlin and Ottaway 1998, Roberts and Ottaway 2003), there is still no clear, easily applicable method for establishing the function of some objects. Because of their depositional contexts in scrap, votive, and safety hoards (e.g. Ryan 1987), and as part of burial deposits (Bradley 1990b), the state in which metal objects enter the ground, whether they are used items or unused, exhausted, broken, or deliberately deformed, can all be important pieces of information. However there has not been the same need to identify the wear traces on metal edge tools as there is for ones of flint and bone. This is because metal edge tools tend to be more similar in at least the use action, if not the use material, to our own experiences of metal edge tools than is the case with flint. With flint there are many edges and uses which we simply do not have in our mindset, whereas most people would regard metal edge tools or metal fittings as, at a basic level, understandable. What is more, it might be unrealistic to think that one edge tool, perhaps a bronze axe, was going to be reserved for working only one material in one particular way. Whilst they are traditionally associated with tree clearance and woodworking, there might well have been a much greater variety of tasks performed with these tools in the past. In some respects, axes, palstaves, and the like may have been more general-purpose tools used to collect firewood, provide browse for animals, lay hedging for field boundary maintenance, cut coppice for making hurdles and basketry, work timber and fell trees, all of which are tasks involving contact with wood, as well as perhaps having a role in the killing and butchering of animals.

In later periods or more sustained industries, excavating metalworking sites can involve dealing with huge quantities of waste materials. It can be impossible to keep all such material but it is also difficult to take representative samples of a highly varied process from which the main product is missing. Selecting fired clay pieces which show a process can include keeping fragments of refractory ceramics for moulds, furnace linings, crucibles, and tuyères (ceramic tubes used to direct air into furnaces). Slag occurs in a wide variety of forms depending on which part of the metal production process it is derived from, thus providing valuable information concerning technical processes. Some combinations of charcoal, ore, and clay may indicate a particular area of the furnace and provide information on the specific procedure. Metallurgy is very varied as a process between smelts, and effects vary greatly even within a single smelt (the weather, wall height, proximity to wind source, vagaries in charge mixture, compass point aspect, or time). Other archaeological materials can have well-defined information relating a fragment to the whole – for example rim sherd to pot, or bone fragment to animal – but there is no such safety in using fragments to represent the whole in metallurgical studies. Samples are often thought of as 'small' amounts but small fragments as individual samples in metallurgical studies may not be representative of the whole. Big pieces as samples may be better and some may even give the diameter or limits on furnace heights or breadths. When sampling it may be tempting to look for the unique, either to establish the range of variation (colours, flows, vitreous, shape, composition) or hoping to gain highly individual clues to the whole by a rare survival, but selective samples cannot be seen as typical, so they need to be complemented by sampling for common traits. Even then samples will be very varied on examination by hand, let alone under the microscope. The polished sections shown in figure 10.9 include ones with inclusions (a, d, e, and f), all of which offer information on the purity of the metal and, in the case of figure 10.9e, a suggestion as to the material being smelted. Such sections also provide the chance to see the structure, for example the fully eutectoid high-carbon steel in figure 10.9b and the three phases in the iron slag in 10.9c. (Eutectic mixtures are distinctive because the temperature at which the mixture is liquid differs from the melting points of the individual components and, in metallurgy, the proportions of the different constituents and the way in which these solidify can create advantageous effects.) If carried out on samples from shaped finished implements, traces of working such as hammering (which flattens crystalline structures and eventually causes fragmentation as metal fatigue) and annealing (that is, using heat to allow recrystallisation) can be seen.

The more social aspects of metallurgy are exciting because metals are used as orna-mention, implements, and containers as these examples show. Metalwork as fittings and as decoration on perishable items of material culture are the subjects of work by Stig-Sørenson (1991, 1997), for Bronze Age costume, suggesting ethnic identity and gender constructions expressed and traceable in the archaeological record. But a wider trawl through the literature also shows some interesting aspects in areas with a strong tradition of research into colonial history and relatively recent material culture, for example table cutlery (Dunning 2000) and beer cans (Maxwell 2000). More recent studies with historical information also offer insights into what is missing from the archaeological record where the material is ultimately very recyclable, for example the lead alloy, pewter (Martin 2000).

Metallurgy is often regarded as a great achievement in technological breakthroughs and to some extent, it seems, improvement and progress; but it is also true that achieving high-quality metalwork requires not just physical skills but also certain kinds of knowledge which it might be easy to keep secret and which might also be quite difficult to replicate even where the process has been observed previously. However there are arguments for metals changing societies, for example iron (Stig-Sørenson 1989). These sorts of issues, along with the social place of smiths (Miller 2002), the way in which a furnace is conceived, firmly embed metallurgy in the social context. In Herbert's excellent discussion of iron, gender, and power (1993), there are two interesting examples: the reuse of slag sometimes in making up the furnace wall, so that there is a continuity in tradition that has a physical embodiment, and also the metaphor of the smelting process as giving birth, with female features added to the furnace though living women are excluded from the smelt. There are many interesting questions as to how gender and social attitudes work in those sorts of contexts.

If we hold in our hands a metal object from an excavation, it is usually possible to say what kinds of metal it might be, although this might have to be confirmed by more expert analysis and, unfortunately, most metal objects will have been corroded so that the surface is lost and careful conservation of some objects is likely to be necessary, especially thin sheet metals or very corroded materials. None the less metals, perhaps more than any other of the materials studied, have exerted a fascination with typological seriation and social overtones. In some cases, one won-ders whether this is truly warranted. Many of the objects that we find as metal are deliberately deposited, especially in the Bronze Age. This has skewed some attitudes towards other aspects of material culture in those periods. Reflecting on figure 3.1 it is clear that metalwork is split into process and product in archaeological studies and that the by-products from its production (slags, furnaces, moulds, anvils) can be as important to understanding the exploitation of metals as debitage analysis is for stone tools. Metal finds are also at particular periods especially selected for by distinctive cultural depositional practices which have left a very rich record for study, though the nature of the raw material and the variation in corrosion in post-depositional processes have also coloured what remains to be studied and the style of that analysis. In the past, the quantities and nature of metalwork deposition in burial mounds made these a target of antiquarian barrow-digging, but the modern advent of metal detectors has also created a bias in the recovery of metalwork. Though some such discoveries have no context or go entirely unreported, there are archaeological responses to this new wealth of information, ranging from metal finds stimulating excavation projects to the portable antiquities scheme in Britain which tries to provide a means of recording such finds. The possibilities for recycling metal in the past make it a particularly challenging material to study, while the practical difficulties of successful prospection, extraction, and smelting allied with the ubiquity or rarity of the raw material deposits have created a distinctive character to the way in which metal finds are viewed and studied.

Technologies

In the past, whilst most people might have experienced metal tools and metal objects, the number directly involved in the metalworking process might have been very limited indeed. The techniques for working native metals are straightforward. The earliest uses of materials have allowed for beating materials into different shapes, and burnishing as can be seen in figure 10.4 which shows part of a gold strip (though here from Iron Age Sutton Common, Yorkshire, UK: Van de Noort et al. 2007). These signs of working are evident, but looking for traces of working on metal objects is just one part of the technological study of metals. There are also casting, alloying (that is, mixing metals), and forging techniques, and sheet metalworking. Major distinctions can be drawn between metals soft enough to be hammered and drawn into shape, those which can be melted, and those which cannot. Copper and copper alloys contrast in their performance and associated technologies with iron, which could not be cast until relatively late in Europe although the relevant technology did exist in China. Later developments involve higher temperatures and greater technical knowledge. Fuel usage, perhaps involving woodland management for charcoal production and preferential selection of wood species, together with the production of crucibles, moulds, and wax models, form an essential part of the exploitation of metal in later periods.

One aspect of metallurgy is finding the raw materials, but then there is the added step of constructing a suitable structure to contain, in close proximity, the right materials under the right physical and chemical conditions in order to produce a successful smelt. It is true that sulphides and some of the more complex minerals may require extra phases to those illustrated in the relatively more straightforward techniques described in figures 10.5 and 10.7. These give some indication of why the metalworking process would have preferred to use material which could be more simply transformed in the smelt. For example, not much copper smelting was done on a large scale until very recently, so figure 10.5 illustrates small-scale smelting using a crucible. Here the ore, in this case malachite, is crushed up and placed in a ceramic crucible suitable for the temperatures required, along with combustible material. The resulting copper can be seen after a successful smelt, when the crucible was held in the furnace at the right temperature and chemical conditions for the reactions listed in figure 10.5 to take place. Essentially, the copper carbonates decompose to copper oxide at high temperatures, and this is then reduced in two stages by carbon monoxide produced by the burning fuel to the metal, copper, and carbon dioxide, a gas which escapes through the furnace. Bellows or some other means of directing air are necessary for maintaining the flow of air and thus the temperature to allow the sequence of combustion and roasting of the ore, and then reduction of the ore, to take place.

A similar kind of sequence can be outlined for reducing cassiterite to tin. Both tin, which is used as a modern solder, and copper have relatively low melting points. That is why they can be cast, but small amounts of tin together with copper have a lower melting point than copper alone. It is thus easier to melt and cast the alloys of copper and tin than to melt and cast pure copper. Figure 10.6 shows the furnace and the arrangement of the bellows and the ceramic pipes (tuyères) leading into the furnace, alongside some of the kinds of moulds that can be used for producing simple metal objects. At their simplest moulds can be depressions in sand, or hollows carefully shaped into solid rock, and at the more complex level can comprise several pieces of ceramic mould which together will make up a three-dimensional object. In all these cases of casting, the furnace itself will leave traces of burning; the moulds, where these were made of inorganic materials, may survive to be found archaeologically, as may the crucibles and the tuyères from the process. The cast items require further finishing to remove material that is extraneous to the basic shape required, for example seams from moulds, and to hammer and then hone the material into its desired shape. The casting seams are clearly visible in figure 10.6e and the granular internal structure of the metals can be seen in the sections.

A more complicated process is involved for iron smelting, where the iron is not usually melted. If copper is successfully smelted in a furnace, the metal would run to the bottom of the furnace or crucible at 1083°C; however the melting point of iron is 1535°C, which is more difficult to achieve using simple technologies, even though the melting point of iron is lowered by enough carbon to allow localised spots of melting in a bloomery furnace. A bloomery furnace produces bloom, a spongy mass of both iron and the waste product known as slag (unlike the latter blast furnace which produces pig iron); the process is otherwise much the same as for smelting copper. The ore, after extraction, is crushed and placed with charcoal in a structure that can both withstand heat and act as insulation, while air into the structure has to be controlled to make sure that the required temperatures and conditions are produced. The outcome, if successful, is the reduction of the iron oxide to iron and gasses; however there are many impurities and these form a glassy, vitreous slag. In many cases, the original desired end product, the bloom, is taken away to be further processed, and what is left is the slag or waste materials. The slag from iron production is basically the same as that produced from copper smelting or any other form of smelt, because the same kinds of silica impurities are present in these ores. The metal bloom produced in an iron smelting furnace must then be hammered to squeeze out the non-metallic slag remaining as part of the bloom. For this a forge is necessary, although this need leave very little trace in the archaeological record, as shown in figure 10.7. Other traces of this process in the archaeological record can include very fine hammerscale debris caused by working metal on an anvil, or furnace walls and furnace structure remains. Frequently the fragments of the inside of the clay furnace, fired hard and vitrified because of the temperatures involved, are found in archaeological contexts. Where successive smelts have taken place in the same place, there is a series of these hard fired cores forming concentric rings, as seen in figure 10.7. This process produces iron, but it is a relatively pure form of iron which can be worked but does not have as high a tensile strength as steel. Steel is iron with small amounts of carbon (up to 2 per cent). To anyone who has taken part in experimental smelts it is all too obvious just how difficult it is to get the right combinations and factors, and it is essential to have air directed into the furnace and to maintain high temperatures and suitable conditions for sufficient time for smelting to take place.

Once metals have been obtained, the major way of extending their range of performance characteristics is by combining or alloying them. When two metals are combined in alloy, small quantities of one metal will completely transform the properties of the parent or base metal. This is because in pure metal the atoms move easily over one another because they are all the same size. Adding even a small amount of a different metal gives different-sized atoms which increase the hardness, because it is less easy for the metal atoms to move over one another. Because of this, the alloy bronze (roughly 90 per cent copper and 10 per cent tin) is a harder material than pure copper. Sometimes the alloy is formed by adding a non-metal, as in the case of iron with small additions of carbon which greatly improves its strength, hardness, and ability to take a keen edge. Steel with about 1 per cent carbon in it is much harder than iron. Adding more carbon hardens the steel even further until it contains about 2–4 per cent carbon, when it is classified as cast iron. In this form, it is very hard but it loses tensile strength and is easily fractured, while malleability and ductility are reduced.

The other effect of making alloys is that the melting points decrease, potentially improving casting properties, a key archaeological point for understanding tech-nologies. They also may stay fluid for longer and flow better into complex moulds before solidifying. Small amounts of lead improve the flow of copper alloys, although that same addition can reduce the strength of the metal in a similar way to that described for iron. Alloys may also be more resistant to corrosion. The melting point is also always lower for an alloy than that of the main parent metal. Indeed, the melting point can be lower than that of either of the metals involved. Solder (an alloy of lead and tin) makes such a good sealer in modern plumbing because of its low melting point of 180°C, which is below that of either pure lead (327°C) or tin (231°C). Furthermore, different percentage mixtures of alloys of the same two metals will have different melting points, and since the manner of mixing the elements together need not result in a perfectly homogenous composition, in effect, alloys do not melt at one point but at a range of temperatures. This range can mean that, in the solidification process after casting, they remain workable for longer periods and thus aspects of their ability to be worked can be improved.

Finally, alloys are also beneficial where they result in a change of colour, if this is perceived as significant for the ultimate purpose of the metal being produced. Although pink copper forms the base metal of the copper/tin alloy of bronze, this metal is yellow. Gold, silver, and copper alloys are also effective, especially for decorative purposes. Because they are all equally soluble in one another, a wide range of colour effects can be achieved from the yellow of gold, the white of silver and the pink of copper, to all the shades in between. That is why gold with high carat value is richly yellow, compared to gold of less purity, which tends to be a more silvery, pale version of gold. A carat, which is the unit normally employed to measure gold purity, is a system where 24 parts represents the whole, so that 18 carat gives 75 per cent purity. But, as with other alloys, it can be important to alloy gold in order to strengthen it, as otherwise it is a very soft metal and, even for jewellery, may be too soft to be practically effective. Iron carbon alloys are much more restrictive, given that a maximum of 5 per cent carbon can be dissolved in iron.

The technology of producing alloys can be simply that of placing ores of both copper and tin or copper and zinc into the smelting process together, a process called natural alloying. But it is impossible to control the exact composition and, if the desirability of an alloy rests on the qualities that are given using particular combinations of compositions, then more control is necessary. In these cases, it is much simpler to smelt the different metals separately and then combine them as pure forms of the metal, using estimated compositions as a mental recipe. In the alloying process, the major metal is usually melted first and then the additional metal is added to it. Once the mixture is thoroughly dissolved, it can be poured into a mould and allowed to cool, producing not necessarily an object but simply an ingot. The exception is that iron carbon alloys are difficult to make because carbon is not readily dissolved in iron and that is why the technology of steel making is a complex process and one which is relatively late in the working of metals.

Figure 10.8 shows the highly unusual process of directly obtaining high-quality steel. The steel is obtained in a complex process of combining different materials present in the original charge. It is a direct method for producing steel and iron, rather than making the iron and then adding carbon. That is why the reconstruction experiment depicted in 10.8 has caused so much interest (Juleff 1996, 1998). It is highly unusual to be able to find archaeological evidence of high-carbon steel produced directly, and furthermore the style of the furnace does not follow that of the European-style tradition in 10.7, but is instead a different arrangement utilising the trade winds of Sri Lanka, with a line of tuyères at the base of the furnace which is crescent-shaped and set back into the hillside to take advantage of the wind. However, the technical aspects of the process are much the same, with the slag running out of the bottom of the furnace, as can be seen in 10.8c. This has contradicted the accepted concept of furnace shapes in very exciting ways and has been established via careful attention to the archaeological evidence and ethnographic accounts, with a confirmatory set of experiments (Juleff 1996 and 1998).

Functions

The earliest use of metal objects was for decoration, but copper was the first metal to be used as an edge tool. Metals have since been used for a wide range of functions: farming equipment from shears to ploughshares and hedging tools; personal equipment from daggers, axes, and razors to weapons and shields; cooking equipment from pots to cauldrons, feasting sets and cutlery; figures and decorative goods such as mirrors, handles, fastenings, and jewellery; and musical instruments. They also serve as coinage and as fittings such as hinges, locks, and buckles. There are a number of ways in which metals stand out. In general, they are hard, yet they are also able to be shaped via compression, for example hammering, or by drawing them out, deforming them under tension. As well as being hard, they tend to be heavy and dense in comparison with other raw materials and respond differently to heat. Whereas a stone heated beyond a certain temperature will become too brittle to be of use, some metals, once heated, will attain different qualities of an edge that will actually be seen as an improvement. Most metals can be polished to take a shine and, with the exception of mercury, have high melting points. Their colours when new are usually white, other than the pink of freshly polished copper, and the yellow of gold. In combination, the alloys bronze (copper and tin) and brass (copper and zinc) also have a yellow hue. Lead, wrought iron, or relatively pure iron and copper are all soft enough to be bent if they are in fine rods, or to be sawn with other metal tools, or hammered.

Another important property of metals that affects archaeological perception and survival is the ease with which they combine with other elements, especially oxygen, and corrode. Those metals which readily form oxides, that is corrode easily, are known as base metals, whereas those which do not are known as noble metals, such as gold and silver. Even silver does indeed tarnish, and copper will form oxides quite readily, whereas metals such as iron are highly corrodible. On some objects, the mineralisation of the surface can actually act to protect the interior and stop further corrosion. In this sense, it is akin to a patina, and although corrosion has happened, the object is stable. In most cases, the stabilisation either requires this formation of an outer layer of corrosion, which in effect seals the interior, or the metal must be placed in a controlled dry atmosphere. There are two unusual effects that this ability or affinity to oxidise creates. Firstly, if objects are made from more than one metal, the one which corrodes more easily will do so at the expense of those that are more resistant. Secondly, if organic materials are close to metal objects, the corrosion products from the metal will preserve details of the organic object, for example textile patterning, or fragments of skin or leather.

Overview

Table 10.1 outlines some of the ways in which key questions are addressed in metallurgy, and shows some contrasts. Whilst bronze and copper are the foci of a range of element/isotope analyses designed to show sources of origin for the raw material, the same is not the case for iron, which both has more ubiquitous deposits of the raw ores and also has fewer possible element markers for distinguishing these. This marks a distinction which is also period-based because of the general sequence of Bronze then Iron Ages. There are also no direct dating techniques for metal artefacts except using classic shape-based typological chronologies, although in principle small amounts of carbon in steel may provide radiocarbon dates. The function of metalwork is assumed rather than understood in a more complex way and the manner

Table 10.1 Techniques of analysis for metal artefacts

METALS	What is it made from?	What is the character of the material and can it be grouped?	Where did the raw material(s) come from?	How was it made?	When was it made? Or when was it deposited?	Was it used? What for?
	Identification	Characterisation	Sourcing/provenance	Technology	Direct dating	Function
Copper plus alloys Lead plus alloys Occasional/frequent	Gross identification by eye and density but requires chemical analysis to confirm	Some trace elements may allow groups to be determined but recycling and alloying can obscure these	Trace elements and isotope sets may characterise some sources but mixture of materials and recycling can make matching source characteristics difficult	By eye and polished sections	No technique	Usually based on shape though potentially wear traces may add to this if surface is not too corroded
Iron and steel Frequent	Usually by eye and corrosion products	Can be analysed for carbon content, but structures and working histories revealed by polished sections may allow sets to be established	No generally applied technique	By eye and polished sections to look at structure and working history	No common technique though it is theoretically possible to extract carbon	Usually based on shape; often too corroded
Precious metals Rare	By eye but samples can be chemically analysed	Rarely found in multiple groups so not often relevant	Potentially see left but requires comparative reference collection from known locations and for these to show distinctive characteristics	By eye, or non-destructive or non-invasive techniques	No technique	Usually based on shape although observations of wear may add to this

in which the category of objects called 'fittings' is used downplays the possibilities for using these inorganic remains to say something about the organic components of material culture which are less often preserved.

Metalwork and metalworking technology can be restricted within a society but also involve a knowledge of and access to resources from other industries. There is the use of clay as refractory materials, furnace walls, crucibles, and moulds; not all clay will withstand the necessary high temperatures. The clay for the furnace will need to be constructed and may not last more than one firing without having to be replaced or mended. Tuyères may also be needed. Furthermore bellows or other methods of directing air are needed, most often involving some arrangement of skin and wood and the use of pipes, perhaps of hollowed-out wood, to direct the air into the furnace. One method of producing finely detailed, three-dimensional metal objects such as figurines is the lost wax technique where a model is made in wax, clay is pressed around it, the clay is then fired into ceramic with the wax burning away, leaving a hole which is then filled with molten metal. It is worth pointing out that the addition of small amounts of lead to bronze will not only make the metal go further but also improve the flow qualities when it is molten, and where complex moulds are used this might be a desirable quality. Smelting, casting, and forging all require combustible materials which use fuel resources in the area. Certainly in later periods the management of woodlands and the production of charcoal are features of metal industries.

Metallurgy is one area of material culture where scientific analyses are widely seen as the norm, but Juleff's (1996, 1998) Sri Lankan work demonstrates an important point. The furnace shapes discovered and the production of steel in such a context were unknown. Though samples were taken and duly analysed under the microscope it was not these that demonstrated the concept or constituted a 'proof'. It was the archaeological record which showed the physical entity and the problem, and the experimental and ethnographic research which showed the feasibility. Furthermore the experiment was full-scale and in the right location. This is not an experiment that could have been undertaken in a scaled-down model or in the laboratory. It is this solid combination of detailed archaeological recording and experimental and ethnographic evidence which has allowed the interpretation to be accepted: no scientific sample result has been required for this acceptance.

Metallurgy wraps up a lot of resources in human and material terms within the society that produces it, and one way of trying to improve our understanding of it is to address questions of scale. There is a hierarchy of studies at different levels: the evidence from one individual event such as a smelt; repeated such events and the combinations of different activities taking place giving site assemblages; and the landscape assemblage where the integration of the whole into a pattern interacting with woodland management and refractory clays may be informative. In archaeometallurgy it is rare that specialist studies are allowed to focus on the broader ranges of this hierarchy such as landscape; they are much more often reduced to the first and most narrow aspects of this hierarchy: individual finds bags or samples selected by other non-specialists. As explained in Chapter 2, there is a separatist vision of 'specialists' who may never be invited to the site and have no chance to work alongside the director or volume editor or other specialists. This is perhaps at its extreme in the highly technical analyses such as occur for metalwork. Nowhere in most contract budgets is there room for general comparative research to contextualise the specialist study; this is seen as inherent in the specialist's own built-up knowledge or something to be researched in their personal time, despite the fact that mini-seminars to present findings would aid the flow of information from analytical work across specialist studies resulting in better-quality information overall.

Analytical approaches divide into those who specialise in process or composition versus those who look chiefly at finished objects. It is healthy to critique the interpretations made on scientific evidence and the way contemporary attitudes colour what is studied and how the evidence is interpreted. For example Budd and Taylor (1995) re-examined the value of the scientific information and the assumptions of some sets of analyses and stressed the more social ways in which metal technology might be seen. Whilst their paper garnered a lot of comment it made more explicit some of the underpinning reasoning in interpretations. That is always a useful process. However, some of the most interesting studies in recent years have been not on the technical systems but on the combinations of the social, technical, and symbolic aspects of metals such as the power of sound, colour, and symbols all working through metallurgy in ancient West Mexico (Hosler 1995). This study undoubtedly used a concept of materiality in its analysis of the metallurgy of this society.

11 Artefacts as material culture: past, present, and future

At the outset three interest groups dealing with artefacts were identified: the professional field and museum archaeologists who recover the finds and then store and display them; the researchers bringing social theory to material culture studies; and those who study artefacts using highly technical analyses. In many ways the book has covered the past, and dealt with the present. It has sought to contextualise and evaluate some of these approaches, but what of the future? Here there is a divide between what would happen in an ideal world and what is likely to happen in reality.

Field archaeology used to be the preserve of antiquarians but has moved to the paid professional. The modern fieldworker is very constrained by time and money, and is expected to provide a basic level of analysis rather than deploy the latest techniques. The pressure to save money, especially on developer-funded excavations, may result in further reduction of the sample size for evaluative excavation work and perhaps the increasing use of sophisticated non-invasive survey equipment. This will limit the number and range of finds but conversely the pace of development can be expected to offset this. The finds will be more of a selective sample from an increased number of development sites. Research digs are rare and, with funding bodies hard-pressed, are likely to become rarer still. The professional museum archaeologist presents some finds and conserves others in their care. In the past, museum objects were presented confidently, but a more self-critical discipline has left them with a multiplicity of briefs and the desire to have more open dialogues about presentations serving multiple needs in the future. The presented objects will remain fairly constant but the curator's greatest challenge will be pressure to increase public access to reserve collections whilst at the same time facing the knowledge that individual objects can be studied minutely for chemical residues, AMS, and genetic data, all of which have a better chance of success if the artefact is kept carefully pristine. Might collections have to be separated into a fourfold system of presented display objects and handling collections for educational visits, as happens now, and the present idea of reserve collections formally divided up into those objects subject to 'ultra-care' with the rest accessible to interested parties on request? This could see museums performing a retrenchment in some respects and yet allowing greater access in others. All of this will be further challenged by an ever increasing demand to store objects in perpetuity as they are retrieved from new fieldwork.

Scientific studies of objects have moved on. What was once wide-scale accessible science undertaken by archaeologists with relevant expertise using microscopes, and with the main goal as characterisation and technology, has come to the present breakthroughs in residue studies as genetic and chemical traces, and as the new fields of phytoliths, starch, and other residues analysis. Only some of these techniques can be undertaken by archaeologists. There is increasingly a sense that the level of science brought to bear on archaeological issues requires the work to be undertaken by individuals at postgraduate and even post-doctoral level in the relevant field of science. Archaeologists will concentrate on morphological and statistical work and reference-collection-based interpretations, rather than on the genetic and chemical analyses. The future will see this trend continue with even fewer archaeologists directly engaged in pursuing the scientific analyses, which will increasingly be done on trace-level 'artefact as site' samples. Museum collections will be mined for such samples. Fewer samples will be analysed, but with more techniques used on particular case studies so that techniques integrate and interact as the costs increase and the potential techniques proliferate.

Social approaches to material cultures have moved from typological seriation, culture histories, and the language of objects to the present-day positions where objects are seen as intimately entangled with people and where the language of expressing this can be argued to be equally entangled. I would like to think that the language in which the archaeological ideas are expressed will become more accessible and that there will be an increased awareness of different perspectives and critical reflection on practice. There will also be an increasingly varied set of disciplines contributing to the debates. In this context, archaeology should stop being a Cinderella discipline and theoretical borrower and export its theoretical developments to interdisciplinary debates about material culture and promote its data recovery techniques as a forensic-style science.

Experimental archaeology and ethnographic data have much in common, and experimental archaeology borrows heavily from ethnography. The close links between ethnoarchaeology and experimental archaeology should be formalised as 'actualistic studies'. The often untapped resource of the analysis of traditions within our own societies will flourish rather than relying on the ethnographic 'other' culture for this kind of actualistic data. It is not always necessary to travel to the other side of the world to get ethnographic data when the extant craft traditions closer to home have much to offer. Furthermore, experimental archaeology will clarify the divide between the experiential archaeology which is so valuable as an educational and promotional tool and the no less powerful but different research agenda of 'archaeology by experiment'. Actualistic studies should increase and the new robust soft science of archaeology should have issues of materiality in primacy. In the same way that someone studying the social construct of gender will need to consider biological sex as basic underpinning strata, so the study of the social construction of material culture needs to be predicated upon an understanding of materials and materiality. The second section of the book has tried to clarify the strong links between materials and the series of possibilities they create because this affects both the way they have been used in the past and the manner in which they have been studied by archaeologists. Multi-sensory issues and interconnections between thoughts, feelings, sounds, and symbols will all become discussion points in material culture studies.

Some other issues have been crystallised by the writing process. In particular, the primacy given to science and theory at the expense of close practical observation is not sustainable. The fact that a skill is practical does not make it easy to acquire nor any less valid to deploy. In my view the primacy given to 'science' in our society and its perception as an opposite to 'arts' is not helpful and perpetuates a vision of a scientific approach as rigorous and factual (implying infallible and valuable) and an 'arts' (or social science) approach as more esoteric and different (implying fallible and of less value). In the former communist bloc there is a refreshingly different attitude where all researchers, no matter what their subject, are regarded as 'scientists'. Science is seen as a manner of thinking through ideas and data, and not a way of demarcating a set of disciplines.

In general, less will be excavated and more will be expected from those excavations. Research fieldwork will be even more restricted than at present but with ever more techniques deployed onto pristine excavated or stored material. Many research projects will return to previously excavated collections to mine them for different kinds of information or apply different techniques. The archaeologists will try to find funding to do the work they want, and the scientific money will go on developing new techniques that further refine a concept of an artefact as a site. It is to be hoped that scientific specialists take location-specific samples from objects and feel that they learn from the archaeological specialists, and that the archaeologists endeavour to understand the potential of the techniques even if the implementation of them is left to a specialist. The science of genetic and chemical trace analyses will increase further our understanding of who used the tool and what it was used on. In the past and at present the evidence bases have allowed a major focus on the questions of 'where from?' and 'how was it made?' with less attention paid to 'how was it used?' and 'why was it made?' If current advances continue there could be a fundamental shift to redress this balance. Such a shift would open up new research avenues because it has always been anomalous that the reason for an object's existence is often the most difficult aspect to appreciate. Objects can be debris from manufacture, and function can be pragmatic and highly social often in combination. No function is only about utility, and the manner of that use can be equally important: debris, tool, icon, heirloom, relic, and toy all reveal social information.

Artefacts are objects that often endure from remote periods and transcend the scale of human lives. We know about people we will never meet because of them. It is humbling to think that one day, in the remote future, others might know about us because of the objects we create and use.

Bibliography

Abbott, M. (1989) *Green Woodwork: working with wood the natural way*, Lewes: Craftsman Publications.

Abbott, M. (2004) *Living Wood: from buying a woodland to making a chair*, Bishop's Frome: Living Wood Books.

Adams, J.L. (2002) *Ground Stone Analysis: a technological approach*, Salt Lake City: University of Utah Press.

Adams, M.J. (1977) 'Style in southeast Asian materials processing: some implications for ritual and art', in H. Lechtman and R.S. Merrill (eds) *Material Culture: styles, organization, and the dynamics of technology*, New York: West Publishing Co., pp. 21–52.

Adams, W.H. and Boling, S.J. (2000) 'Status and ceramics for planters and slaves on three Georgia plantations', in D.R. Brauner (ed.) *Approaches to Material Culture Research for Historical Archaeologists*, California, PA: The Society for Historical Archaeology, pp. 111–138.

Adams, W.Y. and Adams, E.W. (1991) *Archaeological Typology and Practical Reality: a dialectical approach to artifact classification and sorting*, Cambridge: Cambridge University Press.

Adan-Bayewitz, D., Asaro, F., and Giaque, R.D. (2006) 'The discovery of anomalously high silver abundances in pottery from early Roman excavation contexts in Jerusalem', *Archaeometry*, 48.3: 377–398.

Adkins, L. and Adkins, R.A. (1989) *Archaeological Illustration*, Cambridge: Cambridge University Press.

Adovasio, J.M. (1970) 'The origin, development and distribution of Western Archaic Textiles', *Tebiwa*, 13: 1–40.

Adovasio, J.M. (1977) *Basketry Technology: a guide to identification and analysis*, Chicago: Aldine.

Ahler, S. and Geib, P.R. (2000) 'Why flute? Folsom point design and adaptation', *Journal of Archaeological Science*, 27.9: 799–820.

Aitken, M. (1990) *Science-Based Dating in Archaeology*, London: Longman.

Akerman, K., Fullagar, R., and van Gijn, A.L. (2002) 'Weapons and Wunan: production, function and exchange of Kimberley Points', *Australian Aboriginal Studies*, 1: 13–42.

Alberti, B. (2001) 'Faience goddesses and ivory bull-leapers: the aesthetics of sexual difference at Late Bronze Age Knossos', *World Archaeology*, 33: 189–205.

Albrethson, S.E. and Brinch Petersen, E. (1976) 'Excavation of a Mesolithic cemetery at Vedbaek, Denmark', *Acta Archaeologica*, 47: 1–28.

Alexander, J. (1970) *The Directing of Archaeological Excavations*, London: John Baker.

Alishan Yener, K. (2000) *The Domestication of Metals: the rise of complex metal industries in Anatolia*, Leiden: Brill.

Allason-Jones, L. and Jones, J.M. (2001) 'Identification of "jet" artefacts by reflected light microscopy', *European Journal of Archaeology*, 4.2: 233–251.

Allchin, B. (ed.) (1994) Living Traditions: studies in the ethnoarchaeology of South Asia, Columbia, MO: South Asia Publications.

Allen, T. (1995) Lithics and Landscape: archaeological discoveries on the Thames Water pipeline at Gatehampton Farm, Goring, Oxfordshire, 1985–92, Oxford: Oxford University Committee for Archaeology.

Ambrose, W.R. (1993) 'Obsidian hydration dating', in B.L. Fankauser and J.R. Bird (eds) Archaeometry: current Australasian research, Canberra: Australian National University (Occasional Papers in Prehistory 22), pp. 79–84.

Ambrose, W.R. (2001) 'Obsidian hydration dating', in D.R. Brothwell and A.M. Pollard (eds) Handbook of Archaeological Sciences, Chichester: Wiley, pp. 81–92.

Amick, D.S. and Mauldin, R.P. (eds) (1989) Experiments in Lithic Technology, Oxford: British Archaeological Reports International Series 528.

Amirkhanov, H.A. (ed.) (1998) The Eastern Gravettian, Moscow: Russian Academy of Sciences, Institute of Archaeology.

Ammerman, A. and Feldman, M. (1974) 'On the "making" of an assemblage of stone tools', American Antiquity, 39: 610–616.

Andersen, P. (1967) Brikvævning, Copenhagen: Borgen.

Andersen, S. (1987) 'Tybrind Vig: a submerged Ertebølle settlement in Denmark', in J. Coles and A. Lawson (eds) European Wetlands in Prehistory, Oxford: Clarendon, pp. 253–280.

Anderson, J. (2002a) 'Butser Ancient Farm', Bulletin of Primitive Technology, 23: 15–17.

Anderson, J. (2002b) 'The beginnings – living archaeology or applied technology', Bulletin of Primitive Technology, 23: 19–20.

Anderson, P.C. (1980) 'A testimony of prehistoric tasks: diagnostic residues on stone tool working edges', World Archaeology, 12: 181–194.

Anderson, P.C. (ed.) (1999) The Prehistory of Agriculture: new experimental and ethnographic approaches, Berkeley: University of California Press.

Anderson, P.C., Beyries, S., Otte, M. and Plisson, H. (eds) (1993a) Traces et fonction: les gestes retrouvés, vol. 1, Liège: Centre de Recherches Archéologiques du CNRS.

Anderson, P.C., Beyries, S., Otte, M., and Plisson, H. (eds) (1993b) Traces et fonction: les gestes retrouvés, vol. 2, Liège: Centre de Recherches Archéologiques du CNRS.

Anderson, P.C., Georges, J.-M., Vargiolu, R., and Zahouani, H. (2006) 'Insights from a tribological analysis of the tribulum', Journal of Archaeological Science, 33.11: 1559–1568.

Anderson-Gerfaud, P. (1986) 'A few comments concerning residue analysis of stone plant-processing tools', in L.R. Owen and G. Unrath (eds) Technical Aspects of Microwear Studies on Stone Tools, Parts I and II, Early Man News 9/10/11, Tübingen, pp. 69–82 and plates 18–19.

Andrefsky, W. (1998; 2nd edn 2005) Lithics: macroscopic approaches to analysis, Cambridge: Cambridge University Press.

Andrefsky, W. (ed.) (2001) Lithic debitage: context, form and meaning, Salt Lake City: University of Utah.

Andrefsky, W. (2005) 'Lithic studies', in H.D.G. Maschner and C. Chippindale (eds) Handbook of Archaeological Methods, Lanham, MD: AltaMira Press, pp. 715–772.

Andrews, G. (1991) Management of Archaeological Projects, London: English Heritage.

Andrews, P. (1995) 'Experiments in taphonomy', Journal of Archaeological Science, 22: 147–153.

Antipina, Y. (2001) 'Bone tools and wares from the site of Gorny (1690–1410 BC) in the Kargaly mining complex in the south Ural part of the east European steppe', in A.M. Choyke and L. Bartosiewicz (eds) Crafting Bone: skeletal technologies through time and space, proceedings of the 2nd meeting of the (ICAZ) Worked Bone Research Group Budapest, 31 August – 5 September 1999, Oxford: British Archaeological Reports International Series 937, pp. 171–178.

Appadurai, A. (ed.) (1986) The Social Life of Things: commodities in cultural perspective, Cambridge: Cambridge University Press.

Armitage, R.A., Minc, L., Hill, D.V., and Hurry, S.D. (2006) 'Characterization of bricks and tiles from the 17th-century brick chapel, St Mary's City, Maryland', *Journal of Archaeological Science*, 33: 615–627.

Arnold, Béat (1990) *Cortalloid-Est et les village du Lac de Neuchâtelel au bronze final*, *Archéologie Neuchâteloise* 6, Sainte Blaise: Editions du Ruau.

Arnold, Bettina (1990) 'The past as propaganda: totalitarian archaeology in Nazi Germany', *Antiquity*, 64: 464–478.

Arnold, B. and Wieker, N.L. (eds) (2001) *Gender and the Archaeology of Death*, Walnut Creek, CA: AltaMira Press.

Arnold, D.E. (1971) 'Ethnomineralogy of Ticul, Yucatan potters: etics and emics', *American Antiquity*, 36: 20–40.

Arnold, D.E. (1985) *Ceramic Theory and Cultural Process*, Cambridge: Cambridge University Press.

Arnold, D.E., Neff, H., and Bishop, R.L. (1991) 'Compositional analysis and "sources" of pottery: an ethnoarchaeological approach', *American Antiquity*, 93: 70–90.

Arnold, D.E., Neff, H.A., Bishop, R.L., and Glascock, M.D. (1999) 'Testing interpretative assumptions of neutron activation analysis: contemporary pottery in Yucatán, 1964–1994', in E.S. Chilton (ed.) *Material Meanings: critical approaches to the interpretation of material culture*, Salt Lake City: University of Utah Press, pp. 61–84.

Arnold III, P.J. (1991) *Domestic Ceramic Production and Spatial Organisation: a Mexican case study in ethnoarchaeology*, Cambridge: Cambridge University Press.

Arnold III, P.J. (1999) 'On typologies, selection, and ethnoarchaeology in ceramic production studies', in E.S. Chilton (ed.) *Material Meanings: critical approaches to the interpretation of material culture*, Salt Lake City: University of Utah Press, pp. 103–117.

Arthur, J.W. (2002) 'Pottery use-alteration as an indicator of socioeconomic status: an ethnoarchaeological study of the Gamo of Ethiopia', *Journal of Archaeological Method and Theory*, 9.4: 331–355.

Arthur, J.W. and Weedman, K.J. (2005) 'Ethnoarchaeology', in H.D.G. Maschner and C. Chippindale (eds) *Handbook of Archaeological Methods*, Lanham, MD: AltaMira, pp. 216–269.

Ascher, R. (1961a) 'Experimental archaeology', *American Anthropologist*, 63.4: 739–816.

Ascher, R. (1961b) 'Analogy in archaeological interpretation', *Southwestern Journal of Anthropology*, 17: 317–325.

Ashton, N. and David, A. (eds) (1994) *Stories in Stone*, London: Lithic Studies Society.

Aston, B.A. (1994) *Ancient Egyptian Stone Vessels: materials and forms*, Heidelberg: Heidelberger Orientverlag.

Aston, B.A., Harrel, J. and Shaw, I. (2000) 'Stone', in P.T.Nicholson and I. Shaw (eds) *Ancient Egyptian Materials and Technology*, Cambridge: Cambridge University Press, pp. 5–77.

Atchison, J. and Fullagar, R. (1998) 'Starch residues on pounding implements from Jinmium rock-shelter', in R. Fullagar (ed.) *A Closer Look: recent Australian studies of stone tools*, Sydney: University of Sydney, Sydney University Archaeological Methods Series 6, pp. 109–126.

Aten, A., Faraday-Innes, R., and Knew, E. (1955) *Flaying and Curing of Hides and Skins as a Rural Industry*, Rome: Food and Agriculture Organization of the United Nations.

Atherton, J. (1983) 'Ethnoarchaeology in Africa', *The African Archaeological Review*, 1: 75–104.

Audouin, F. and Plisson, H. (1982) 'Les Ocres et leurs témoins au paléolithique en France: enquête et expériences sur leur validité archéologique', *Cahiers du Centre de Recherches Préhistoriques*, 8: 33–80.

Audouze, F. (ed.) (1992) *Ethnoarchéologie: justification, problèmes, limites*, Juan-les-Pins: Editions APDCA.

Aveling, E.M. and Heron, C. (1998) 'Identification of birch bark tar at the Mesolithic site of Starr Carr', *Ancient Biomolecules*, 2: 69–80.

Aveling, E.M. and Heron, C. (1999) 'Chewing tar in the early Holocene: an archaeological and ethnographic evaluation', *Antiquity*, 73: 579–584.

Bagshawe, T.W. (1949) 'Romano-British hoes or rakes', *Antiquaries' Journal*, 29: 86–87.

Bahn, P.G. and Vertut, J. (1988) *Images of the Ice Age*, Leicester: Windward.

Bahnson, A. (2005) 'Women's skin coats from West Greenland – with special focus on formal clothing of caribou skin from the early nineteenth century', in J.C.H. King, B. Pauksztat, and R. Storrie (eds) *Arctic Clothing of North America – Alaska, Canada, Greenland*, London: The British Museum Press, pp. 84–90.

Bailey, G. (ed.) (1983) *Hunter-Gatherer Economy in Prehistory: a European perspective*, Cambridge: Cambridge University Press.

Baillie, M. (1995) *A Slice through Time: dendrochronology and precision dating*, London: Batsford.

Balfour-Paul, J. (1997) *Indigo in the Arab World*, Richmond: Curzon.

Balme, J. and Paterson, A. (eds) (2005) *Archaeology in Practice: a student guide to archaeological analyses*, Oxford: Blackwell.

Bamforth, D.B. (1986) 'Technological efficiency and tool curation', *American Antiquity*, 51: 38–50.

Bamforth, D.B. (1988) 'Investigating microwear polishes with blind tests: the institute results in context', *Journal of Archaeological Science*, 15: 11–24.

Bamforth, D.B., Burns, G.R., and Woodman, C. (1990) 'Ambiguous use traces and blind test results: new data', *Journal of Archaeological Science*, 17: 413–430.

Banghard, K. (2000) 'Jungneolithische Rindendächer', in S. Heinrichs and M. Passlick (eds) *Experimentelle Archäologie: Bilanz 1999*, Oldenburg: Isensee, pp. 7–12.

Banks, W. and Greenwood, C. (1975) *Starch and Its Components*, Edinburgh: Edinburgh University Press.

Banning, E.B. (2000) *The Archaeologist's Laboratory: the analysis of archaeological data*, New York: Kluwer/Plenum.

Barber, E.J.W. (1991) *Prehistoric Textiles: the development of cloth in the Neolithic and Bronze Ages with special reference to the Aegean*, Oxford: Princeton University Press.

Barber, E.W. (1994) Women's Work: the first 20,000 years, London: W.W. Norton & Company.

Barber, M., Field, D., and Topping, P. (1999) *The Neolithic Flint Mines of England*, Swindon: English Heritage.

Barclay, K. (2001) *Scientific Analyses of Archaeological Ceramics*, Oxford: Oxbow.

Barfield, L. (1994) 'The Iceman reviewed', *Antiquity*, 68: 10–26.

Barfield, L. and Hodder, M. (1987) 'Burnt mounds as saunas and the prehistory of bathing', *Antiquity*, 61: 370–379.

Barker, P. (1979) (2nd edn) *Techniques of Archaeological Excavation*, London: Batsford.

Barley, N. (1983) *The Innocent Anthropologist: notes from a mud hut*, London: British Museum Press.

Barley, N. (1994) *Smashing Pots: feats of clay from Africa*, London: British Museum Press.

Barnatt, J. and Herring, P. (1986) 'Stone circles and megalithic geometry: an experiment to test alternative design practices', *Journal of Archaeological Science*, 13: 431–450.

Barnett, W.K. and Hoopes, J.W. (1995) *The Emergence of Pottery: technology and innovation in ancient societies*, Washington DC: Smithsonian Institution Press.

Barratt, J.C., Freeman, W.M., and Woodward, A. (2000) *Cadbury Castle, Somerset: the later prehistoric and early historic archaeology*, London: English Heritage.

Bartoll, J. and Ikeya, M. (1997) 'ESR dating: a trial', *Applied Radiation and Isotopes*, 48: 981–984.

Barton, H., Torrence, R., and Fullagar, R. (1998) 'Clues to stone tool function re-examined: comparing starch grain frequencies on used and unused obsidian artefacts', *Journal of Archaeological Science*, 25: 1231–1238.

Bataille, G. and Sontag, S. (2001) *Story of the Eye*, London: Penguin.

Baxter, E.J. (2005) The Archaeology of Childhood: children, gender and material culture, Walnut Creek, CA: AltaMira.

Baxter, M.J. (2001) 'Multivariate analysis in archaeology', in D.R. Brothwell and A.M. Pollard (eds) Handbook of Archaeological Sciences, Chichester: Wiley, pp. 685–694.

Baxter, M.J. and Buck, C.E. (2000) 'Data handling and statistical analysis', in E. Ciliberto and G. Spoto (eds) Modern Analytical Methods in Art and Archaeology, New York: Wiley, pp. 681–746.

Baxter, M.J. and Jackson, C.M. (2001) 'Variable selection in artefact compositional studies', Archaeometry, 43: 253–268.

Baxter, M.J., Cool, H.E.M., and Jackson, C.M. (2006) 'Comparing glass compositional analyses', Archaeometry, 48: 399–414.

Bayley, J. (ed.) (1998) Science in Archaeology: an agenda for the future, London: English Heritage.

Bayman, J.M. (2002) 'Hohokam craft economies and the materialization of power', Journal of Archaeological Method and Theory, 9: 69–95.

Beausang, E. (2000) 'Childbirth in prehistory: an introduction', European Journal of Archaeology, 3: 69–87.

Becher, T. (1989) Academic Tribes and Territories: intellectual enquiry and the cultures of disciplines, Milton Keynes: The Society for Research into Higher Education and Open University Press.

Beck, C.W. (1985) 'The role of the scientist: the amber trade, the chemical analysis of amber, and the determination of Baltic provenience', Journal of Baltic Studies, 16: 191–199.

Beck, C.W. and Borromeo, C. (1990) 'Ancient pine pitch: technological perspectives from a Hellenistic shipwreck', in A.R. Biers and P.E. McGovern (eds) Organic Contents of Ancient Vessels: materials analysis and archaeological investigation, Philadelphia: University of Pennsylvania Museum, Research Papers in Science and Archaeology 7, pp. 51–58.

Beck, C.W. and Shennan, S. (1990) Amber in Prehistoric Britain, Oxford: Oxbow Books.

Beck, C.W., Loze, I.B., and Todd, J.M. (2003) Amber in Archaeology: proceedings of the fourth International Conference on Amber in Archaeology, Talsi, 2001, Riga: Institute of the History of Latvia Publishers.

Beck, C.W., Smart, C.J., and Ossenkop, D.J. (1989) 'Residues and linings in ancient Mediterranean transport amphoras', in R.O. Allen (ed.) Archaeological Chemistry IV, Washington DC: American Chemical Society, Advances in Chemistry 220, pp. 369–380.

Begemann, F., Schmitt-Strecker, S., Pernicka, E., and Lo Schiavo, F. (2001) 'Chemical composition and lead isotopy of copper and bronze from Nuraghic Sardinia', European Journal of Archaeology, 4: 43–85.

Bell, H.R. (1998) Men's Business, Women's Business: the spiritual role of gender in the world's oldest culture, Rochester, VT: Inner Traditions.

Bell, M., Fowler, P.J., and Hillson, S. (1996) The Experimental Earthwork 1962–90, York: Council for British Archaeology.

Bellot-Gurlet, L., Poupeau, G., Dorighel, O., Calligaro, T., Dran, J.-C., and Salomon, J. (1999) 'A PIXE/fission-track dating approach to sourcing studies of obsidian artefacts in Colombia and Ecuador', Journal of Archaeological Science, 26: 855–860.

Beloe, E.M. (1892) 'Quern with iron handle from Leziate', Proceedings of the Society of Antiquaries (2nd series), 14: 183.

Beloyianni, M.P. (2000) 'Baskets in the fresco of the "Saffron Gatherers" at Akrotiri, Thera: relevance to the present', in S. Sherratt (ed.) The Wall Paintings of Thera: proceedings of the first international symposium, vol. 2, Athens: Petros M. Nomikos and the Thera Foundation, pp. 568–579.

Bender-Jørgensen, L. (1986) Forhistoriske Textiler I Skandinavien (Prehistoric Scandinavian Textiles), Copenhagen: Det Kongelige Nordiske Oldskriftselskab.

Bender-Jørgensen, L. (1992) North European Textiles until AD 1000, Aarhus: Aarhus University Press.

Bender-Jørgensen, L. and Munksgaard, E. (eds) (1992) *Archaeological Textiles in Northern Europe*, Tidens Tand, 5, Copenhagen: Kons Skol.

Bennike, P., Ebbeson, K., and Bender-Jørgensen, L. (1986) 'Early neolithic skeletons from Bolkilde bog, Denmark', *Antiquity*, 60: 199–209.

Benson, L.V., Hattori, E.M., Taylor, H.E., Poulson, S.R., and Jolies, E.A. (2006) 'Isotope sourcing of prehistoric willow and tule textiles recovered from western Great Basin rock shelters and caves: proof of concept', *Journal of Archaeological Science*, 33: 1588–1599.

Bergen, P.F. van, Bull, I.D., Poulton, P.R., and Evershed, R.P. (1997) 'Organic geochemical studies of soils from the Rothamstead classical experiments 1. Total lipid extracts, solvent insoluble residues and humic acids from Broadbalk wilderness', *Organic Geochemistry*, 26: 117–135.

Bernick, K. (1998). 'Stylistic characteristics of basketry from Coast Salish area wet sites', in K. Bernick (ed.) *Hidden Dimensions: the cultural significance of wetland archaeology*, Vancouver: University of British Columbia, pp. 139–156.

Berquist, A. and Taylor, T. (1987) 'The origin of the Gundestrup Cauldron', *Antiquity*, 61: 10–24.

Betancourt, P. (1985) *The History of Minoan Pottery*, Princeton: Princeton University Press.

Beuker, J.R. (1983) *Vakmanschap in vuursteen: de vervaardiging en het gebruik van vuurstenen verktuigen in de prehistorie*, Assen: Provincial Museum van Drenthe.

Beuker, J.R. (1990) *Werken met steen*, Assen: Provincial Museum van Drenthe.

Binford, L.R. (1962) 'Archaeology as anthropology', *American Antiquity*, 28: 217–225.

Binford, L.R. (1967) 'Smudge pits and hide smoking: the use of analogy in archaeological reasoning', *American Antiquity*, 32: 1–12.

Binford, L.R. (1972) *An Archaeological Perspective*, New York: Seminar Press.

Binford, L.R. (1973) 'Interassemblage variability – the Mousterian and the "functional" argument', in C. Renfrew (ed.) *The Explanation of Culture Change: models in prehistory*, London: Duckworth, pp. 227–254.

Binford, L.R. (1978) *Nunamiut Ethnoarchaeology*, New York: Academic Press.

Binford, L.R. (1979) 'Organization and formation processes: looking at curated technologies', *Journal of Anthropological Research*, 35: 255–73.

Binford, L.R. (1981) 'Behavioural archaeology and the "Pompeii Premise"', *Journal of Anthropological Research*, 37: 195–208.

Binford, L.R. (2001) *Constructing Frames of Reference: an analytical method for archaeological theory building using hunter-gatherer and environmental data sets*, Berkeley: University of California Press.

Binford, S.R. and Binford, L.R. (eds) (1968) *New Perspectives in Archaeology*, Chicago: Aldine.

Bird, C.F.M. (1993) 'Woman the toolmaker: evidence for women's use and manufacture of flaked stone tools in Australia and New Guinea', in H. du Cros and L. Smith (eds) *Women in Archaeology: a feminist critique*, Canberra: The Australian National University Occasional Paper 23, pp. 22–30.

Bíró, M.T. (2003) 'Recycling worked bone in Pannonia: data on curation of workshop debitage and worn/damaged objects in the Roman bone manufacturing industry', in I. Riddler (ed.) *Materials of Manufacture: the choice of materials in the working of bone and antler in northern and central Europe during the first millennium AD*, Oxford: British Archaeological Reports International Series 1193, pp. 19–24.

Bisson, M.S. (2000) 'Nineteenth-century tools for twenty-first century archaeology? Why the Middle Paleolithic typology of François Bordes must be replaced', *Journal of Archaeological Method and Theory*, 7: 1–48.

Bisson, M.S., Childs, S.T., de Barros, P., and Holl, A.F.C. (2000) *Ancient African Metallurgy: the sociocultural context*, Walnut Creek, CA: AltaMira Press.

Blinman, E. and Swink, C. (1997) 'Technology and organization of Anasazi trench kilns', in P.M. Rice (ed.) *The prehistory and history of ceramic kilns: ceramics and civilisation, vol. 7*, Colombus: The American Ceramic Society, pp. 85–102.

Blumenschine, R.J., Marean, C.W., and Capaldo, S.D. (1996) 'Blind tests of inter-analyst correspondence and accuracy in the identification of cut marks, percussion marks, and carnivore tooth marks on bone surfaces', *Journal of Archaeological Science*, 23: 493–507.

Bocquet, A. (1994) 'Charavines il y a 5000 ans', *Dossiers d'Archéologie*, 199: 1–104.

Bodribb, G. (1987) *Roman Brick and Tile*, Gloucester: Alan Sutton.

Boetzkes, M. and Lüth, J.B. (eds) (1991) *Woven Messages – Indonesian Textile Tradition in Course of Time*, Hildesheim: Roemer-Museum.

Boileau, M.-C. (2005) *Production et distribution des céramiques au IIIe millénaire en Syrie du Nord-Est: étude technologique des céramiques de Tell'Atij et Tell Gudeda*, Paris: Editions Epistèmes (Maison des sciences de l'homme).

Boivin, N. (2004) 'Geoarchaeology and the goddess Laksmi: Rajasthani insights into geoarchaeological methods and prehistoric soil use', in N. Boivin and M.A. Owoc (eds) *Soils, Stones and Symbols: cultural perceptions of the mineral world*, London: UCL Press, pp. 165–186.

Boivin, N. and Owoc, M.A. (eds) (2004) *Soils, Stones and Symbols: cultural perceptions of the mineral world*, London: UCL Press.

Bonnichsen, R., Hodges, L., Ream, W., Field, K.G., Kirner, D.L., Selsor, K., and Taylor, R.E. (2001) 'Methods for the study of ancient hair: radiocarbon dates and gene sequences from individual hairs', *Journal of Archaeological Science*, 28: 775–785.

Bordaz, J. (1970) *Tools of the Old and New Stone Age*, New York: Dover Publications.

Bosson, M.S. (2001) 'Interview with a Neanderthal: an experimental approach for reconstructing scraper production rules, and their implications for imposed form in Middle Palaolithic tools', *Cambridge Archaeological Journal*, 11: 165–184.

Bourdieu, P. (1977) *Outline of a Theory of Practice*, Cambridge: Cambridge University Press.

Bourke, L. (2001) *Crossing the Rubicon: Bronze Age metalwork from Irish rivers*, Galway: National University of Ireland Press.

Bourraiu, J.D., Nicholson, P.T., and Rose, P.J. (2000) 'Pottery', in P.T. Nicholson and I. Shaw (eds) *Ancient Egyptian Materials and Technology*, Cambridge: Cambridge University Press, pp. 121–147.

Bouzek, J., Koutecky, D., and Simon, K. (1989) 'Tin and prehistoric mining in the Erzgebirge (Ore Mountains): some new evidence', *Oxford Journal of Archaeology*, 8: 203–212.

Bowers, P.M., Bonnichsen, R., and Hoch, D. M. (1983) 'Flake dispersal experiments: non-cultural transformation of the archaeological record', *American Antiquity*, 48: 553–572.

Bradley, B., Winkler, M.H., INTERpark and Primitive Tech. Enterprises (1989) *Flintknapping with Dr. Bruce Bradley* [video], Cortez, CO: INTERpark.

Bradley, B.A. (1975) 'Lithic reduction sequences: a glossary and discussion', in E. Swanson (ed.) *Stone Tool Use and Manufacture*, The Hague: Mouton, pp. 5–14.

Bradley, B.A. (2000a) 'Getting to the point: arrowheads at Stix and Leaves Pueblo', *Indian Artifact Magazine*, 20–1 (http://www.primtech.net/iam/article.html).

Bradley, B.A. (2000b) 'Points from two Pueblo Sites in Southwestern Colorado', http://www.primtech.net/chips/Points.htm.

Bradley, C.S. (2000) 'Smoking pipes for the archaeologist', in K. Karklins (ed.) *Studies in Material Culture Research*, California, PA: The Society for Historical Archaeology, pp. 104–133.

Bradley, R. (1990a) 'Perforated stone axe-heads in the British Neolithic: their distribution and significance', *Oxford Journal of Archaeology*, 9: 299–304.

Bradley, R. (1990b) *The Passage of Arms: an archaeological analysis of prehistoric hoards and votive deposits*, Cambridge: Cambridge University Press.

Bradley, R. (1997) *Rock Art and the Prehistory of Atlantic Europe: signing the land*, London: Routledge.

Bradley, R. (2000) *An Archaeology of Natural Places*, London: Routledge.

Bradley, R. (2002) *The Past in Prehistoric Societies*, London: Routledge.

Bradley, R. (2006) 'Bridging the two cultures: commercial archaeology and the study of British prehistory', *The Antiquaries Journal*, 86: 1–13.

Bradley, R. and Edmonds, M. (1988) 'Fieldwork at Great Langdale, Cumbria 1985–1987: preliminary report', *Antiquaries' Journal*, 68: 181–209.

Bradley, R. and Edmonds, M. (1993) *Interpreting the Axe Trade*, Cambridge: Cambridge University Press.

Bradley, R. and Ford, S. (1986) 'The siting of Neolithic stone quarries – experimental archaeology at Great Langdale, Cumbria', *Oxford Journal of Archaeology*, 5: 123–128.

Bradley, R. and Suthren, R. (1990) 'Petrographic analysis of hammerstones from the Neolithic quarries at Great Langdale', *Proceedings of the Prehistoric Society*, 56: 117–122.

Bradley, R., Meredith, P., Smith, J., and Edmonds, M. (1992) 'Rock physics and the Neolithic axe trade in Great Britain', *Archaeometry*, 34: 223–234.

Bradshaw, R.H.W., Coxon, P., Greig, J.R.A., and Hall, A.R. (1981) 'New fossil evidence for the past cultivation and processing of hemp (Cannabis sativa L.) in Eastern England', *New Phytologist*, 89: 503–510.

Brandt, S.A. and Weedman, K.J. (1997) 'The ethnoarchaeology of hide working and flakes stone tool use in southern Ethiopia', in K. Fukui, E. Kurimoto, and M. Shigeta (eds) *Ethiopia in Broader Perspective: papers of the 13th International Conference of Ethiopian Studies, Vol. 1*, Kyoto: Shokado Book Sellers, pp. 351–361.

Braun, D. (1980) 'Experimental interpretation of ceramic vessel use on the basis of rim and neck formal attributes', Appendix 1 in D.C. Fiero, R.W. Munson, M.T. McClain, S.M. Wilson, and A.H. Zier (eds) *The Navajo Project*, Flagstaff, AZ: Museum of Northern Arizona, Research Paper 11, pp. 171–231.

Braun, D.P. (1983) 'Pots as tools', in J. Moore and A. Keene (eds) *Archaeological Hammers and Theories*, New York: Academic Press, pp. 107–134.

Brauner, D.R. (ed.) (2000) *Approaches to Material Culture Research for Historical Archaeologists*, California, PA: The Society for Historical Archaeology.

Briard, J. (1976) *L'Age de Bronze en Europe barbare*; trans. M. Turton (1979) *The Bronze Age in Barbarian Europe: from the megaliths to the Celts*, London: Book Club Associates with Routledge and Kegan Paul Ltd.

Bridgford, S. (1997) 'Mightier than the pen? An edgewise look at Irish Bronze Age swords', in Carman, J. (ed.) *Material Harm: archaeological studies of war and violence*, Glasgow: Cruithne Press, pp. 95–115.

Briuer, F.L. (1976) 'New clues to stone tool function: plant and animal residues', *American Antiquity*, 41: 478–483.

Brodie, N. Doole, J., and Renfrew, C. (eds) (2001) *Trade in Illicit Antiquities: the destruction of the world's archaeological heritage*, Cambridge: McDonald Institute.

Broholm, H.C. and Hald, M. (1948) *Bronze Age Fashion*, Copenhagen: Gyldendalske Boghandel Nordisk Forlag.

Bronitsky, G. and Hamer, R. (1986) 'Experiments in ceramic technology: the effects of various tempering materials on impact and thermal shock resistance', *American Antiquity*, 51: 89–101.

Brose, D. (1975) 'Functional analysis of stone tools: a cautionary note on the role of animal fats', *American Antiquity*, 40: 86–94.

Broshi, M. (1994) 'Archaeological museums in Israel: reflections on problems of national identity', in F.E.S. Kaplan (ed.) *Museums and the Making of 'Ourselves'*, pp. 314–329.

Brothwell, D.R. and Pollard, A.M. (eds) (2001) Handbook of Archaeological Sciences, Chichester: Wiley.

Brown, J. (1995) Traditional Metalworking in Kenya, Oxford: Oxbow.

Brown, R. (1995, 3rd edn) Beeswax, Burrowbridge: Bee Books.

Brown, T.A. (2001) 'Ancient DNA', in D.R. Brothwell and A.M. Pollard (eds) Handbook of Archaeological Sciences, Chichester: Wiley, pp. 301–312.

Brück, J. (1995) A place for the dead: the role of human remains in Late Bronze Age Britain', Proceedings of the Prehistoric Society, 61: 245–277.

Brück, J. (1999a) 'Houses, lifecycles and deposition on Middle Bronze Age settlements in Southern Britain', Proceedings of the Prehistoric Society, 65: 145–166.

Brück, J. (1999b) 'The nature of the upper secondary fill in the outer ditch, Trench B', in A. Whittle, J. Pollard, and C. Grigson (eds) The Harmony of Symbols: the Windmill Hill causewayed enclosure, Oxford: Oxbow, pp. 375–380.

Brück, J. (2001) Bronze Age Landscapes: tradition and transformation, Oxford: Oxbow.

Brugmann, B. (2004) Glass Beads from Early Anglo-Saxon Graves: a study of the provenance and chronology of glass beads from Early Anglo-Saxon graves, based on visual examination, Oxford: Oxbow Books.

Brumm, A. (2004) 'An axe to grind: symbolic considerations of stone axe use in ancient Australia', in N. Boivin and M.A. Owoc (eds) Soils, Stones and Symbols: cultural perceptions of the mineral world, London: UCL Press, pp. 143–163.

Brysting Damm, C. (2000) 'Time, gender and production: a critical evaluation of archaeological time concepts', in M. Donald and L. Hurcombe (eds) Gender and Material Culture in Archaeological Perspective, London: Macmillan, pp. 110–122.

Brzeziński, W. and Piotrowski, W. (eds) (1997) Proceedings of the First International Symposium on Wood Tar and Pitch: held by the Biskupin Museum (department of the State Archaeological Museum in Warsaw) and the Museumsdorf Düppel (Berlin) at Biskupin Museum, Poland, July 1st–4th 1993, Warsaw: Domu Wydawniczym Pawła Dąbrowskiego.

Buchli, V. (ed.) (2004) Material Culture: critical concepts in the social sciences (3 vols), London: Routledge.

Buckley, V. (ed.) (1990) Burnt Offerings: international contributions to burnt mound archaeology, Dublin: Wordwell.

Budd, P. and Taylor, T. (1995) 'The faerie smith meets the bronze industry: magic versus science in the interpretation of prehistoric metal-making', World Archaeology, 27: 133–143.

Budd, P., Gale, D., Pollard, A.M., Thomas, R.G., and Williams, P.A. (1992) 'The early development of metallurgy in the British Isles', Antiquity, 66: 677–686.

Budd, P., Pollard, A.M., Scaife, B., and Thomas, R.G. (1995) 'Oxhide ingots, recycling and the Mediterranean metals trade', Journal of Mediterranean Archaeology, 8: 1–32, 70–75.

Buford Price, P. (2005) 'Science and technology with nuclear tracks in solids', Radiation Measurements, 40: 146–159.

Buijs, C. (2005) 'Clothing as a visual representation of identities in East Greenland', in J.C.H. King, B. Pauksztat, and R. Storrie (eds) Arctic Clothing of North America – Alaska, Canada, Greenland, London: The British Museum Press, pp. 108–114.

Burkitt, M.C. (1920) 'Classification of burins or gravers', Proceedings of the Prehistoric Society of East Anglia, 3: 306–310.

Burley, D.V. (2000) 'Function, meaning and context: ambiguities in ceramic use by the Hivernant Metis of the Northwestern Plains', in D.R. Brauner (ed.) Approaches to Material Culture Research for Historical Archaeologists, California, PA: The Society for Historical Archaeology, pp. 399–408.

Burov, G.M. (1998) 'The use of vegetable materials in the Mesolithic of northeast Europe', in M. Zvelebil, L. Domańska, and R. Dennell (eds) Harvesting the Sea, Farming the Forest: the *emergence of Neolithic societies in the Baltic Region*, Sheffield: Sheffield Academic Press Ltd, pp. 53–63.

Buzon, M.R., Eng, J.T., Lambert, P.T., and Walker, P.L. (2005) 'Bioarchaeological methods', in H.D.G. Maschner and C. Chippindale (eds) *Handbook of Archaeological Methods*, Lanham, MD: AltaMira, pp. 871–918.

Cahen, D. and Keeley, L.H. (1980) 'Not less than two, not more than three', *World Archaeology* 12: 166–180.

Callahan, E. (1999) 'What is experimental archaeology?', in D. Westcott (ed.) *Primtive Technology: a book of earth skills*, Layton, UT: Gibbs Smith, pp. 4–6.

Callahan, E. (2002) 'Hans de Haas: the gentle giant', *Bulletin of Primitive Technology*, 23: 27–29.

Cameron, C.M. and Tomka, S.A. (eds) (1993) *Abandonment of Settlements and Regions: ethnoarchaeological and archaeological approaches*, Cambridge: Cambridge University Press.

Cameron, E. (ed.) (1998) *Leather and Fur: aspects of early medieval trade and technology*, London: Archetype Publications Ltd.

Campbell, P. (2002) 'Mortar and pestle', *Bulletin of Primitive Technology*, 24: 19–24.

Caple, C. (2000) *Conservation Skills: judgement, method and decision making*, London: Routledge.

Caple, C. (2001) 'Degradation, investigation and preservation of archaeological evidence', in D.R. Brothwell and A.M. Pollard (eds) *Handbook of Archaeological Sciences*, Chichester: Wiley, pp. 587–594.

Carey, J. (2003) *Braids and Beyond: a broad look at narrow wares*, Ottery St Mary, Devon: Carey Company/Braid Society.

Carpenter, A.J. and Feinman, G.M. (1999) 'The effects of behaviour on ceramic composition: implications for the definition of production locations', *Journal of Archaeological Science*, 26: 783–797.

Carr, C. (1990) 'Advances in ceramic radiography and analysis: applications and potentials', *Journal of Archaeological Science*, 17: 13–34.

Carr, P.J. (ed.) (1994) *The Organisation of North American Prehistoric Chipped Stone Tool Technologies*, Ann Arbor, MI: International Monographs in Prehistory.

Carter, T., Poupeau, G., Bressy, C., and Pearce, N.J.G. (2006) 'A new programme of obsidian characterization at Çatalhöyük, Turkey', *Journal of Archaeological Science*, 33: 893–909.

Carver, M.O.H. (1985) 'Theory and practice in urban pottery seriation', *Journal of Archaeological Science*, 12: 353–366.

Castoldi, G.L. (1981) 'Erythrocytes', in D. Zucker-Franklin, M.F. Greaves, C.E. Grossi, and A.M. Marmont (eds) *Atlas of Blood Cells: function and pathology*, Milan and Philadelphia: Ermes/Lea & Febiger, pp. 35–145.

Catling, D. and Grayson, J. (1998) *Identification of Vegetable Fibres*, London: Archetype.

Cattaneo, C., Gelsthorpe, K., Phillips, P., and Sokal, R.J. (1993) 'Blood residues on stone tools: indoor and outdoor experiments', *World Archaeology*, 25: 29–43.

Cattaneo, C., Gelsthorpe, K., Dixon, P., Gale, J., Phillips, P., and Sokal, R.J. (1994) 'Erratic survival: blood on stones', in N. Aston and A. David (eds) *Stories in Stone*, London: Lithic Studies Society, Occasional Paper 4, pp. 24–27.

Caulfield, S. (1977) 'The beehive quern in Ireland', *Journal of the Royal Society of Antiquaries of Ireland*, 107: 104–138.

Cecil, L.G. and Neff, H. (2006) 'Postclassic Maya slips and paints and their relationship to socio-political groups in El Petén, Guatemala', *Journal of Archaeological Science*, 33: 1482–1491.

Cernych, E.N. (1978) 'Aibunar, a Balkan copper mine of the 4th millennium BC', *Proceedings of the Prehistoric Society*, 44: 203–217.

Chapman, J. (2000) *Fragmentation in Archaeology: people, places and broken objects in the prehistory of south eastern Europe*, London: Routledge.

Charles, D.K., Nest, J. van, and Buikstra, J.E. (2004) 'From the earth: minerals and meaning in the Hopewellian World', in N. Boivin and M.A. Owoc (eds) *Soils, Stones and Symbols: cultural perceptions of the mineral world*, London: UCL Press, pp. 43–70.

Charles, R. (1997) 'The exploitation of carnivores and other fur-bearing mammals during the north-western European Late Upper Palaeolithic and Mesolithic', *Oxford Journal of Archaeology*, 16: 253–277.

Charters, S., Evershed, R.P., Goad, L.J., Heron, C., and Blinkhorn, P. (1993a) 'Identification of an adhesive used to repair a Roman jar', *Archaeometry*, 35: 91–101.

Charters, S., Evershed, R.P., Goad, L.J., Leyden, A., Blinkhorn, P.W., and Denham, V. (1993b) 'Quantification and distribution of lipids in archaeological ceramics: implications for sampling potsherds for organic residue analysis', *Archaeometry*, 35: 211–223.

Chataigner, C., Badalin, R., Bigazzi, G., Cauvin, M.-C., Jrbashian, R., Karapetian, S.G., Norelli, P., Oddone, M., and Poidevin, J.-L. (2003) 'Provenance studies of obsidian artifacts from Armenian archaeological sites using the fission-track dating method', *Journal of Non-Crystalline Solids*, 323: 167–171.

Childe, V.G. (1925) *The Dawn of European Civilisation*, London: Kegan Paul.

Childe, V.G. (1926) *The Aryans: a study of Indo-European origins*, London: Kegan Paul.

Chilton, E.S. (ed.) (1999a) *Material Meanings: critical approaches to the interpretation of material culture*, Salt Lake City: University of Utah Press.

Chilton, E.S. (1999b) 'One size fits all: typology and alternatives for ceramic research', in E.S. Chilton (ed.) *Material Meanings: critical approaches to the interpretation of material culture*, Salt Lake City: University of Utah Press, pp. 44–60.

Choyke, A.M. (2001) 'Late Neolithic Red Deer canine beads and their imitations', in A.M. Choyke and L. Bartosiewicz (eds) *Crafting Bone: skeletal technologies through time and space, proceedings of the 2nd meeting of the (ICAZ) Worked Bone Research Group Budapest, 31 August – 5 September 1999*, British Archaeological Reports International Series 937, Oxford: Archaeopress, pp. 251–266.

Choyke, A.M. and Bartosiewicz, L. (eds) (2001) *Crafting Bone: skeletal technologies through time and space, proceedings of the 2nd meeting of the (ICAZ) Worked Bone Research Group Budapest, 31 August – 5 September 1999*, British Archaeological Reports International Series 937, Oxford: Archaeopress.

Christensen, M., Walter, P.H., and Menu, M. (1992) 'Usewear characterisation of prehistoric flints with IBA', *Nuclear Instruments and Methods in Physics Research*, B64: 488–493.

Ciliberto, E. and Spoto, G. (eds) (2000) *Modern Analytical Methods in Art and Archaeology*, New York: Wiley.

Claassen, C. (ed.) (1992) *Exploring Gender through Archaeology*, Madison, WI: Prehistory Press.

Claassen, C. (1998) *Shells*, Cambridge: Cambridge University Press.

Claassen, C. and Joyce, R. (1997) *Women in Prehistory*, Philadelphia: University of Pennsylvania Press.

Claris, P. and Quartermaine, J. (1989) 'The Neolithic quarries and axe-factory sites of Great Langdale and Scafell Pike: a new field survey', *Proceedings of the Prehistoric Society*, 55: 1–25.

Clark, J.D. and Kurashina, H. (1981) 'A study of the work of a modern tanner in Ethiopia and its relevance for archaeological interpretation', in R. Gould and M.B. Schiffer (eds) *Modern Material Culture: the archaeology of us*, New York: Academic Press, pp. 303–321.

Clark, J.E. (1991) 'Flintknapping and debitage disposal among the Lacandon Maya of Chiapas, Mexico', in E. Staski and L.D. Sutro (eds) *The Ethnoarchaeology of Refuse Disposal*, Tempe: Arizona State University, pp. 63–78.

Clark, J.G.D. (1929) 'Discoidal polished knives', *Proceedings of the Prehistoric Society of East Anglia*, 6: 40–54.

Clark, J.G.D. (1952) *Prehistoric Europe: the economic basis*, London: Methuen.

Clark, J.G.D. (1965) 'Traffic in stone axe and adze blades', *Economic History Review*, 18: 1–28.

Clark, J.G.D. and Thompson, M.W. (1953) 'The groove and splinter technique of working antler in Upper Palaeolithic and Mesolithic Europe', *Proceedings of the Prehistoric Society*, 6: 148–160.

Clarke, D.L. (1968) *Analytical Archaeology*, London: Methuen.

Clarke, D.L. (1970) *Beaker Pottery of Great Britain and Ireland*, Cambridge: Cambridge University Press.

Clarke, D.L. (1973) 'Archaeology: the loss of innocence', *Antiquity*, 47: 6–18.

Clarke, D.V., Cowie, T.G., and Foxon, A. (1985) *Symbols of Power at the Time of Stonehenge*, Edinburgh: National Museum of Antiquities of Scotland.

Classen, C. (1997) 'Foundations for an anthropology of the senses', *International Social Sciences Journal*, 153: 401–412.

Classen, C. (2005) *The Book of Touch*, Oxford: Berg.

Classen, C. and Howes, D. (2006) 'The museum as sensescape: Western sensibilities and indigenous artefacts', in E. Edwards, C. Gosden and R.B. Phillips (eds) *Sensible Objects: colonialism, museums and material culture*, Oxford: Berg, pp. 199–222.

Classen, C., Howes, D., and Synnott, A. (1994) *Aroma: the cultural history of smell*, London: Routledge.

Cleal, R. (1988) 'The occurrence of drilled holes in Later Neolithic pottery', *Oxford Journal of Archaeology*, 7: 139–146.

Cleal, R. and MacSween, A. (eds) (1999) *Grooved Ware in Great Britain and Ireland*, Oxford: Oxbow.

Cleal, R.M.J., Walker, K.E., and Montague, R. (1995) *Stonehenge in Its Landscape: twentieth-century excavations*, London: English Heritage.

Cleghorn, P.L. (1986) 'Organisational structure at the Mauna Kea adze quarry complex, Hawaii', *Journal of Archaeological Science*, 13: 375–380.

Clough, T.H.McK. and Cummins, W.A. (eds) (1979) *Stone Axe Studies*. London: CBA Report 67.

Clutton-Brock, J. (1984) 'Excavation at Grimes Graves, Norfolk 1972–1976', *Fascicule 1: Neolithic antler picks from Grimes Graves, Norfolk, and Durrington Walls, Wiltshire: a biometrical analysis*, London: British Museum Publication.

Coates, J.F. (1989) 'The trireme sails again', *Scientific American*, 260: 68–75.

Coghlan, H.H. (1951; 2nd edn 1975) *Notes on the Prehistoric Metallurgy of Copper and Bronze in the Old World*, Oxford: Pitt Rivers Museum.

Coles, B.J. (1990) 'Anthropomorphic wooden figurines from Britain and Ireland', *Proceedings of the Prehistoric Society*, 56: 315–333.

Coles, B.J. (ed.) 1992 *The Wetland Revolution in Prehistory*. Southampton: Prehistoric Society and WARP.

Coles, B.J. (1998) 'Wood species for wooden figures: a glimpse of a pattern', in A. Gibson and D. Simpson (eds) *Prehistoric Ritual and Religion: essays in honour of Aubrey Burl*, Stroud: Sutton Publishing, pp. 163–173.

Coles, B.J. and Coles, J.M. (1989) *People of the Wetlands*, London: Guild Publishing.

Coles, J.M. (1962) 'European Bronze Age shields', *Proceedings of the Prehistoric Society*, 28: 156–190.

Coles, J.M. (1963) 'Irish Bronze Age horns and their relations with Northern Europe', *Proceedings of the Prehistoric Society*, 29: 326–356.

Coles, J.M. (1967) 'Some Irish horns of the late Bronze Age', *Journal of the Royal Society of Antiquaries of Ireland*, 97: 113–117.

Coles, J.M. (1973) *Archaeology by Experiment*, London: Hutchinson.

Coles, J.M. (1979) *Experimental Archaeology*, London: Academic Press.

Coles, J.M. (1982) 'The Bronze Age in northwestern Europe: problems and advances', in F. Wendorf and A.E. Close (eds) *Advances in World Archaeology*, vol. 1, London: Academic Press, Inc. (London) Ltd, pp. 265–321.

Coles, J.M., Heal, S.V.E., and Orme, B.J. (1978) 'The use and character of wood in prehistoric Britain and Ireland', *Proceedings of the Prehistoric Society*, 44: 1–45.

Coles, J.M., Hibbert, F.A., and Orme, B.J. (1973) 'Prehistoric roads and tracks in Somerset: 3 the Sweet Track', *Proceedings of the Prehistoric Society*, 39: 256–293.

Collingwood, P. (1974) *The Techniques of Sprang: plaiting on stretched threads*, London: Faber and Faber.

Collingwood, P. (1982) *The Techniques of Tablet Weaving*, London: Batsford.

Collingwood, P. (1998) *The Techniques of Ply-Split Braiding*, London: Bellew.

Collins, M.B. and Fenwick, J.M. (1974) 'Heat treating of chert: methods of interpretation and their application', *Plains Anthropologist*, 19: 134–145.

Conkey, M.W. (2006) 'Style, design and function', in C. Tilley, W. Keane, S. Küchler, M. Rowlands, and P. Spyer (eds) *Handbook of Material Culture*, London: Sage, pp. 355–372.

Conkey, M. and Spector, J. (1984) 'Archaeology and the study of gender', in M. Schiffer (ed.) *Advances in Archaeological Method and Theory*, 7, London: Academic Press, pp. 1–38.

Connan, J. (1999) 'Use and trade of bitumen in antiquity and prehistory: molecular archaeology reveals secrets of past civilizations', *Philosophical Transactions of the Royal Society of London*, B354: 33–50.

Connan, J. and Nissenbaum, A. (2003) 'Conifer tar on the keel and hull planking of the Ma'agan Mikhael Ship (Israel, 5th century BC): identification and comparison with natural products and artefacts employed in boat construction', *Journal of Archaeological Science*, 30: 709–719.

Connolly, T., Erlandson, J.M., and Norris, S.E. (1995) 'Early Holocence basketry and cordage from Daisy Cave, San Miguel Island, California', *American Antiquity*, 60: 309–318.

Cooney, G. (1989) 'Stone axes of northern Leinster', *Oxford Journal of Archaeology*, 8: 145–158.

Cooney, G. (1998) 'Breaking stones, making places: the social landscape of axe production sites', in A. Gibson and D. Simpson (eds) *Prehistoric Ritual and Religion: essays in honour of Aubrey Burl*, Stroud: Sutton Publishing Ltd, pp. 108–118.

Copeland, R. (1972) *A Short History of Pottery Raw Materials and the Cheddleton Flint Mill*, Leek: Cheddleton Flint Mill Industrial Heritage Trust.

Copley, M.S., Berstan, R., Dudd, S.N., Aillaud, S., Mukherjee, A.J., Straker, V., Payne, S., and Evershed, R.P. (2005) 'Processing of milk products in pottery vessels through British prehistory', *Antiquity*, 79: 895–908.

Costin, C.L. (1996) 'Exploring the relationship between gender and craft in complex societies: methodological and theoretical issues of gender attribution', in R.P. Wright (ed.) *Gender and Archaeology*, Philadelphia: University of Pennsylvania Press, pp. 111–140.

Costin, C.L. (1999) 'Formal and technological variability and the social relations of production: *crisoles* from San José de Moro, Peru', in E.S. Chilton (ed.) *Material Meanings: critical approaches to the interpretation of material culture*, Salt Lake City: University of Utah Press, pp. 85–102.

Costin, C.L. (2000) 'The use of ethnoarchaeology for the archaeological study of ceramic production', *Journal of Archaeological Method and Theory*, 7: 377–403.

Costin, C.L. (2005) 'Craft production', in H.D.G. Maschner and C. Chippindale (eds) *Handbook of Archaeological Methods*, Lanham, MD: AltaMira, pp. 1034–1107.

Cotkin, S.J., Carr, C., Cotkin, M.L., Dittert, A.E., and Kremser, D.T. (1999) 'Analysis of slips and other inorganic surface materials on Woodland and Early Fort ancient ceramics, south-central Ohio', *American Antiquity*, 64: 316–342.

Cotterell, B. and Kamminga, J. (1987) 'The formation of flakes', *American Antiquity*, 52: 675–708.

Coudart, A. (1992) 'Sur l'analogie ethnographique et l'ethnoarchéologie et sur l'histoire des rapports entre archéologie et ethnologie', in J. Garanger (ed.) La Préhistoire dans le monde, Paris: Presses Universitaires de France, pp. 248–263.

Crabtree, D.E. (1972) An Introduction to Flintworking, Pocatello: Idaho State University Museum, Occasional Paper 28.

Crabtree, D.E. (1973) 'The obtuse edge as a functional edge', Tebiwa, 16: 46–53.

Crabtree, D.E. and Butler, B.R. (1964) 'Notes on experiments in flint knapping: 1. Heat treatment of silica materials', Tebiwa, 7: 1–6.

Craddock, P.T. (ed.) (1980) Scientific Studies in Early Mining and Extractive Metallurgy, London: British Museum Research Laboratory.

Craddock, P.T. (1989) 'The scientific investigation of early mining and metallurgy', in J. Henderson (ed.) Scientific Analysis in Archaeology and Its Interpretation, Oxford: Oxford University Committee for Archaeology, pp. 178–212.

Craddock, P.T. (1995) Early Mining and Production, Edinburgh: Edinburgh University Press.

Craddock, P.T. and Hughes, M.J. (eds) (1985) Furnaces and Smelting Technology in Antiquity, London: British Museum Press.

Craddock, P.T. and Lang, J. (eds) (2003) Mining and Metal Production Through the Ages, London: British Museum Press.

Craig, O.E., Chapman, J., Figler, A., Patay, P., Taylor, G., and Collins, M.J. (2003) 'Milk jugs and other myths of the Copper Age of Central Europe', European Journal of Archaeology, 6: 251–265.

Crane, E. (1983) The Archaeology of Beekeeping, London: Duckworth.

Creighton, O. and Higham, R. (2005) Medieval Town walls: an archaeology and social history of urban defence, Stroud: Tempus.

Cribb, J. (ed.) (1986) Money: from cowrie shells to credit cards, London: published for the Trustees of the British Museum by British Museum Publications.

Croes, D.R. (1997) 'The north-central cultural dichotomy: its evolution as suggested by wet-site basketry and wooden fish hooks'. Antiquity, 71: 594–615.

Croes, D.G. (1995) The Hoko River Archaeological Site Complex: the wet/dry site (45CA213), 3,000–1,700 BP, Pullman: Washington State University Press.

Cronyn, J. (1990) The Elements of Archaeological Conservation, London: Routledge and Kegan Paul.

Cronyn, J.M. (2001) 'The deterioration of organic materials', in D.R. Brothwell and A.M. Pollard (eds) Handbook of Archaeological Sciences, Chichester: Wiley, pp. 627–636.

Cros, H. du and Smith, L. (eds) (1993) Women in Archaeology: a feminist critique, Canberra: Australian National University.

Crosby, D.D.B. and Mitchell, J.G. (1987) 'A survey of British metamorphic hone stones of the 9th–15th century AD in the light of potassium-argon and natural remnant magnetisation studies', Journal of Archaeological Science, 14: 483–506.

Çukur, A. and Kunç, S. (1989) 'Development of bronze production technologies in Anatolia', Journal of Archaeological Science, 16: 225–231.

Cumberpatch, C.G. and Blinkhorn, H.P. (1997) Not So Much a Pot, More a Way of Life: current approaches to artefact analysis in archaeology, Oxford: Oxbow.

Cummings, V. (2002) 'Experiencing texture and transformation in the British Neolithic', Oxford Journal of Archaeology, 21.3: 249–261.

Curran, J.M., Meighan, I.G., Simpson, D.D.A., Rogers, G., and Fallick, A.E. (2001) '87Sr/86Sr: a new discriminant for provenancing Neolithic porcellanite artifacts from Ireland', Journal of Archaeological Science, 28: 713–720.

Curwen, E.C. (1937) 'Querns', Antiquity, 17: 19–26.

Cushing, F.H. (1894) 'Primitive copper working: an experimental study', *American Anthropologist*, 7: 93–117.

Custer, J.F., Ilgenfritz, J., and Doms, K.R. (1988) 'A cautionary note on the use of chemstrips for the detection of blood residues on prehistoric tools', *Journal of Archaeological Science*, 15: 343–346.

Dahlberg, F. (1981) *Woman the Gatherer*, London: Yale University Press.

Dance, S.P. (ed.) (1974) *The Encyclopedia of Shells*, London: Blandford Press.

Daugherty, R.T. (1986) *Splintwoven Basketry*, Colorado: Interweave Press.

Davey, N. (1961) *A History of Building Materials*, London: Phoenix House.

David, N. (1972) 'On the life span of pottery, type frequencies and archaeological inference', *American Antiquity*, 37: 141–142.

David, N. and Kramer, C. (2001) *Ethnoarchaeology in Action*, Cambridge: Cambridge University Press.

David, N., Sterner, J.A., and Gavua, K.B. (1988) 'Why pots are decorated', *Current Anthropology*, 29: 365–389.

Davis, S. and Payne, S (1993) 'A barrow full of cattle skulls', *Antiquity*, 67: 12–22.

Dawson, P., Levy, R., Gardner, D., and Walls, M. (2007) 'Simulating the behaviour of light inside Arctic dwellings: implications for assessing the role of vision in task performance', *World Archaeology*, 39.1: 17–35.

Deal, M. (1982) 'Functional variation of Maya spiked vessels: a practical guide', *American Antiquity*, 47: 614–633.

Deal, M. (1985) 'Household pottery disposal in the Maya Highlands: an ethnoarchaeological interpretation', *Journal of Anthropological Archaeology*, 4: 243–291.

Deal, M. and Silk, P. (1988) 'Absorption residues and vessel function: a case study from the Maine-Maritimes region', in C.C. Kolb and L.M. Lackey (eds) *A Pot for All Reasons: ceramic ecology revisited*, Philadelphia: Laboratory of Anthropology, Temple University, pp. 105–125.

DeBoer, W.R. (1974) 'Ceramic longevity and archaeological interpretation: an example from the Upper Ucayali, Peru', *American Antiquity*, 39: 335–344.

DeBoer, W.R. (2005) 'Colours for a North American past', *World Archaeology*, 37: 66–91.

DeBoer, W.R. and Lathrap, D.W. (1979) 'The making and breaking of Shipibo-Conibo ceramics', in C. Kramer (ed.) *Ethnoarchaeology: implications of ethnography for archaeology*, Tucson: University of Arizona Press, pp. 102–138.

Deetz, J. (1967) *Invitation to Archaeology*, New York: Natural History Press.

Degryse, P., Schneider, J., Haack, U., Lauwers, V., Poblome, J., Waelkens, M., and Muchez, P. (2006) 'Evidence for glass "recycling" using Pb and Sr isotopic ratios and Sr-mixing lines: the case of early Byzantine Sagalassos', *Journal of Archaeological Science*, 33: 494–501.

Deguilloux, M.F., Bertel, L., Celant, A., Pemonge, M.H., Sadori, L., Magri, D., and Pett, R.J. (2006) 'Genetic analysis of archaeological wood remains: first results and prospects', *Journal of Archaeological Science*, 33: 1216–1227.

Dehn, T. and Hansen, S.I. (2006) 'Birch bark in Danish passage graves', *Journal of Danish Archaeology*, 14: 23–44.

Del Mar, F. (1924) *A Year among the Maoris: a study of their arts and customs*, London: Ernest Benn.

DeMarrais, E., Gosden, C., and Renfrew, C. (eds) (2004) *Rethinking Materiality: the engagement of mind with the material world*, Cambridge: McDonald Institute for Archaeological Research.

Demars, P.-Y. and Laurent, P. (1989) *Types d'outils lithiques du Paléolithique Superior en Europe*, Bordeaux: CNRS.

Densmore, F. (1928; new printing 1974) *How Indians Use Wild Plants for Food, Medicine and Crafts*, New York: Dover Publications.

Derndarsky, M. and Ocklind, G. (2001) 'Some preliminary observations on subsurface damage on experimental and archaeological quartz tools using CLSM and dye', *Journal of Archaeological Science*, 28.11: 1149–1158.

D'Errico, F. and Vanhaeren, M. (2002) 'Criteria for identifying Red Deer (*Cervus elaphus*) age and sex from their canines: application to the study of Upper Palaeolithic and Mesolithic ornaments', *Journal of Archaeological Science*, 29: 211–232.

Dhavalikar, M.K. (1994) 'Chalcolithic architecture at Inamgaon and Walki: an ethnoar-chaeological study', in B. Allchin (ed.) *Living Traditions: studies in the ethnoarchaeology of South Asia*, Columbia, MO: South Asia Publications, pp. 31–52.

Diallo, B., Vanhaelen, M., and Gosselain, O.P. (1995) 'Plant constituents involved in coating practices among traditional African potters', *Experientia*, 51: 95–97.

Dibble, H.L. (1987) 'The interpretation of Middle Paleolithic scrapers morphology', *American Antiquity*, 52: 109–117.

Dobres, M.-A. (1995) 'Beyond gender attribution: some methodological issues for engendering the past', in J. Balme and W. Beck (eds) *Gendered Archaeology: the second Australian Women in Archaeology Conference*, Canberra: ANH Publications, pp. 51–66.

Dobres, M.-A. (1999) 'Of paradigms and ways of seeing: artifact variability as if people mattered', in E.S. Chilton (ed.) *Material Meanings: critical approaches to the interpretation of material culture*, Salt Lake City: University of Utah Press, pp. 7–23.

Dobres, M.-A. (2000) *Technology and Social Agency: outlining a practice framework for archaeology*, Oxford: Blackwell.

Dobres, M.-A. and Hoffman, C.R. (eds) (1999) *The Social Dynamics of Technology: practice, politics and world views*, Washington DC: Smithsonian Institution Press.

Dobres, M.-A. and Robb, J.E. (eds) (2000) *Agency in Archaeology*, London: Routledge.

Dobres, M.-A. and Robb, J. (2005) '"Doing" agency: introductory remarks on methodology', *Journal of Archaeological Method and Theory*, 12: 159–166.

Dommelen, van, P. (2006) 'Colonial matters: material culture and postcolonial theory in colonial situations', in C. Tilley, W. Keane, S. Küchler, M. Rowlands and P. Spyer (eds) *Handbook of Material Culture*, London: Sage, pp. 104–124.

Donald, M. and Hurcombe, L. (eds) (2000a) *Gender and Material Culture in Archaeological Perspective*, London: Macmillan.

Donald, M. and Hurcombe, L. (eds) (2000b) *Gender and Material Culture in Historical Perspective*, London: Macmillan.

Donald, M. and Hurcombe, L. (eds) (2000c) *Gender and Material Culture: representations of gender from prehistory to the present*, London: Macmillan.

Dornan, J.L. (2002) 'Agency and archaeology: past, present, and future directions', *Journal of Archaeological Method and Theory*, 9: 303–329.

Doumas, C.G. (1983) *Thera, Pompeii of the Ancient Aegean*, London: Thames and Hudson.

Downs, E.F. and Lowenstein, J.M. (1995) 'Identification of blood proteins: a cautionary note', *Journal of Archaeological Science*, 22: 11–16.

Dowson, T. (2000) 'Why queer archaeology? An introduction', *World Archaeology*, 32: 161–165.

Drennan, R.D. (1996) *Statistics for Archaeologists: a commonsense approach*, New York: Plenum.

Driel-Murray, C. van (2000) 'Leatherwork and skin products', in P.T. Nicholson and I. Shaw (eds) *Ancient Egyptian Materials and Technology*, Cambridge: Cambridge University Press, pp. 299–319.

Driel-Murray, C. van (2002) 'Practical evaluation of a field test for the identification of ancient vegetable tanned leathers', *Journal of Archaeological Science*, 29: 17–21.

Dries, M.H. van den (1998) *Archaeology and the Application of Artificial Intelligence: case studies on use-wear analysis of prehistoric flint tools*, Leiden: Leiden University.

Driesch, A. von den and Peters, J. (1995) 'Zur Ausrüstung des Mannes im Eis: gegenstände und knochenreste tierischer Herkunft', in K. Spindler, H. Rastbichler-Zissernig, H. Wilfing, D. zur Nedden and H. Nothdurfter (eds) *Der Mann im Eis: neue Funde und Ergebnisse*, Vienna: Springer-Verlag, pp. 59–66.

Drucker, P. (1965) *Cultures of the North Pacific Coast*, San Franciso: Chandler Publishing Co.

Dubreuil, L. (2004) 'Long-term trends in Natufian subsistence: a use wear analysis of ground stone tools', *Journal of Archaeological Science*, 31: 1613–1629.

Dubreuil, L. (2006): 'Mortar versus grinding-slabs and the neolithization process in the Near East', in L. Longo and N. Skakun (eds) *Prehistoric Technology 40 Years Later: function studies and the Russian legacy*, Book of Abstracts, Verona: Comune di Verona, pp. 55–56.

Dudd, S.N. and Evershed, R.P. (1998) 'Direct demonstration of milk as an element of archaeological economies', *Science*, 282: 1478–1481.

Dudd, S.N., Regert, M., and Evershed, R.P. (1998) 'Assessing microbial lipid concentrations during laboratory degradations of fats and oils and pure triacylglycerols absorbed in ceramic potsherds', *Organic Geochemistry*, 29: 1345–1354.

Dunbar, R. (1995) *The Trouble with Science*, London: Faber and Faber.

Dungworth, D.B. (1997) 'Roman copper alloys: analysis of artefacts from northern Britain', *Journal of Archaeological Science*, 24: 901–10.

Dunnell, R.C. and Hunt, T.L. (1990) 'Elemental composition and inference of ceramic vessel functioning', *Current Anthropology*, 31: 330–336.

Dunning, P. (2000) 'Composite table cutlery from 1700 to 1930', in K. Karklins (ed.) *Studies in Material Culture Research*, California, PA: The Society for Historical Archaeology, pp. 32–45.

Dunsmore, S. (1985) *The Nettle in Nepal: a cottage industry*, Surbiton: Land Resources Development Centre.

Duttine, M., Villeneuve, G., Poupeau, G., Rossi, A.M., and Scorzelli, R.B. (2003) 'Electron spin resonance of Fe^{3+} ion in obsidians from Mediterranean islands: application to provenance studies', *Journal of Non-Crystalline Solids*, 323, 193–199.

Earwood, C. (1993) *Domestic Wooden Artefacts*, Exeter: Exeter University Press.

Earwood, C. (1998) 'Primitive ropemaking: the archaeological and ethnographic evidence', *Folk Life*, 36: 45–51.

Eckardt, H. and Williams, H. (2003) 'Objects without a past?', in H. Williams (ed.) *Archaeologies of Remembrance: death and memory in past societies*, New York: Kluwer/Plenum.

Edmonds, M. (2001) 'Lithic exploitation and use', in D.R. Brothwell and A.M. Pollard (eds) *Handbook of Archaeological Sciences*, Chichester: Wiley, pp. 461–470.

Edmonds, M. (1995) *Stone Tools and Society*, London: Batsford.

Edwards, E., Gosden, C., and Phillips, R.B. (eds) (2006) *Sensible Objects: colonialism, museums and material culture*, Oxford: Berg.

Egg, M., Goedecker-Ciolek, R., Groenman-van Waateringe, W., and Spindler, K. (1993) *Die Geltschermumie vom Ende der Steinzeit aus den Ötztaler Alpen*, Mainz: Römisch-Germanischen Zentralmuseums.

Ehrenberg, M. (1989) *Women in Prehistory*, London: British Museum Publications.

Ehrenreich, R.M. (1985) 'Blacksmithing technology in Iron Age Wessex', *Oxford Journal of Archaeology*, 5: 165–184.

Ehrenreich, R.M. (ed.) (1991) *Metals in Society: theory beyond analysis*, MASCA research papers in science and technology vol. 8.2, Philadelphia: University Museum, University of Pennsylvania.

Eisele, J.A., Fowler, D.D., Haynes, G., and Lewis, R.A. (1995) 'Survival and detection of blood residues on stone tools', *Antiquity*, 6: 36–46

Ellis, L. (ed.) (2000) *Archaeological Method and Theory: an encyclopedia*, New York: Garland.

Ellis, L. (2006) 'Ceramics', in J. Balme and A. Paterson (eds) *Archaeology in Practice: a student guide to archaeological analyses*, Oxford: Blackwell, pp. 235–259.

Emerson, T.E. and Hughes, R.E. (2000) 'Figurines, flint clay sourcing, the Ozark Highlands, and Cahokian acquisition', *American Antiquity*, 65: 79–101.

Emery, K.F. (2001) 'The economics of bone artifact production in the ancient Maya lowlands', in A.M. Choyke and L. Bartosiewicz (eds) *Crafting Bone: skeletal technologies through time and space, proceedings of the 2nd meeting of the (ICAZ) Worked Bone Research Group Budapest, 31 August – 5 September 1999*, Oxford: British Archaeological Reports International Series 937, pp. 73–83.

Eogan, G. (1994) *The Accomplished Art*, Oxford: Oxbow Monograph 42.

Ericson, J.E. and Purdy, B.A. (eds) (1984) *Prehistoric Quarries and Lithic Production*, Cambridge: Cambridge University Press.

Ericson, J.E., Read, D., and Burke, C. (1972) 'Research design: the relationship between primary function and the physical properties of vessels', *Anthropology UCLA*, 3: 84–95.

Evans, A.A. and Donahue, R.E. (2005) 'The elemental chemistry of lithic microwear: an experiment', *Journal of Archaeological Science*, 32: 1733–1740.

Evans, A.J. (1905) *Preliminary Scheme for the Classification and Approximate Chronology of the Periods of Minoan Culture in Crete from the Close of the Neolithic to the Early Iron Age*, privately printed.

Evans, C. (1989) 'Perishables and worldly goods – artifact decoration and classification in the light of wetlands research', *Oxford Journal of Archaeology*, 8: 179–202.

Evans, Sir John (1864) 'On the coinage of the ancient Britons and natural selection', *Journal of the Royal Institution of Great Britain*, 7: 476–487; reproduced by Pitt-Rivers in J. Myers (ed.) (1906) *The Evolution of Culture and Other Essays*, Oxford: Clarendon.

Evans, Sir John (1897) *The Ancient Stone Implements, Weapons and Ornaments of Great Britain*, London: Longmans, Green and Co.

Evershed, R.P. (2000) 'Biomolecular analysis by organic mass spectrometry', in E. Ciliberto and G. Spoto (eds) *Modern Analytical Methods in Art and Archaeology*, New York: Wiley, pp. 177–240.

Evershed, R.P. and Tuross, N. (1996) 'Proteinaceous material from potsherds', *Journal of Archaeological Science*, 23: 429–436.

Evershed, R.P., Heron, C., and Goad, L.J. (1991) 'Epicuticular wax components preserved in potsherds as chemical indicators of leafy vegetables in ancient diets', *Antiquity*, 65: 540–544.

Evershed, R.P., Heron, C., Charters, S., and Goad, L.J. (1992) 'The survival of food residues: new methods of analysis, interpretation and application', in A.M. Pollard (ed.) *New Developments in Archaeological Science*, Oxford: Oxford University Press, Proceedings of the British Academy 77, pp. 187–208.

Evershed, R.P., van Bergen, P.F., Peakman, T.M., Firbank, E.C., Horton, M.C., Edwards, D., Biddle, M., Kjolby-Biddle, B., and Rowley-Conwy, P.A. (1997a) 'Archaeological frankincense', *Nature*, 390: 667–668.

Evershed, R.P., Vaughan, S.J., Dudd, S.N., and Soles, J.S. (1997b) 'Fuel for thought? Beeswax in lamps and conical cups from Late Minoan Crete', *Antiquity*, 71: 979–985.

Evershed, R.P., Dudd, S.N., Charters, S., Mottram, H., Stott, A.W., Raven, A., van Bergen, P.F., and Bland, H.A. (1999) 'Lipids as carriers of anthropogenic signals from prehistory', *Philosophical Transactions of the Royal Society*, B354: 19–31.

Evershed, R.P., Dudd, S.N., Lockheart, M.J., and Jim, S. (2001) 'Lipids in archaeology', in D.R. Brothwell and A.M. Pollard (eds) *Handbook of Archaeological Sciences*, Chichester: Wiley, pp. 331–350.

Fansa, M. (ed.) (2002) *Experimentelle Archäologie in Europa, Bilanz 2002, Heft 1*, Oldenburg: Isensee Verlag.

Farley, M. (1979) 'Flint flake dimensions in the British Neolithic', *Proceedings of the Prehistoric Society*, 45: 322–323.

Fiedel, S. (1996) 'Blood from stones? Some methodological and interpretive problems in blood residue analysis', *Journal of Archaeological Science*, 23: 139–147.

Fienup-Riordan, A. (2005) '*Tupigat* (twined things): Yup'ik grass clothing, past and present', in J.C.H. King, B. Pauksztat, and R. Storrie (eds) *Arctic Clothing of North America – Alaska, Canada, Greenland*, London: The British Museum Press, pp. 53–61.

Finlay, N. (1997) 'Kid knapping: the missing children in lithic analysis', in J. Moore and E. Scott (eds) *Invisible People and Processes*, Leicester: Leicester University Press, pp. 203–212.

Fischer, A. (1989) 'A late Palaeolithic "school" of flint-knapping at Trollesgave, Denmark', *Acta Archaeologica*, 60: 33–49.

Fischer, C. (undated) *The Tollund Man and the Elling Woman*, Silkeborg: Silkeborg Museum.

Fleckinger, A. and Steiner, H. (1999; 2nd edn 2003) *The Fascination of the Neolithic Age: the Iceman*, Vienna: Folio.

Fleming, S. (1997) *Roman Glass: reflections of everyday life*, Philadelphia: University of Pennsylvania Press.

Fleming, S. (1999) *Roman Glass: reflections on cultural change*, Philadelphia: Museum of Archaeology and Anthropology, University of Pennsylvania.

Flenniken, J.J. and Raymond, A.W. (1986) 'Morphological projectile point typology: replication experimentation and technological analysis', *American Antiquity*, 51: 603–614.

Fletcher, J. (2000) 'Hair', in P.T. Nicholson and I. Shaw (eds) *Ancient Egyptian Materials and Technology*, Cambridge: Cambridge University Press, pp. 495–504.

Fletcher, M. and Lock, G.R. (1991) *Digging Numbers: elementary statisitics for archaeologists*, Oxford: Oxford University Committee for Archaeology.

Florance, N. (1962) *Rush-work*, London: G. Bell & Sons.

Forest Products Research Laboratory (1953) *An Atlas of End Grain Photomicrographs for the Identification of Hardwoods*, London: HMSO.

Forrest, A.J. (1983) *Masters of Flint*, Lavenham: Terrace Dalton.

Foster, G.M. (1960) 'Life expectancy of utilitarian pottery in Tzintzuntzan, Michoacan, Mexico', *American Antiquity*, 25: 606–609.

Frank, B.E. (1998) *Mande Potters and Leather-workers: art and heritage in West Africa*, Washington DC: Smithsonian Institution Press.

Freeman, L. (1983) 'More on the Mousterian: flaked bone from Cueva Morin', *Current Anthropology*, 24.3: 366–372.

Freestone, I.C. (2001) 'Post-depositional changes in archaeological ceramics and glasses', in D.R. Brothwell and A.M. Pollard (eds) *Handbook of Archaeological Sciences*, Chichester: Wiley, pp. 615–626.

Freestone, I. and Gaimster, D. (1997) *Pottery in the Making*, London: British Museum Press.

Freter, A. (1993) 'Obsidian-hydration dating: its past, present and future application in Mesoamerica', *Ancient Mesoamerica*, 4: 285–303.

Friedl, E. (1989) *Women of Deh Koh: lives in an Iranian village*, London: Smithsonian Institution Press.

Frison, R.E. and Stanford, D.J. (1982) *The Agate Basin Site: a record of the paleoindian occupation of the Northwestern High plains*, New York: Academic Press.

Fritz, G.J. (2005) 'Paleoethnobotanical methods and applications', in H.D.G. Maschner and C. Chippindale (eds) *Handbook of Archaeological Methods*, Lanham, MD: AltaMira Press, pp. 773–834.

Fullagar, R. (1991) 'The role of silica in polish formation', *Journal of Archaeological Science*, 18: 1–25.

Fullagar, R. (1993) 'Taphonomy and tool-use: a role for phytoliths in use-wear and residue analysis', in B. Fankhauser and R. Bird (eds) *Archaeometry: current Australasian research*, Canberra: Australian National University (Occasional Papers in Prehistory 22), pp. 21–27.

Fullagar, R. (ed.) (1998) *A Closer Look: recent Australian studies of stone tools*, Sydney: University of Sydney, Sydney University Archaeological Methods Series 6.

Fullagar, R. and Field, J. (1997) 'Seed grinding implements from the Pleistocene Australian arid zone', *Antiquity*, 71: 300–307.

Fullagar, R. Furby, J., and Hardy, B. (1996) 'Residues on stone artifacts: state of a scientific art', *Antiquity*, 70: 740–745.

Fullagar, R., Loy, T., and Cox, S. (1998) 'Starch grains, sediments and stone tool function: evidence from Bitokara, Papua New Guinea', in R. Fullagar (ed.) *A Closer Look: recent Australian studies of stone tools*, Sydney: University of Sydney, Sydney University Archaeological Methods Series 6, pp. 49–60.

Fullagar, R., Field, J., Denham, T., and Lentfer, C. (2006) 'Early and mid Holocene tool-use and processing of taro (*Colocasia esculenta*), yam (*Dioscorea* sp.) and other plants at Kuk Swamp in the highlands of Papua New Guinea', *Journal of Archaeological Science*, 33: 595–614.

Gabriel, S. and Goymer, S. (1991) *The Complete Book of Basketry Techniques*, Newton Abbot: David & Charles.

Gaffney, C., Gaffney, V., and Tingle, M. (1985) 'Settlement, economy or behaviour? Micro-regional land use models and the interpretation of surface artefact patterns', in C. Haselgrove, M. Millett, and I. Smith (eds) *Archaeology from the Ploughsoil*, Sheffield: Department of Archaeology and Prehistory, pp. 95–107.

Gage, J., Jones, A., Bradley, R., Spence, K., Barber, E., and Taçon, P. (1999) 'What meaning had colour in early societies?', *Cambridge Archaeoogical Journal*, 9: 110–129.

Gale, N.H. (2001) 'Archaeology, science-based archaeology and the Mediterranean Bronze Age metals trade: a contribution to the debate', *European Journal of Archaeology*, 4.1: 113–130.

Gale, N.H. and Stos-Gale, Z. (2000) 'Lead isotope analyses applied to provenance studies', in E. Ciliberto and G. Spoto (eds) *Modern Analytical Methods in Art and Archaeology*, New York: Wiley, pp. 503–584.

Gale, N.H., Einfalt, H.C., Hubberten, H.W., and Jones, R.E. (1988) 'The sources of Mycenaean gypsum', *Journal of Archaeological Science*, 15: 57–72.

Gale, R., Gasson, P., Hepper, N., and Killen, G. (2000) 'Wood', in P.T. Nicholson and I. Shaw (eds) *Ancient Egyptian Materials and Technology*, Cambridge: Cambridge University Press, pp. 334–371.

Gallager, J.P. (1977) 'Contemporary stone tools in Ethiopia: Implications for archaeology', *Journal of Field Archaeology*, 4: 407–414.

Gansser-Burckhardt, A. (1942) *Das Leder und seine Verarbeitung im Römischen Legionslager Vindonissa*, Basel: Konnissionsverlag von Birkhäuser.

Gardiner, J. (ed.) (2005) *Before the Mast: Life and death aboard the Mary Rose. The archaeology of the Mary Rose vol. 4*, London: English Heritage.

Garling, S.J. (1998) 'Megafauna on the menu? Haemoglobin crystallisation of blood residues from stone artefacts at Cuddie Springs', in R. Fullagar (ed.) *A Closer Look: recent Australian studies of stone tools*, Sydney: University of Sydney, Sydney University Archaeological Methods Series 6, pp. 29–48.

Geary, K. (2005) 'Training the next generation of finds specialists', *The Archaeologist*, 58: 9.

Gell, A. (1998) *Art and Agency: an anthropological theory*, Oxford: Clarendon.

Gelvin-Reymiller, C., Reuther, J.D., Potter, B.A., and Bowers, P.M. (2006) 'Technical aspects of a worked proboscidean tusk from Inmachuk River, Seward Peninsular, Alaska', *Journal of Archaeological Science*, 33: 1088–1094.

Gernaey, A.M., Waite, E.R., Collins, M.J., Craig, O.E., and Sokol, R.J. (2001) 'Survival and interpretation of archaeological proteins', in D.R. Brothwell and A.M. Pollard (eds) *Handbook of Archaeological Sciences*, Chichester: Wiley, pp. 323–330.

Gero, J.M. (1991) 'Genderlithics: women's roles in stone tool production', in J.M. Gero and M.W. Conkey (eds) *Engendering Archaeology*, Oxford: Blackwell, pp. 163–193.

Gero, J. (1994) 'Gender division of labor in the construction of archaeological knowledge in the USA', in G. Bond and A. Gilliam (eds) *The Social Construction of the Past: representation as power*, New York: Routledge, pp. 144–153.

Gero, J.M. (1996) 'Archaeological practice and gendered encounters with field data', in R.P. Wright (ed.) *Gender and Archaeology*, Philadelphia: University of Pennsylvania Press, pp. 251–280.

Gero, J.M. and Conkey, M. (eds) (1991) *Engendering Archaeology*, Oxford: Blackwell.

Gianno, R. (1990) *Semelai Culture and Resin Technology*, New Haven: The Connecticut Academy of Arts and Sciences.

Gibson, A.M. (2002) *Prehistoric Pottery in Britain and Ireland*, Stroud: Tempus.

Gibson, A.M. and Woods, A.J. (1990; 2nd edn 1997) *Prehistoric Pottery for the archaeologist*, Leicester: Leicester University Press.

Gibson, J.J. (1986) *The Ecological Approach to Visual Perception*, Hillsdale: Lawrence Erlbaum.

Gibson, K.R. and Ingold, T. (eds) (1993) *Tools, Language and Cognition in Human Evolution*, Cambridge: Cambridge University Press.

Gifford-Gonzalez, D.P., Damrosch, D.B., Damrosch, D.R., Pryor, J., and Thunen, R.L. (1985) 'The third dimension in site structure: an experiment in trampling and vertical dispersal', *American Antiquity*, 50: 803–818.

Gijn, A. van (1990) *The Wear and Tear of Flint: principles of functional analysis applied to Dutch Neolithic assemblages*, Leiden: Analecta Praehistorica Leidensia 22.

Gijn, A. van (1998a) 'A closer look: a realistic attempt to "squeeze blood from stones"', in R. Fullagar (ed.) *A Closer Look: recent Australian studies of stone tools*, Sydney: University of Sydney, Sydney University Archaeological Methods Series 6, pp. 189–192.

Gijn, A. van (1998b; for 1994) 'Traditions in tool-use behaviour: evidence from the Dutch Neolithic', *Helinium*, 34: 261–280.

Gijn, A. van (1998c) 'Craft activities in the Dutch Neolithic: a lithic viewpoint', in M. Edmonds and C. Richards (eds) *Understanding the Neolithic of North-Western Europe*, Glasgow: Cruithne, pp. 328–350.

Gijn, A. van (2005) 'A functional analysis of some Late Mesolithic bone and antler implements from the Dutch coastal zone', in H. Luik, A.M. Choyke, C.E. Batey, and L. Lougas (eds) *From Hooves to Horns, from Mollusc to Mammoth: manufacture and use of bone artefacts from prehistoric times to the present*, Research into Ancient Times 15, Tartu: Ajaloo Instituut, pp. 47–66.

Gijn, A. van (2006) 'Implements of bone and amber: a Mesolithic tradition continued', in L.P. Louwe Kooijmans and P.F.B. Jongste (eds) *Analecta Praehistorica Leidensia*, 37/38, 'Schipluiden: a Neolithic settlement on the Dutch North Sea coast c.3500 CAL BC', Leiden: Faculty of Archaeology, Leiden University, pp. 207–224.

Gijn, A. van and Boon, J. (2006) 'Birch bark tar', in L.P. Louwe Kooijmans and P.F.B. Jongste (eds) *Analecta Praehistorica Leidensia*, 37/38, 'Schipluiden: a Neolithic settlement on the Dutch North Sea coast c.3500 CAL BC', Leiden: Faculty of Archaeology, Leiden University, pp. 261–266.

Gijn, A. van and Houkes, R. (2006) 'Stone, procurement and use', in L.P. Louwe Kooijmans and P.F.B. Jongste (eds) *Analecta Praehistorica Leidensia*, 37/38, 'Schipluiden: a Neolithic settlement on the Dutch North Sea coast c.3500 CAL BC', Leiden: Faculty of Archaeology, Leiden University, pp. 167–193.

Gijn, A. van and Niekus, M.J.L.Th. (2001) 'Bronze Age settlement flint from the Netherlands: the Cinderella of lithic research', in W.H. Metz, B.L. van Beek, and H. Steegstra (eds) *Patina: essays presented to Jay Jordan Butler on the occasion of his 80th birthday*, Groningen: Metz, Van Beek, and Steegstra, pp. 305–320.

Gijn, A. van and Raemaekers, C.M. (1999) 'Tool use and society in the Dutch Neolithic: the inevitability of ethnographic analogies', in L.R. Owen and M. Porr (eds) *Ethno-Analogy and the Reconstruction of Prehistoric Artefact Use and Production*, Urgeschichtliche Materialhefte 14, Tübingen: Mo Vince Verlag, pp. 43–52.

Gijn, A. van, Betuw, V. van, Verbaas, A., and Wentink, K. (2006) 'Flint, procurement and use', in L.P. Louwe Kooijmans and P.F.B. Jongste (eds) *Analecta Praehistorica Leidensia*, 37/38, 'Schipluiden: a Neolithic settlement on the Dutch North Sea coast c.3500 CAL BC', Leiden: Faculty of Archaeology, Leiden University, pp. 129–166.

Gillooly, M. (ed.) (1992) *Natural Baskets*, Pownal, VT: Storey Publishing.

Gillow, J. and Sentence, B. (2004) *A Visual Guide to Traditional Techniques: world textiles*, London: Thames and Hudson.

Gilman, P.A. (1987) 'Architecture as artefact: pit structures and pueblos in the American south west', *American Antiquity*, 52: 538–564.

Gilman, P.A. (1989) 'A response to Wilhusen', *American Antiquity*, 54: 834–836.

Gilman, P.A., Canouts, V., and Bishop, R.L. (1994) 'The production and distribution of classic Mimbres black on white pottery', *American Antiquity*, 59: 695–709.

Gimbutas, M. (1985) 'East Baltic amber in the fourth and third millennia B.C.', *Journal of Baltic Studies*, 16: 231–256.

Giria, Y. and Bradley, B. (1998) 'Blade technology at Kostenski 1/1, Avdeevo and Zaraysk', in H.A. Amirkhanov (ed.) *The Eastern Gravettian*, Moscow: Russian Academy of Sciences, Institute of Archaeology, pp. 191–213.

Given, M. (2004) *The Archaeology of the Colonized*, London: Routledge.

Glowacki, M. (2005) 'Food of the gods or mere mortals? Hallucinogenic *Spondylus* and its interpretive implications for early Andean society', *Antiquity*, 79: 257–268.

Godfrey, E. and Nie, van, M. (2004) 'A Germanic ultra-high carbon steel punch of the late Roman-Iron Age', *Journal of Archaeological Science*, 31: 1117–1125.

Godwin, H. (1967) 'The ancient cultivation of Hemp', *Antiquity*, 41: 42–49, 137–138.

Goedecker-Ciolek, R. (1993) 'Zur Herstellungstechnik von Kleidung und Ausrüstungsgegenständen', in M. Egg, R. Goedecker-Ciolek, W. Groenman-van Waateringe, and K. Spindler (eds) *Die Geltschermumie vom Ende der Steinzeit aus den Ötztaler Alpen*, Mainz: Römisch-Germanischen Zentralmuseums, pp. 110–113.

Golde, P. (ed.) (1986) *Women in the Field: anthropological experiences*, Berkeley: University of California Press.

Golden, J., Levy, T.A., and Hauptmann, A. (2001) 'Recent discoveries concerning Chalcolithic metallurgy at Shiqmim, Israel', *Journal of Archaeological Science*, 28: 951–963.

Gordon, A. and Keating, R.C. (2001) 'Light microscopy and determination of *Eryngium yuccifolium* (Michaux) leaf material in twined slippers from Salts Cave, Kentucky', *Journal of Archaeological Science*, 28: 55–60.

Gordon, R.B. (1983) 'Laboratory evidence of the use of metal tools at Machu Picchu (Peru) and environs', *Journal of Archaeological Science*, 12: 311–327.

Gordon, R.B. and Killick, D. (1993) 'Adaption of technology to culture and environment: bloomery iron smelting in America and Africa', *Technology and Culture*, 34: 243–270.

Gorman, A. (1995) 'Gender, labour and resources: the female knappers of the Andaman islanders', in J. Balme and W. Beck (eds) *Gendered Archaeology: the second Australian Women in Archaeology Conference*, Canberra: Australian National University, pp. 87–91.

Gosden, C. (1999) *Anthropology and Archaeology: a changing relationship*, London: Routledge.

Gosden, C. (2005) 'What do objects want?', *Journal of Archaeological Method and Theory*, 12: 193–211.

Gosden, C. (2006) 'Material culture and long-term change', in C. Tilley, W. Keane, S. Küchler, M. Rowlands, and P. Spyer (eds) *Handbook of Material Culture*, London: Sage, pp. 425–442.

Gosden, C. and Marshall, Y. (1999) 'The cultural biography of objects', *World Archaeology*, 31: 169–178.

Gosselain, O.P. (1992) 'Bonfire of the enquiries: pottery firing temperatures in archaeology: what for?', *Journal of Archaeological Science*, 19: 243–259.

Gosselain, O.P. (1999) 'In pots we trust: the processing of clay and symbols in sub-Saharan Africa', *Journal of Material Culture*, 4: 205–230.

Gosselain, O.P. (2000) 'Materializing identities: an African perspective', *Journal of Archaeological Method and Theory*, 7: 187–217.

Gosselain, O.P. and Livingstone-Smith, A. (1995) 'The "Ceramic and Society Project": an ethnographic and experimental approach to technological style', in A. Lindhal and O. Stilborg (eds) *The Aim of Laboratory Analyses of Ceramics in Archaeology, April 7–9, 1995 in Lund, Sweden: in honour of Birgitta Huthén*, Stockholm: Kungl. Vitterhets historie och antikvitets akademien, pp. 147–160.

Gostenčnik, K. (2003) 'Elk antler as a material of manufacture: finds from Late Republican/Early Imperial "Old Virunum" on the Magdalensberg in Carinthia, southern Austria', in I. Riddler (ed.) *Materials of Manufacture: the choice of materials in the working of bone and antler in northern and central Europe during the first millennium AD*, British Archaeological Reports International Series 1193, Oxford: Archaeopress, pp. 1–14.

Gould, R.A. (ed.) (1978) *Explorations in Ethnoarchaeology*, Albuquerque: University of New Mexico Press.

Gould, R.A. (1980) *Living Archaeology*, Cambridge: Cambridge University Press.

Gould, R.A. and Schiffer, M.B. (1981) *Modern Material Culture: the archaeology of us*, New York: Academic Press.

Gould, R.A. and Watson, P.J. (1982) 'A dialogue on the meaning and use of analogy in ethnoarchaeological reasoning', *Journal of Anthropological Archaeology*, 1: 255–281.

Gowan, L. (1991) *The Craft of Stickmaking*, Swindon: Crowood Press.

Gowlett, J.A.J. and Hedges, R.E.M. (1986) *Archaeological Results from Accelerator Dating*, Oxford: Oxford University Committee for Archaeology.

Grace, R. (1989) *Interpreting the Function of Stone Tools: the quantification and computerisation of micro-wear analysis*, Oxford: British Archaeological Reports, International Series 474.

Gramsch, B. (1992) 'Friesack Mesolithic wetlands', in B. Coles (ed.) *The Wetland Revolution in Prehistory*, Exeter: WARP Occasional Paper 6, pp. 65–72.

Gräslund, B., Knutsson, H., Knutsson, K. and Taffinder, J. (eds) (1990) *The Interpretative Possibilities of Microwear Studies*, Uppsala: Societas Archaeologica Upsaliensis.

Graves-Brown, P. (ed.) (2000) *Matter, Materiality and Modern Culture*, London: Routledge

Green, H.S. (1980) *The Flint Arrowheads of the British Isles: a detailed study of material from England and Wales with comparanda from Scotland and Ireland*, British Archaeological Reports British Series 75, Oxford: Archaeopress.

Greenfield, H.J. (1999) 'The origins of metallurgy: distinguishing stone from metal cut-marks on bones from archaeological sites', *Journal of Archaeological Science*, 26: 797–809.

Greenfield, P. (2000) 'Children, material culture and weaving; historical change and developmental change', in J. Sofaer Derevenski (ed.) *Children and Material Culture*, London: Routledge, pp. 72–86.

Grieve, M. (1931) *A Modern Herbal: the medicinal, culinary, cosmetic and economic properties, cultivation and* folklore of herbs, grasses, fungi, shrubs and trees with all their modern scientific uses, London: Jonathan Cape Ltd; revised edition published 1973 and reprinted 1998, London: Tiger Books.

Griffin, P.B. and Solheim, W.G. (1988–9) 'Ethnoarchaeological research in Asia', Asian Perspectives, 28: 145–162.

Griffiths, D.M. (1978) 'Use-marks on historic ceramics: a preliminary study', Historical Archaeology, 12: 68–81.

Griffiths, N. and Jenner, A. with Wilson, C. (1990) Drawing Archaeoologcial Finds: a handbook, London: Institute of Archaeology.

Griffiths, W.E. (1951) 'Decorated rotary querns from Wales and Ireland', Ulster Journal of Archaeology, 14: 49–61.

Griffitts, J. and Bonsall, C. (2001) 'Experimental determination of the function of antler and bone "bevel-ended tools" from prehistoric shell middens in western Scotland', in A.M. Choyke and L. Bartosiewicz (eds) Crafting Bone: skeletal technologies through time and space, proceedings of the 2nd meeting of the (ICAZ) Worked Bone Research Group Budapest, 31 August – 5 September 1999, British Archaeological Reports International Series 937, Oxford: Archaeopress, pp. 207–220.

Grimm, L. (2000) 'Apprentice flint-knapping: relating material culture and social practice in the Upper Palaeolithic', in J. Sofaer Derevenski (ed.) Children and Material Culture, London: Routledge, pp. 53–71.

Grimshaw, A. (2001) The Ethnographer's Eye: ways of seeing in anthropology, Cambridge: Cambridge University Press.

Grinsell, L.V. (1960) 'The breaking of objects as a funeral rite', Folklore, 71: 475–491.

Groenewoudt, B.J. and Nie, M. van (1995) 'Assessing the scale and organisation of Germanic iron production at Heeten (the Netherlands)', Journal of European Archaeology, 3: 187–215.

Groenman-van Waateringe, W. (1993) 'Analyses of the hides and skins from the Hauslabjoch', in M. Egg, R. Goedecker-Ciolek, W. Groenman-van Waateringe, and K. Spindler (eds) Die Geltschermumie vom Ende der Steinzeit aus den Ötztaler Alpen, Mainz: Römisch-Germanischen Zentralmuseums, pp. 114–128.

Grün, R. (2001) 'Trapped charge dating (ESR, TL, OSL)', in D.R. Brothwell and A.M. Pollard (eds) Handbook of Archaeological Sciences, Chichester: Wiley, pp. 47–62.

Guerra, M.F. and Calligaro, T. (2004) 'Gold traces to trace gold', Journal of Archaeological Science, 31: 1199–1208.

Guibert, P., Ney, C., Bechtel, F., Schvoerer, M., and Araguas, P. (1998) 'Datation par thermoluminescence d'éléments architecturaux en terre cuite de la "Seo del Salvador", église cathédrale de Saragosse, Espagne', Revue d'Archéométrie, 22: 125–135.

Gurfinkel, D.M. and Franklin, U.M. (1988) 'A study of the feasibility of detecting blood residues on artefacts', Journal of Archaeological Science, 15: 83–98.

Gustafson, P. (1980) Salish Weaving, Vancouver: Douglas & McIntyre.

Gutheil, G., Bloom, P., Valderrama, N., and Freedman, R. (2004) 'The role of historical institutions in children's and adult's naming of artifacts', Cognition, 91: 23–42.

Haagen, C. (1994) Bush Toys: Aboriginal children at play. Canberra: Aboriginal Studies Press.

Hageneder, F. (2001) The Heritage of Trees: history, culture, symbolism, Edinburgh: Floris.

Hageneder, F. (2005) The Living Wisdom of Trees, London: Duncan Baird.

Hald, M. (1980) Ancient Danish Textiles from Bogs and Burials, Copenhagen: National Museum of Denmark.

Hall, A.R., Tomlinson, P.R., Hall, R.A., Taylor, G.W., and Walton, P. (1984) 'Dyeplants from Viking York', Antiquity, 58: 58–60.

Hally, D.J. (1986) 'The identification of vessel function: a case study from Northwest Georgia', American Antiquity, 51: 267–295.

Hamann, B. (1997) 'Weaving and the iconography of prestige: the royal gender symbolism of Lord 5 Flower's/Lady 4 Rabbit's family', in C. Claassen and R.A. Joyce (eds) *Women in Prehistory: North America and Mesoamerica*, Philadelphia: University of Pennsylvania, pp. 153–172.

Hamilakis, Y. and Yalouri, E. (1996) 'Antiquities as symbolic capital in modern greek society', *Antiquity*, 70: 117–129.

Hamon, C. (2003) 'De l'utilisation des outils de mouture, broyage et polissage au Néolithique en Bassin Parisien: apports de la tracéologie', *Bulletin de la Société Préhistorique Française*, 100: 101–116.

Hamon, C. (2004) 'Le statut des outils de boyage et d'abrasion dans l'espace domestique que Néolithique Ancien en Basin Parisien', *Notae Praehistoricae*, 24: 117–128.

Hamon, C. (2005) 'Quelle signification archéologique pour les dépôts de meules Néolithiques dans la Vallée de l'Aisne?', *RAP*, 22: 39–48.

Hamon, C. and Samzun, A. (2004) 'Une fosse Villeneuve-Saint-Germain final à Saint Denis "Rue du Landy": un dépôt de meules inédit en Ile-de-France', *Interneo*, 5: 17–27.

Hancock, R.G.V. (2000) 'Elemental analysis', in E. Ciliberto and G. Spoto (eds) *Modern Analytical Methods in Art and Archaeology*, New York: Wiley, pp. 11–20.

Hancocks, A. and Powell, N. (2005) 'Finds workers are archaeologists too! The work of IFA's Finds Group', *The Archaeologist*, 58: 8.

Hannus, L.A. (1997) 'Mammoth bone flake tools from the Lange/Ferguson site, South Dakota', in L.A. Hannus, L. Rossum, and R.P. Winham (eds) *Proceedings of the 1993 Bone Modification Conference, Hot Springs, South Dakota*, Sioux Falls, SD: Archaeology Laboratory, Augustana College, pp. 220–235.

Hannus, L.A., Rossum, L., and Winham, R.P. (eds) (1997) *Proceedings of the 1993 Bone Modification Conference, Hot Springs, South Dakota*, Sioux Falls, SD: Archaeology Laboratory, Augustana College.

Hansen, H.-O. (1977) *The Prehistoric Village at Lejre*, Roskilde: The Historical-Archaeological Research Center.

Harding, A. (2004) 'Warfare: a defining characteristic of Bronze Age Europe?', in J. Carman and A. Harding (eds) *Ancient Warfare: archaeological perspectives*, Stroud: Sutton, pp. 157–173.

Harding, A.F. (ed.) (1999) *Experiment and Design*, Oxford: Oxbow.

Harris, J. (ed.) (1999) *5000 Years of Textiles*, London: British Museum Press.

Harrison, R. (2000) '"Nowadays with glass": regional variation in Aboriginal bottle glass artefacts from Western Australia', *Archaeology in Oceania*, 35: 34–47.

Harrison, R. (2003) '"The Magical Virtue of These Sharp Things": colonialism, mimesis and knapped bottle glass artefacts in Australia', *Journal of Material Culture*, 8: 311–336.

Harsema, O.H. (1979) *Maalstenen en Handmolens in Drenthe van het Neolithicum tot ca. 1300 A.D.*, Zwolle: The Provincial Museum of Drenthe at Assen.

Hart, F.A., Storey, J.M.V., Adams, S.J., Symonds, R.P., and Walsh, J.N. (1987) 'An analytical study, using inductively coupled plasma (ICP) spectrometry, of Samian and colour-coated wares from the Roman town at Colchester together with related continental Samian wares', *Journal of Archaeological Science*, 14: 577–598.

Harvey, J. (1996) *Traditional Textiles of Central Asia*, London: Thames and Hudson Ltd.

Haslam, M. (2004) 'The decomposition of starch grains in soils: implications for archaeological residue analysis', *Journal of Archaeological Science*, 31: 1715–1734.

Hastorf, C.A. and DeNiro, M.J. (1985) 'Reconstruction of prehistoric plant production and cooking practices by a new isotopic method', *Nature*, 315: 489–491.

Hather, J.G. (2000) *The Identification of the Northern European Woods: a guide for archaeologists and conservators*, London: Archetype.

Haughton, C. and Powlesland, D. (1999) *West Heslerton: The Anglian cemetery*, Yedingham: Landscape Research Centre.

Hauptmann, A., Pernicka, E., Rehren, T., and Yalcin, U. (1999) *The Beginnings of Metallurgy: the proceedings of the international conference 'The Beginnings of Metallurgy', Bochum, 1995*, Bochum: Deutsches Bergbau-Museum.

Hayden, B. (ed.) (1979) *Lithic Use-Wear Analysis*, New York: Academic Press.

Hayden, B. (1984) 'Are emic types relevant to archaeology', *Ethnohistory*, 31: 79–92.

Hayden, B. (1990) 'The right rub: hide working in high ranking households', in B. Gräslund, H. Knutsson, K. Knutsson, and J. Taffinder (eds) *The Interpretive Possibilities of Microwear Studies*, AUN 14, Uppsala: Societas Archaeologia Upsaliensis, pp. 89–102.

Hayden, B. (1992) 'Observing prehistoric women', in C. Claassen (ed.) *Exploring Gender through Archaeology*, Madison, WI: Prehistory Press, pp. 33–48.

Hays-Gilpin, K. (2000) 'Gender constructs in the material culture of seventh-century Anasazi farmers in north-eastern Arizona', in M. Donald and L. Hurcombe (eds) *Representations of Gender from Prehistory to the Present*, Basingstoke: Macmillan, pp. 31–44.

Hayward, L.G. (1990) 'The origin of the raw elephant ivory used in Greece and the Aegean during the Bronze Age', *Antiquity*, 64: 103–109.

Healy, F. (1994) 'Typology: The maker's or the analyst's?', in N. Ashton and A. David (eds) *Stories in Stone: Proceedings of Anniversary Conference at St. Hilda's College, Oxford, April 1993*, Oxford: Lithic Studies Society, pp. 179–181.

Heckman, A.M. (2005) 'Cultural communication of ethnicity through clothing: the Qocha-Lake symbol in contemporary textiles from Ausangate, Peru', in R.M. Reycraft (ed.) *Us and Them: archaeology and ethnicity in the Andes*, Los Angeles: The Cotsen Institute of Archaeology, University of California, pp. 104–114.

Hedges, J.W. and Wait, G.A. (1987) 'Cooper's crozes', *Antiquity*, 61: 257–259.

Hedges, R.E.M. (2001) 'Dating in archaeology: past, present and future', in D.R. Brothwell and A.M. Pollard (eds) *Handbook of Archaeological Sciences*, Chichester: Wiley, pp. 3–8.

Hegmon, M. and Kulow, S. (2005) 'Painting as agency, style as structure: innovations in Mimbres pottery designs from southwest New Mexico', *Journal of Archaeological Method and Theory*, 12: 313–334.

Heimann, R.B., Kreher, U., Spazier, I., and Wetzel, G. (2001) 'Mineralogical and chemical investigations of bloomery slags from prehistoric (8th century BC to 4th century AD) iron production sites in Upper and Lower Lusatia, Germany', *Archaeometry*, 43: 227–252.

Hein, A., Tsolakidou, A., Iliopoulos, I., Mommsen, H., Buxeda I Garrigós, J., Montana, G., and Kilikoglou, V. (2002) 'Standardisation of elemental analytical techniques applied to provenance studies of ancient ceramics', *The Analyst*, 127: 542–553.

Heizer, R.F. and Kroeber, T. (eds) (1979) *Ishi, the Last Yahi: a documentary history*, Berkeley: University of California Press.

Helms, M.W. (1988) *Ulysses' Sail: an ethnographic odyssey of power, knowledge and geographical distance*, Princeton: Princeton University Press.

Helms, M.W. (1993) *Craft and the Kingly Ideal: art, trade and power*, Austin: The University of Texas Press.

Henderson, J. (ed.) (1989) *Scientific Analysis in Archaeology*. Oxford: Oxford University Committee for Archaeology.

Henderson, J. (2000) *The Science and Archaeology of Materials: an investigation of inorganic materials*, London: Routledge.

Henderson, J. (2001) 'Glass and glazes', in D.R. Brothwell and A.M. Pollard (eds) *Handbook of Archaeological Sciences*, Chichester: Wiley, pp. 471–482.

Hendon J.A. (1997) 'Women's work, women's space, and women's status among the Classic-Period Maya elite of the Copan Valley, Honduras', in C. Claassen and R.A. Joyce (eds) *Women* in Prehistory: North America and Mesoamerica, Philadelphia: University of Pennsylvania Press, pp. 33–46.

Henry, D.O. and Odell, G.H. (1989) Alternative Approaches to Lithic Analysis: proceedings of the University of Tulsa Conference on Lithic Analysis, Arlington, VA: American Anthropological Association.

Henshall, A. (1950) 'Textiles and weaving appliances from prehistoric Britain', Proceedings of the Prehistoric Society, 16: 130–62.

Herbert, E.W. (1984) Red Gold of Africa: copper in precolonial history and culture, Madison: The University of Wisconsin Press.

Herbert, E.W. (1993) Iron, Gender, and Power: rituals of transformation in African Societies, Indianapolis: Indiana University Press.

Heron, C. and Evershed, R.P. (1993) 'The analysis of organic residues and the study of pottery use', in M. Schiffer (ed.) Archaeological Method and Theory 5, Tucson: University of Arizona Press, pp. 247–284.

Heron, C. and Pollard, A.M. (1988) 'The analysis of natural resinous materials from Roman amphoras', in E.A. Slater and J.O. Tate (eds) Science and Archaeology, Oxford: British Archaeological Reports, British Series 196, pp. 429–448.

Heron, C., Evershed, R.P., and Goad, L.J. (1991a) 'Effects of migration of soil lipids on organic residues associated with buried potsherds', Journal of Archaeological Science, 18: 641–659.

Heron, C.L., Evershed, R.P., Goad, L.J., and Denham, V. (1991b) 'New approaches to the analysis of organic residues from archaeological remains', in P. Budd, B. Chapman, C. Jackson, R. Janaway and B. Ottaway (eds) Archaeological Sciences 1989: Proceedings of a Conference on the Application of Scientific Techniques to Archaeology, Bradford, September 1989, Oxford: Oxbow, Monographs in Archaeology 9, pp. 332–339.

Hester, T.R. (1972) 'Ethnographic evidence for the thermal alteration of siliceous stone', Tebiwa, 15: 63–65.

Hester, T.R. and Heizer, R.F. (1981) Making Stone Vases: ethnoarchaeological studies at an alabaster workshop in Upper Egypt, Malibu, CA: Undena Publications.

Hetherington, K. (2003) 'Spatial textures. place, touch and praesentia', Environment and Planning A, 35: 1933–1944.

Hildebrand, J.A. (1978) 'Pathways revisited: a quantitative model of discard', American Antiquity, 43: 274–279.

Hilgeman, S.L. (2000) Pottery and Chronology at Angel, Tuscaloosa: University of Alabama.

Hill, H.E. and Evans, J. (1989) 'Crops of the Pacific: new evidence from chemical analysis of organic residues in pottery', in D.R. Harris and G.C. Hillman (eds) Foraging and Farming: the evolution of plant exploitation, London: Unwin Hyman, pp. 418–425.

Hill, J.D. (1995) Ritual and Rubbish in the Iron Age of Wessex, Oxford: British Archaeological Reports, British Series 242.

Hill, R.G.P. (ed.) (1960) The Lapps Today in Finland, Norway and Sweden, Paris: Mouton.

Hiscock, P. (2002) 'Quantifying the size of artefact assemblages', Journal of Archaeological Science, 29.3: 251–258.

Hodder, I. (1983) Symbols in Action: ethnoarchaeological studies of material culture, Cambridge: Cambridge University Press.

Hodder, I. (ed.) (1987) The Archaeology of Contextual Meanings, Cambridge: Cambridge University Press.

Hodder, I. (ed.) (1989) The Meaning of Things: material culture and symbolic expression, London: Unwin Hyman.

Hodder, I. (ed.) (1996) On the Surface: Çatalhöyük 1993–95, Cambridge: McDonald Institute for Archaeological Research; London: British Institute of Archaeology at Ankara.

Hodder, I. (2005) 'Post-processual and interpretive archaeology', in C. Renfrew and P. Bahn (eds) *Archaeology: the key concepts*, London: Routledge, pp. 207–212.

Hodges, H.W.M. (1955) 'The excavation of a group of cooking-places at Ballycroghan, Co. Down', *Ulster Journal of Archaeology*, 18: 17–36.

Hodos, T., Knappett, C., and Kilikoglou, V. (in press) 'Middle and Late Iron Age painted ceramics from Kinet Höyük: macro, micro and elemental analyses', *Anatolian Studies*, 55.

Hofman, J.L. and Enloe, J.G. (ed.) (1992) *Piecing Together the Past: applications of refitting studies in archaeology*, Oxford: Tempus Reparatum.

Holdaway, S. and Stern, N. (2004) *A Record in Stone: the study of Australia's flaked stone artefacts*, Canberra: Aboriginal Studies Press.

Holtorf, C. (2002) 'Notes on the life history of a pot sherd', *Journal of Material Culture*, 7: 49–71.

Höpfel, F., Platzer, W., and Spindler, K. (eds) (1992) *Der Mann im Eis 1: Bericht über das Internationale Symposium 1992 in Innsbruck*, Innsbruck: Universität Innsbruck.

Horne, L. (1994) 'Itinerant brasscasters of eastern India', in B. Allchin (ed.) *Living Traditions: studies in the ethnoarchaeology of South Asia*, Columbia, MO: South Asia Publications, pp. 265–280.

Hortolà, P. (1992) 'SEM analysis of red blood cells in aged human bloodstains', *Forensic Science International*, 55: 139–159

Hortolà, P. (2001a) 'Experimental SEM determination of game mammalian bloodstains on stone tools', *Environmental Archaeology*, 6: 99–104.

Hortolà, P. (2001b) 'Morphological characterisation of red blood cells in human bloodstains on stone: a systematical SEM study', *Anthropologie* (Brno), 39: 235–240.

Hortolà, P. (2002) 'Red blood cell haemotaphonomy of experimental human bloodstains on techno-prehistoric lithic raw materials', *Journal of Archaeological Science*, 29: 733–739.

Hoskins, J. (2006) 'Agency, biography and objects', in C. Tilley, W. Keane, S. Küchler, M. Rowlands, and P. Spyer (eds) *Handbook of Material Culture*, London: Sage, pp. 74–84.

Hosler, D. (1994) *The Sounds and Colors of Power: the sacred metallurgical technology of ancient West Mexico*, Cambridge, MA: MIT Press.

Hosler, D. (1995) 'Sound, color and meaning in the metallurgy of ancient West Mexico', *World Archaeology*, 27: 100–115.

House, J.H. and Smith, J.W. (1975) 'Experiments in the replication of fire-cracked rock', in M.B. Schiffer and J.H. House (eds) *The Cache River Archaeological Project*, Fayetteville: Arkansas Archaeological Survey, pp. 75–80.

Hovers, E., Ilani, S, Bar-Yosef, O., Vandermeersch, B., Barham, L., Belfer-Cohen, A., Klein, R.G., Knight, C., Power, C., Watts, I., Mc Brearty, S., Marshack, A., and Sagona, A. (2003) 'An early case of color symbolism', *Current Anthropology*, 44: 491–522.

Howard-Johnston, J. (1998) 'Trading in fur, from Classical Antiquity to the early Middle Ages', in E. Cameron (ed.) *Leather and Fur: aspects of early medieval trade and technology*, London: Archetype Publications Ltd, pp. 65–79.

Howes, D. (ed.) (1991) *The Varieties of Sensory Experience: a source book in the anthropology of the senses*, Toronto: University of Toronto Press.

Howes, D. (2006) 'Scent, sound and synaesthesia: intersensoriality and material culture theory', in C. Tilley, W. Keane, S. Küchler, M. Rowlands, and P. Spyer (eds) *Handbook of Material Culture*, London: Sage, pp. 161–172.

Hughes, G. (2000) *The Lockington Gold Hoard: excavations at the Early Bronze Age cemetary at Lockington, Leicestershire*, Oxford: Oxbow.

Hunter, F.J. and Davis, M. (1994) 'Early Bronze Age lead – a unique necklace from southeast Scotland', *Antiquity*, 68: 824–830.

Hurcombe, L.M. (1985) 'The potential of functional analyses of obsidian tools: a closer view', in C. Malone and S. Stoddart (eds) *Papers in Italian Archaeology*, Oxford: British Archaeological Reports, International Series 244, pp. 50–60.

Hurcombe, L.M. (1986) 'Residue studies on obsidian tools', in L.R. Owen and G. Unrath (eds) *Technical Aspects of Microwear Studies on Stone Tools, Parts I and II, Early Man News* 9/10/11, Tübingen, pp. 83–90 and plates 20–21.

Hurcombe, L.M. (1988) 'Some criticisms and suggestions in response to Newcomer et al. 1986', *Journal of Archaeological Science*, 15: 1–10.

Hurcombe, L.M. (1992) *Use Wear Analysis and Obsidian: theory, experiments and results*, Sheffield: Sheffield Academic Press

Hurcombe, L.M. (1993) 'Experimentell arkeologi och stenredskap (experimental archaeology and stone tools)', *Forntida Teknik*, 2.93: 4–16.

Hurcombe, L.M. (1994) 'From functional interpretation to cultural choices in tool use', in N. Ashton and A. David (eds) *Stories in Stone*, Lithic Studies Society, Occasional Paper 4, London: British Museum, pp. 145–155.

Hurcombe, L.M. (1995) 'Our own engendered species', *Antiquity*, 69: 87–100.

Hurcombe, L.M. (2000a) 'Plants as the raw materials for crafts', in A. Fairbairn (ed.) *Plants in Neolithic Britain and Beyond*, Oxford: Oxbow/Neolithic Studies Group.

Hurcombe, L.M. (2000b) 'Time, skill and craft specialisation as gender relations', in M. Donald and L. Hurcombe (eds) *Gender and Material Culture in Archaeological Perspective*, London: Macmillan, pp. 88–109.

Hurcombe, L.M. (2004a) 'Experimental archaeology', in C. Renfrew and P. Bahn (eds) *Archaeology: the key concepts*, London: Routledge, pp. 110–115.

Hurcombe, L.M. (2004b) 'The lithic evidence from the Pabbi Hills', in R.W. Dennell, with contributions by M. Anwar, M. Beech, R. Coard, L.M. Hurcombe, H.M. Rendell and A. Turner, *Early Hominin Landscapes in Northern Pakistan: investigations in the Pabbi Hills*, Oxford: British Archaeological Reports International Series 1265, pp. 222–291.

Hurcombe, L.M. (2006 in press) 'Looking for prehistoric basketry and cordage using inorganic remains: the evidence from stone tools', in L. Longo and N. Skakun (eds) *'Prehistoric Technology' 40 years later: functional studies and the Russian legacy*, Oxford: British Archaeological Reports International Series.

Hurcombe, L. (2007) 'A sense of materials and sensory perception in concepts of materiality', *World Archaeology*, 39.4.

Hurcombe, L.M. (forthcoming) 'Skeuomorphs'.

Hurcombe, L.M. and Lemieux, L. (2005) 'Basketry', in J. Gardiner (ed.) *Before the Mast: life and death aboard the Mary Rose. The archaeology of the Mary Rose vol. 4*, London: English Heritage, pp. 400–408.

Hurcombe, L.M. and Williams, L. (2002) 'Fish skin as a prehistoric material', *Bulletin of Primitive Technology*, 23: 39–41.

Hurley, W.M. (1979) *Prehistoric Cordage: identification of impressions on pottery*, Washington DC: Taraxacum Inc.

Huth, C. (2000) 'Metal circulation, communication and traditions of craftsmanship in Late Bronze Age and early Iron Age Europe', in C.F.E. Pare (ed.) *Metals Make the World Go Round: the supply and circulation of metals in Bronze Age Europe. Proceedings of a conference held at the University of Birmingham in June 1997*, Oxford: Oxbow, pp. 175–193.

Hutson, S. (2006) 'Self-citation in archaeology: age, gender, prestige, and the self', *Journal of Archaeological Method and Theory*, 13: 1–18.

Hyland, D.C., Tersak J.M., and Adovasio J.M. (1990) 'Identification of the species of origin of residual blood on lithic material', *American Antiquity*, 55: 104–112.

Ingersoll, D., Yellen, J., and MacDonald, W. (eds) (1977) *Experimental Archeology*, New York: Columbia University Press.

Ingold, T. (1990) 'Society, nature and the concept of technology', *Archaeological Review from Cambridge*, 9: 5–17.

Ingold, T. (2000) *The Perception of the Environment: essays in livelihood, dwelling and skill*, London: Routledge.

Ingold, T. (2007) 'Materials against materiality', *Archaeological Dialogues* 14: 1–16.

Inizan, M.-L., Roche, H., and Tixier, J. (1992) *Technology of Knapped Stone*, Meudon: Centre National de la Recherche Scientifique, Préhistorie de la Pierre Taillée 3.

Inizan, M.-L., Reduron-Ballinger, M., Roche, H., and Tixier, J. (1999) *Technology and Terminology of Knapped Stone: followed by a multilingual vocabulary*, Nanterre: CREP.

Iriarte, J., Holst, I., Marozzi, O., Listopad, C., Alonso, E., Rinderknecht, A., and Montaña, J. (2004) 'Evidence for cultivar adoption and emerging complexity during the Mid-Holocene in the La Plata Basin, Uruguay', *Nature*, 432: 614–617.

Jagiella, C. (1987) *Atlas der Hölzer Saudi Arabiens: die Holzanatomie der Wichtigsten Bäume und Sträucher Arabiens mit einem Holzanatomischen Bestimmungsschlüssel*, Wiesbaden: L. Reichert.

Jahren, A.H., Toth, N., Schick, K., Clark, J.D., and Amundson, R.G. (1997) 'Determining stone tool use: chemical and morphological analyses of residues on experimentally manufactured stone tools', *Journal of Archaeological Science*, 24: 245–250.

Jakes, K.A., Sibley, L.R., and Yerkes, R. (1994) 'A comparative collection for the study of fibres used in prehistoric textiles from eastern North America', *Journal of Archaeological Science*, 21: 641–650.

James, S.R. (2001) 'Prehistoric Hohokam bone artifacts from southern Arizona: craft specialization, status and gender', in A.M. Choyke and L. Bartosiewicz (eds) *Crafting Bone: skeletal technologies through time and space, proceedings of the 2nd meeting of the (ICAZ) Worked Bone Research Group Budapest, 31 August – 5 September 1999*, Oxford: British Archaeological Reports International Series 937, pp. 331–241.

Janusek, J.W. (2005) 'Of pots and people: ceramic style and social identity in the Tiwanaku state', in R.M. Reycraft (ed.) *Us and Them: archaeology and ethnicity in the Andes*, Los Angeles: The Cotsen Institute of Archaeology, University of California, pp. 34–53.

Jensen, G. (2001) 'Macro wear patterns on Danish Late Mesolithic antler axes', in A.M. Choyke and L. Bartosiewicz (eds) *Crafting Bone: skeletal technologies through time and space, proceedings of the 2nd meeting of the (ICAZ) Worked Bone Research Group Budapest, 31 August – 5 September 1999*, Oxford: British Archaeological Reports International Series 937, pp. 165–170.

Jesus, P.S. de (1980) *The Development of Prehistoric Mining and Metallurgy in Anatolia*, Oxford: British Archaeological Reports International Series 74.

Jewell, P.A. (ed.) (1963) *The Experimental Earthwork on Overton Down*, London: British Association for the Advancement of Science.

Johnson, E. (1985) 'Current developments in bone technology', in M.B. Schiffer (ed.) *Advances in Archaeological Method and Theory*, vol. 8: London: Academic Press, pp. 157–236.

Johnson, L.L. (1978) 'A history of flintknapping experimentation 1838–1976', *Current Anthropology*, 19: 337–372.

Johnson, M. (1999) *Archaeological Theory: an introduction*, Oxford: Blackwell.

Johnson, M.H. (1989) 'Conceptions of agency in archaeological interpretation', *Journal of Anthropological Archaeology*, 8: 189–211.

Jones, A. (2001) 'Drawn from memory: the archaeology of aesthetics and the aesthetics of archaeology in Earlier Bronze Age Britain and the present', *World Archaeology*, 33: 335–356.

Jones, A. (2004) 'Archaeometry and materiality: materials-based analysis in theory and practice', *Archaeometry*, 46: 327–338, and comments in *Archaeometry*, 47: 175–207.

Jones, A. and MacGregor, G. (eds) (2002) *Colouring the Past*, Oxford: Berg.

Jones, D. and Cloke, P. (2002) *Tree Culture: the place of trees and trees in their place*, Oxford: Berg.

Jones, S. and Pay, S. (1990) 'The legacy of Eve', in P. Gathercole and D. Lowenthal (eds) *The Politics of the Past*, London: Unwin Hyman, pp. 160–171.

Jørgensen, L. and Vang Petersen, P. (1998) *Gold, Power and Belief: Danish gold treasures from prehistory and the Middle Ages*, Copenhagen: Thaning and Appel with the Danish National Museum.

José-Yacamán, M. and Ascencio, J.A. (2000) 'Electron microscopy and its application to the study of archaeological materials and art preservation', in E. Ciliberto and G. Spoto (eds) *Modern Analytical Methods in Art and Archaeology*, New York: Wiley, pp. 405–444.

Joyce, R.A. and Lopiparo, J. (2005) Postscript: doing agency in archaeology', *Journal of Archaeological Method and Theory*, 12: 365–374.

Juel Jensen, H. (1994) *Flint Tools and Plant Working: hidden traces of Stone Age technology*, Copenhagen: Aarhus University Press.

Juleff, G. (1996) 'An ancient wind-powered iron smelting technology in Sri Lanka', *Nature*, 379: 60–63.

Juleff, G. (1998) *Early Iron and Steel in Sri Lanka: a study of the Samanalawewa area*, Mainz am Rhein: Verlag Philipp von Zabern.

Kamminga, J. (1982) *Over the Edge: functional analysis of Australian stone tools*, St Lucia: University of Queensland, Occasional Papers in Anthropology 12.

Kamp, K.A. (2001) 'Where have all the children gone? The archaeology of childhood', *Journal of Archaeological Method and Theory*, 8: 1–34.

Karali, L. (1999) *Shells in Aegean Prehistory*, Oxford: British Archaeological Report International Series 761.

Karklins, K. (ed.) (2000) *Studies in Material Culture Research*, California, PA: The Society for Historical Archaeology.

Kars, E.A.K., Kars, H., and McDonnell, R.D. (1992) 'Greenstone axes from eastern central Sweden: a technological-petrological approach', *Archaeometry*, 34: 213–222.

Karsten, P. and Knarrström, B. (2003) *The Tågerup Excavations*, Trelleborg: National Heritage Board (Sweden).

Kealhofer, L., Torrence, R., and Fullagar, R. (1999) 'Integrating phytoliths within use-wear/residue studies of stone tools', *Journal of Archaeological Science*, 26: 527–546.

Keates, S. (2002) 'The flashing blade: copper, colour and luminosity in North Italian Copper Age society', in A. Jones and G. MacGregor (eds), *Colouring the Past*, Oxford: Berg, pp. 109–125.

Keeley, L.H. (1980) *Experimental Determination of Stone Tool Uses*, Chicago: Chicago University Press.

Keeley, L.H. and Newcomer, M.H. (1977) 'Microwear analysis of experimental flint tools: a test case', *Journal of Archaeological Science*, 4: 29–62.

Keeley, L.H. and Toth, N. (1981) 'Microwear polishes on early stone tools from Koobi Fora, Kenya', *Nature*, 293: 464–465.

Keller, C.M. and Keller, J.D. (1996) *Cognition and Tool Use: the blacksmith at work*, Cambridge: Cambridge University Press.

Kelterborn, P. (2002) 'Measurable flintknapping', in M. Fansa (ed.) *Experimentelle Archäologie in Europa, Bilanz 2002, Heft 1*, Oldenburg: Isensee Verlag, pp. 35–49.

Kemp, B. (2000) 'Soil (including mud-brick architecture)', in P.T. Nicholson and I. Shaw (eds) *Ancient Egyptian Materials and Technology*, Cambridge: Cambridge University Press, pp. 78–103.

Kempe, D. and Harvey, A.P. (eds) (1983) *The Petrology of Archaeological Artefacts*, Oxford: Clarendon Press.

Kenmotsu, N. (2000) 'Gunflints: a study', in D.R. Brauner (ed.) *Approaches to Material Culture Research for Historical Archaeologists*, California, PA: The Society for Historical Archaeology, pp. 340–372.

Kenoyer, J.M. (1986) 'The Indus bead industry: contributions to bead technology', *Ornament*, 10: 18–23.

Kenoyer, J.M., Vidale, M., and Bhan, K.K. (1991) 'Contemporary stone bead making in Khambhat, India: patterns in craft specialization and organization of production as reflected in the archaeological record', *World Archaeology*, 23: 44–63.

Kenoyer, J.M., Vidale, M., and Bhan, K.K. (1994) 'Carnelian bead production in Khambhat, India: an ethnoarchaeological study', in B. Allchin (ed.) *Living Traditions: studies in the ethnoarchaeology of South Asia*, Columbia, MO: South Asia Publications, pp. 281–306.

Kent, K.P. (1983) *Pueblo Indian Textiles: a living tradition*, Santa Fe, NM: School of American Research Press.

Kent, S. (1993) 'Models of abandonment and material culture frequencies', in C.M. Cameron and S.A. Tomka (eds) *Abandonment of Settlements and Regions: ethnoarchaeological and archaeological approaches*, Cambridge: Cambridge University Press, pp. 54–73.

Kidder, A.V. (1915) 'Pottery of the Pajarito plateau and of some adjacent regions in New Mexico', *Memoir* 2: 407–462. Washington DC: American Anthropological Association.

Kidder, A.V. (1917) 'A design-sequence from New Mexico', *Proceedings of the National Academy of Sciences*, 3: 369–370.

Kidder, M.A. and Kidder, A.V. (1917) 'Notes on the pottery of Pecos', *American Anthropologist*, 19: 325–360.

Kienlin, T.L. and Ottaway, B.S. (1998) 'Flanged axes of the north-alpine region: an assessment of the possibilities of use wear analysis on metal artifacts', in C. Mordant, M. Pernot and V. Rychner (eds) *L'Atelier du Bronzier en Europe du XXe au VIIIe Siècle avant notre Ere*, actes du colloque international Bronze '96, Neuchâtel et Dijon, tome II: Du minerai au métal, du métal à l'objet, Paris: CTHS, pp. 271–286.

Killick, D. (1996) 'Optical and electron microscopy in material culture studies', in D.W. Kingery (ed.) *Learning from Things: method and theory of material culture studies*, Washington DC: Smithsonian Institution, pp. 204–230.

Killick, D. (2001) 'Science, speculation and the origins of extractive metallurgy', in D.R. Brothwell and A.M. Pollard (eds) *Handbook of Archaeological Sciences*, Chichester: Wiley, pp. 483–492.

Killick, D. (2007 in press) 'Archaeological science in the USA and Britain', in A. Sullivan (ed.) *Archaeological Concepts for the Study of the Cultural Past*, Salt Lake City: University of Utah Press.

Kimura, B., Brandt, S.A., Hardy, B.L., and Hauswirth, W. (2001) 'Analysis of DNA from ethnoarchaeological stone scrapers', *Journal of Archaeological Science*, 28: 45–53.

Kingery, W.D. (1996a) 'A role for materials science', in D.W. Kingery (ed.) *Learning from Things: method and theory of material culture studies*, Washington DC: Smithsonian Institution, pp. 175–180.

Kingery, W.D. (1996b) 'Materials science and material culture', in D.W. Kingery (ed.) *Learning from Things: method and theory of material culture studies*, Washington DC: Smithsonian Institution, pp. 181–203.

Kingery, W.D. (1997) 'The operational principles of ceramic kilns', in P.M. Rice (ed.) *Ceramics and Civilisation, vol. 3: the prehistory and history of ceramic kilns*, Colombus: The American Ceramic Society, pp. 11–19.

Kinnes, I. and Varndell, G. (eds) (1995) *'Unbaked Urns of Rudely Shape': essays on British and Irish pottery for Ian Longworth*, Oxford: Oxbow Monograph 5.

Klokkernes, T. and Sharma, N. (2005) 'The Roald Amundsen Collection: the impact of a skin preparation method on preservation', in J.C.H. King, B. Pauksztat, and R. Storrie (eds) *Arctic*

Clothing of North America – Alaska, Canada, Greenland, London: The British Museum Press, pp. 91–94.

Knappett, C. (1994) 'Traditional pottery technologies in two North West Frontier Villages, Pakistan', *South Asian Studies*, 10: 99–111.

Knappett, C. (2002) 'Photographs, skeuomorphs and marionettes: some thoughts on mind, agency and object', *Journal of Material Culture*, 7: 97–117.

Knappett, C. (2005a) *Thinking through Material Culture: an interdisciplinary perspective*, Philadelphia: University of Pennsylvania Press.

Knappett, C. (2005b) 'Pottery', in H.D.G. Maschner and C. Chippindale (eds) *Handbook of Archaeological Methods*, Lanham, MD: AltaMira, pp. 673–714.

Knappett, C. (2005c) 'The affordances of things: a post-Gibsonian perspective on the relationality of mind and matter', in E. DeMarrais, C. Gosden, and C. Renfrew (eds), *Rethinking Materiality: the engagement of mind with the material world*, Cambridge: McDonald Institute Monographs, pp. 43–51.

Knappett, C. (2007) 'Materials with materiality?', *Archaeological Dialogues*, 14: 20–23.

Knappett, C. (in press) 'Pottery fabrics and technology', in J.N. Postgate and D. Thomas (eds) *Kilise Tepe: Excavations 1994–98*, Cambridge: McDonald Institute, with the British Institute of Archaeology at Ankara.

Knappett, C., Pirrie, D., Power, M., Nikolakopoulou, I., and Hilditch, J. (forthcoming) 'Analyzing ceramics through Qemscan: a pilot study on LB I pottery from Akrotiri, Thera', *Journal of Archaeological Science*.

Knarrström, B. (2001) *Flint: a Scanian hardware*, Lund: National Heritage Board.

Knöpfli, H. (1997) *Crafts and Technologies*, London: British Museum Press.

Knutsson, K. (1988) *Patterns of Tool Use: scanning electron microscopy of experimental quartz tools*, Uppsala: Societas Archaeologica Uppsaliensis.

Koller, J., Baumer, U., and Mania, D. (2001) 'High-tech in the middle Palaeolithic: Neandertal-manufactured pitch identified', *European Journal of Archaeology*, 4: 385–397.

Kooistra, L. (2006) 'Fabrics of fibres and strips of bark', in L.P. Louwe Kooijmans and P.F.B. Jongste (eds) *Analecta Praehistorica Leidensia*, 37/38, 'Schipluiden: a Neolithic settlement on the Dutch North Sea coast c.3500 CAL BC', Leiden: Faculty of Archaeology, Leiden University, pp. 253–259.

Kooyman, B.P. (2000) *Understanding Stone Tools and Archaeological Sites*, Calgary: University of Calgary Press.

Kooyman, B.P., Newman, M.E., and Ceri, H. (1992) 'Verifying the reliability of blood residue analysis on archaeological tools', *Journal of Archaeological Science*, 19: 265–269.

Kooyman, B.P., Newman, M.E., Cluney, C., Lobb, M., Tolman, S., McNeil, P., and Hills, L.V. (2001) 'Identification of horse exploitation by Clovis hunters based on protein analysis', *American Antiquity*, 66: 686–691.

Kopytoff, I. (1986) 'The cultural biography of things: commodities as a process', in A. Appadurai (ed.) *The Social Life of Things: commodities in cultural perspective*, Cambridge: Cambridge University Press, pp. 64–91.

Korbe-Grohne, U. (1988) 'Microscopic methods for identification of plant fibres and animal hairs from the Princes' Tomb of Hochdorf, SW Germany', *Journal of Archaeological Science*, 15: 73–83.

Kossinna, G. (1911) *Die Herkunft der Germanen*, Leipzig: Kabitzsch.

Kramer, C. (1979) *Ethnoarchaeology: implications of ethnography for archaeology*, New York: Columbia University Press.

Kramer, C. (1994) 'A tale of two cities: ceramic ethnoarchaeology in Rajasthan', in B. Allchin (ed.) *Living Traditions: studies in the ethnoarchaeology of South Asia*, Columbia, MO: South Asia Publications, pp. 307–322.

Krzyszkowska, O. (1990) *Ivory and Related Materials: an illustrated guide*, London: Institute of Classical Studies, Classical Handbook 3, Bulletin Supplement 59.

Krzyszkowska, O. and Morkot, R. (2000) 'Ivory and related materials', in P.T. Nicholson and I. Shaw (eds) *Ancient Egyptian Materials and Technology*, Cambridge: Cambridge University Press, pp. 320–331.

Küchler, S. (2002) 'Binding in the Pacific: between loops and knots', in V. Buchli (ed.) *The Material Culture Reader*, Oxford: Berg, pp. 63–80.

Kuhn, S.L. (1995) *Mousterian Lithic Technology: an ecological perspective*, Princeton, NJ: Princeton University Press.

Kuhn, T.S. (1962) *The Structure of Scientific Revolutions*, Chicago: Chicago University Press.

Kuniholm, P.I. (2001) 'Dendrochronology and other applications of tree-ring studies in archaeology', in D.R. Brothwell and A.M. Pollard (eds) *Handbook of Archaeological Sciences*, Chichester: Wiley, pp. 35–46.

Kuoni, B. (1981) *Cestería Tradicional Ibérica*, Barcelona: Ediciones del Serbal.

Kuzmin, Y.K., Hall, S., Tite, M.S., Bailey, R., O'Malley, J.M., and Medvedev, V.E. (2001) 'Radiocarbon and thermoluminescence dating of the pottery from the early Neolithic site of Gasya (Russian Far East): initial results', *Quaternary Science Reviews*, 20: 945–948.

Kvamme, K.L., Stark, M.T., and Longacre, W.A. (1996) 'Alternative procedures for assessing standardization in ceramic assemblages', *American Antiquity*, 61: 116–126.

La Violette, A. (2000) *Ethno-Archaeology in Jenne, Mali*, Oxford: British Archaeological Reports, International Series S838.

Lacorre, F. (1960) *La Gravette: le Gravétien et le Bayacien*, Paris: CNRS.

Lahiri, N. (1995) 'Indian metal and metal-related artifacts as cultural signifiers: an ethnographic perspective', *World Archaeology*, 27: 116–132.

Lambert, J.B. (1997) *Traces of the Past: unraveling the secrets of archaeology through chemistry*, Reading, MA: Addison-Wesley.

Lambert, J.B. (2005) 'Archaeological chemistry', in H.D.G. Maschner and C. Chippindale (eds) *Handbook of Archaeological Methods*, Lanham, MD: Altamira Press, pp. 478–500.

Lancaster, J. (1986) 'Wind action on stone artifacts: an experiment in site modification', *Journal of Field Archaeology*, 13: 359–363.

Langdon, J. (2004) *Mills in the Medieval Economy: England, 1300–1540*, Oxford: Oxford University Press.

Langenheim, J.H. (2003) *Plant Resins: chemistry, evolution, ecology and ethnobotany*, Cambridge: Timber Press.

Langsner, D. (1995) *Green Woodworking: a hands-on approach*, Asheville, NC: Lark Books.

Larick, R. (1986) 'Age grading and ethnicity in the style of Loikop (Samburu) spears', *World Archaeology*, 18: 268–283.

Larick, R. (1991) 'Warriors and blacksmiths: mediating ethnicity in East African spears', *Journal of Anthropological Archaeology*, 10: 299–331.

Larkin, P. (1964) *The Whitsun Weddings*, London: Faber and Faber.

Larsson, L. (2000) 'The passage of axes: fire transformation of flint objects in the Neolithic of southern Sweden', *Antiquity*, 74: 602–610.

Lassen, H. (2000) 'Introduction to weight systems in the Bronze Age East Mediterranean: the case of Kalavasos-Ayios Dhimitrios', in C.F.E. Pare (ed.) *Metals Make the World Go Round: the supply and circulation of metals in Bronze Age Europe. Proceedings of a conference held at the University of Birmingham in June 1997*, Oxford: Oxbow, pp. 233–246.

Latham, A.G. (2001) 'Uranium-series dating', in D.R. Brothwell and A.M. Pollard (eds) *Handbook of Archaeological Sciences*, Chichester: Wiley, pp. 63–72.

Latz, P. (1995) *Bushfires and Bushtucker: Aboriginal plant use in Central Australia*, Alice Springs: Iad Press.

Lautridou, J.P., Letavernier, G., Lindé, K., Etlicher, B., and Ozouf, J.C. (1986) 'Porosity and frost susceptibility of flints and chalk: laboratory experiments, comparison of "glacial" and "periglacial" surface texture of flint materials, and field investigations', in G. de G. Sieveking and M.B. Hart (eds) The Scientific Study of Flint and Chert, proceedings of the 4th International Flint Symposium held at Brighton Polytechnic 10–15 April 1983, Cambridge: Cambridge University Press, pp. 269–282.

Lawrence, S. (2006) 'Artifacts of the modern world', in J. Balme and A. Paterson (eds) Archaeology in Practice: a student guide to archaeological analyses, Oxford: Blackwell, pp. 362–388.

Lawson, G. (1999) 'Getting to grips with music's prehistory: experimental approaches to function, design and operational wear in excavated musical instruments', in A. Harding (ed.) Experiment and Design: archaeological studies in honour of John Coles, Oxford: Oxbow, pp. 133–138.

Lazzari, M. (2003) 'Archaeological visions: gender, landscape and optic knowledge', Journal of Social Archaeology, 3.2: 194–222.

Lazzari, M. (2005) 'The texture of things: objects, people and landscape in Northwest Argentina (first millennium A.D.)', in L. Meskell (ed.). Archaeologies of Materiality, Oxford: Blackwell, pp. 126–161.

Lea, V. (2005) 'Raw, pre-heated or ready to use: discovering specialist supply systems for flint industries in mid-Neolithic (Chassey culture) communities in southern France', Antiquity, 79: 51–65.

Leach, B. and Tait, J. (2000) 'Papyrus', in P.T. Nicholson and I. Shaw (eds) Ancient Egyptian Materials and Technology, Cambridge: Cambridge University Press, pp. 227–253.

Leakey, M. with Roe, D. (1995) Olduvai Gorge, volume 5: excavations in Beds III, IV and the Masek Beds, 1968–1971, Cambridge: Cambridge University Press.

Lechtman, H. (1996) 'Arsenic bronze: dirty copper or chosen alloy? A view from the Americas', Journal of Field Archaeology, 23: 477–514.

Lee, M. (2005) 'Hairnets and fishnets: the Yup'ik Eskimo Kaapaaq in historical context', in J.C.H. King, B. Pauksztat, and R. Storrie (eds) Arctic Clothing of North America – Alaska, Canada, Greenland, London: The British Museum Press, pp. 127–130.

Leeuw, S. van der, (1993) 'Giving the potters a choice: conceptual aspects of pottery techniques', in P. Lemonnier (ed.) Technological Choices: transformation in material cultures since the Neolithic, London: Routledge, pp. 238–288.

Leeuw, S. van der, and Pritchard, A.C. (1984) The Many Dimensions of Pottery, Amsterdam: Amsterdam University Press.

Leigh, D. (1972) First Aid for Finds: a practical guide for archaeologists, Southampton: RESCUE.

LeMoine, G.M. (1997) Usewear Analysis on Bone and Antler Tools of the Mackenzie Inuit, Oxford: British Archaeological Reports, International Series 679.

LeMoine, G.M. and Darwent, C.M. (1998) 'The Walrus and the Carpenter: late Dorset ivory working in the High Arctic', Journal of Archaeological Science, 25: 73–83.

Lemonnier, P. (1976) 'La description des chaînes opératoires: contribution à l'analyse des systèmes techniques', Techniques et Culture, 1: 100–151.

Lemonnier, P. (1986) 'The study of material culture today: toward an anthropology of technical systems', Journal of Anthropological Archaeology, 5: 147–186.

Lemonnier, P. (1989) 'Towards an anthropology of technology', Man, 24: 526–527.

Lemonnier, P. (ed.) (1993) Technological Choices: transformations in material cultures since the Neolithic, London: Routledge.

Lemorini, C., Stiner, M.C., Gopher, A., Shimelmitz, R., and Barkai, R. (2006) 'Use-wear analysis of an Amudian laminar assemblage from the Acheuleo-Yabrudian of Qesem Cave, Israel', Journal of Archaeological Science, 33: 921–934.

Lentfer, C., Therin, M., and Torrence, R. (2002) 'Starch grains and environmental reconstruction: a modern test case from West New Britain, Papua New Guinea', *Journal of Archaeological Science*, 29: 687–698.

Lentz, D.L., Yaeger, J., Robin, C., and Ashmore, W. (2005) 'Pine, prestige and politics of the Late Classic Maya at Xunantunich, Belize', *Antiquity*, 79: 573–585.

Leroi-Gourhan, A. (1964) *Le Geste et la parole, vol. I: Technique et langage; vol. II: La Mémoire et les rythmes*, Paris: Albin Michel; trans. A. Bostock Berger (1993) *Gesture and Speech*, Cambridge, MA: MIT.

Lewenstein, S.M. (1987) *Stone Tool Use at Cerros: the ethnoarchaeological and use-wear evidence*, Austin: University of Texas Press.

Light, J.D. (2000) 'A field guide to the identification of metal', in K. Karklins (ed.) *Studies in Material Culture Research*, California, PA: The Society for Historical Archaeology, pp. 3–19.

Lightfoot, R.R. (1993) 'Abandonment processes in prehistoric pueblos', in C.M. Cameron and S.A. Tomka (eds) *Abandonment of Settlements and Regions: ethnoarchaeological and archaeological approaches*, Cambridge: Cambridge University Press, pp. 165–177.

Lillehammer, G. (1996) 'Death, family and gender – life's starting point', *KAN (Kvinner i Archaeologi I Norge)*, 26: 61–81.

Lillie, M.C., Zhilin, M., Shavchenko, S., and Taylor, M. (2005) 'Carpentry dates back to the Mesolithic', *Antiquity*, 79: project gallery. Online. Available http://0-antiquity.ac.uk.lib.ex.ac.uk/projgall/lillie/index.html (accessed 3 July 2006).

Lindahl, A. and Stilborg, O. (eds) (1995) *The Aim of Laboratory Analyses of Ceramics in Archaeology: papers read at the workshop held at Odengarden, April 7–9, 1995 in honour of Birgitta Hulthén*, Stockholm: Kungl. Vitterhets historie och antikvitets akademien.

Liritzis, I. (2006) 'SIMS-SS, a new obsidian hydration dating method: analysis and theoretical principles', *Archaeometry*, 48: 533–547.

Livingstone Smith, A. (2001) 'Bonfire II: the return of pottery firing temperatures', *Journal of Archaeological Science*, 28: 991–1003.

Loney, H.L. (2000) 'Social and technological control: a critical review of models of technological change in ceramic studies', *American Antiquity*, 65: 646–668.

Longacre, W.A. (1985) 'Pottery use-life among the Kalinga, northern Luzon, the Philippines', in B. Nelson (ed.) *Decoding Prehistoric Ceramics*, Carbondale: Southern Illinois University Press, pp. 334–346.

Longacre, W.A. (ed.) (1991) *Ceramic Ethnoarchaeology*, Tucson: University of Arizona Press.

Longacre, W.A. and Skibo, J.M. (eds) (1994) *Kalinga Ethnoarchaeology: expanding archaeological method and theory*, Washington D.C.: Smithsonian Institution Press.

Longo, L. and Skakun, N. (eds) (2007 in press) *'Prehistoric Technology' 40 years later: functional studies and the Russian legacy*, Oxford: British Archaeological Reports International Series.

López Varela S.L., van Gijn, A.L., and Jacobs, L. (2002) 'De-mystifying pottery production in the Maya Lowlands: detection of traces of use-wear on pottery sherds through microscopic analysis and experimental replication', *Journal of Archaeological Science*, 29: 1133–1147.

Lord, J. (1993) *The Nature and Subsequent Uses of Flint*, privately published.

Louwe Kooijmans, L.P. and Jongste, P.F.B. (eds) (2006) *Analecta Praehistorica Leidensia*, 37/38, 'Schipluiden: a Neolithic settlement on the Dutch North Sea coast c.3500 CAL BC', Leiden: Faculty of Archaeology, Leiden University.

Louwe Kooijmans, L.P. and Kooistra, L. (2006) 'Wooden artefacts', in L.P. Louwe Kooijmans and P.F.B. Jongste (eds) *Analecta Praehistorica Leidensia*, 37/38, 'Schipluiden: a Neolithic settlement on the Dutch North Sea coast c.3500 CAL BC', Leiden: Faculty of Archaeology, Leiden University, pp. 225–251.

Lovick, S.K. (1983) 'Fire-cracked rock as tools: wear pattern analysis', *Plains Anthropologist*, 28: 41–52.

Loy, T.H. (1983) 'Prehistoric blood residues: detection on tool surfaces and identification of species of origin', *Science*, 220: 1269–1271.

Loy, T.H. (1998) 'Organic residues on Oldowan tools from Sterkfontein Cave, South Africa', in M.A. Raath, H. Soodyall, K.L.K.D. Barkhan, and P.V. Tobias (eds) *Dual Congress of the International Association for the Study of Human Paleontology, and International Association of Human Biologists*, Johannesburg: Department of Anatomical Sciences, University of the Witwatersrand Medical School, pp. 74–75.

Loy, T.H. and Dixon, E.J. (1998) 'Blood residues on fluted points from eastern Beringia', *American Antiquity*, 63: 21–46.

Loy, T.H. and Hardy, B.G. (1992) 'Blood residue analysis of 90,000 year old stone tools from Tabun Cave, Israel', *Antiquity*, 66: 24–35.

Loy, T.H. and Matthaei, K.I. (1994) 'Species of origin determination from prehistoric blood residues using ancient genomic DNA', *Australasian Biotechnology*, 4: 161–162.

Loy, T.H. and Wood, A.R. (1989) 'Blood residue analysis at Çayönü Tepesi, Turkey', *Journal of Field Archaeology*, 16: 451–460.

Loy, T.H., Spriggs, M., and Wickler, S. (1992) 'Direct evidence for human use of plants 28,000 years ago: starch residues on stone artefacts from the northern Solomon Islands', *Antiquity*, 66: 898–912.

Lubar, S. and Kingery, W.D. (eds) (1993) *History from Things: essays on material culture*, London: Smithsonian Institution Press.

Luedtke, B.E. (1992) *An Archaeologist's Guide to Chert and Flint*, Los Angeles: Institute of Archaeology, Universiy of California.

Luik, H., Choyke, A.M., Batey, C.E., and Lougas, L. (eds) (2005) *From Hooves to Horns, from Mollusc to Mammoth: manufacture and use of bone artefacts from prehistoric times to the present*, Research into Ancient Times 15, Tartu: Ajaloo Instituut.

Lundström, I. and Adolfsson, G. (1993) *The Exhibitions at the Archaeological Museum in Stavanger, Norway*, Stavanger: Arkeologisk Museum I Stavanger.

Lupo, K.D. and Schmitt, D.N. (2002) 'Upper Palaeolithic net-hunting, small prey exploitation, and women's work effort: a view from the ethnographic and ethnoarchaeological record of the Congo basin', *Journal of Archaeological Method and Theory*, 9: 147–179.

Lyman, R. L., O'Brien, M.J., and Hayes, V. (1998) 'Mechanical and functional study of bone rods from the Richey-Roberts Clovis Cache, Washington, U.S.A.', *Journal of Archaeological Science*, 25: 887–906.

Lynch, F. (1998) 'Colour in Prehistoric architecture', in A. Gibson and D. Simpson (eds) *Prehistoric Ritual and Religion: essays in honour of Aubrey Burl*, Stroud: Sutton Publishing Ltd, pp. 62–67.

Lyons, C. and Papadopoulos, J. (eds) (2002) *The Archaeology of Colonialism: issues and debates*, Los Angeles: Getty Research Institute.

Lyons, C.L. (2000) 'Gender and burial in early colonial Sicily: the case of Morgantina', in M. Donald and L. Hurcombe (eds) *Representations of Gender from Prehistory to the Present*, vol. 3, London: Macmillan, pp. 87–103.

Mabry, J., Skibo, J.M., Schiffer, M.B., and Kvamme, K. (1988) 'Use of a falling-weight tester for assessing ceramic impact strength', *American Antiquity*, 53: 830–839.

McBrearty, S., Bishop, L., Plummer, T., Dewar, R., and Conard, N. (1998) 'Tools underfoot: human trampling as an agent of lithic artefact edge modification', *American Antiquity*, 63: 108–129.

McCarthy, F.D. (1967; 2nd edn 1976) *Australian Aboriginal Stone Implements: including bone, shell and tooth implements*, Sydney: The Australian Museum Trust.

McClure, S.B., Bernabeu, J., García, O., Aura, E., Molina, L., Descantes, C., Speakman, R.J., and Glascock, M.D. (2006) 'Testing technological practices: neutron activation analysis of Neolithic ceramics from Valencia, Spain', *Journal of Archaeological Science*, 33: 671–680.

McDonnell, J.G. (2001) 'Pyrotechnology', in D.R. Brothwell and A.M. Pollard (eds) *Handbook of Archaeological Sciences*, Chichester: Wiley, pp. 493–506.

McGee, E. (1978; 2nd edn 1982) *No Need to Die: real techniques of survival*, London: Paul H. Crompton Ltd.

McGhee, R. (1977) 'Ivory for the sea woman: the symbolic attributes of a prehistoric technology', *Canadian Journal of Archaeology*, 1: 141–149.

Macgillivray, J.A. (1998) *Knossos: pottery groups of the Old Palace Period*, Athens: British School at Athens Studies 5.

McGrail, S. (1982) *Woodworking techniques before A.D. 1500: papers presented to a symposium at Greenwich in September, 1980, together with edited discussion*, Oxford: British Archaeological Reports, International Series S129.

McGrail, S. (1987) *Ancient Boats in North-Western Europe: the archaeology of water transport to AD 1500*, London: Longmans.

McGrail, S. (2002) *Boats of the World: from the stone age to medieval times*, Oxford: Oxford University Press.

MacGregor, A. (1976) 'Bone skates: a review of the evidence', *Archaeological Journal*, 133: 57–74.

MacGregor, A. (1985) *Bone, Antler, Ivory and Horn*, Beckenham: Croom Helm.

MacGregor, A. (1998) 'Hides, horns and bone: animals and interdependent industries in the early urban context', in E. Cameron (ed.) *Leather and Fur: aspects of early medieval trade and technology*, London: Archetype Publications Ltd, pp. 11–26.

MacGregor, A. and Currey, J. (1983) 'Mechanical properties as conditioning factors in the bone and antler industry of the 3rd to the 19th century', *Journal of Archaeological Science*, 10: 71–77.

MacGregor, A. and Mainman, A. (2001) 'The bone and antler industry in Anglo-Scandinavian York: the evidence from Coppergate', in A.M. Choyke and L. Bartosiewicz (eds) *Crafting Bone: skeletal technologies through time and space, proceedings of the 2nd meeting of the (ICAZ) Worked Bone Research Group Budapest, 31 August – 5 September 1999*, Oxford: British Archaeological Reports International Series 937, pp. 343–354.

MacGregor, G. (1999) 'Making sense of the past in the present: analysis of carved stone balls', *World Archaeology*, 31.2: 258–271.

McGregor, R. (1992) *Prehistoric Basketry of the Lower Pecos, Texas*, Madison, WI: Prehistory Press.

McGrew, W.C. (1992) *Chimpanzee Material Culture*, Cambridge: Cambridge University Press.

McIntosh, R.J. (1974) 'Archaeology and mud wall decay in a west African village', *World Archaeology*, 6: 154–171.

McIntosh, R.J. (1977) 'The excavation of mud structures: an experiment from West Africa', *World Archaeology*, 9: 185–199.

MacKenzie, M. (1991) *Androgynous Objects: string bags and gender in central New Guinea*, Chur: Harwood Academic.

McNabb, J. (1989) 'Sticks and stones: a possible experimental solution to the question of how the Clacton spear point was made', *Proceedings of the Prehistoric Society*, 55: 251–257.

McNeil, M. and Selwyn, L.S. (2001) 'Electrochemical processes in metallic corrosion', in D.R. Brothwell and A.M. Pollard (eds) *Handbook of Archaeological Sciences*, Chichester: Wiley, pp. 605–614.

Maggi, R. and Pearce, M. (2005) 'Mid fourth-millennium copper mining in Liguria, north-west Italy: the earliest known copper mines in Western Europe', *Antiquity*, 79: 66–77.

Malafouris, L. (2004) 'The cognitive basis of material engagement: where brain, body and culture conflate', in E. DeMarrais, C. Gosden, and C. Renfrew (eds) *Rethinking Materiality: the Engagement of Mind with the Material World*, Cambridge: McDonald Institute for Archaeological Research, pp. 53–62.

Manby, T.G. (1995) 'Skeuomorphism: some reflections of leather, wood and basketry in Early Bronze Age pottery', in I. Kinnes and G. Varndell (eds) *'Unbaked Urns of Rudely Shape': essays on British and Irish pottery for Ian Longworth*, Oxford: Oxbow Monograph 5, pp. 81–88.

Mandeville, M.D. (1973) 'A consideration of the thermal pre-treatment of chert', *Plains Anthropologist*, 18: 177–202.

Mandeville, M.D. (1983) 'Experiments to investigate the effects of heat treatment on the use wear of flint tools', *Proceedings of the Prehistoric Society*, 49: 1–13.

Mann, I. (1962) *Animal By-Products: processing and utilization*, Rome: Food and Agriculture Organization of the United Nations.

Mansur-Franchomme, M.E. (1983) 'Scanning electron microscopy of dry hide working tools: the role of abrasives and humidity in microwear polish formation', *Journal of Archaeological Science*, 10: 223–230.

Marlar, R.A., Leonard, B.L., Billman, B.R., Lambert, P.M., and Marlar, J.E. (2002) 'Biochemical evidence of cannibalism at a prehistoric Puebloan site in southwestern Colorado', *Nature*, 407: 74–78.

Martin, A.S. (2000) 'The role of pewter as missing artefact: consumer attitudes toward tablewares in late 18th century Virginia', in D.R. Brauner (ed.) *Approaches to Material Culture Research for Historical Archaeologists*, California, PA: The Society for Historical Archaeology, pp. 248–274.

Maschner, H.D.G. and Chippindale, C. (eds) (2005) *Handbook of Archaeological Methods*, Lanham, MD: AltaMira.

Mason, H.J. (1978) *Flint: the versatile stone*, Ely: Providence Press.

Mason, O. Tufton (1895) *Woman's Share of Primitive Culture*, London: Macmillan.

Mathieu, J.R. (eds) (2002) *Experimental Archaeology: replicating past objects, behaviours and processes*, Oxford: British Archaeological Reports, International Series 1035.

Matthews, K. (2000) 'The material culture of the homosexual male: a case for archaeological exploration', in M. Donald and L. Hurcombe (eds) *Gender and Material Culture in Archaeological Perspective*, Basingstoke: Macmillan, pp. 3–19.

Mattingley, D.J. (1990) 'Painting, presses and perfume production at Pompeii', *Oxford Journal of Archaeology*, 9: 71–90.

Maxfield, V.A. and Peacock, D.P.S. (2001) *Mons Claudianus II: survey and excavation*, Cairo: Institut Français d'Archéologie Orientale.

Maxfield, V.A. and Peacock, D.P.S. (eds) (2006) *Mons Claudianus III: ceramic vessels and related objects*, Cairo: Institut Français d'Archéologie Orientale.

Maxwell, D.B.S. (2000) 'Beer cans: a guide for the archaeologist', in D.R. Brauner (ed.) *Approaches to Material Culture Research for Historical Archaeologists*, California, PA: The Society for Historical Archaeology, pp. 290–308.

Maynard, B. (1989) *Modern Basketry Techniques*, London: Batsford.

Mayo, E. (1944) *Shells and How They Live*, London: Pleiades Books.

Mazza, P.P.A., Martini, F., Sala, B., Magi, M., Colombini, M.P., Giachi, G., Landucci, F., Lemorini, C., Modugno, F., and Ribechini, E. (2006) 'A new Palaeolithic discovery: tar-hafted stone tools in a European Mid-Pleistocene bone-bearing bed', *Journal of Archaeological Science*, 33.9: 1310–1318.

Meaney, A. L. (1981) *Anglo-Saxon Amulets and Curing Stones*, Oxford: British Archaeological Reports, British Series 96.

Mears, R. (1990) The Survival Handbook, Oxford: Oxford Illustrated Press.

Mears, R. (2002) Bushcraft, London: Hodder and Stoughton.

Mears, R. (2005) 'Making string from nettle', skills section, Bushcraft [DVD]. London: BBC.

Médart, F. (2000) L'Artisanat textile au Néolithique, Préhistoires 4, Montagnac: Monique Mergoil.

Meehan, B. and Jones, R. (eds) (1988) Archaeology with Ethnography: an Australian perspective, Canberra: Australian National University Press.

Meeks, N.D. and Cartwright, C.R. (2005) 'Caribou and seal hair: examination by scanning electron microscope', in J.C.H. King, B. Pauksztat, and R. Storrie (eds) Arctic Clothing of North America – Alaska, Canada, Greenland, London: The British Museum Press, pp. 42–44.

Melcher, C.L. and Zimmerman, C.W. (1977) 'Thermoluminescence determination of prehistoric heat treatment of chert artefacts', Science, 197: 1359–1362.

Meskell, L. (ed.) (2005) Archaeologies of Materiality, Oxford: Blackwell.

Michels, J.W. (1986) 'Obsidian hydration dating', Endeavour, 10: 97–100.

Millard, A. (2001) 'The deterioration of bone', in D.R. Brothwell and A.M. Pollard (eds) Handbook of Archaeological Sciences, Chichester: Wiley, pp. 637–648.

Miller, D. (1985) Artefacts as Categories: a study of ceramic variability in central India, Cambridge: Cambridge University Press.

Miller, D. (1987) Material Culture and Mass Consumption, Oxford: Blackwell.

Miller, D. (ed.) (1995) Acknowledging Consumption: a review of new studies, London: Routledge.

Miller, D. (ed.) (1998) Material Cultures: why some things matter, London: UCL Press.

Miller, D. (2002) 'Smelter and smith: Iron Age metal fabrication technology in Southern Africa', Journal of Archaeological Science, 29: 1083–1131.

Miller, D. (ed.) (2005) Materiality: an introduction, Durham and London: Duke University Press.

Miller, D. (2006) 'Consumption', in C. Tilley, W. Keane, S. Küchler, M. Rowlands, and P. Spyer (eds) Handbook of Material Culture, London: Sage, pp. 341–354.

Miller, G.L. (2000) 'A revised set of CC index values for classification and economic scaling of English ceramics from 1787 to 1880', in D.R. Brauner (ed.) Approaches to Material Culture Research for Historical Archaeologists, California, PA: The Society for Historical Archaeology, pp. 86–110.

Milliken, S. and Cook, G. (eds) (2001) A Very Remote Period Indeed: papers on the Palaeolithic presented to Derek Roe, Oxford: Oxbow Books.

Mills, B.J. (1989) 'Integrating functional analyses of vessels and sherds through models of ceramic assemblage formation', World Archaeology, 21: 133–147.

Mills, J.S. and White, R. (1994) The Organic Chemistry of Museum Objects, 2nd edn, London: Butterworths.

Mitchell, C. (1992) 'Activating women in Arikara ceramic production', in C. Claassen (ed.) Exploring Gender Through Archaeology: selected papers from the 1991 Boone Conference, Monograph 11, Madison, WI: Prehistory Press, pp. 89–94.

Mithen, S. (1996) The Prehistory of the Mind, London: Thames and Husdon.

Mobley-Tanaka, J.L. and Griffitts, J.L. (1997) 'Spatulate and notched tools from the American southwest: a lesson in function-based typologies', in L.A. Hannus, L. Rossum, and R.P. Winham (eds) Proceedings of the 1993 Bone Modification Conference, Hot Springs, South Dakota, Sioux Falls, SD: Archaeology Laboratory, Augustana College, pp. 247–255.

Moens, L., von Bolen, A., and Vandenabeele, P. (2000) 'X-ray fluorescence', in E. Ciliberto and G. Spoto (eds) Modern Analytical Methods in Art and Archaeology, New York: Wiley, pp. 55–80.

Moir, B.G. (1990) 'Comparative studies of "fresh" and "aged" Tridacna gigas shell: preliminary investigations of a reported technique for pre-treatment of tool material', Journal of Archaeological Science, 17: 329–346.

MOLAS (1994) (3rd edn) *Archaeological Site Manual*, London: Museum of London Archaeologcial Services.

Molleson, T. (1994) 'The eloquent bones of Abu Hureyra', *Scientific American*, 271: 70–75.

Momigliano, N. (ed.) (2007) *Knossos Pottery Handbook: Neolithic and Bronze Age (Minoan)*, BSA Studies Series 14, London: British School at Athens.

Momigliano, N. and Knappett, C. (forthcoming) *Pottery Fabrics at Iasos, Southwest Turkey*. Rome: Bretschneider.

Montgomery, B.K. (1993) 'Ceramic analysis as a tool for discovering processes of pueblo abandonment', in C.M. Cameron and S.A. Tomka (eds) *Abandonment of Settlements and Regions: ethnoarchaeological and archaeological approaches*, Cambridge: Cambridge University Press, pp. 157–166.

Moore, A.M.T., Hillman, G.C., and Legge, A.J. (2000) *Village on the Euphrates: from foraging to farming at Abu Hureyra*, Oxford: Oxford University Press.

Moore, D.T. and Oddy, W.A. (1985) 'Touchstones: some aspects of their nomenclature, petrography and provenance', *Journal of Archaeological Science*, 12: 59–80.

Moore, H. (1996) *Space, Text and Gender: an anthropological study of the Marakwet of Kenya*, Cambridge: Cambridge University Press.

Moore, J. and Scott, E. (eds) (1997) *Invisible People and Processes*, Leicester: Leicester University Press.

Moritz, L.A. (1958, reprinted 2002) *Grain-Mills and Flour in Classical Antiquity*, Oxford: Oxbow Books.

Moss E.H. (1983) *The Functional Analysis of Flint Implements. Pincevent and Pont d'Ambon: two case studies from the French Final Palaeolithic*, Oxford: British Archaeological Reports, International Series 177.

Moss, E.H. (1987) 'A review of "Investigating microwear polishes with blind tests"', *Journal of Archaeological Science*, 14: 473–482.

Mottram, H.R., Dudd, S.N., Lawrence, G.J., Stott, A.W., and Evershed, R.P. (1999) 'New chromatographic, mass-spectrometric and stable isotope approaches to classification of degraded animal fats preserved in archaeological pottery', *Journal of Chromatography*, 833: 209–221.

Mowat, L., Morphy, H., and Dransart, P. (1992) *Basketmakers: meaning and form in Native American baskets*, Oxford: Pitt Rivers Museum.

Muir, R. (2005) *Ancient Trees and Living Landscapes*, Stroud: Tempus.

Mulholland, J.A. (1981) *A History of Metals in Colonial America*, Tuscaloosa, AL: University of Alabama Press.

Mulville, J. and Outram, A.K. (eds) (2005) *The Zooarchaeology of Fats, Oils, Milk and Dairying*, Oxford: Oxbow Books.

Mussi, M. (1995) 'The earliest occupation of Europe: Italy', in W. Roebroeks and T. van Kolfschoten (eds) *The Earliest Occupation of Europe*, Leiden: Leiden University Press, pp. 27–49.

Nadel, D., Grinberg, U., Boaretto, E., and Werker, E. (2006) 'Wooden objects from Ohalo II (23,000 cal BP), Jordan Valley, Israel', *Journal of Human Evolution*, 50: 644–662.

Nagar, M. and Misra, V.N. (1994) 'Survival of the hunter-gathering tradition in the Ganga Plains and Central India', in B. Allchin (ed.) *Living Traditions: studies in the ethnoarchaeology of South Asia*, Columbia, MO: South Asia Publications, pp. 169–192.

Needham S.P. (1989) 'Selective deposition in the British Early Bronze Age', *World Archaeology*, 20: 229–248.

Needham, S.P. and Spence T. (1997) 'Refuse and the formation of middens', *Antiquity*, 71: 77–90.

Neff, H. (2000) 'Neutron activation analysis for provenance determination in archaeology', in E. Ciliberto and G. Spoto (eds) *Modern Analytical Methods in Art and Archaeology*, New York: Wiley, pp. 81–134.

Neff, H. (2001) 'Synthesizing analytical data – spatial results from pottery provenance', in D.R. Brothwell and A.M. Pollard (eds) *Handbook of Archaeological Sciences*, Chichester: Wiley, pp. 733–748.

Nelson, B.A. (1991) 'Ceramic frequency and use-life: a Highland Mayan case in cross-cultural perspective', in W.A. Longacre (ed.) *Ceramic Ethnoarchaeology*, Tucson: University of Arizona Press, pp. 162–181.

Nelson, N.C. (1916) 'Flint working by Ishi', reprinted (1979) in R.F. Heizer and T. Kroeber (eds) *Ishi, the Last Yahi: a documentary history*, Berkeley: University of California Press, pp. 168–171.

Nelson, S. (1997) *Gender in Archaeology: analyzing power and prestige*, Walnut Creek, CA: AltaMira.

Nelson, S. and Rosen-Ayalon, M. (eds) (2001) *In Pursuit of Gender: worldwide archaeological approaches*, Walnut Creek, CA: AltaMira Press.

Nettl, B. (1965) 'Songs of Ishi', reprinted (1979) in R.F. Heizer and T. Kroeber (eds) *Ishi, the Last Yahi: a documentary history*, Berkeley: University of California Press, pp. 203–216.

Neupert, M.A. (2000) 'Clays of contention: an ethnoarchaeological study of factionalism and clay composition', *Journal of Archaeological Method and Theory*, 7: 249–272.

Neupert, M.A. and Longacre, W.A. (1994) 'Informant accuracy in pottery use-life studies: a Kalinga example', *Kalinga Ethnoarchaeology: expanding archaeological method and theory*, Washington DC: Smithsonian Institution Press, pp. 71–82.

Newcomer, M.H., Grace, R., and Unger-Hamilton, R. (1986) 'Investigating microwear polishes with blind tests', *Journal of Archaeological Science*, 13: 203–217.

Newman, M.E. and Julig, P. (1989) 'The identification of protein residues on lithic artifacts from a stratified boreal forest site', *Journal Canadien d'Archéologie/Canadian Journal of Archaeology*, 13: 119–132.

Newman, M.E., Yohe, R.M., Ceri, H., and Sutton, M.Q. (1993) 'Immunological protein residue on non-lithic archaeological materials', *Journal of Archaeological Science*, 20: 93–100.

Newman, M.E., Ceri, H., and Kooyman, B. (1996) 'The use of immunological techniques in the analysis of archaeological materials – a response to Eisele; with report of studies at Head-Smashed-In Buffalo Jump', *Antiquity*, 70: 677–682.

Newman, M.E., Yohe II, R.M., Kooyman, B., and Ceri, H. (1997) '"Blood" from stones? Probably: a response to Fiedel', *Journal of Archaeological Science*, 24: 1023–1027.

Newman, M.E., Byrne, G., Ceri, H., Dimnik, L.S., and Bridge, P.J. (1998) 'Immunological and DNA analysis of blood residues from a surgeon's kit used in the American Civil War', *Journal of Archaeological Science*, 25: 553–557.

Newman, R. and Serpico, M. (2000) 'Adhesives and binders', in P.T. Nicholson and I. Shaw (eds) *Ancient Egyptian Materials and Technology*, Cambridge: Cambridge University Press, pp. 475–494.

Nicholson, P.T. and Henderson, J. (2000) 'Glass', in P.T. Nicholson and I. Shaw (eds) *Ancient Egyptian Materials and Technology*, Cambridge: Cambridge University Press, pp. 195–226.

Nicholson, P.T. and Patterson, H.L. (1985) 'Pottery making in Upper Egypt: an ethno-archaeological study', *World Archaeology*, 17: 222–239.

Nicholson, P.T. and Patterson, H.L. (1989) 'Ceramic technology in Upper Egypt: a study of pottery firing', *World Archaeology*, 21: 71–86.

Nicholson, P.T. and Patterson, H.L. (1991) 'The Ballas Pottery Project: ethnoarchaeology in Upper Egypt', in G.J.I. Bey and C.A. Pool (eds) *Ceramic Production and Distribution: an integrated approach*, Boulder: Westview Press, pp. 25–47.

Nicholson, P.T. with Peltenburg, E. (2000) 'Egyptian faience', in P.T. Nicholson and I. Shaw (eds) *Ancient Egyptian Materials and Technology*, Cambridge: Cambridge University Press, pp. 177–194.

Nicolson, R.A. (2005) 'Oil from troubled waters: historical and archaeological investigations into the use of fish and sea mammal oil in the Northern Isles of Scotland', in J. Mulville and A.K. Outram (eds) *The Zooarchaeology of Fats, Oils, Milk and Dairying*, Oxford: Oxbow Books, pp. 142–147.

Nielsen, A.E. (1991) 'Trampling the archaeological record: an experimental study', *American Antiquity*, 56: 483–503.

Nieuwenhuis, C.J. (2002) *Traces on Tropical Tools: a functional study of chert artefacts from preceramic sites in Colombia*, Leiden: Faculty of Archaeology, University of Leiden.

Noort, R. van de, Chapman, H., and Collis, J. (2007 in press) *Sutton Common: the excavation of an Iron Age 'marsh-fort'*, York: Council for British Archaeology Research Report 154.

Norbach, L.C. (ed.) (1996) *Early Iron Production: archaeology, technology and experiments*, Lejre: Historical-Archaeological Experimental Centre Technical Report No. 3.

Noshiro, S., Suzuki, M., and Yamada, M. (1992) 'Species selection for wooden artefacts by prehistoric and early historic people in the Kanto plain, Central Japan', *Journal of Archaeological Science*, 19: 429–444.

Nowakowski, J.A. (1991) 'Trethellan Farm, Newquay: the excavation of a lowland Bronze Age settlement and Iron Age cemetery', *Cornish Archaeology*, 30: 5–242.

Nowakowski, J.A. (2001) 'Leaving home in the Cornish Bronze Age: Insights into Planned Abandonment Processes', in J. Brück (ed.) *Bronze Age Landscapes: tradition and transformation*, Oxford: Oxbow, pp. 139–148.

O'Brien, P. (1990) 'An experimental study of the effects of salt erosion on pottery', *Journal of Archaeological Science*, 17: 393–401.

O'Brien, W. (1994) *Mount Gabriel: Bronze Age mining in Ireland*, Galway: Galway University Press.

O'Brien, W. (1996) *Bronze Age Copper Mining in Britain and Ireland*, Princes Risborough: Shire Archaeology.

O'Brien, W. (1998) 'Approaches to the study of metal in the insular Bronze Age', in J. Bayley (ed.) *Science in Archaeology: an agenda for the future*, London: English Heritage, pp. 109–122.

O'Brien, W. (2005) *Ross Island: mining, metal and society in early Ireland*, Galway: National University of Ireland.

O'Connell, J.F. (1995) 'Ethnoarchaeology needs a general theory of behaviour', *Journal of Archaeological Research*, 3: 205–255.

O'Connor, S. and Veth, P. (2005) 'Early Holocene shell fish hooks from Lene Hara Cave, East Timor establish complex fishing technology was in use in Island South East Asia five thousand years before Austronesian settlement', *Antiquity*, 79: 249–256.

O'Riordain, B. and Waddell, J. (1993) *The Funerary Bowls and Vases of the Irish Bronze Age*, Galway: Galway University Press.

Oakes, J.E. (1987) *Factors Influencing Kamik Production in Arctic Bay, Northwest Territories*, Ottawa: Canada Museum Mercury Series.

Oakley, K.P. (1965a) 'Folklore of Fossils part I', *Antiquity* 39: 9–16.

Oakley, K.P. (1965b) 'Folklore of Fossils part II', *Antiquity* 39: 117–125.

Oakley, K.P. (1981) 'Emergence of higher thought 3.0–0.2 Ma B.P.', *Philosophical Transactions of the Royal Society of London*, Series B, 292 (1057): 205–211.

Oddy, W.A. (ed.) (1980) *Aspects of Early Metallurgy*, London: British Museum Press.

Odell, G.H. (1994) 'Prehistoric hafting and mobility in the North American mid-continent: examples from Illinois', *Journal of Anthropological Archaeology*, 13: 51–73.

Odell, G.H. (1996a) *Stone Tools and Mobility in the Illinois Valley: from hunter-gatherer camps to agricultural villages*, Ann Arbor: International Monographs in Prehistory.

Odell, G.H. (ed.) (1996b) *Stone Tools: theoretical insights into human prehistory*, New York: Plenum Press.

Odell, G.H. (2000a) 'Stone tool research at the end of the millennium: procurement and technology', *Journal of Archaeological Research*, 8: 269–330.

Odell, G.H. (2000b) 'Usewear analysis', in Ellis, L. (ed.) *Archaeological Method and Theory: an encyclopedia*, New York: Garland, pp. 651–655.

Odell, G.H. (2001) 'Stone tool research at the end of the millennium: classification, function, and behavior', *Journal of Archaeological Research*, 9: 45–100.

Odell, G.H. and Cowan, F. (1986) 'Experiments with spears and arrows on animal targets', *Journal of Field Archaeology*, 13: 195–212.

Odell, G.H. and Odell-Vereecken, F. (1980) 'Verifying reliability of lithic use-wear assessments by "blind tests": the low-power approach', *Journal of Field Archaeology*, 7: 87–120.

Odell, G.H., Hayden, B.D., Johnson, J.K., Kay, M., Morrow, T.A., Nash, S.E., Nassaney, M.S., Rick, J.W., Rondeau, M.F., Rosen, S.A., Shott, M.J., and Thacker, P.T. (1996) 'Some comments on a continuing debate', in G.H. Odell (ed.) *Stone Tools: theoretical insights into human prehistory*, New York: Plenum Press, pp. 377–392.

Ogden, J. (2000) 'Metals', in P.T. Nicholson and I. Shaw (eds) (2000) *Ancient Egyptian Materials and Technology*, Cambridge: Cambridge University Press, pp. 148–176.

Olausson, D.S. and Larsson, L. (1982) 'Testing for the presence of thermal pre-treatment of flint in the Mesolithic and Neolithic of Sweden', *Journal of Archaeological Science*, 9: 275–285.

Olcott, M.D. (1985) 'Tacitus on the ancient amber-gatherers: a re-evaluation of the *Germania*', *Journal of Baltic Studies*, 16: 302–315.

Oliveira, M.A. de and Oliveira, L. de (1991) *The Cork*, Mozelos: Grupo Amorim.

Olsen, B. (2006) 'Scenes from a troubled engagement: post-structuralism and material culture studies', in C. Tilley, W. Keane, S. Küchler, M. Rowlands, and P. Spyer (eds) *Handbook of Material Culture*, London: Sage, pp. 85–103.

Olsen, S.L. (1988) 'Applications of scanning electron microscopy in archaeology', *Advances in Electronics and Electron Physics*, 71: 357–380.

Olsen, S.L. (1989) 'On distinguishing natural from cultural damage on archaeological antler', *Journal of Archaeological Science*, 16: 125–136.

Olsen, S.L. (2001) 'The importance of thong-smoothers at Botal, Kazakstan', in A.M. Choyke and L. Bartosiewicz (eds) *Crafting Bone: skeletal technologies through time and space, proceedings of the 2nd meeting of the (ICAZ) Worked Bone Research Group Budapest, 31 August – 5 September 1999*, Oxford: British Archaeological Reports International Series 937, pp. 197–206.

Orme, B. (1973) 'Archaeology and ethnography', in C. Renfrew (ed.) *The Explanation of Culture Change: models in prehistory*, London: Duckworth, pp. 481–492.

Orme, B. (1974) 'Twentieth century prehistorians and the idea of ethnographic parallels', *Man N.S.*, 9: 199–212.

Orme, B. (1981) *Anthropology for Archaeologists: an introduction*, Ithica: Cornell University Press.

Orme, B.J. and Coles, J.M. (1983) 'Prehistoric wood-working from the Somerset Levels', *Somerset Levels Papers*, 9: 19–43.

Orozco-Kohler, T. (2000) *Aprovisionamiento e Intercambio: analisis petrologico del utillaje pulimentado en la prehistoria reciente del Pais Valenciano (España)*. Oxford: British Archaeological Reports, International Series 867.

Ortman, S. (2000) 'Conceptual metaphor in the archaeological record: methods and an example from the American southwest', *American Antiquity*, 65: 613–645.

Orton, C., Tyers, P., and Vince, A. (1993) *Pottery in Archaeology*, Cambridge: Cambridge University Press.

Orton, C.R. and Tyers, P.A. (1992) 'Counting broken objects: the statistics of ceramic assemblages', in A.M. Pollard (ed.) *New Developments in Archaeological Science*, Oxford: Oxford University Press, Proceedings of the British Academy 77, pp. 163–186.

Osborne, K. (2005) 'Sharing the fun of finds', *The Archaeologist*, 58: 34–35.

Osgood, C. (1940) *Ingalik Material Culture*, New Haven: Yale University Press.

Osgood, R. and Monks, S. (2000) *Bronze Age Warfare*, Stroud: Sutton Publications.

Oswald, A. (1975) *Clay Pipes for the Archaeologist*, Oxford: British Archaeological Reports British Series 14.

Otak, L.A. (2005) 'Iniqsimajuq: caribou skin preparation in Igloolik, Nunavut', in J.C.H. King, B. Pauksztat and R. Storrie (eds) *Arctic Clothing of North America – Alaska, Canada, Greenland*, London: The British Museum Press, pp. 74–79.

Ottaway, B.S. (1998) 'The settlement as an early smelting place for copper', in BUMA-IV Organizing Committee, *Proceedings of the Fourth International Conference on the Beginning of the Use of Metals and Alloys*, Shimane: The Japan Institute of Metals, pp. 165–172.

Ottaway, B.S. (2003) 'Experimental archaeometallurgy', in T. Stöllner, G. Körlin, G. Steffens and J. Cierny (eds) *Man and Mining: studies in honour of Gerd Weisgerber on occasion of his 65th birthday*, Anschnitt Beiheft, 16, Bochum: Deutsches Bergbau-Museum, pp. 341–348.

Ottaway, B.S. and Seibel, S. (1998) 'Dust in the wind: experimental casting of bronze in sand moulds', in M.-C. Frère-Sautot and J.-P. Millotte (eds) *Paléométallurgie des Cuivres: actes du colloque de Bourg-en-Bresse et Baune, 17–18 oct. 1997*, Monographies Instrumentum, 5, Montagnac: Editions Monique Mergoil, pp. 59–63.

Outram, A.K. (2005) 'Publishing archaeological experiments: a quick guide for the uninitiated', *EuroREA*, 2: 1–3.

Outram, A.K. and Rowley-Conwy, P. (1998) 'Meat and marrow utility indices for horse (Equus)', *Journal of Archaeological Science*, 25: 839–849.

Outram, A.K., Knüsel, C.J., Knight, S., and Harding, A.F. (2005) 'Understanding complex fragmented assemblages of human and animal remains: a fully integrated approach', *Journal of Archaeological Science*, 32: 1699–1710.

Owen, L.R. (1997) 'Geschlechterrollen und die Interpretation von Grabbeigaben: Nadeln, Pfrieme, Spitzen', *Ethnographisch-Archäologische Zeitschrift*, 38: 495–504.

Owen, L.R. (1998; for 1994) 'Gender, crafts and the reconstruction of tool use', *Helinium*, 34: 186–200.

Owen, L.R. (1999) 'Questioning stereo-typical notions of prehistoric tool functions: ethno-analogy, experimentation and functional analysis', in L.R. Owen and M. Porr (eds) *Ethno-Analogy and the Reconstruction of Prehistoric Artefact Use and Production*, Tübingen: Mo Vince Verlag, pp. 17–30.

Owen, L.R. (2000) 'Lithic functional analysis as a means of studying gender and material culture in prehistory', in M. Donald and L. Hurcombe (eds) *Gender and Material Culture in Archaeological Perspective*, Basingstoke: Macmillan, pp. 185–205.

Owen, L.R. and Porr, M. (eds) (1999) *Ethno-Analogy and the Reconstruction of Prehistoric Artefact Use and Production*, Tübingen: Mo Vince Verlag.

Owen, L.R. and Unrath, G. (eds) (1986) *Technical Aspects of Microwear Studies on Stone Tools, Parts I and II*, Early Man News 9/10/11, Tübingen.

Owoc, M. (2005) 'From the ground up: agency, practice, and community in the Southwestern British Bronze Age', *Journal of Archaeological Method and Theory*, 12: 257–281.

Owoc, M.A. (2007 forthcoming) 'Just an impression? Materialising the invisible on southwestern British Bronze Age ceramics', in P. Blinkhorn, C. Cumberpatch, and A. Teather (eds), *The Chiming of Cracked Bells*, Oxford: Oxbow Books.

Paine, S. (1990) *Embroidered Textiles: traditional patterns from five continents, with a worldwide guide to identification*, London: Thames and Hudson Ltd.

Paine, S. (1994) *The Afghan Amulet: travels from the Hindu Kush to Razgrad*, London: Penguin Books Ltd.

Pals, J.P. and Dierendonck, M.C. van (1988) 'Between flax and fibre: cultivation and processing of flax in a mediaeval peat reclamation settlement near Midwoud (Prov. Noord Holland)', *Journal of Archaeological Science*, 15: 237–251.

Palyvou, C. (2005) *Akrotiri, Thera: an architecture of affluence 3,500 years old*, Philadelphia: The Institute for Aegean Prehistory Academic Press.

Panagiotakopulu, E., Buckland, P.C., Day, P.M., Doumas, C., Sarpaki, A., and Skidmore, P. (1997) 'A lepidopterous cocoon from Thera and evidence for silk in the Aegean Bronze Age', *Antiquity*, 71: 420–429.

Pare, C.F.E. (ed.) (2000) *Metals Make the World Go Round: the supply and circulation of metals in Bronze Age Europe*, Oxford: Oxbow.

Park, R.W. (1998) 'Size counts; the miniature archaeology of childhood in Inuit societies' *Antiquity*, 72: 269–281.

Parker Pearson, M. (2001) 'Food, fertility and front doors in the first millennium BC', in T.C. Champion and J.R. Collis (eds) *The Iron Age in Britain and Ireland: recent trends*, Sheffield: Sheffield Academic Press, pp. 117–132.

Parker Pearson, M. and Ramilisonina (1998) 'Stonehenge for the ancestors: the stones pass on the message', *Antiquity* 72: 308–326.

Parker Pearson, M., Pollard, J., Tilley, C., Welham, K., and Albarella, U. (2006) 'Materialising Stonehenge: the Stonehenge Riverside Project and new discoveries', *Journal of Material Culture*, 11: 227–261.

Parkes, P.A. (1986) *Current Scientific Techniques in Archaeology*, London: Croom Helm.

Patrick, M., Koning, A.J. de and Smith, B. (1985) 'Gas liquid chromatographic analysis of fatty acids in food residues from ceramic in the southwestern Cape, South Africa', *Archaeometry*, 27: 231–236.

Paterson, M. (2005) 'The forgetting of touch: re-membering geometry with eyes and hands', *Angelaki*, 10.3: 115–132.

Patterson, L.W. (1981) 'Fracture force changes from heat treating and edge grinding', *Flintknapper's Exchange*, 4.3: 6–9.

Patterson, L.W. (1995) 'Thermal damage of chert', *Lithic Technology*, 20.1: 72–80.

Pauksztat, B. (2005) 'Kayak clothing in contemporary Greenlandic kayak clubs', in J.C.H. King, B. Pauksztat, and R. Storrie (eds) *Arctic Clothing of North America – Alaska, Canada, Greenland*, London: The British Museum Press, pp. 115–120.

Pavlish, L.A. and Sheppard, P.J. (1983) 'Thermoluminescent determination of Paleoindian heat treatment in Ontario, Canada', *American Antiquity*, 48: 793–799.

Peabody Turnbaugh, S. and Turnbaugh, W.A. (1986, 2nd edn 2004) *Indian Baskets*, Atglen, PA: Schiffer Publishing.

Peachy, A. (2005) 'Urning a living? A survey of Roman pottery specialists', *The Archaeologist*, 58: 14–15.

Peacock, D. (1977) *Pottery and Early Commerce*, London: Academic Press.

Peacock, D. (1980) 'The Roman millstone trade: a petrological sketch', *World Archaeology*, 12: 43–53.

Peacock, D. (1998) 'Ceramics and lithics: into the future', in J. Bayley (ed.) *Science in Archaeology: an agenda for the future*, London: English Heritage, pp. 157–160.

Peacock, D.P.S. (1967) 'Heavy mineral analysis', *Archaeometry*, 10: 97–100.

Peacock, D.P.S. (1968) 'Thin sectioning', *Proceedings of the Prehistoric Society*, 34: 414–427.

Peacock, D.P.S. and Maxfield, V.A. (1997) *Mons Claudianus I: topography and quarries*, Cairo: Institut Français d'Archéologie Orientale.

Pearsall, D.M., Chandler-Ezell, K., and Zeidler, J.A. (2004) 'Maize in ancient Ecuador: results of residue analysis of stone tools from the Real Alto site', *Journal of Archaeological Science*, 31: 423–442.

Pedersen, K. (2005) 'Eskimo sewing techniques in relation to contemporary sewing techniques – seen through a copy of a Qilakitsoq costume', in J.C.H. King, B. Pauksztat, and R. Storrie (eds) *Arctic Clothing of North America – Alaska, Canada, Greenland*, London: The British Museum Press, pp. 70–73.

Peer, van, P. (1995) *The Levallois Reduction Strategy*, Madison: Prehistory Press.

Pelegrin, J. (1993) 'A framework for analysing prehistoric stone tools manufacture and a tentative application to some early lithic industries', in A. Berthelet and J. Chavaillon (eds) *The Use of Tools by Human and Non-Human Primates*, Oxford: Clarendon, pp. 302–314.

Penhallurick, R.D. (1986) *Tin in Antiquity*, London: Institute of Metals.

Penniman, T.K. (1984) *Pictures of Ivory and other Animal Teeth, Bone and Antler, with a Brief Commentary on their Use and Identification*, 2nd edn, Oxford: Pitt Rivers Museum, Occasional Paper on Technology 5.

Perry, L. (2005) 'Reassessing the traditional interpretation of "Manioc" artifacts in the Orinoco Valley of Venezuela', *Latin American Antiquity*, 16: 409–426.

Petersen, P.V. (1993) *Flint fra Danmarks Oldtid*, Copenhagen: Høst & Søns.

Petraglia, M., Knepper, D., Glumac, P., Newman, M., and Sussman, C. (1996) 'Immunological and microwear analysis of chipped-stone artifacts from Piedmont contexts', *American Antiquity*, 61: 127–135.

Pétrequin, A.-M. and Pétrequin, P. (1988) *Le Néolithique du lacs*, Montligeon: Errance.

Pétrequin, P. and Pétrequin, A.-M. (2000) *Ecologie d'un outil: la hache de pierre en Irian Jaya (Indonésie)*, CRA Monograph 12, Paris: CNRS.

Pétrequin, P., Jeunesse, C., and Jeudy, F. (1995) *La Hache de pierre: carrières vosgiennes et échanges de lames polies pendant le Néolithique (5400–2100 av. J.-C.)*, Paris: Editions Errance.

Petrussen, F. (2005) 'Arctic clothing from Greenland', in J.C.H. King, B. Pauksztat, and R. Storrie (eds) *Arctic Clothing of North America – Alaska, Canada, Greenland*, London: The British Museum Press, pp. 45–47.

Pettitt, P.B. (2005) 'Radiocarbon dating', in H.D.G. Maschner and C. Chippindale (eds) *Handbook of Archaeological Methods*, Lanham, MD: AltaMira, pp. 309–336.

Phillips, J. (2000) 'Ostrich eggshells', in P.T. Nicholson and I. Shaw (eds) *Ancient Egyptian Materials and Technology*, Cambridge: Cambridge University Press, pp. 332–333.

Phillips, P. (1988) 'Traceology (microwear) studies in the USSR', *World Archaeology*, 19: 349–356.

Pierce, C. (2005) 'Reverse engineering the ceramic cooking pot: cost and performance properties of plain and textured vessels', *Journal of Archaeological Method and Theory*, 12.2: 117–157.

Pigeot, N. (1990) 'Technical and social actors: flintknapping specialists at Magdalenian Etiolle', *Archaeological Review from Cambridge*, 9: 126–141.

Piggott, S. (1962) 'Head and hooves', *Antiquity* 36: 110–118.

Pigott, V.C. (ed.) (1999) *The Archaeometallurgy of the Asian Old World*, Philadelphia: University Museum, University of Pennsylvania.

Pike, A.W.G. and Pettitt, P.B. (2005) 'Other dating techniques', in H.D.G. Maschner and C. Chippindale (eds) *Handbook of Archaeological Methods*, Lanham, MD: AltaMira, pp. 337–372.

Piperno, D.R. (2006) *Phytoliths: a comprehensive guide for archaeologists and palaeoecologists*, Lanham, MD: AltaMira.

Piperno, D.R. and Holst, I. (1998) 'The presence of starch grains on prehistoric stone tools from the lowland Neotropics: indications of early tuber use and agriculture in Panama', *Journal of Archaeological Science*, 25: 765–776.

Piperno, D.R., Ranere, A.J., Holst, I., and Hansell, P. (2000) 'Starch grains reveal early root crop horticulture in the Panamanian tropical forest', *Nature*, 407: 894–897.

Piperno, D.R., Weis, E., Holst, I., and Nadel, D. (2004) 'Processing of wild cereal grains in the Upper Palaeolithic revealed by starch grain analysis', *Nature*, 430: 670–673.

Pitt-Rivers, Lt-Gen. A. Lane-Fox (1867) 'Primitive warfare II', *Journal of the Royal United Service Institution*; reprinted in J. Myers (ed.) (1906) *The Evolution of Culture and Other Essays*, Oxford: Clarendon.

Pitt-Rivers, Lt-Gen. A. Lane-Fox (1875) 'Principles of classification'; reprinted in J. Myers (ed.) (1906) *The Evolution of Culture and Other Essays*, Oxford: Clarendon, pp. 1–19.

Pitts, M. (1978) 'On the shape of waste flakes as an index of technological change in lithic industries', *Journal of Archaeological Science*, 5: 17–37.

Pitts, M. and Roberts, M. (1997) *Fairweather Eden: life in Britain half a million years ago as revealed by the excavations at Boxgrove*, London: Century.

Pleiner, R. (2000) *Iron in Archaeology: the European bloomery smelters*, Prague: Archaeologický ústav AVŮR.

Plisson, H. and Gijn, A. van (1989) 'La Tracéologie: mode d'emploi', *L'Anthropologie*, 93: 631–642.

Ploux, S. (1991) 'Technologie, technicité, technicians: méthode de détermination d'auteurs et comportements techniques individuels', in *25 Ans d'Etudes Technologiques en Préhistoire*, Juans-les-Pins: Editions APDCA, pp. 201–214.

Pokines, J.T. (1998) 'Experimental replication and use of Cantabrian Lower Magdalenian antler projectile points', *Journal of Archaeological Science*, 25: 875–887.

Pole, L., Doyal, S., with Burkinshaw, J. (2004) *Second Skin: everyday and sacred uses of bark*, Exeter: Royal Albert Memorial Museum and Art Gallery.

Pollard, A.M. (ed.) (1992) *New Developments in Archaeological Science*, Oxford: Oxford University Press, Proceedings of the British Academy 77.

Pollard, A.M., and Heron, C. (1996) *Archaeological Chemistry*, Cambridge: Royal Society of Chemistry.

Pollard, J. (2001) 'The aesthetics of depositional practice', *World Archaeology*, 33: 315–334.

Pope, S.T. (1918) 'Yahi archery', reprinted in R.F. Heizer and T. Kroeber (eds) *Ishi the Last Yahi: a documentary history*, Berkely: University of California Press, pp. 172–200.

Pope, S.T. (1979) 'Yahi archery', in R.F. Heizer and T. Kroeber (eds) *Ishi, the Last Yahi: a documentary history*, Berkeley: University of California Press, pp. 172–200.

Popper, Sir Karl (1959) *The Logic of Scientific Discovery*, London: Hutchinson.

Porr, M. (1999) 'Archaeology, analogy, material culture, society: an exploration', in L.R. Owen and M. Porr (eds) *Ethno-Analogy and the Reconstruction of Prehistoric Artefact Use and Production*, Tübingen: Mo Vince Verlag, pp. 3–15.

Powers, A., Padmore, J., and Gilbertson, D. (1989) 'Studies of late prehistoric and modern opal phytoliths from coastal sand dunes and machair in northwest Britain', *Journal of Archaeological Science*, 16: 26–46.

Pretola, J.P. (2001) 'A feasibility study using silica polymorph ratios for sourcing chert and chalcedony lithic materials', *Journal of Archaeological Science*, 28: 721–739.

Price, T.D., Chappell, S., and Ives, D.J. (1982) 'Thermal alteration in Mesolithic assemblages', *Proceedings of the Prehistoric Society*, 48: 467–485.

Pringle, H. (1997) 'Ice age communities may be earliest known net hunters', *Science* 277: 1203–1204.

Procter, H.R. (1903; 2nd edn 1922) *The Principles of Leather Manufacture*, London: E. & F.N. Spon.

Provenzano, N. (2001) 'Worked bone assemblages from northern Italian Terramares: a technological approach', in A.M. Choyke and L. Bartosiewicz (eds) *Crafting Bone: skeletal technologies through time and space, proceedings of the 2nd meeting of the (ICAZ) Worked Bone Research Group Budapest, 31 August – 5 September 1999*, Oxford: British Archaeological Reports International Series 937, pp. 93–109.

Pryor, F. (1998) *Etton: excavations at a Neolithic causewayed enclosure near Maxey, Cambridgeshire 1982–7*, London: English Heritage.

Pryor, F. (2001) *The Flag Fen Basin: archaeology and environment of a Fenland landscape*, Swindon: English Heritage.

Pugsley, P. (2005) 'The origins of medieval vessel turning', *The Antiquaries Journal*, 85: 1–22.

Pulak, C. (2000) 'The balance weights from the Late Bronze Age shipwreck at Uluburun', in C.F.E. Pare (ed.) *Metals Make the World Go Round: the supply and circulation of metals in Bronze Age Europe. Proceedings of a conference held at the University of Birmingham in June 1997*, Oxford: Oxbow, pp. 247–266.

Purdy, B.A. and Clark, D.E. (1971) 'Thermal alterations of silica materials: an archaeological approach', *Science*, 173: 322–325.

Purdy, B.A. and Clark, D.E. (1979) 'Weathering of thermally altered prehistoric stone implements', *Lithic Technology*, 8: 20–21.

Pyburn, K.A. (ed.) (2004) *Ungendering Archaeology*, London: Routledge.

Quarino, L. and Kobilinsky, L. (1988) 'Development of a radioimmunoassay technique for the detection of human hemoglobin in dried bloodstains', *Journal of Forensic Sciences*, 33: 1369–1378.

Raheel, M. (1994) 'History, identification, and charaterisation of old world fibers and dyes', in S.U. Wisseman and W.S. Williams (eds) *Ancient Technologies and Archaeological Materials*, Reading: Gordon and Breach, pp. 21–153.

Ramis, D. and Alcover, J.A. (2001) 'Bone needles in Mallorcan prehistory: a reappraisal', *Journal of Archaeological Science*, 28: 907–911.

Ramseyer, D. (ed.) (2001) *Objets méconnus*, Paris: Société Préhistorique Française (English summaries).

Rapp, G., Balescu, S., and Lamothe, M. (1999) 'The identification of granitic fire-cracked rocks using luminescence of alkali feldspars', *American Antiquity*, 64: 71–78.

Rapp, G., Allert, J., Vitali, V., Jing, Z., and Henrickson, E. (2000) *Determining Geologic Sources of Artifact Copper*, Walnut Creek, CA: AltaMira Press.

Raven, A.M., van Bergen, P.F., Stott, A.W., Dudd, S.N., and Evershed, R.P. (1997) 'Formation of long-chain ketones in archaeological pottery vessels by pyrolysis of acyl lipids', *Journal of Analytical and Applied Pyrolysis*, 40/41: 267–285.

Read, D.W. and Russell, G. (1996) 'A method for taxonomic typology construction and an example: utilized flakes', *American Antiquity*, 61: 663–684.

Redman, C.L. (1973) 'Multistage fieldwork and analytical techniques', *American Antiquity*, 38: 61–79.

Reed, F. (2005) 'The poor man's raincoat: Alaskan fish-skin garments', in J.C.H. King, B. Pauksztat, and R. Storrie (eds) *Arctic Clothing of North America – Alaska, Canada, Greenland*, London: The British Museum Press, pp. 48–52.

Reed, I.W. (1990) *1000 Years of Pottery: an analysis of pottery trade and use*, Trondheim: Riksantokvaren.

Reed, R. (1972) *Leathers, Skins and Parchments*, London: Academic Press.

Rega, E. (1997) 'Age, gender and biological reality in the Early Bronze Age cemetery at

Mokrin', in J. Moore and E. Scott (eds) *Invisible People and Processes*, London: Leicester University Press, pp. 229–247.

Rega, E. (2000) 'The gendering of children in the Early Bronze Age Cemetery at Mokrin', in M. Donald and L. Hurcombe (eds) *Gender and Material Culture in Archaeological Perspective*, London: Macmillan, pp. 238–249.

Regert, M., Bland, H.A., Dudd, S.N., Bergen, P.F. van, and Evershed, R.P. (1998) 'Free and bound fatty acid oxidation products in archaeological ceramic vessels', *Proceedings of the Royal Society of London*, B265: 2027–2032.

Regert, M., Delacotte, J.-M., Menu, M., Pétrequin, P., and Rolando, C. (1999) 'Identification of Neolithic hafting adhesives from two lake dwellings at Chalain (Jura, France)', *Ancient Biomolecules*, 2: 81–96.

Rehder, J.E. (2000) *The Mastery and Uses of Fire in Antiquity*, Montreal: McGill-Queen's University Press.

Reichart, E.T. (1913) *The Differentiation and Specificity of Starches in Relation to Genera, Species, etc.*, Washington DC: Carnegie Institute.

Reichert, A. (2000) 'Zur rekonstruktion der "Ötzi"-schuhe', in S. Heinrichs and M. Passlick (eds) *Experimentelle Archäologie: Bilanz 1999*, Oldenburg: Isensee, pp. 69–76.

Renfrew, C. (1994) 'Towards a cognitive archaeology', in C. Renfrew and E.B.W. Zubrow (eds) *The Ancient Mind: Elements of Cognitive Archaeology*, Cambridge: Cambridge University Press, pp. 3–12.

Renfrew, C. (1998) *Cognition and Material Culture: the archaeology of symbolic storage*, Cambridge: McDonald Institute for Archaeological Research.

Renfrew, C. (2001) 'Symbol before concept: material engagement and the early development of society', in I. Hodder (ed.) *Archaeological Theory Today*, Cambridge: Polity Press, pp. 122–140.

Renfrew, C. (2004) 'Towards a theory of material engagement', in E. DeMarrais, C. Gosden, and C. Renfrew (eds) *Rethinking Materiality: the engagement of mind with the material world*, Cambridge: McDonald Institute for Archaeological Research, pp. 23–31.

Renfrew, C. and Zubrow, E.B.W. (eds) (1994) *The Ancient Mind: elements of cognitive archaeology*, Cambridge: Cambridge University Press.

Renfrew, C., Gosden, C., and DeMarrais, E. (eds) (2004) *Substance, Memory, Display: archaeology and art*, Cambridge: McDonald Institute of Archaeological Research.

Reynolds, P.J. (1974) 'Experimental Iron-Age storage pits, an interim report', *Proceedings of the Prehistoric Society*, 40: 118–131.

Reynolds, P.J. (1976) *Farming in the Iron Age*, Cambridge: Cambridge University Press.

Reynolds, P.J. (1979) *Iron-Age Farm: The Butser Experiment*, London: British Museum Press.

Rhoads, J.W. (1992) 'Significant sites and non-site archaeology: a case-study from south-east Australia', *World Archaeology*, 24: 198–217.

Rice, P. (1981) 'Prehistoric Venuses: symbols of motherhood or womanhood', *Journal of Anthropological Research*, 37: 402–444.

Rice, P. (1987) *Pottery Analysis*, Chicago: Chicago University Press.

Rice, P.M. (1990) 'Functions and uses of archaeological ceramics', in W.D. Kingery (ed.) *The Changing Role of Ceramics in Society: 26,000 B.P. to the present*, Westerville, OH: American Ceramic Society, pp. 1–12.

Rice, P.M. (ed.) (1997) *Ceramics and Civilisation, vol. 3: the prehistory and history of ceramic kilns*, Colombus: The American Ceramic Society.

Richards, C. and Thomas, J. (1984) 'Ritual activity and structural deposition in Later Neolithic Wessex', in R. Bradley and J. Gardiner (eds) *Neolithic Studies: a review of some current research*, Oxford: British Archaeological Reports, British Series 133, pp. 189–218.

Richards, J.C. (1990) *The Stonehenge Environs Project*, London: English Heritage.

Riciputi, L.R., Ealm, J.M., Anovitz, L.M., and Cole, D.R. (2002) 'Obsidian diffusion dating by Secondary Ion Mass Spectrometry: a test using results from Mound 65, Chalco, Mexico', *Journal of Archaeological Science*, 29: 1055–1075.

Riddler, I. (ed.) (2003) *Materials of Manufacture: the choice of materials in the working of bone and antler in northern and central Europe during the first millennium AD*, Oxford: British Archaeological Reports International Series 1193.

Ridings, R. (1996) 'Where in the world does obsidian hydration dating work?', *American Antiquity*, 61: 136–148.

Rimantiene, R. (1992) 'Neolithic hunter-gatherers at Sventoji in Lithuania', *Antiquity*, 66: 367–376.

Rival, L. (1998) 'Trees, from symbols of life and regeneration to political artefacts', in L. Rival (ed.) *The Social Life of Trees*, Oxford: Berg, pp. 1–36.

Roberts, B. and Ottaway, B.S. (2003) 'The use and significance of socketed axes during the late Bronze Age', *European Journal of Archaeology*, 6: 119–140.

Robins, G.V., Seeley, N.J., McNeil, D.A.C., and Symons, M.C.R. (1978) 'Identification of ancient heat treatment in flint artefacts by ESR spectroscopy', *Nature*, 276: 703–704.

Robinson, N., Evershed, R.P., Higgs, W.J., Jerman, K., and Eglington, G. (1987) 'Proof of a pine wood origin for pitch from Tudor (*Mary Rose*) and Etruscan shipwrecks: application of analytical organic chemistry in archaeology', *Analyst*, 112: 637–644.

Robson, E., Treadwell, L., and Gosden, C. (eds) (2006) *Who Owns Objects: the ethics and politics of collecting cultural artefacts*, Oxford: Oxbow.

Rodaway, P. (1994) *Sensuous Geographies: body, sense and place*, London: Routledge.

Rodman, A.O. and Lopez, G.A.F. (2005) 'North Coast Style after Moche: clothing and identity at El Brujo, Chicama Valley, Perud', in R.M. Reycraft (ed.) *Us and Them: archaeology and ethnicity in the Andes*, Los Angeles: The Cotsen Institute of Archaeology, University of California, pp. 115–133.

Rogers, A. (1994) *Early Prehistoric Textiles, Cordage and Basketry from the Wetland sites of Northern Europe*, unpublished M.Phil thesis, University of Exeter.

Roque, C., Guibert, P., Vartanian, E., Bechtel, F., Treuil, R., Darcque, P., Koukouli-Chryssanthaki, H., and Malamidou, D. (2002) 'Chronology of the Neolithic sequence at Dikili Tash Tell, Macedonia, Greece: TL-dating of domestic ovens', *Archaeometry*, 44: 625–645.

Roque, C., Guibert, P., Vartanian, E., Vieillevigne, E., and Bechtel, F. (2004) 'Changes in luminescence properties induced by thermal treatments; a case study at Sipan and Trujillo Moche sites (Peru)', *Radiation Measurements*, 38: 119–126.

Rosen, S.A. (1997) *Lithics after the Stone Age: a handbook of stone tools from the Levant*, Walnut Creek, CA: AltaMira Press.

Ross, L.A. and Light, J.D. (2000) 'A guide to the description and interpretation of metal files', in K. Karklins (ed.) *Studies in Material Culture Research*, California, PA: The Society for Historical Archaeology, pp. 20–31.

Rostoker, W. and Bronson, B. (1990) *Pre-Industrial Iron: its technology and ethnology*, Philadelphia: privately published.

Rotlander, R.C.A. (1990) 'Lipid analysis in the identification of vessel contents', in W.R. Biers and P.E. McGovern (eds) *Organic Contents of Ancient Vessels*, Philadelphia: University of Pennsylvania, MASCA Research Papers in Science and Archaeology 7, pp. 37–40.

Rots, V., Pirnay, L., Pirson, Ph. and Baudoux, O. (2006) 'Blind tests shed light on possibilities and limitations for identifying stone tool prehension and hafting', *Journal of Archaeological Science*, 33: 935–952.

Rottländer, R. (1975) 'Some aspects of the patination of flint, Second International Symposium of Flint', *Staringia*, 3: 54–56.

Rouse, J. (1960) 'The classification of artefacts and archaeology', *American Antiquity*, 25: 313–323.

Roux, V. (1989) *The Potter's Wheel: craft specialisation and technical competence* (with the collaboration of *Daniela Corbetta*), New Delhi: Oxford and IBH Publishing Co. Pvt. Ltd.

Roux, V. (1990) 'The psychosocial analysis of technical activities: a contribution to the study of craft specialization', *Archaeological Review from Cambridge*, 9.1: 142–153.

Roux, V. (1999) 'Ethnoarchaeology and the generation of referential models: the case of Harappan carnelian beads', in L.R. Owen and M. Porr (eds) *Ethno-Analogy and the Reconstruction of Prehistoric Artefact Use and Production*, Tübingen: Mo Vince Verlag, pp. 153–170.

Roux, V. (2003) 'A dynamic systems framework for studying technological change: application to the emergence of the potter's wheel in the southern Levant', *Journal of Archaeological Method and Theory*, 10: 1–30.

Roux, V. and Courty, M.-A. (1998) 'Identification of wheel fashioning methods: technological analysis of 4th–3rd millennium BC oriental ceramics', *Journal of Archaeological Science*, 25: 747–763.

Roux, V., Bril, B., and Dietrichm G. (1995) 'Skills and learning difficulties involved in stone knapping: the case of stone-bead knapping in Khambhat, India', *World Archaeology*, 27: 63–87.

Rowe, D.J. (1983) *Lead Manufacturing in Britain: a history*, London: Croom Helm.

Rowlands, M.J. (1976) *The Production and Distribution of Metalwork in the Middle Bronze Age in Southern Britain*, Oxford: British Archaeological Reports British Series 31.

Rowlands, M.J. and Warnier, J.-P. (1993) 'The magical production of iron in the Cameroon grassfields', in T. Shaw, P. Sinclair, B.W. Andah, and I.A. Okpoko (eds) *The Archaeology of Africa: foods, metals and towns*, London: Routledge, pp. 512–550.

Ruiz-Gálvez, M. (2000) 'Weight systems and exchange networks in Bronze Age Europe', in C.F.E. Pare (ed.) *Metals Make the World Go Round: the supply and circulation of metals in Bronze Age Europe. Proceedings of a conference held at the University of Birmingham in June 1997*, Oxford: Oxbow, pp. 267–279.

Russell, A.E. (2000) 'Material culture and African-American spirituality at the Hermitage', in D.R. Brauner (ed.) *Approaches to Material Culture Research for Historical Archaeologists*, California, PA: The Society for Historical Archaeology, pp. 423–440.

Russell, M. (1982) *Trees and Timber in the Ancient Mediterranean World*, Oxford: Clarendon Press.

Russell, M. (2000) *Neolithic Flint Mines in Britain*, London: Tempus.

Russell, N. (2001a) 'The social life of bone: a preliminary assessment of bone tool manufacture and discard at Çatalöyük', in A.M. Choyke and L. Bartosiewicz (eds) *Crafting Bone: skeletal technologies through time and space, proceedings of the 2nd meeting of the (ICAZ) Worked Bone Research Group Budapest, 31 August – 5 September 1999*, Oxford: British Archaeological Reports International Series 937, pp. 241–249.

Russell, N. (2001b) 'Neolithic relations of production: insights from the bone tool industry', in A.M. Choyke and L. Bartosiewicz (eds) *Crafting Bone: skeletal technologies through time and space, proceedings of the 2nd meeting of the (ICAZ) Worked Bone Research Group Budapest, 31 August – 5 September 1999*, Oxford: British Archaeological Reports International Series 937, pp. 271–280.

Ryan, M. (1987) 'The Donare hoard', *Antiquity*, 61: 57–63.

Ryder, M.L. (1969) 'Changes in the fleece of sheep following domestication', in P.J. Ucko and G.W. Dimbleby (eds) *The Domestication of Plants and Animals*, London: Duckworth, pp. 495–521.

Ryder, M.L. (1970) 'Remains derived from skin', in D. Brothwell and E.S. Higgs (eds) *Science and Archaeology*, London: Thames and Hudson, pp. 539–554.

Ryder, M.L. (1980) 'Hair remains throw light on early British cattle', *Journal of Archaeological Science*, 7: 389–392.

Ryder, M.L. (1984a) 'Skin, hair and cloth remains from the ancient Kerma civilisation of northern Sudan', *Journal of Archaeological Science*, 11: 477–482.

Ryder, M.L. (1984b) 'The first hair remains from an aurochs (*Bos primigenius*) and some medieval domestic cattle hair', *Journal of Archaeological Science*, 11: 99–101.

Ryder, M.L. (1984c) 'Wools from textiles in the Mary Rose, a 16th-century English warship', *Journal of Archaeological Science*, 11: 337–344.

Ryder, M.L. (1987) 'The evolution of the fleece', *Scientific American*, 255: 112–119.

Ryder, M.L. (1990) 'Skin and wool-textile remains from Hallstatt, Austria', *Oxford Journal of Archaeology*, 9: 37–50.

Ryder, M.L. (1991) 'The last word on the golden fleece legend', *Oxford Journal of Archaeology*, 10: 57–60.

Ryder, M.L. (1992) 'Iron Age haired animal skins from Hallstatt, Austria', *Oxford Journal of Archaeology*, 11: 55–68.

Ryder, M.L. and Gabra-Sanders, T. (1987) 'A microscopic study of remains of textiles made from plant fibres', *Oxford Journal of Archaeology*, 6: 91–108.

Rye, O.S. (1981) *Pottery Technology: principles and reconstruction*, Washington DC: Taraxacum.

Sackett, J.R. (1977) 'The meaning of style in archaeology: a general model', *American Antiquity*, 42: 369–380.

Sackett, J.R. (1990) 'Style and ethnicity in archaeology: the case of isochrestism', in M.W. Conkey and C.A. Hastorf (eds) *The Uses of Style in Archaeology*, Cambridge: Cambridge University Press, pp. 32–43.

Sagona, C. (1999) 'Silo or vat? Observations on the ancient textile industry in Malta and early Phoenician interests in the island', *Oxford Journal of Archaeology*, 18: 23–60.

Sala I.L. (1986) 'Use wear and post-depositional surface modification: a word of caution', *Journal of Archaeological Science*, 13: 229–244.

Salls, R.A. (1985) 'The scraper plane: a functional interpretation', *Journal of Field Archaeology*, 12: 99–106.

Salmon, M.H. (1978) 'What can systems theory do for archaeology', *American Antiquity*, 43: 174–183.

Sanden, W. van der and Capelle, T. (2001) *Mosens Guder: antropomorfe træfigurer fra Nord- og Nordvesteuropas fortid = Immortal Images: ancient anthropomorphic wood carvings from northern and northwest Europe*, Silkeborg: Silkeborg Museum.

Sands, R. (1997) *Prehistoric Woodworking: the analysis and interpretation of Bronze and Iron Age toolmarks*, London: Institute of Archaeology, University College London.

Sargent, C.F. and Friedel, D.A. (1986) 'From clay to metal: culture change and container usage among the Bariba of northern Benin, West Africa', *African Archaeological Review*, 4: 177–195.

Saunders, N.J. (2004) 'The cosmic Earth: materiality and mineralogy in the Americas', in N. Boivin and M.A. Owoc (eds) *Soils, Stones and Symbols: cultural perceptions of the mineral world*, London: UCL Press, pp. 123–141.

Saville, A. (1997) 'The prehistoric exploitation of a flint resource in North-East Scotland: work at Den of Boddam in 1991', in A. Ramos-Millán and A. Bustillo (eds) *Siliceous Rocks and Culture*, Granada: Universidad de Granada, pp. 293–299.

Scarre, C. and Lawson, G. (2006) *Archaeoacoustics*, Cambridge: MacDonald Institute for Archaeological Research.

Scheinsohn, V. and Ferretti, J.L. (1995) 'The mechanical properties of bone materials in relation to the design and function of prehistoric tools from Tierra del Fuego, Argentina', *Journal of Archaeological Science*, 22: 711–718.

Scheinsohn, V. and Ferretti, J.L. (1997) 'Design and function of prehistoric tools of Tierra del Fuego (Argentina) as related to the mechanical properties of bone materials utilized in their manufacture', in L.A. Hannus, L. Rossum, and R.P. Winham (eds) *Proceedings of the 1993 Bone Modification Conference, Hot Springs, South Dakota*, Sioux Falls, SD: Archaeology Laboratory, Augustana College, pp. 65–75.

Schick, K.D. (1986) *Stone Age Sites in the Making: experiments in the formation and transformation of archaeological occurrences*, Oxford: British Archaeological Reports, International Series S319.

Schick, K.D. and Toth, N. (1993) *Making Silent Stones Speak: human evolution and the dawn of technology*, London: Weidenfeld and Nicolson.

Schick, K.D., Toth, N.R., Garufi, G., Savage-Rumbaugh, S., Rumbaugh, D., and Sevcik, R. (1999) 'Continuing investigations into the stone tool-making and tool-using capabilities of a Bonobo (*Pan paniscus*)', *Journal of Archaeological Science*, 26: 821–833.

Schiffer, M.B. (1972) 'Archaeological context and systemic context', *American Antiquity*, 37: 156–165.

Schiffer, M.B. (1983) 'Toward the identification of formation processes', *American Antiquity*, 48: 675–706.

Schiffer, M.B. (1987) *Formation Processes of the Archaeological Record*, Albuquerque: University of New Mexico Press.

Schiffer, M.B. (1988) 'The effects of surface treatment on permeability and evaporative cooling effectiveness of pottery', in R.G.V. Hancock and L.A. Pavlish (eds) *Proceedings of the 26th International Archaeometry Symposium*, Toronto: University of Ontario, Department of Physics, Archaeometry Laboratory, pp. 23–29.

Schiffer, M.B. (1990) 'The influence of surface treatment on heating effectiveness of ceramic vessels', *Journal of Archaeological Science*, 17: 373–382.

Schiffer, M.B. (1995) *Behavioral Archaeology*, Salt Lake City: University of Utah Press.

Schiffer, M.B. and House, J.H. (eds) (1975) *The Cache River Archaeological Project*, Fayetteville: Arkansas Archaeological Survey.

Schiffer, M.B. and Miller, A. (1999) *The Material Life of Human Beings: artifacts, behavior, and communication*, London and New York: Routledge.

Schiffer, M.B. and Skibo, J.M. (1989) 'A provisional theory of ceramic abrasion', *American Anthropologist*, 91: 102–116.

Schiffer, M.B. and Skibo, J.M. (1997) 'The explanation of artifact variability', *American Antiquity*, 62: 27–50.

Schindler, D.L., Hatch, J.W., Hay, C.A., and Bradt, R.C. (1982) 'Aboriginal thermal alteration of central Pennsylvania jasper, analytical and behavioural implications', *American Antiquity*, 47: 526–544.

Schlanger, N. (2004) "Suivre les gestes, éclat par éclat': la chaîne opératoire de Leroi-Gourhan', in F. Adouze and N. Schlanger (eds) *Autour de l'homme: Contexte et actualité de Leroi-Gourhan*, Paris: Editions APDCA.

Schlanger, N. (2005) 'The chaîne opératoire' in C. Renfrew and P. Bahn (eds) *Archaeology: the key concepts*, London: Rouledge, pp. 25–31.

Schlanger, S.H. (1991) 'On manos, metates, and the history of site occupations', *American Antiquity*, 56: 460–474.

Schledermann, P. (1996) *Voices in Stone: a personal journey into the Arctic past*, Calgary: The Arctic Institute of North America of the University of Calgary.

Schmidt, P.R. (1997) *Iron Technology in East Africa*, Bloomingdale and Indianapolis: Indiana University Press.

Schoeser, M. (2003) *World Textiles: a concise history*, London: Thames and Hudson.

Schofield, J. (2000) *Managing Lithic Scatters: archaeological guidance for planning authorities and developers*, London: English Heritage.

Schott, M.J. (2000) 'The quantification problem in stone tool assemblages', *American Antiquity*, 65: 725–738.

Schrüfer-Kolb, I. (2004) *Roman Iron Production in Britain: technological and socio-economic landscape development along the Jurassic Ridge*, Oxford: British Archaeological Reports British Series 380.

Schweingruber, F. H. (1976) *Prähistorisches Holz: die Bedeutung von Holzfunden aus Miteleuropa für die Lösung archäologischer und vegetationskundlicher Probleme*, Bern: Paul Haupt.

Sciama, L.D. and Eicher, J.B. (eds) (1998) *Beads and Bead Makers: gender, material culture and meaning*, Oxford: Berg.

Scott, D.A. (1991) *Metallography and Microstructure of Ancient and Historic Metals*, Los Angeles: Getty Conservation Institute.

Scott, J. (2003) *The Pleasures of Antiquity: British collectors of Greece and Rome*, New Haven: Yale University Press, Paul Mellon Centre for Studies in British Art.

Scott-Jackson, J.E. (2000) *Lower and Middle Paleolithic Artefacts from Deposits Mapped as Clay-with-Flints*, Oxford: Oxbow Books.

Šebesta, G. (1992) *La Via del Rame*, Trento: Mediocredito Trentino.

Semenov, S.A. (1964) *Prehistoric Technology: an experimental study of the oldest tools and artefacts from traces of manufacture and wear*, London: Cory, Adams & Mackay (1957 Russian translated and with a preface by M.W. Thompson).

Senior, L.M. (2000) 'Gender and craft innovation: proposal of a model', in M. Donald and L. Hurcombe (eds) *Gender and Material Culture in Archaeological Perspective*, London: Macmillan, pp. 71–87.

Seremetakis, C.N. (ed.) (1996) *The Senses Still: perception and memory as material culture in modernity*, London: University of Chicago Press.

Serpico, M. and White, R. (2000a) 'Oil, fat and wax', in P.T. Nicholson and I. Shaw (eds) *Ancient Egyptian Materials and Technology*, Cambridge: Cambridge University Press, pp. 390–429.

Serpico, M. with White, R. (2000b) 'Resins, amber and bitumen', in P.T. Nicholson and I. Shaw (eds) *Ancient Egyptian Materials and Technology*, Cambridge: Cambridge University Press, pp. 430–474.

Shackleton, J. and Elderfield, H. (1990) 'Strontium isotope dating of the source of Neolithic European Spondylus shell artefacts', *Antiquity*, 64: 312–315.

Shanks, M. (1998) 'The life of an artefact in an interpretive archaeology', *Fennoscandia Archaeologica*, 15: 15–42.

Shanks, M. and Tilley, C. (1987, 2nd edn 1992) *Re-constructing Archaeology: theory and practice*, London: Routledge.

Shanks, O.C., Bonnichsen, R., Vella, A.T., and Ream, W. (2001) 'Recovery of protein and DNA trapped in stone tool microcracks', *Journal of Archaeological Science*, 28: 965–972.

Shea, J. (2006) 'The origins of lithic projectile point technology: the evidence from Africa, the Levant, and Europe', *Journal of Archaeological Science*, 33: 823–846.

Shea, J., Davis, Z., and Brown, K. (2001) 'Experimental tests of Middle Palaeolithic spear points using a calibrated crossbow', *Journal of Archaeological Science*, 28: 807–816.

Shennan, S. (1985) *Experiments in the Collection and Analysis of Archaeological Survey Data: the East Hampshire Survey*, Sheffield: University of Sheffield, Department of Archaeology and Prehistory.

Shepherd, A. (1985) *Ceramics for the Archaeologist*, Washington DC: Carnegie Institution.

Sheridan, J.A. (1995) 'The faience beads', in I. Banks, 'The excavation of three cairns at Stoneyburn Farm, Crawford, Lanarkshire, 1991', *Proceedings of the Society of Antiquaries of Scotland*, 125: 321–324.

Sheridan, A. (1999) 'Drinking, driving, death and display; Scottish Bronze Age artefact studies since Coles', in Harding, A.F. (ed.) *Experiment and Design: archaeological studies in honour of John Coles*, Oxford: Oxbow, pp. 49–59.

Sheridan, A. and Davis, M. (1998) 'The Welsh "jet set" in prehistory: a case of keeping up with the Joneses?', in A. Gibson and D. Simpson (eds) *Prehistoric Ritual and Religion: essays in honour of Aubrey Burl*, Stroud: Sutton Publishing Ltd, pp. 148–162.

Sherratt, S. (ed.) (2000) *The Wall Paintings of Thera: proceedings of the first international symposium*, 3 vols, Athens: Petros M. Nomikos and the Thera Foundation.

Shimada, I. (2005) 'Experimental archaeology', in H.D.G. Maschner and C. Chippindale (eds) *Handbook of Archaeological Methods*, Lanham, MD: AltaMira, pp. 603–642.

Shopland, N. (2006) *A Finds Manual: excavating, processing and storing*, Stroud: Tempus.

Shortland, A., Schachner, L., Freestone, I., and Tite, M. (2006) 'Natron as a flux in the early vitreous materials industry: sources, beginnings and reasons for decline', *Journal of Archaeological Science*, 33: 521–530.

Shott, M.J. (1989) 'On tool-class use lives and the formation of archaeological assemblages', *American Antiquity*, 54: 9–30.

Shott, M.J. (1996) 'Mortal pots: on use life and vessel size in the formation of ceramic assemblages', *American Antiquity*, 61: 463–482.

Shott, M.J. (2001) 'Quantification of broken objects', in D.R. Brothwell and A.M. Pollard (eds) *Handbook of Archaeological Sciences*, Chichester: Wiley, pp. 711–722.

Shott, M.J. (2005) 'Two cultures: thought and practice in British and North American archaeology', *World Archaeology*, 37: 1–10.

Shott, M.J. and Sillitoe, P. (2001) 'The mortality of things: correlates of use life in Wola material culture using age-at-census data', *Journal of Archaeological Method and Theory*, 8: 269–302.

Shutova, N. (2006) 'Trees in Udmurt religion' *Antiquity*, 80: 318–327.

Sidéra, I. (2001) 'Domestic and funerary bone, antler and tooth objects in the Neolithic of western Europe: a comparison', in A.M. Choyke and L. Bartosiewicz (eds) *Crafting Bone: skeletal technologies through time and space, proceedings of the 2nd meeting of the (ICAZ) Worked Bone Research Group Budapest, 31 August – 5 September 1999*, Oxford: British Archaeological Reports International Series 937, pp. 221–229.

Sieveking, G. and Newcomer, M.H. (1986) *The Human Uses of Flint and Chert*, Cambridge: Cambridge University Press.

Sieveking, G. de G. and Clayton, C.J. (1986) 'Frost shatter and the structure of frozen flint', in G. de G. Sieveking and M.B. Hart (eds) *The Scientific Study of Flint and Chert, proceedings of the 4th International Flint Symposium held at Brighton Polytechnic 10–15 April 1983*, Cambridge: Cambridge University Press, pp. 283–290.

Sieveking, G. de G. and Hart, M.B. (eds) (1986) *The Scientific Study of Flint and Chert, proceedings of the 4th International Flint Symposium held at Brighton Polytechnic 10–15 April 1983*, Cambridge: Cambridge University Press.

Sillar, B. (2000a) 'Dung by preference: the choice of fuel as an example of how Andean pottery production is embedded within wider technical, social and economic practices', *Archaeometry*, 42: 2–20.

Sillar, B. (2000b) *Shaping Cultures: making pots and correcting households*, Oxford: British Archaeological Reports, International Series 883.

Sillar, B. and Tite, M. (2000) 'The challenge of "technological choices" for materials science approaches in archaeology', *Archaeometry*, 42: 2–20.

Sillitoe, P. (1988) *Made in Niugini: technology in the highlands of Papua New Guinea*, London: British Museum Publications.

Silvestre, R. (1994) 'The ethnoarchaeology of Kalinga basketry: a preliminary investigation', in W.A. Longacre and J.M. Skibo (eds) *Kalinga Ethnoarchaeology: expanding archaeological method and theory*, Washington DC: Smithsonian Institution Press, pp. 199–207.

Silvestri, A., Molin, G., Salviulo, G., and Schievenin, R. (2006) 'Sand for Roman glass production: an experimental and philological study on source of supply', *Archaeometry*, 48: 415–432.

Sim, D. and Ridge, I. (eds) (1998) *Beyond the Bloom: bloom refining and iron artefact production in the Roman world*, Oxford: Archaeopress, British Archaeological Reports International Series 725.

Simpson, D.D.A. (1996) '"Crown" antler maceheads and the Later Neolithic in Britain', *Proceedings of the Prehistoric Society*, 62: 293–309.

Skeates, R. (1991) 'Triton's trumpet: a neolithic symbol in Italy', *Oxford Journal of Archaeology*, 10: 17–32.

Skeates, R. (1995) 'Animate objects: a biography of prehistoric "axe-amulets" in the central Mediterranean region', *Proceedings of the Prehistoric Society*, 61: 279–301.

Skibo, J.M. (1992) *Pottery Function: a use alteration perspective*, New York: Plenum.

Skibo, J.M. (1999) *Ants for Breakfast: archaeological adventures among the Kalinga*, Salt Lake City: University of Utah Press.

Skibo, J.M. and Schiffer, M.B. (1987) 'The effects of water on processes of ceramic abrasion', *Journal of Archaeological Science*, 14: 83–96.

Skibo, J.M., Schiffer, M.B., and Reid, K.C. (1989) 'Organic-tempered pottery: an experimental study', *American Antiquity*, 54: 122–146.

Sleeswyk, A. (1987) 'Pre-stressed wheels in ancient Egypt', *Antiquity*, 61: 90–96.

Sloper, D. (1989) 'The experimental production of a replica of an early bronze age shale cup from Farway Down', *Proceedings of the Devon Archaeological Society*, 47: 113–117.

Smirnova, L. (2001) 'Utilization of rare bone material in medieval Novgorod', in A.M. Choyke and L. Bartosiewicz (eds) *Crafting Bone: skeletal technologies through time and space, proceedings of the 2nd meeting of the (ICAZ) Worked Bone Research Group Budapest, 31 August – 5 September 1999*, Oxford: British Archaeological Reports International Series 937, pp. 9–17.

Smith, A.L. (2000) 'Processing clay for pottery in northern Cameroon: social and technical requirements', *Archaeometry*, 42: 21–42.

Smith, E.A. (1978) *Working in Precious Metals*, Edinburgh: A.P. and R. Baker Ltd.

Smith, M.J., Jr (1988) 'Function from whole vessel shape: a method and an application to Anasazi Black Mesa, Arizona', *American Anthropologist*, 90: 912–922.

Smith, P.R. and Wilson, M.T. (1990) 'Detection of haemoglobin in human skeletal remains by Elisa', *Journal of Archaeological Science*, 17: 255–268.

Smith, P.R. and Wilson, M.T. (2001) 'Blood residues in archaeology', in D.R. Brothwell and A.M. Pollard (eds) *Handbook of Archaeological Sciences*, Chichester: Wiley, pp. 313–322.

Sneath, P.H.A and Sokal, R.R. (1962) 'Numerical taxonomy', *Nature*, 193: 855–60.

Snyder, J. (2002) 'Lejre today', *Bulletin of Primitive Technology*, 23: 13–14.

Sofaer Derevenski, J. (1997) 'Age and gender at the site of Tiszapolgár-Basatanya, Hungary', *Antiquity*, 71: 875–889.

Sofaer Derevenski, J. (2000a) 'Rings of life: the role of early metalwork in mediating the gendered life course', *World Archaeology*, 31: 389–406

Sofaer Derevenski, J. (2000b) *Children and Material Culture*, London: Routledge.

Soffer, O., Adovasio, J.M., and Hyland, D.C. (2001) 'Perishable technologies and invisible people: nets, baskets, and "Venus" wear ca. 26,000 B.P.', in B.A. Purdy (ed.) *Enduring Records: the environmental and cultural heritage of wetlands*, WARP Occasional Paper 14, Oxford: Oxbow Books, pp. 233–245.

Spector, J. (1993) *What This Awl Means: feminist archaeology at a Dakota village*, St Paul: Minnesota Historical Society Press.

Spindler, K. (1995) The Man in the Ice, London: Phoenix.

Spindler, K., Rastbichler-Zissernig, H., Wilfing, H., Nedden, D. zur and Nothdurfter, H. (eds) (1995) Der Mann im Eis: neue Funde und Ergebnisse, Vienna: Springer-Verlag.

Spoto, G. and Ciliberto, E. (2000) 'X-ray photoelectron spectroscopy and auger electron spectroscopy in art and archaeology', in E. Ciliberto and G. Spoto (eds) Modern Analytical Methods in Art and Archaeology, New York: Wiley, pp. 363–404.

Sprague, R. (2000) 'Glass trade beads: a progress report', in D.R. Brauner (ed.) Approaches to Material Culture Research for Historical Archaeologists, California, PA: The Society for Historical Archaeology, pp. 202–220.

Stahl, A.B. (2002) 'Colonial entanglements and the practice of taste: an alternative to logo-centric approaches', American Anthropologist, 104.3: 827–845.

Stambolov, T. (1969) Manufacture, Deterioration and Preservation of Leather: a literature survey of theoretical aspects and ancient techniques, Amsterdam: Central Research Laboratory of Objects of Art and Science.

Stark, M.T. (1999) 'Social dimensions of technical choice in Kalinga ceramic traditions', in E.S. Chilton (ed.) Material Meanings: critical approaches to the interpretation of material culture, Salt Lake City: University of Utah Press, pp. 24–43.

Stephenson, R. (2005) 'Integration or independence: what do we do with the finds reports?', The Archaeologist, 58: 31.

Sternberg, R.S. (2001) 'Magnetic properties and archaeomagnetism', in D.R. Brothwell and A.M. Pollard (eds) Handbook of Archaeological Sciences, Chichester: Wiley, pp. 73–80.

Sterner, J. (1989) 'Who is signalling whom? Ceramic style, ethnicity and taphonomy among the Sirak Bulahey', Antiquity, 63: 451–460.

Stevanovic, M. (1997) 'The Age of Clay: the social dynamics of house destruction', Journal of Anthropological Archaeology, 16: 334–395.

Stevenson, I.N. (1974) Andean Village Technology: a introduction to a collection of manufactured articles from Santiago de Chocorvos, Peru, Oxford: Pitt Rivers Museum.

Stewart, H. (1977) Indian Fishing: early methods on the Northwest Coast, Vancouver: Douglas and McIntyre.

Stewart, H. (1984) Cedar – Tree of Life to the Northwest Coast Indians, Vancouver: Douglas and Macintyre.

Stig-Sørenson, M.L. (1989) 'Ignoring innovation – denying change: the role of iron and the impact of external influences on the transformation of Scandinavian societies 800–500 B.C.', in S.E. van der Leeuw and R. Torrence (eds) What's New? A closer look at the process of innovation, One World Archaeology No. 14, London: Unwin Hyman, pp. 182–202.

Stig-Sørenson, M.L. (1991) 'Gender construction through appearance', in D. Walde and N.D. Willows (eds) The Archaeology of Gender, Calgary: Archaeological Association of Calgary, pp. 121–129.

Stig-Sørenson, M.L. (1997) 'Reading dress: the construction of social categories and identities in Bronze Age Europe', Journal of European Archaeology, 5: 93–114.

Stilborg, O. (2001) 'Temper for the sake of coherence: analyses of bone- and chaff-tempered ceramics from Iron Age Scandinavia', European Journal of Archaeology, 4: 398–404.

Stine, L.F., Cabak, M.A., and Groover, M.D. (2000) 'Blue beads as African-American cultural symbols', in D.R. Brauner (ed.) Approaches to Material Culture Research for Historical Archaeologists, California, PA: The Society for Historical Archaeology, pp. 221–247.

Stocks, D. (1989) 'Ancient factory mass-production techniques: indications of large-scale stone bead manufacture during the Egyptian New Kingdom period', Antiquity, 63: 526–31.

Stocks, D. (1993) 'Making stone vessels in ancient Mesopotamia and Egypt', Antiquity, 67: 596–603.

Stone, P.G. and Planel, P.G. (eds) (1999) The Constructed Past: experimental archaeology, education and the public, London: Routledge.

Stott, A.W., Berstan, R., Evershed, R.P., Bronk-Ramsey, C., Hedges, R.E.M., and Humm, M.J. (2003) 'Direct dating of archaeological pottery by compound-specific ^{14}C analysis of preserved lipids', Analytical Chemistry, 75: 5037–5045.

Strassburg, J. (1998) 'Let the "Axe" go! Mapping the meaningful spectrum of the "thin-butted flint axe"', in Å. Gillberg, O. Jensen, H. Karlsson, and M. Rolöf (eds) The Kaleidoscopic Past. Proceedings of the 5th Nordic TAG Conference, Göteborg, 2–5 April 1997, Göteborg: University of Göteborg, Department of Archaeology, pp. 156–169.

Strathern, M. (1988) The Gender of the Gift, Berkeley: University of California Press.

Sulzenbacher, G. (2002) The Glacier Mummy: discovering the Neolithic Age with the Iceman, Vienna: Folio.

Sunshine, P. (2006) Wattle and Daub, Princes Risborough: Shire.

Sussman, C. (1988) A Microscopic Analysis of Use-Wear and Polish Formation on Experimental Quartz Tools, Oxford: British Archaeological Reports, International Series 411.

Sussman, L. (2000) 'Objects vs. sherds: a statistical evaluation', in K. Karklins (ed.) Studies in Material Culture Research, California, PA: The Society for Historical Archaeology, pp. 96–103.

Sutton, D. (2006) 'Cooking skill, the senses, and memory: the fate of practical knowledge', in E. Edwards, C. Gosden, and R.B. Phillips (eds) Sensible Objects: colonialism, museums and material culture, Oxford: Berg, pp. 87–118.

Taçon, P.S.C. (1991) 'The power of stone: sysmbolic aspects of stone use and tool development in western Arnhem Land, Australia', Antiquity, 65: 192–207.

Taçon, P.S.C. (2004) 'Ochre, clay, stone and art: the symbolic importance of minerals as life-force among Aboriginal peoples of northern and central Australia', in N. Boivin and M.A. Owoc (eds) Soils, Stones and Symbols: cultural perceptions of the mineral world, London: UCL Press, pp. 31–42.

Talalay, L.E. (1987) 'Rethinking the function of clay figurine legs from Neolithic Greece: an argument by analogy', American Journal of Archaeology, 91: 161–169.

Talalay, L.E. (1993) Deities, Dolls and Devices. Neolithic figurines from Franchthi Cave, Greece, Bloomington and Indianapolis: Indiana University Press.

Taylor, J. (1980) Prehistoric Goldwork of the British Isles, Cambridge: Cambridge University Press.

Taylor, M. (1992) 'Flag Fen: the wood', Antiquity, 66: 476–498.

Taylor, M. (1998) 'Wood and bark from the enclosure ditch', in F. Pryor (ed.) Etton: Excavations at a Neolithic causewayed enclosure near Maxey, Cambridgeshire, 1982–7, London: English Heritage, pp. 115–160.

Taylor, R.E. (2001) 'Radiocarbon dating', in D.R. Brothwell and A.M. Pollard (eds) Handbook of Archaeological Sciences, Chichester: Wiley, pp. 23–34.

Taylor, T. (1999) 'Envaluing metal: theorising the Eneolithic "hiatus"', in S.M.M. Young, A.M. Pollard, P. Budd, and R.A. Ixer (eds) Metals in Antiquity, Oxford: British Archaeological Reports International Series 792, pp. 22–32.

Tebbs, B. (ed.) (1984) Trees of the British Isles, London: Orbis.

Therin, M. (1998) 'The movement of starch grains in sediments', in R. Fullagar (ed.) A Closer Look: recent Australian studies of stone tools, Sydney: University of Sydney, Sydney University Archaeological Methods Series 6, pp. 61–72.

Therin, M., Torrence, R., and Fullagar, R. (1997) 'Australian Museum starch reference collection', Australian Archaeology, 44: 52–53.

Thery, B., Pétrequin, P., and Pétrequin, A.-M. (1990) Langda, l'herminette de pierre polie en Nouvelle Guinée, Video recording (26 mins), Paris: JVP Films – CNRS Audiovisual – CRAVA.

Thirault, E. (2005) 'The politics of supply: the Neolithic axe industry in Alpine Europe', Antiquity, 79: 34–50.

Thomas, E. (1964) 'The four niches and amuletic figures in the Theban royal tombs', *Journal of the American Research Centre in Egypt*, 3: 71–8.

Thomas, J. (1971) *The Rise of the Staffordhire Potteries*, London: Adams and Dart.

Thomas, J. (1996) *Time, Culture and Identity: an interpretive archaeology*, London: Routledge.

Thomas, J. (2006) 'Phenomenology and material culture', in C. Tilley, W. Keane, S. Küchler, M. Rowlands, and P. Spyer (eds) *Handbook of Material Culture*, London: Sage, pp. 43–59.

Thomas, N. (1991) *Entangled Objects: exchange, colonialism and material culture in the Pacific*, Cambridge, MA: Harvard University Press.

Thomson, R. (1998) 'Leather working processes', in E. Cameron (ed.) *Leather and Fur: aspects of early medieval trade and technology*, London: Archetype Publications Ltd, pp. 1–9.

Tilley, C. (1999) *Metaphor and Material Culture*, Oxford: Blackwell.

Tilley, C. (2002) 'The metaphorical transformations of Wala canoes', in V. Buchli (ed.) *The Material Culture Reader*, Oxford: Berg, pp. 27–55.

Tilley, C. (2004) *The Materiality of Stone: explorations in landscape phenomenology*, Oxford: Berg.

Tilley, C. (2006) 'Objectification', in C. Tilley, W. Keane, S. Küchler, M. Rowlands, and P. Spyer (eds) *Handbook of Material Culture*, London: Sage, pp. 60–73.

Tilley, C., Keane, W., Küchler, S, Rowlands, M., and Spyer, P. (eds) (2006) *Handbook of Material Culture*, London: Sage.

Tillman, D.A. (1978) *Wood as an Energy Resource*, New York: Academic Press.

Tillman, D.A., Rossi, A.J., and Kitto, W.D. (1981) *Wood Combustion: principles, processes, and economics*, New York: Academic Press.

Tite, M.S. (1969) 'Determination of the firing temperature of ancient ceramics by measurement of thermal expansion: a reassessment', *Archaeometry*, 11: 131–143.

Tite, M.S. (1992) 'The impact of electron microscopy on ceramic studies', in A.M. Pollard (ed.) *New Developments in Archaeological Science*, Oxford: Oxford University Press, Proceedings of the British Academy 77, pp. 111–132.

Tite, M.S. (1995) 'Firing temperature determination: how and why?', in A. Lindhal and O. Stilborg (eds) *The Aim of Laboratory Analyses of Ceramics in Archaeology, April 7–9, 1995 in Lund, Sweden: in honour of Birgitta Huthén*, Stockholm: Kungl. Vitterhets historie och antikvitets akademien, pp. 37–42.

Tite, M.S. (1996) 'Dating, provenance, and usage in material culture studies', in D.W. Kingery (ed.) *Learning from Things: method and theory of material culture studies*, Washington DC: Smithsonian Institution, pp. 231–260.

Tite, M. (1999) 'Pottery production, distribution and consumption – the contribution of the physical sciences', *Journal of Archaeological Method and Theory*, 6: 181–233.

Tite, M.S. (2001) 'Materials study in archaeology', in D.R. Brothwell and A.M. Pollard (eds) *Handbook of Archaeological Sciences*, Chichester: Wiley, pp. 443–448.

Tomášková, S. (2000) *The Nature of Difference: history and lithic use-wear at two Upper Paleolithic sites in Central Europe*, Oxford: British Archaeological Reports, International Series 880.

Tomášková, S. (2005) 'What is a burin? Typology, technology, and interregional comparison', *Journal of Archaeological Method and Theory*, 12.2: 79–115.

Tomka, S.A. (1993) 'Site abandonment behaviour among transhumant agro-pastoralists: the effects of delayed curation on assemblage composition', in C.M. Cameron and S.A. Tomka (eds) *Abandonment of Settlements and Regions: ethnoarchaeological and archaeological approaches*, Cambridge: Cambridge University Press, pp. 11–24.

Tomlinson, P. (1985) 'Use of vegetative remains in the identification of dyeplants from water-logged 9–10th century AD deposits at York', *Journal of Archaeological Science*, 12: 269–283.

Topping, P. and Lynott, M.J. (eds) (2005) *The Cultural Landscape of Prehistoric Mines*, Oxford: Oxbow Books.

Torrence, R. (1983) 'Time budgeting and hunter-gatherer technology', in G. Bailey (ed.) *Hunter-Gatherer Economy in Prehistory: a European perspective*, Cambridge: Cambridge University Press, pp. 11–22.

Torrence, R. (1986) *Production and Exchange of Stone Tools: prehistoric obsidian in the Aegean*, Cambridge: Cambridge University Press.

Torrence, R. (1989a) 'Tools as optimal solutions', in R. Torrence (ed.) *Time, Energy and Stone Tools*, Cambridge: Cambridge University Press, pp. 1–6.

Torrence, R. (ed.) (1989b) *Time, Energy and Stone Tools*, Cambridge: Cambridge University Press.

Torrence, R. (1989c) 'Re-tooling: towards a behavioral theory of stone tools', in R. Torrence (ed.) *Time, Energy and Stone Tools*, Cambridge: Cambridge University Press, pp. 57–66.

Torrence, R. and Barton, H. (eds) (2006) *Ancient Starch Research*, Walnut Creek, CA: Left Coast Press.

Torrence, R., Wright, R., and Conway, R. (2004) 'Identification of starch granules using image analysis and multivariate techniques', *Journal of Archaeological Science*, 31: 519–532.

Toth, N., Clark, D., and Ligabue, G. (1992) 'The last stone axe-makers', *Scientific American*, 267: 88–93.

Trigger, B. (1989) *A History of Archaeological Thought*, Cambridge: Cambridge University Press.

Tringham, R. (1978) 'Experimentation, ethnoarchaeology, and leapfrogs in archaeological methodology', in R.A. Gould (ed.) *Explorations in Ethnoarchaeology*, Albuquerque: University of New Mexico Press, pp. 169–199.

Tringham, R. (1991) 'Households with faces: the challenge of gender in prehistoric architecture remains', in J.M. Gero and M.W. Conkey (eds) *Engendering Archaeology*, Oxford: Blackwell, pp. 95–102.

Tringham, R. (1994) 'Engendered places in prehistory', *Gender, Place and Culture*, 1: 169–203.

Tringham, R. and Krstić, D. (1990) *Selevac: a Neolithic village in Yugoslavia*, Los Angeles: University of California.

Tringham, R. and Stevanović, M (1990) 'The non-ceramic uses of clay', in Tringham, R. and Krstić, D. (1990) *Selevac: a Neolithic village in Yugoslavia*, Los Angeles: University of California, pp. 323–396.

Tringham, R., Cooper, G., Odell, G., Voytek, B., and Whitman, A. (1974) 'Experimentation in the formation of edge damage: a new approach to lithic analysis', *Journal of Field Archaeology*, 1: 171–196.

Troja, S.O. and Roberts, R.G. (2000) 'Luminescence dating', in E. Ciliberto and G. Spoto (eds) *Modern Analytical Methods in Art and Archaeology*, New York: Wiley, pp. 585–640.

Tuohy, T. (2001) 'Bone and antler working on the Iron Age sites of Glastonbury and Meare in Britain', in A.M. Choyke and L. Bartosiewicz (eds) *Crafting Bone: skeletal technologies through time and space, proceedings of the 2nd meeting of the (ICAZ) Worked Bone Research Group Budapest, 31 August – 5 September 1999*, Oxford: British Archaeological Reports International Series 937, pp. 157–164.

Turner, M.N.J., Boelscher Ignace, M., and Ignace, R. (2000) 'Traditional ecological knowledge and wisdom of aboriginal peoples in British Columbia', *Ecological Applications* 10: 1275–1287.

Tuross, N. and Dillehay, T.D. (1995) 'The mechanism of organic preservation at Monte Verde, Chile, and one use of biomolecules in archaeological interpretation', *Journal of Field Archaeology*, 22: 97–110.

Tuross, N., Barnes, I., and Potts, R. (1996) 'Protein identification of blood residues on experimental stone tools', *Journal of Archaeological Science*, 23: 289–296.

Tylecote, R.F. (1976; 2nd edn 1991) *A History of Metallurgy*, London: The Institute of Materials.

Tylecote, R.F. (1986) *The Prehistory of Metallurgy in the British Isles*, London: Institute of Metals.

Tylecote, R. (1987) *The Early History of Metallurgy in Europe*, London: Longman.

Tylecote, R.F. and Gilmore, B.J.J. (1986) *The Metallography of Early Ferrous Edge Tools and Edged Weapons*, Oxford: British Archaeological Reports British Series 155.

Tzachili, I. (1990) 'All important yet illusive: looking for evidence of cloth-making at Akrotiri', in D.A. Hardy (ed.) *Thera and the Aegean World 3: third international congress*, London: Thera Foundation, pp. 327–349.

Unrath, G., Owen, L.R., Gijn, A. van, Moss, E.H., Plisson, H., and Vaughan, P. (1986) 'An evaluation of microwear studies: a multi-analyst approach', in L.R. Owen and G. Unrath (eds) *Technical Aspects of Microwear Studies on Stone Tools, Parts I and II*, Early Man News 9/10/11, Tübingen, pp. 117–176 and plates 30–56.

Vandiver, P.B., Soffer, O., Klima, B., and Svoboda, J. (1989) 'The origins of ceramic technology at Dolni Vestonice, Czechoslavakia', *Science* 246: 1002–1009.

Vanhaeren, M. and d'Errico, F. (2006) 'Aurignacian ethno-linguistic geography of Europe revealed by personal ornaments', *Journal of Archaeological Science*, 33: 1105–1128.

Vanhaeren, M., d'Errico, F., Stringer, C., James, S.L., Todd, J.A., and Mienis, H.K. (2006) 'Middle Palaeolithic shell beads in Israel and Algeria', *Science*, 312: 1785–1788.

Varien, M.D. and Potter, J.M. (1997) 'Unpacking the discard equation: simulating the accumulation of artifacts in the archaeological record', *American Antiquity*, 62: 194–213.

Varndell, G. (1999) 'An engraved chalk plaque from Hanging Cliff, Kilham', *Oxford Journal of Archaeology*, 18: 351–355.

Vaughan, P. (1985) *Use-wear Analysis of Flaked Stone Tools*, Tucson: The University of Arizona Press.

Vaz Pinto, I., Schiffer, M.B., Smith, S., and Skibo, J.M. (1987) 'Effects of temper on ceramic abrasion resistance: a preliminary investigation', *Archaeomaterials*, 1: 119–134.

Velde, B. and Druc, I.C. (1999) *Archaeological Ceramic Materials: origin and utilization*, Berlin: Springer.

Verlaeckt, K. (2000) 'Hoarding and the circulation of metalwork in Late Bronze Age Denmark: quantification and beyond', in C.F.E. Pare (ed.) *Metals Make the World Go Round: the supply and circulation of metals in Bronze Age Europe. Proceedings of a conference held at the University of Birmingham in June 1997*, Oxford: Oxbow, pp. 194–208.

Verri, G., Barkai, R., Gopher, A., Hass, M., Kubik, P.W., Paul, M., Ronen, A., Weiner, S., and Boaretto, E. (2005) 'Flint procurement strategies in the Late Lower Palaeolithic recorded by in situ produced cosmogenic ^{10}Be in Tabun and Qesem Caves (Israel)', *Journal of Archaeological Science*, 32: 207–213.

Vīkis-Freibergs, V. (1985) 'Amber in Latvian folk songs and folk beliefs', *Journal of Baltic Studies*, 16: 320–340.

Vitelli, K.D. (1989) 'Were pots first made for foods? Doubts from Franchthi', *World Archaeology*, 21: 17–29.

Vitelli, K. (ed.) (1996) *Archaeological Ethics*, Walnut creek: Altamira.

Vogelsang-Eastwood, G. (2000) 'Textiles', in P.T. Nicholson and I. Shaw (eds) *Ancient Egyptian Materials and Technology*, Cambridge: Cambridge University Press, pp. 268–298.

Waddell, J. (1998) *The Prehistoric Archaeology of Ireland*, Galway: Galway University Press.

Waddington, C. (2005) *The Joy of Flint*, Newcastle-upon-Tyne: Museum of Antiquities.

Wall, J. (1987) 'The role of daggers in Early Bronze Age Britain: the evidence of wear analysis', *Oxford Journal of Archaeology*, 6: 115–120.

Wallis L. and O'Connor, S. (1998) 'Residues on a sample of stone points from the west Kimberley', in R. Fullagar (ed.) *A Closer Look: recent studies of Australian stone tools*, Sydney: Sydney University Archaeological Methods Series 6, pp. 150–178.

Waly, N.M. (1999) 'The selection of plant fibers and wood in the manufacture of organic household items from the El-Gabalein area, Egypt', in M. van der Veen (ed.) *The Exploitation of Plant Resources in Ancient Africa*, London: Kluwer Academic, pp. 261–272.

Warnier, J.-P. (2006) 'Inside and outside: surfaces and containers', in C. Tilley, W. Keane, S. Küchler, M. Rowlands, and P. Spyer (eds) Handbook of Material Culture, London: Sage, pp. 186–196.

Washburn, D.K. (2001) 'Remembering things seen: experimental approaches to the process of information transmittal', Journal of Archaeological Method and Theory, 8: 67–99.

Washburn, D.K. and Petitto, A. (1993) 'An ethnoarchaeological perspective on textile categories of identification and function', Journal of Anthropological Archaeology, 12: 150–172.

Watkinson, D. (1987) First Aid for Finds, London: Rescue, British Archaeological Trust.

Watson, J. (1998) 'Organic artefacts and their preservation', in J. Bayley (ed.) Science in Archaeology: an agenda for the future, London: English Heritage, pp. 225–236.

Watts, M. (2002) The Archaeology of Mills and Milling, Stroud: Tempus.

Wayman, M.L., Smith, R.R., Hickey, C.G., and Duke, M.J.M. (1985) 'The analysis of copper artefacts of the Copper Inuit', Journal of Archaeological Science, 12: 367–376.

Weiner, J. and Dreshsel, K. (2002) 'German experimental archaeology', Bulletin of Primitive Technology, 23: 31–33.

Welander, R., Breeze, D.J., and Clany, T.O. (eds) (2003) The Stone of Destiny: artefact and icon, Edinburgh: Society of Antiquaries of Scotland.

Wendrich, W. (1991) Who Is Afraid of Basketry, Leiden: Leiden University.

Wendrich, W. (1999) The World According to Basketry: an ethno-archaeological interpretation of basketry production in Egypt, Leiden: Leiden University Press (book and video).

Wendrich, W.Z. (2000) 'Basketry', in P.T. Nicholson and I. Shaw (eds) Ancient Egyptian Materials and Technology, Cambridge: Cambridge University Press, pp. 254–267.

Wentink, K. (2006) Ceci n'est pas une hache: Neolithic depositions in the northern Netherlands, Leiden: Faculty of Archaeology.

Wertime, T.A. (1964) 'Man's first encounter with metallurgy', Science, 146: 1257–1267.

West, A. (1989) Aboriginal Australia: culture and society, Woden: Aboriginal and Torres Strait Islander Commission.

Whallon R., Jr (1972) 'A new approach to pottery typology', American Antiquity, 37: 13–33.

Whitbread, I.K. (2001) 'Ceramic petrology, clay geochemistry and ceramic production – from technology to the mind of the potter', in D.R. Brothwell and A.M. Pollard (eds) Handbook of Archaeological Sciences, Chichester: Wiley, pp. 449–460.

White, J.P., Modjeska, N., and Hipuya, I. (1977) 'Group definitions and mental templates: an ethnographical experiment', in R.V.S. Wright (ed.) Stone Tools as Cultural Markers, Canberra: Australian Institute of Aboriginal Studies, pp. 380–90.

White, L.A. (1959) The Evolution of Culture, New York: McGraw-Hill.

White, R. (1989a) 'Production complexity and standardization in early Aurignacian bead and pendant manufacture: evolutionary implications', in P. Mellars and C. Stringer (eds) The Human Revolution, Edinburgh: Edinburgh University Press, pp. 366–390.

White, R. (1989b) 'Toward a contextual understanding of the earliest body ornaments', in E. Trinkaus (ed.) The Emergence of Modern Humans: biocultural adaptations in the Later Pleistocene, Cambridge: Cambridge University Press, pp. 211–231.

White, R. (1989c) 'Visual thinking in the Ice Age', Scientific American, 260: 92–99.

White, R. (1992) 'Beyond art: toward an understanding of the origins of material representation in Europe', Annual Review of Anthropology, 21: 537–564.

Whittaker, J.C. (1994) Flintknapping: making and understanding stone tools, Austin: University of Texas Press.

Wickens, H. (1983) Natural Dyes for Spinners and Weavers, London: Batsford.

Wicker, N.L. and Arnold, B. (eds) (1999) From the Ground Up: beyond gender theory in archaeology, Oxford: British Archaeological Reports, International Series S812.

Wiessner, P. (1984) 'Reconsidering the behavioural basis for style: a case study among the Kalahari San', *Journal of Anthropological Archaeology*, 3: 190–234.

Wild, J.P. (1970) *Textile Manufacture in the Northern Roman Provinces*, London: Cambridge University Press.

Wild, J.P. (1988) *Textiles in Archaeology*, Aylesbury: Shire Publications.

Wildman, A.B. (1954) *The Microscopy of Animal Textile Fibres, Including Methods for the Complete Analysis of Fibre Blends*, Headingley, Leeds: Wool Industries Research Association.

Wilkie, L.A. (2000) 'Glass-knapping at a Louisiana plantation: African-American tools?', in D.R. Brauner (ed.) *Approaches to Material Culture Research for Historical Archaeologists*, California, PA: The Society for Historical Archaeology, pp. 189–201.

Wilkie, L.A. (2003) *The Archaeology of Mothering: an African-American midwife's tale*, London: Routledge.

Williams-Thorpe, O. (1995) 'Obsidian in the Mediterranean and near east: a provenancing success story', *Archaeometry*, 37: 17–248.

Williams-Thorpe, O. and Thorpe, R.S. (1992) 'Geochemistry, sources and transport of the Stonehenge bluestones', in A.M. Pollard (ed.) *New Developments in Archaeological Science*, Oxford: Oxford University Press, Proceedings of the British Academy 77.

Willis, S. (1997) 'Samian: beyond dating', in K. Meadows, C. Lemke, and J. Heron (eds) *TRAC 96: Proceedings of the 6th Theoretical Roman Archaeology Conference*, Oxford: Oxbow, pp. 38–54.

Willoughby, P.R. (1987) *Spheroids and Battered Atones in the African Early and Middle Stone Age*, Oxford: British Archaeological Reports International Series 321.

Wilshusen, R.H. (1989) 'Architecture as artefact. Part II a comment on Gilman', *American Antiquity*, 54: 826–833.

Wilson, D.C., Rathje, W.L., and Hughes, W.W. (1991) 'Household discards and modern refuse: a principle of household resource use and waste', in E. Staski and L.D. Sutro (eds) *The Ethnoarchaeology of Waste Disposal*, Tempe: Arizona State University, Anthropological Research Papers 42, pp. 41–51.

Wilson, L. and Pollard, A.M. (2001) 'The provenance hypothesis', in D.R. Brothwell and A.M. Pollard (eds) *Handbook of Archaeological Sciences*, Chichester: Wiley, pp. 507–584.

Wilson, T. (1899) *Arrowheads, Spearheads and Knives of Prehistoric Times*, Washington DC: Smithsonian Institution Press.

Windes, T.C. and McKenna, P.J. (2001) 'Going against the grain: wood production in Chacoan society', *American Antiquity*, 66: 119–140.

Winiger, J. (1995) 'Die Bekleidung des Eismannes und die Anfänge der Weberei nördlich der Alpen', in K. Spindler, H. Rastbichler-Zissernig, H. Wilfing, D. zur Nedden, and H. Nothdurfter (eds) *Der Mann im Eis: neue Funde und Ergebnisse*, Vienna: Springer-Verlag, pp. 119–187.

Wintle, A. (1996) 'Archaeologically-relevant dating techniques for the next century: small, hot and identified by acronyms', *Journal of Archaeological Science*, 23: 123–138.

Wiseman, J. (1986) *The SAS Survival Handbook*, London: William Collins Sons & Co. Ltd.

Wobst, H.M. (1978) 'The archaeo-ethnography of hunter-gatherers or the tyranny of the ethnographic record in archaeology', *American Antiquity*, 43: 303–409.

Wobst, H.M. (1999) 'Style in archaeology or archaeologists in style', in E.S. Chilton (ed.) *Material Meanings: critical approaches to the interpretation of material culture*, Salt Lake City: University of Utah Press, pp. 118–132.

Woodbury, S.E., Evershed, R.P., Russell, J.B., Griffiths, R.E., and Farnell, P. (1995) 'Detection of vegetable oil adulteration using gas chromatography combustion/isotope ratio mass spectrometry', *Analytical Chemistry*, 67: 2685–2690.

Woodroffe, D. (ed.) (1949) *Standard Handbook of Industrial Leathers: dealing with the production, testing, application and care and maintenance of industrial leathers*, London: The National Trade Press Ltd.

Woodward, A. (2000) 'The prehistoric pottery', in G. Hughes (ed.) The Lockington Gold Hoard: an Early Bronze Age barrow cemetery at Lockington, Leicestershire, Oxford: Oxbow, pp. 48–61.

Woodward, A. (2002) 'Beads and beakers: heirlooms and relics in the British Early Bronze Age', Antiquity, 76: 1040–1047.

Wright, D. (1983, 2nd edn) The Complete Book of Baskets and Basketry, Newton Abbot: David and Charles.

Wright, K.I. (1994) 'Ground-stone tools and hunter-gatherer subsistence in Southwest Asia: implications for the transition to farming', American Antiquity, 59: 238–263.

Wright, K.I. (2000) 'The social origins of cooking and dining in early villages of Western Asia', Proceedings of the Prehistoric Society, 66: 89–121.

Wright, R. (1991) 'Women's labor and pottery production in prehistory', in J. Gero and M. Conkey (eds) Engendering Prehistory: women and production, Oxford: Basil Blackwell, pp. 194–223.

Wright, R. (1993) 'Technological styles: transforming a natural material into a cultural object', in W.D. Kingery and S. Luber (eds) History from Things: essays on material culture, Washington DC: Smithsonian Institution Press.

Wright, R.P. (1996) 'Technology, gender and class: worlds of difference in UR III Mesopotamia', in R.P. Wright (ed.) Gender and Archaeology, Philadelphia: University of Pennsylvania Press, pp. 79–110.

Wright, R.V.S. (ed.) (1977) Stone Tools as Cultural Markers: change, evolution and complexity, Canberra: Australian Institute of Aborignal Studies.

Wylie, A. (1985) 'The reaction against analogy', in M.B. Schiffer (ed.) Advances in Archaeological Method and Theory, vol. 8, New York: Academic Press, pp. 63–111.

Wylie, A. (1989) 'The interpretive dilemma', in V. Pinsky and A. Wylie (eds) Critical Traditions in Contemporary Archaeology, Cambridge: Cambridge University Press, pp. 18–27.

Wylie, A. (1992) 'On "Heavily decomposing red herrings": scientific method in archaeology and the ladening of evidence with theory', in L. Embree (ed.) Metaarchaeology, Dordrecht: Kluwer, pp. 269–288.

Wylie, A. (1997) 'Good science, bad science, or science as usual? Feminist critiques of science', in L. Hager (ed.) Women in Human Evolution, London: Routledge, pp. 29–55.

Yellen, J.E. (1977) Archaeological Approaches to the Present: models for reconstructing the past, New York: Academic Press.

Yener, K.A. and Ozbal, H. (1987) 'Tin in the Taurus Mountains: the Bokardag mining district', Antiquity, 61: 220–226.

Yerkes, R.W. and Gaertner, L.M (1997) 'Micro-wear analysis of Dalton artifacts', in D.F. Morse (ed.) Sloan: a Palaeoindian Dalton Cemetery in Arkansas, Washington DC: Smithsonian Institution Press, pp. 58–71.

Yerkes, R.W. and Kardulias, P.N. (1994) 'Microwear analysis of the treshing sledge flints from Cyprus and Greece: implications for the study of ancient agriculture', Helinium, 34: 281–293.

Yoffee, N. and Sherratt, A. (eds) (1993) Archaeological Theory: who sets the agenda?, Cambridge: Cambridge University Press.

Yohe II, R.M., Newman, M.E., and Schneider, J.S. (1991) 'Immunological identification of small-mammal proteins on Aboriginal milling equipment', American Antiquity, 56: 659–666.

Yorston, R.M., Gaffney, V.L., and Reynolds, P.J. (1990) 'Simulation of artefact movement due to cultivation', Journal of Archaeological Science, 17: 67–83.

Young, D. (2006) 'The colours of things', in C. Tilley, W. Keane, S. Küchler, M. Rowlands, and P. Spyer (eds) Handbook of Material Culture, London: Sage, pp. 173–185.

Young, L.C. and Stone, T. (1990) 'The thermal properties of textured ceramics: an experimental study', Journal of Field Archaeology, 17: 195–203.

Young, R. and Humphrey, J. (1999) 'Flint use in England after the Bronze Age: time for a re-evaluation?', *Proceedings of the Prehistoric Society*, 65: 231–242.

Young, S.M.M., Pollard, A.M., Budd, P., and Ixer, R.A. (eds) (1999) *Metals in Antiquity*, Oxford: British Archaeological Reports International Series 792.

Young, S.M.M. and Pollard, A.M. (2000) 'Atomic spectroscopy and spectrometry', in E. Ciliberto and G. Spoto (eds) *Modern Analytical Methods in Art and Archaeology*, New York: Wiley, pp. 21–54.

Zhilin, M.G. (2001) 'Technology of the manufacture of Mesolithic bone and antler daggers on Upper Volga', in A.M. Choyke and L. Bartosiewicz (eds) *Crafting Bone: skeletal technologies through time and space, proceedings of the 2nd meeting of the (ICAZ) Worked Bone Research Group Budapest, 31 August – 5 September 1999*, Oxford: British Archaeological Reports International Series 937, pp. 149–155.

Zola, N. and Gott, B. (1992) *Koorie Plants, Koorie People*, Melbourne: Koorie Heritage Trust.

Index

Note: Colour figures are shown in **bold.** Page numbers in *italics* denote visual elements within the text, with 'f.' indicating figures, and 't.' indicating tables.

eBooks – at www.eBookstore.tandf.co.uk

A library at your fingertips!

eBooks are electronic versions of printed books. You can store them on your PC/laptop or browse them online.

They have advantages for anyone needing rapid access to a wide variety of published, copyright information.

eBooks can help your research by enabling you to bookmark chapters, annotate text and use instant searches to find specific words or phrases. Several eBook files would fit on even a small laptop or PDA.

NEW: Save money by eSubscribing: cheap, online access to any eBook for as long as you need it.

Annual subscription packages

We now offer special low-cost bulk subscriptions to packages of eBooks in certain subject areas. These are available to libraries or to individuals.

For more information please contact webmaster.ebooks@tandf.co.uk

We're continually developing the eBook concept, so keep up to date by visiting the website.

www.eBookstore.tandf.co.uk